The Range of Philosophy

INTRODUCTORY READINGS

THE RANGE
OF PHILOSOPHY

Introductory Readings

HAROLD H. TITUS
MAYLON H. HEPP

Denison University

SECOND EDITION

VAN NOSTRAND REINHOLD COMPANY

New York Cincinnati Toronto London Melbourne

Van Nostrand Reinhold Company Regional Offices:
Cincinnati, New York, Chicago, Millbrae, Dallas

Van Nostrand Reinhold Company Foreign Offices:
London, Toronto, Melbourne

PUBLISHED BY VAN NOSTRAND REINHOLD COMPANY
450 West 33rd Street, New York, N.Y. 10001

Published simultaneously in Canada by
D. Van Nostrand Company (Canada), Ltd.

10 9 8 7 6 5 4 3 2 1

Preface

THE FIRST EDITION of *The Range of Philosophy* (published under the imprint of American Book Company) pointed out that the editors wished to emphasize both the scope and the immediacy of philosophic thinking. To convey range and relevance has been the primary objective in building this collection. The editors have tried to select material that is clear and readable and that is stated in language not too technical for the beginner to understand with some effort on his part. There is an attempt to introduce the beginner to the live issues in philosophy and to deal with questions that have a close relation to life and are, therefore, of general human interest.

Many of the selections used in the first edition, especially those from the classical philosophers, have been retained, but the new edition has given an opportunity to include more recent or contemporary selections and to make changes which, in the light of classroom experience, are thought to strengthen the book as a whole. We envision two principal class uses for the book: as a book of readings in conjunction with an expository text and as a basic source book to be used perhaps with other original writings by selected philosophers. The chapters in this reader parallel the chapters in the Fifth Edition of *Living Issues in Philosophy* by Harold H. Titus (New York: Van Nostrand Reinhold Company, 1970), but this book of selections can be readily adapted for use with other texts, if such are desired, or used separately.

An examination of the Table of Contents will show that we have included selections both from the philosophical "greats" of the past, such as Plato, Aristotle, Aquinas, Descartes, Berkeley, Hume, Kant, and Mill, and from more recent representatives of the traditional systems or types of philosophy. Selections are also included from such contemporary movements as philosophical analysis, and existentialism, and from some leading philosophical scientists. On the whole, the emphasis is on present-day thinkers and issues.

In some instances there is a single selection covering a chapter or topic. When two or three selections or authors are used in one chapter, these selections have been chosen because they expand and develop the line of thought, or because they present contrasting views on controversial issues. The extent of our editing has varied with the nature of the material; throughout, we have tried to keep the needs of the beginning student in mind. When selections are cut or parts omitted, an effort has been made to preserve the main argument or point of view and to eliminate less relevant or repetitious material or points not essential or appropriate in an introductory book of readings. When an author refers to works not readily available to the student, to questions that are now obsolete, or to events of passing interest only, the editors have seen no point in including that material merely to be able to say that the selection has not been cut. Another factor in determining the length of selections has been adaptability for classroom use. We have tried to keep the selections short enough so that they may be used with expository material, if that is desired.

Harold H. Titus
Maylon H. Hepp

Contents

1 Philosophy and Our Changing World

SIDNEY HOOK / The Uses of Philosophy *

Sidney Hook (1902–   ), professor and chairman of philosophy at New York University, is the author of *Education for Modern Man; Heresy, Yes—Conspiracy, No; The Quest for Being; The Paradoxes of Freedom*, and many other books and articles.

IN PERIODS of world and national crisis, such as we are passing through, many individuals are wont to turn to philosophy and philosophers in hope of finding a faith to sustain them in time of troubles. . . . Those who ask questions find that the answer which the philosopher gives them is an invitation to inquiry, not a conclusion or credo. Philosophy, they are sometimes told, is not so much an activity that offers definite answers to questions as one that questions answers. But surely philosophy does not question answers to anything or everything.

This failure to get a specific answer sometimes leads to frustration and to a series of other questions. What is philosophical inquiry as distinct from other forms? What is philosophy, after all? What has it to say? Why study it?

I propose to discuss briefly some of the uses of philosophy without offering a formal definition of it, because any definition presupposes some con-

* Sidney Hook, from "Does Philosophy Have a Future?", *Saturday Review*, 50 (November 11, 1967) pp. 21–23, 62. Used by permission of the author and the publisher. Copyright 1967 Saturday Review, Inc.

ception not likely to be shared by all philosophers. Further, it seems possible to convey a notion of what philosophy is by describing its common uses.

The first and most obvious use of the study of philosophy is that it helps us to understand the nature and history of our civilization. We cannot grasp the pattern of its events and the character of its institutions without some knowledge of the ideas of Plato, Aristotle, Plotinus, Aquinas, Kant, Hegel, and Marx. We cannot understand the political history of the United States without some appreciation of the philosophy of Locke. We cannot appreciate the recent history of Europe and Asia without a grasp of the social philosophy of Marx. I am not saying that the philosophical ideas of these thinkers alone are the forces which entered into the determination of history. Obviously, economic and national interests as well as outstanding personalities played a large role, too; but I am saying that philosophical conceptions of the nature of man, of the nature of justice, of social welfare, of human personality, of freedom, had some influence upon events, and that without reference to them we cannot explain the shape of the past.

Ideas—philosophical ideas—also have a direct relevance to present-day religious, social, and political movements. They are not merely a part of the heritage of the West. They are the means by which we seek to preserve and defend the West. That is why ideas are among the most practical things in the world. Whoever wants to understand our world, and the world of the past out of which it grew, must therefore pay some attention to philosophical ideas. The study of philosophy, in other words, gives us a perspective upon our human history and our present-day experience. It reveals, in John Dewey's words, "the predicaments, the prospects, and aspirations of men."

But philosophy has an even more important use. It has a bearing not only on the shape of the past, but on the shape of things to come. To the extent that fundamental ideas determine our actions, they flow from our basic commitments. Philosophy is a mode of thought which analyzes our presuppositions and assumptions in every field of action and thought. It enables us to make explicit our allegiances to the ideals in behalf of which we are prepared to live, to fight, sometimes even to die. Its primary concern here is with meaning, not truth, and it aims to produce an awareness of what we are about. This awareness or self-consciousness is not easy to achieve. The fruit of ancient wisdom was expressed in the Greek injunction, "Know thyself," but this is a difficult task. Very few of us can answer the questions: "What do we really want?" ; "What do we really mean by the large terms which play a role in human discourse?" We inherit a large mass—usually a mess—of traditional beliefs. Some of these we call first principles. Others, who do not share them, dub them prejudices. How do we sort them out?

This suggests the third use of philosophy. Awareness and self-consciousness do not come about by revelation. For the revelations—"the moments of truth," as the phrase goes—which overtake us are themselves in need of understanding. This can be reliably achieved only by the activity of logical analysis. A person may utter statements that are true or false and yet not be clear about their meaning or their justification or relevance. Whatever else philosophy is, it is an activity of logical analysis which seeks to locate issues in dispute and to help clarify them. When properly pursued, philosophy gives a methodological sophistication that can be achieved by no other discipline. It is not a mere matter of reasoning from premises to conclusion, as in mathematics or chess, because it scrutinizes the premises and basic terms which all subjects take for granted. It enables us to distinguish between statements of fact and disguised definitions, between hypotheses which may be true or false and resolutions which are adequate or inadequate. It is always prepared to consider alternatives to the familiar. William James actually defines philosophy as a quest for alternatives and their investigation. In summary, then, philosophy consists of an analysis of concepts and ideas in an attempt to cut through slogans to genuine issues and problems.

Let us consider a few simple illustrations:

1) The most fashionable slogan in intellectual and educational circles during recent years has been "Down with conformity and conformism." The conformist is the yes man, the man who agrees. He is at the bottom of the cultural ladder. But everyone who denounces conformism can be made to realize that one of the greatest nonconformists of the twentieth century was Adolf Hitler. Would that he had conformed to the accepted decencies of his time! To make a fetish of nonconformity won't do at all—especially when we run into a lunatic who refuses to conform to the traffic laws and rams our car, or a man who shortchanges us and tosses our complaint off with the observation that he is an arithmetical nonconformist. It is or should be obvious that conformism is a relational term. Conformity or nonconformity is no virtue in itself. Unless we know what we are conforming with or not conforming with, the term is meaningless. What we sometimes have in mind when we praise nonconformity is intellectual independence, the intelligence and courage to agree or disagree on the basis of evidence.

2) Another illustration is the slogan which originated in high places and which has been often repeated: "There are no alternatives to peace!" How many who mouth this sentence are aware that it commits them to unconditional surrender if an enemy threatens attack? What those who utter this sentence mean to say is that peace is desirable. The meaning of what they actually said is that peace at any price, even at the cost of free-

dom, is desirable. People who speak this way don't say what they really mean. More important—and this is not the same thing—they don't mean what they really say.

3) Another confusion is the belief that the equality or inequality of races necessarily has a bearing on the question of segregation or integration in housing, transportation, schooling. The view which condemns discrimination against human beings on the basis of religion or race is primarily a moral view. It flows from our belief in the validity of the democratic ideal which rests upon an equality of concern for all human beings to develop their personality to their highest potential. Some facts may have a bearing on this policy, but not the discovery that there is a greater distribution of natural capacity in one race or group than another. Whatever be the facts about the distribution of capacity in group A or B, each member of that group is morally entitled to the rights and privileges which flow from the obligation of a democratic community to all its citizens.

Consider a family which has several children with varying natural capacities—very bright, normal, and dull. Would any responsible parent deprive any of these children of food, clothing, and shelter because of difference in their capacities? If the question of their schooling arose, their educational opportunities would be commensurate with their educational capacities. So with the educational opportunities for the children of members of different groups. The question is not whether the distribution of capacity is inherently the same or different among them, but whether they are to be given educational opportunities on the basis of their capacities or on the basis of their color. This would mean that children, white or nonwhite, Christian or Jewish, would find themselves in the same class in the same school if their educational capacities were the same. Once this analysis is made we can see where the issue lies. It lies in the field of social morality. It is not a question of physical anthropology at all, but rather of the extent to which we accept democracy.

I could have taken other illustrations for analysis from popular philosophy, such as the vulgar notion that because all human action is interested, everyone therefore acts for his own interests, that willy-nilly everyone is selfish. I wanted, however, to show how a little elementary logical analysis has relevance to practical affairs.

But a word about that old chestnut of adolescent cynicism—everyone is selfish, everyone acts for his own pleasure. If I say that all men have two eyes, I am saying something which is confirmed by universal observation. Were I to ask, however, under what possible circumstance one could show that this statement were false, you would be able to describe a state of affairs I could observe—the presence of only one natural eye or three; or, if the mother, when pregnant, had taken thalidomide, none. But suppose you could not describe any possible state of affairs which would invalidate your position; what meaning could be assigned to not having two eyes? Obviously, none. Now suppose I ask: Under what circumstances would you be prepared to say that a person is unselfish; how would he have to *behave* for you to count him as unselfish? As soon as you indicated the specifiable respects, observation of which would lead you to the conclusion, you could know what to do to put it to a test. But if you can't describe the behavior which you are prepared to describe as unselfish, then you are using the term "selfish" in such a way that it has no empirical meaning. You are claiming that the statement, "Everyone is selfish," is true no matter what the facts are or will be—and, therefore, you are not making a statement of fact at all.

4) There is a further use of philosophy. It concerns itself with the place of man in the universe from the point of view of certain large and perennial questions which all reflective men at some time or another ask. These questions are not raised or answered in any of the special sciences, but to answer them intelligently one must be familiar with the best science and theology of the day, and approach them in a rational spirit. These are questions such as: In what sense, if any, does the universe show a design? Does this design imply a designer or a God or a Friend behind the phenomena? Is man a tenement of clay inhabited by an immortal soul or a handful of wonderful salts in a solution of water? Are human beings responsible for their actions? If they are, does this mean that they have free wills? If the will is free, does this mean that the will is uncaused? If the will is uncaused, does this mean that actions are a matter of chance, and if so, in what sense are men morally responsible for their conduct?

This leads on to all sorts of exacting and intricate questions. What do we mean by a cause? Can there be a first cause? Are these questions answerable? What is a genuine question anyhow? Does every sentence which has the form of a question possess the sense of one? Concerning these questions there is dogmatic belief and often dogmatic disbelief. Philosophy is the discipline which considers the fundamental questions in such a way that no matter what answers one makes to them, one can give reasons or grounds for belief or disbelief.

5) Finally, I come to what I regard as the most important use of philosophy, to which all the other uses of philosophy are ancillary—philosophy as the quest for wisdom. Everyone knows that there is a difference between knowledge and wisdom, but not everyone can tell in what this difference consists. We are aware that a man can have a great deal of knowledge about many things and still be a learned fool. We sometimes say he has been educated beyond his capacities. We also know there are wise men who are not encyclopedias of learning, and that wise men of the past often lacked the knowledge of present-day schoolboys. This has led some thinkers to contrast knowledge and wisdom as if they belonged to entirely differ-

ent orders or dimensions of insight. But if we speak of a wise man, we are entitled to ask: "What is he wise about?" If he were ignorant of everything, he couldn't be wise.

Consequently, we must conclude that wisdom is a species of knowledge —it is knowledge of the origin, careers, interrelations, and reliabilities of human values in our experience. Wisdom is an affair of values, and of value judgments. It is intelligent conduct of human affairs. It is knowledge of what is of most worth in our experience, of the ends which we can justifiably pursue, of the good, the better, and the best, the bad, the worse, and the worst in those concrete situations in which, confronted by alternatives of policy or action, we ask: "What shall I do?"

This raises a very large question. How can we be wise or even rational about our values or our ends? What does it mean to be rational or reasonable about them? The term "rational," or "reasonable," has many meanings, but some eminent thinkers claim that they can all be reduced to variations of one meaning, viz., the appropriate or economical use of means to achieve ends. They assert that once we have an end we can be rational about the means of realizing it, but that it makes no sense to speak of ends being rational or reasonable. This suggests that ultimately all ends are on the same plane and that no good reason or rational ground can be given for accepting one or rejecting others. If one accepts Gandhi's ends, one can be rational about achieving them. If one accepts Hitler's ends, one can be rational about achieving them. But we cannot be rational in choosing between Gandhi's and Hitler's ends.

This is the position of Bertrand Russell, who says, "There is no such thing as an irrational end except one impossible of realization." Now, this is false on its face because in one sense there are many ends which are impossible of realization, but are not irrational to pursue because of the desirable consequences of our pursuit of them. Suppose I take all knowledge as my province. It is impossible to achieve literal mastery of the whole of knowledge, but it may not be irrational to pursue it as a goal, because I may thereby acquire more knowledge in this fashion than if I had taken a more restricted end. Or, suppose I take as my end kindness in all circumstances to everyone. This, too, given men as we know them, is impossible, but the world would be a far better place if I try to be invariably kind than if I take as my ideal a more restricted sort of kindness or an ideal of indifference.

One might retort that what Russell means is still valid, for in these cases what I am really taking as my end are those consequences which are realizable. The problem then is: How can you rationally decide concerning alternative ends, all of which are equally realizable?

The answer, it seems to me, is suggested by analyzing how we proceed in any concrete situation in which we must make a choice between ends. If we have only one end, we have no moral problem. It is only a question of means. But the obvious truth is that we always have more than one end—usually a cluster of ends or values—to which we are committed. Our problem is, which end should we commit ourselves to? Now, the answer I suggest is that we always proceed by checking the alternative possible ends in terms of the consequences of the means used to achieve them and in the light of all the other ends which, on the basis of past experience, we have accepted as having prima facie validity. Of course, every one of these other ends may itself be questioned. Every end in human experience is also a means to some other end. How do we test them? By the same process. But does this not set up an infinite regress? No, not if we take our problems one at a time.

Consider a simple example. A student comes to me in distress and wants to know whether he should remain in school or exploit some opportunity for remunerative employment. I point out the relative advantages and disadvantages of both, stressing the fact that in the modern world he is more likely to find a creative vocation through continuing his schooling. Now, this assumes that a creative vocation is a good thing to have. How do we know that? Suppose it is denied. Again, we point to the alternative uses of the concrete goals or possibilities of living. A creative vocation is a center around which to organize experience; it is a source of satisfaction and delight; it also provides occasions for companionship and friendship. But are *these* worthwhile? To which I reply that they enrich living. Yes, comes the rejoinder, but is life worthwhile? Now, at this point we can very well question the validity of the process. A student who wants to know whether to continue his schooling or discontinue it is not interested in knowing whether life is worth living. That is a legitimate question, too, in its context. But it is out of context here.

What I have been trying to illustrate is the general method by which we do, in fact, seek to answer specific moral questions. They are much more complicated, of course, when they concern other human beings. (I am not giving any answers here or claiming to be wise. A philosopher in his own life need be no more wise than a physician need be healthy.) I am particularly concerned to challenge the view that all our values are ultimate values that are inarbitrable. Indeed, I question whether it is true that any value in a specific context is an ultimate value rather than a penultimate one which is tested by its successive consequences. At any rate, I believe I have shown that we can be wise or foolish about the ends of action, that it makes good sense to undertake rational criticism of our ends, and that the originally desired end may sometimes appear in the light of our reflective analysis as undesirable.

Although the philosopher does not himself have to be a wise man, at his best he knows more than the methods and techniques by which the process of reflection is carried out. He has vision of possibilities. He is not only a critic but a seer. His vision is often expressed as a glimpse into what can make our society better for our time, into what can most enrich our life and give it abiding worth, an insight into human possibilities and how to realize them. When the philosopher is a man of vision, he leaves his mark upon the experience of others, whose ordinary life acquires new dimensions of significance.

Of such philosophers, Santayana says: "It is not easy for him to shout or to address a crowd; he must be silent for long periods; for he is watching stars that move slowly and in courses that it is possible though difficult to see; and he is crushing all things in his heart as in a winepress, until his life and their secret flow out together."

C. D. BROAD / Philosophy: Critical and Speculative *

C. D. Broad (1887–   ) is an outstanding British philosopher who taught for many years at Cambridge University. Among his well-known works are *Five Types of Ethical Theory*; *Mind and Its Place in Nature*; and the book from which we quote.

Now the most fundamental task of Philosophy is to take the concepts that we daily use in common life and science, to analyse them, and thus to determine their precise meanings and their mutual relations. Evidently this is an important duty. In the first place, clear and accurate knowledge of anything is an advance on a mere hazy general familiarity with it. Moreover, in the absence of clear knowledge of the meanings and relations of the concepts that we use, we are certain sooner or later to apply them wrongly or to meet with exceptional cases where we are puzzled as to how to apply them at all. For instance, we all agree pretty well as to the place of a certain pin which we are looking at. But suppose we go on to ask: "Where is the image of that pin in a certain mirror; and is it in this place (whatever it may be) in precisely the sense in which the pin itself is in *its* place?" We

* C. D. Broad, from "Introduction," in *Scientific Thought* (New York: Humanities Press, 1952), pp. 16–22. Used by permission of the publisher.

shall find the question a very puzzling one, and there will be no hope of answering it until we have carefully analysed what we mean by *being in a place*.

Again, this task of clearing up the meanings and determining the relations of fundamental concepts is not performed to any extent by any other science. Chemistry *uses* the notion of substance, geometry that of space, and mechanics that of motion. But they assume that you already know what is meant by *substance* and *space* and *motion*. So you do in a vague way; and it is not their business to enter, more than is necessary for their own special purposes, into the meaning and relations of these concepts as such. Of course the special sciences do in some measure clear up the meanings of the concepts that they use. A chemist, with his distinction between elements and compounds and his laws of combination, has a clearer idea of substance than an ordinary layman. But the special sciences only discuss the meanings of their concepts so far as this is needful for their own special purposes. Such discussion is incidental to them, whilst it is of the essence of Philosophy, which deals with such questions for their own sake. Whenever a scientist begins to discuss the concepts of his science in this thorough and disinterested way we begin to say that he is studying, not so much Chemistry or Physics, as the *Philosophy* of Chemistry or Physics. It will therefore perhaps be agreed that, in the above sense of Philosophy, there is both room and need for such a study, and that there is no special reason to fear that it will be beyond the compass of human faculties.

At this point a criticism may be made which had better be met at once. It may be said: "By your own admission the task of Philosophy is purely verbal; it consists entirely of discussions about the meanings of words." This criticism is of course absolutely wide of the mark. When we say that Philosophy tries to clear up the meanings of concepts we do not mean that it is simply concerned to substitute some long phrase for some familiar word. Any analysis, when once it has been made, is naturally *expressed* in words; but so too is any other discovery. When Cantor gave his definition of Continuity, the final result of his work was expressed by saying that you can substitute for the word "continuous" such and such a verbal phrase. But the essential part of the work was to find out exactly what properties are present in objects when we predicate continuity of them, and what properties are absent when we refuse to predicate continuity. This was evidently not a question of words but of things and their properties.

Philosophy has another and closely connected task. We not only make continual use of vague and unanalysed concepts. We have also a number of uncriticised beliefs, which we constantly assume in ordinary life and in the sciences. We constantly assume, *e.g.* that every event has a cause, that nature obeys uniform laws, that we live in a world of objects whose existence and behaviour are independent of our knowledge of them, and so on.

Now science takes over these beliefs without criticism from common-sense, and simply works with them. We know by experience, however, that beliefs which are very strongly held may be mere prejudices. Negroes find it very hard to believe that water can become solid, because they have always lived in a warm climate. Is it not possible that we believe that nature as a whole will always act uniformly simply because the part of nature in which the human race has lived has happened to act so up to the present? All such beliefs then, however deeply rooted, call for criticism. The first duty of Philosophy is to state them clearly; and this can only be done when we have analysed and defined the concepts that they involve. Until you know exactly what you mean by *change* and *cause* you cannot know what is meant by the statement that *every change has a cause*. And not much weight can be attached to a person's most passionate beliefs if he does not know what precisely he is passionately believing. The next duty of Philosophy is to test such beliefs; and this can only be done by resolutely and honestly exposing them to every objection that one can think of oneself or find in the writings of others. We ought only to go on believing a proposition if, at the end of this process, we still find it impossible to doubt it. Even then of course it may not be true, but we have at least done our best.

These two branches of Philosophy—the analysis and definition of our fundamental concepts, and the clear statement and resolute criticism of our fundamental beliefs—I call *Critical Philosophy*. It is obviously a necessary and a possible task, and it is not performed by any other science. The other sciences *use* the concepts and *assume* the beliefs; Critical Philosophy tries to analyse the former and to criticise the latter. Thus, so long as science and Critical Philosophy keep to their own spheres, there is no possibility of conflict between them, since their subject-matter is quite different. Philosophy claims to analyse the general concepts of substance and cause, *e.g.*; it does not claim to tell us about particular substances, like gold, or about particular laws of causation, as that *aqua regia* dissolves gold. Chemistry, on the other hand, tells us a great deal about the various kinds of substances in the world, and how changes in one cause changes in another. But it does not profess to analyse the general concepts of substance or causation, or to consider what right we have to assume that every event has a cause.

It should now be clear why the method of Philosophy is so different from that of the natural sciences. Experiments are not made, because they would be utterly useless. If you want to find out how one substance behaves in presence of another you naturally put the two together, vary the conditions, and note the results. But no experiment will clear up your ideas as to the meaning of *cause* in general or of *substance* in general. Again, all conclusions from experiments rest on some of those very assumptions which it is the business of Philosophy to state clearly and to criticise. The experimenter assumes that nature obeys uniform laws, and that similar results will follow always and everywhere from sufficiently similar conditions. This is one of the assumptions that Philosophy wants to consider critically. The method of Philosophy thus resembles that of pure mathematics, at least in the respect that neither has any use for experiment.

There is, however, a very important difference. In pure mathematics we start either from axioms which no one questions, or from premises which are quite explicitly assumed merely as hypotheses; and our main interest is to deduce remote consequences. Now most of the tacit assumptions of ordinary life and of natural science claim to be true and not merely to be hypotheses, and at the same time they are found to be neither clear nor self-evident when critically reflected upon. Most mathematical axioms are very simple and clear, whilst most other propositions which men strongly believe are highly complex and confused. Philosophy is mainly concerned, not with remote conclusions, but with the analysis and appraisement of the original premises. For this purpose analytical power and a certain kind of insight are necessary, and the mathematical method is not of much use.

Now there is another kind of Philosophy; and, as this is more exciting, it is what laymen generally understand by the name. This is what I call *Speculative Philosophy*. It has a different object, is pursued by a different method, and leads to results of a different degree of certainty from Critical Philosophy. Its object is to take over the results of the various sciences, to add to them the results of the religious and ethical experiences of mankind, and then to reflect upon the whole. The hope is that, by this means, we may be able to reach some general conclusions as to the nature of the Universe, and as to our position and prospects in it.

There are several points to be noted about Speculative Philosophy. (i) If it is to be of the slightest use it must presuppose Critical Philosophy. It is useless to take over masses of uncriticised detail from the sciences and from the ethical and religious experiences of men. We do not know what they mean, or what degree of certainty they possess till they have been clarified and appraised by Critical Philosophy. It is thus quite possible that the time for Speculative Philosophy has not yet come; for Critical Philosophy may not have advanced far enough to supply it with a firm basis. In the past people have tended to rush on to Speculative Philosophy, because of its greater practical interest. The result has been the production of elaborate systems which may quite fairly be described as moonshine. The discredit which the general public quite rightly attaches to these hasty attempts at Speculative Philosophy is reflected back on Critical Philosophy, and Philosophy as a whole thus falls into undeserved disrepute.

(ii) At the best Speculative Philosophy can only consist of more or less happy guesses, made on a very slender basis. There is no hope of its reaching the certainty which some parts of Critical Philosophy might quite well attain. Now speculative philosophers as a class have been the most dogmatic of men. They have been more certain of everything than they had a right to be of anything.

(iii) A man's final view of the Universe as a whole, and of the position and prospects of himself and his fellows, is peculiarly liable to be biased by his hopes and fears, his likes and dislikes, and his judgments of value. One's Speculative Philosophy tends to be influenced to an altogether undue extent by the state of one's liver and the amount of one's bank-balance. No doubt livers and bank-balances have their place in the Universe, and no view of it which fails to give them their due weight is ultimately satisfactory. But their due weight is considerably less than their influence on Speculative Philosophy might lead one to suspect. But, if we bear this in mind and try our hardest to be "ethically neutral," we are rather liable to go to the other extreme and entertain a theory of the Universe which renders the existence of our judgments of value unintelligible.

A large part of Critical Philosophy is almost exempt from this source of error. Our analysis of truth and falsehood, or of the nature of judgment, is not very likely to be influenced by our hopes and fears. Yet even here there is a slight danger of intellectual dishonesty. We sometimes do our Critical Philosophy, with half an eye on our Speculative Philosophy, and accept or reject beliefs, or analyse concepts in a certain way, because we feel that this will fit in better than any alternative with the view of Reality as a whole that we happen to like.

(iv) Nevertheless, if Speculative Philosophy remembers its limitations, it is of value to scientists, in its methods, if not in its results. The reason is this. In all the sciences except Psychology we deal with objects and their changes, and leave out of account as far as possible the mind which observes them. In Psychology, on the other hand, we deal with minds and their processes, and leave out of account as far as possible the objects that we get to know by means of them. A man who confines himself to either of these subjects is likely therefore to get a very one-sided view of the world. The pure natural scientist is liable to forget that minds exist, and that if it were not for them he could neither know nor act on physical objects. The pure psychologist is inclined to forget that the main business of minds is to know and act upon objects; that they are most intimately connected with certain portions of matter; and that they have apparently arisen gradually in a world which at one time contained nothing but matter. Materialism is the characteristic Speculative Philosophy of the pure natural scientist, and subjective idealism that of the pure psychologist. To the scientist subjective idealism seems a fairy tale, and to the psychologist materialism seems sheer lunacy. Both are right in their criticisms, but neither sees the weakness of his own position. The truth is that both these doctrines commit the fallacy of over-simplification; and we can hardly avoid falling into some form of this unless at some time we make a resolute attempt to think *synoptically* of all the facts. Our *results* may be trivial; but the *process* will at least remind us of the extreme complexity of the world, and teach us to reject any cheap and easy philosophical theory, such as popular materialism or popular theology.*

For Further Study

Adler, Mortimer J. *The Conditions of Philosophy*. New York: Dell Publishing Co., 1967 (Delta Book).

Emmet, E. R. *Learning to Philosophise*. New York: Philosophical Library, 1965, Chs. 1–4.

Ewing, A. C. *Fundamental Questions of Philosophy*. London: Routledge & Kegan Paul, 1951, Ch. 1, "What Philosophy Is and Why It Is Worth Studying." (Also Collier Book AS250V.)

Flay, Joseph C. "What is Philosophy?" *Personalist*, 47 (Spring, 1967): 206–217.

Hahn, Lewis. "Philosophy as Comprehensive Vision," *Philosophy and Phenomenological Research*, 22 (September, 1961): 16–25.

Jaspers, Karl. *Way to Wisdom*. New Haven: Yale U. Press, 1954, Ch. 1, "What is Philosophy?"

Marcel, Gabriel. *Men Against Humanity*. London: Harvill, 1952, Part 2, Ch. 1, "The Philosopher and the Contemporary World."

Russell, Bertrand. *The Problems of Philosophy*. London and New York: Oxford U. Press, 1912, Ch. 15, "The Value of Philosophy." (Also Galaxy Book GB21, 1959.)

* For a different conception, and a more favorable evaluation of speculative philosophy, see the Whitehead selection in Ch. 18.

PART 1

Methods of Inquiry

2 The Sources of Knowledge

ELMER SPRAGUE / Matters of Fact and Matters of Logic *

Elmer Sprague (1924–   ) holds a Doctorate of Philosophy from Oxford University, where he was a Rhodes Scholar. He has taught philosophy at Brooklyn College since 1953.

IN THIS CHAPTER I shall discuss man's powers to know and the kinds of knowledge which these powers guarantee. The discussion will center on two kinds of knowledge: matters of fact, which depend on man's senses, or his powers of perceiving; and matters of logic, which depend on man's reason, or his powers of conceiving. This chapter is a necessary preface to all the rest. If what is said here seems formal, empty, and uninteresting, I must beg the reader to remember that until we settle questions about the *ways* in which we can know, we cannot settle questions about *what* we can know. This is one of the central problems in philosophy, and one to which philosophers turn again and again as the key to all of their other problems.

In what follows I shall consider knowledge as declarative sentences or statements, which someone knows how to prove or to use. There is more than one way of proving and using declarative sentences, but the example of the Pythagorean Theorem will illustrate my point in a general way. The theorem: "In any right-angled triangle, the square which is described on

* Elmer Sprague, from "Philosophy and Man: Intellectual Powers," in *What is Philosophy?* (New York: Oxford University Press, Inc., 1961), pp. 13–29. Used by permission of the publisher.

the side opposite the right angle is equal to the squares described on the sides which contain the right angle." Now I may be said to know the theorem when I can prove it by appeal to the necessary definitions, postulates, axioms, and preceding theorems in Euclidean geometry, when I can use it to prove further theorems, and when I can use it to find the length of unknown sides, and so on.

Knowledge may also be spoken of as knowing some object. For example, philosophers like to talk about our knowledge of material objects; and they like to talk in general about objects of knowledge. But talk about objects of knowledge can always be translated into talk about knowing whether a statement about the object is true or false. The reader will find it a salutary move to translate an awesome question like "Can I really know material objects?" into the more manageable question, "How do I know that the statement, 'There is a tea cup on my desk,' is true?" What is more, talk about knowledge as statements puts us in a favorable position to deal with the social aspect of knowledge. Whatever my object of knowledge, if I want to call someone's attention to it or to discuss it with him, I must make statements about it. Statements are the medium for exchanging knowledge; and this consideration makes them additionally interesting as a clue to man's powers to know.

MATTER-OF-FACT STATEMENTS

We may begin with matter-of-fact statements, and see what can be made of them in their own right. Later, when we have also examined matter-of-logic statements, we may consider the differences between the two kinds of statement. Here are some sample matter-of-fact statements:

> The cows are in the corn field.
> Alice always talks too much.
> The sun will rise tomorrow.
> Aristotle gave philosophy lectures.
> Alexander swam the Hellespont.
> The Eiffel Tower is in New York City.

These statements differ in many ways. All are about different subjects. Some are in the present tense, while others are about the past and the future. Some are statements about a particular subject at a particular time. Some are generalizations about a particular subject, and thus are meant to describe that subject at all times (e.g. Alice always talks too much). But despite their many differences, the characteristic which these statements have in common is that they may be proved true or false by experience.

It is easy to say that matter-of-fact statements are confirmed or disproved by experience; but it is not easy to give any general account of what is meant by experience. What is usually meant is that someone who wants to confirm a matter-of-fact statement must use his senses in some way to find out whether the statement does describe the world. When we find that a matter-of-fact statement does describe the world, we say that it is confirmed. When we find that a matter-of-fact statement fails to describe the world, we say that it is disproved. Here, we may consider the following examples which are meant to illustrate in a general way the confirmation of a matter-of-fact statement by experience.

(1) When someone tells me, "The cows are in the corn field," I look in the corn field to see whether I can find the cows there. If they are in the corn field, my finding them there has confirmed the statement. My failing to find them in the corn field would disprove it. But I must not minimize the difficulties in proving this statement false, or, to put the matter another way, the difficulties in proving that the statement "The cows are not in the corn field" is true. To be sure, I must have searched, and searched carefully. Of course, looking for cows in a corn field requires less care than hunting for a needle in a haystack; but nonetheless I must be certain that I have looked in all those places big enough to conceal a herd of cows before I can assert confidently that there are no cows in the corn field in question. The proof of the affirmative statement "The cows are in the corn field" is, however, fairly easy. All I have to do is find the cows. But the proof of the negative statement is more difficult. No matter how exhaustive a search I conduct before I conclude that the cows are not in the corn field, it is still possible that they might be hidden in a spot that I have missed.

(2) While riding with me in my car, someone tells me, "The radiator is boiling." I can neither see nor hear anything unusual from the direction of the radiator; so I look at the temperature gauge. If the indicator is in the red section of its arc, I agree with my passenger. His statement is true. But here confirmation by experience is more complicated than in the case above, where I looked into the corn field and saw the cows. Why does my seeing the temperature indicator in the red section prove true the statement "The radiator is boiling"? It proves it for me because I believe another statement, which links the behavior of the indicator and the behavior of the radiator: "If the indicator is in the red, the radiator is boiling." And why do I believe this last statement? I believe it because in the past each time the indicator has gone into the red section of its arc, I have found the car's radiator to be boiling. So now when I find the indicator in the red I believe that the radiator must be boiling.

But one may very well ask why my memory of the indicator's riding in the red when the radiator was boiling in the past in any way guarantees that my radiator is now boiling because the indicator is riding in the red section. Strictly speaking, there is no guarantee that there is now a connection between the position of the indicator and my radiator's boiling. Matter-of-fact statements are meant to describe the world, and it is possible that the world may have changed since I last experienced a link between the position of the indicator and the radiator's boiling. My temperature gauge may now be broken, to name the most probable way in which the world may have changed. But even though there is no guarantee that there is a connection between the position of the indicator and my radiator's boiling, it usually happens in cases of this kind that our belief that the present resembles the past outweighs our knowledge that the world may have changed. Our belief about a particular kind of connection grows stronger each time we experience it. On the other hand, those occasions when experience disproves our matter-of-fact statements (The gauge was broken. The radiator was not even hot.) are salutary reminders that matter-of-fact statements are meant to describe the world rather than to prescribe it.

(3) "The sun will rise tomorrow" is yet another and different example of a statement that we say is true because of experience. But here there is no present experience comparable to looking at an indicator in the red portion of its arc, that leads from the seen to belief in the unseen. It is the regularity of our past experience of sunrises that leads us to expect that the sun will rise tomorrow, and thus leads us to say that the statement is true. Of course, neither my past experience of sunrises nor the expectation it engenders makes the statement true. Only the sun's rising on the morrow can do that.

These three examples show that confirmation of a matter-of-fact statement by experience may have at least these three meanings: (1) I am directly observing what the statement describes, and what I observe justifies my saying that the statement is true. (2) I am directly observing one thing, which I have regularly found to be conjoined with the state of affairs described by the statement, and this observation leads me to believe that the state of affairs which the statement describes, but which I have not observed, does exist; and I say that the statement is true. In principle we argue for the truth of statements about the past or the future in the same way when we say that what we can see implies the existence of past events which we have not seen or when we argue that what we can see implies the probability of events yet to come. (3) I remember something that I have regularly observed in the past; and I am led to believe that a similar state of affairs which the statement describes, but which I have not yet observed, will exist; and I say that the statement is true.

To these remarks about confirming by experience must be added the rule that no one can confirm a matter-of-fact statement who does not know what observations will confirm it. If I do not know the difference between cows and the rest of the world, and corn fields and the rest of the world, the statement "The corn field is in the cows" will make as much sense to me as the statement "The cows are in the corn field." Philosophers say that someone who does not know how to confirm a matter-of-fact statement does not understand it. To him, it is meaningless. To him, it makes no sense.

After this consideration of proving and disproving matter-of-fact statements, we are in a position to notice one of their characteristics that is their defining characteristic. For every matter-of-fact statement, its denial is as meaningful as the statement itself. For instance, "The cows are not in the corn field" is as meaningful as "The cows are in the corn field." It is because each is as meaningful as the other that we must appeal to experience to determine which is true. Later we shall find this characteristic to be of the greatest importance in distinguishing matter-of-fact statements from matter-of-logic statements.

THE SENSES AND KNOWLEDGE

Matter-of-fact statements are the kind of knowledge we may gain by the use of our senses; but not all philosophers have thought that our senses are fit instruments for gaining knowledge of the world. Their views deserve some notice. At the outset, however, I wish to announce that I am not claiming that the only knowledge we have is knowledge confirmed by our senses. Therefore, neither does the position I am describing hold its place by belittling other sources of knowledge, nor does it deserve belittlement for the purpose of enhancing other sources of knowledge.

The criticism of the senses as powers for knowing falls under two main heads: the claim that the fallibility of the senses makes all sensory knowledge untrustworthy; and the claim that the senses can never be used to gain knowledge of the real world.

The claim that the senses are fallible rests on evidence that the senses deceive. The classic examples fall into two varieties: the failure to perceive things as they are, and the mistake of perceiving things that are not. Examples of the failure to perceive things as they are, are the straight stick that looks bent in water; the penny at one's feet that turns out to be a bottle cap; the mountain that seems quite near but turns out to be a hundred miles away; the man in the night who turns out to be a wind-blown bush; and the burglar's footsteps that turn into a dripping faucet. The problems in these examples arise largely from assuming more than the sensory evidence warrants. The fault lies not with the senses but with the hasty assumption; and its avoidance lies not in abandoning the senses because they are untrustworthy, but in seeking more sensory knowledge to confirm or disprove one's first assumption. What is more, as soon as one learns the tricks one's senses can play, one learns to be careful in judging water effects, distance, and shadows.

But if we pursue the fallibility of the senses a little further, we discover that a good part of the trouble comes from personifying the senses: from my thinking of my use of my senses as a communication between *me* and my senses. I say, "My eyes deceived me," when I ought to say, "I should have taken another look." I say, "My ears tricked me," when I ought to say, "I should have listened more carefully." I say, "My nose knows," when I ought to say, "I smell it." The problem of the fallibility of the senses turns into the problem of the careless observer when we make ourselves the subject of verbs of sense. Then we know that we have only ourselves to blame for our perceptual mistakes. Ordinary people know this; but philosophers have to be reminded from time to time.

The mistake of perceiving things that are not is exemplified by mirages, unrecognized mirror images, and the one-legged man who still feels rheumatic pains in his amputated member. The solution of the problems raised by these examples requires again a greater use of the senses. Three tests are possible: the test of two or more observers; the test of observations at different times; and the test of two or more senses. Do I see an oasis or do I see a mirage? If I can see it at different times, and if my fellow travelers can see it at the same times I do, my answer is a tentative "Oasis." Tentative, because the test of an optical experience is, can I touch what I see? It may be objected, of course, that sensory tests are circular. Touch confirms sight, and sight confirms touch. One illusion leads to another, and all is illusion. This objection leads us to the second main head under which criticism of the senses is made: The senses can never be used to gain knowledge of the real world.

"Real" is a loaded word. If it is used to describe a world that transcends the powers of our senses, then by definition we can never learn anything of that world by our senses. But here I understand the denial of sensory knowledge of a real world to be a claim that the world is a creation of one's senses, and that one cannot tell what to credit to the world and what to attribute to one's senses. The claim is that the knower and his knowledge run together indistinguishably.

The distinction between the knower and the known is not always an easy one to make; and it often depends on where the philosopher wants to draw the line. Consider, for example, the Wizard of Oz and his Emerald City. To achieve the absolute greenness of Oz, the Wizard equipped all of his subjects and visitors with green spectacles, which they were compelled to wear at all times. Now here is a nice philosophical question: Was the city of Oz really green or was its greenness merely in the eyes of its beholders? (Said eyes being properly assisted by green spectacles, of course.) Whether or not a philosopher says that Oz was really green depends on where he draws the line between the beholders and the world. If the philosopher says that Oz was really not green, he is ready to argue that if the inhabitants had taken off their colored spectacles, they would have found the city to be not wholly green. Such a philosopher is answering the question from a viewpoint above the relation of the beholder to the city; and thus he finds green not in the world but in the eye of the beholder. On the other hand, a philosopher might argue that the question about Oz's greenness must always be answered from within the relationship of the beholder and the world. For such a philosopher, when someone says, "Oz isn't really green," he is only saying, "I am not looking at Oz through green spectacles." So, from the point of view of those subject to the Wizard's spectacles, Oz is really green.

The philosophical moral is that only when we can distinguish between two different ways of knowing the world (without green spectacles and with green spectacles) are we in any position to distinguish between what is the world and what is a condition for knowing the world. Without the correction of other perceptions—in the way that clear-eyed observers can penetrate the Wizard of Oz's color-scheming—the world of sense is as real as we perceive it. There is some truth in saying that we are the prisoners of our senses; but we may take consolation in the fact that our prison is not a cave-like dungeon, but a house of correction.

MATTER-OF-LOGIC STATEMENTS

I want now to turn to matter-of-logic statements. As always, it will be best to proceed by way of examples:

> The whole is equal to the sum of its parts.
> In any right-angled triangle the square which is described on the side opposite the right angle is equal to the squares described on the sides which contain the right angle. (Pythagorean Theorem)
> Three times five is equal to one-half of thirty.
> That which is red is colored.

Why do we accept or reject these statements? In a general way, the answer is that matter-of-logic statements are confirmed by an appeal to the way in which we use the words in the statement. How does this sort of confirmation work? I shall illustrate it by considering "The whole is equal to the sum of its parts."

In the case of "The whole is equal to the sum of its parts," the appeal is to the way in which we are to use the words "whole," "part," and "equal to" in this statement. That into which a whole can be divided is its parts. That into which parts can be assembled is a whole. Further, there is a question of the kind of whole that we will allow this statement to describe. The rough rule is that the wholes and their parts must be subject to some system of measurement as of area or weight or volume. What "equal to" means in "The whole is equal to the sum of its parts" is that whatever quantitative measurement can be applied to the whole can also be applied to the sum of the parts. Now the confirmation of "The whole is equal to the sum of its parts" depends solely on my understanding the way in which these words are to be used and by agreeing to use them in this way. This is why I call such a statement a matter-of-logic statement, for our "logic" comes from the Greek *logos* meaning "word." In addition, I must digress for a moment to give a little historical perspective to what I have spoken of as "understanding the way in which words are to be used." For a very long time, philosophers thought about matter-of-logic statements as being about ideas or concepts rather than about words. This was their way of distinguishing between matter-of-fact statements, which were about perceptions, and matter-of-logic statements, which were about conceptions. In addition, just as perceptions were perceived by the senses, so a faculty called reason was thought of as conceiving conceptions, or ideas. Thus many philosophers speak of confirming matter-of-logic statements as an appeal to reason; but I want to follow those philosophers who speak of confirming matter-of-logic statements as reminding ourselves of the ways in which we may use these statements.

We can carry our understanding of matter-of-logic statements a little further if we consider the way in which we use "The whole is equal to the sum of its parts." This matter-of-logic statement is really a rule which allows me the convenience of mentioning the whole rather than listing all of the parts. For example, when you ask me how much money I have, I can tell you that I have two dollars and thirty-six cents rather than having to say that I have three nickels, two dimes, a penny, two quarters, and three half-dollars. But notice that the confirmation of "The whole is equal to the sum of its parts" never depends on any example of its usefulness. I do not say that the statement is true because my pocketful of coins is the same as two dollars and thirty-six cents. I say that the statement is true because I understand the way in which the words are used. On the other hand, I never allow that any example can disprove the statement either. My tactics are to show that any example which someone believes disproves "The whole is equal to the sum of its parts" is really not a case to which the rule can be applied; and anyone who supposes that it is such a case misunderstands the way in which the rule is to be used. An example will illustrate my point.

Suppose that someone argues in the following way: I can show you that the whole is not equal to the sum of its parts. Look at this medicine dropper full of liquid. Now, I squeeze it ten times, and let ten drops fall into this saucer; and they run together to make one drop. That shows you that the whole is not equal to the sum of its parts, for the sum of the parts is ten drops, but the whole in the saucer is only one drop.

My reply to this argument must be that I am being taken in a numbers game. When I said that the whole is equal to the sum of its parts, I never meant to claim that one is equal to ten. Indeed, enumerative equality is not the sort of equality which can be sought between a whole and its parts, since the whole will always be one, and the number of its parts will always be greater than one. What has happened is that the drops case has been presented in such a way that it does not fit the rule. So it can in no way disprove my claim that the whole is equal to the sum of its parts. I can, however, turn the example to my own account by showing how it can be made to fit the rule. I can talk about the volume of the drop in the saucer and the volume of the ten drops that were squeezed from the medicine dropper. When their volume is considered, the whole is equal to the sum of the parts. What is required here is discretion in summing. Notice, however, that by showing how the drops case can be made to fit the rule, I am not appealing to the case to confirm the matter-of-logic statement, "The whole is equal to the sum of its parts." What I am doing is showing a case in which the rule can be used.

I now want to distinguish two sorts of matter-of-logic statements. The sorts which I have in mind are exemplified by "That which is red is colored," and the Pythagorean Theorem. To bring out their characteristics, I shall discuss each of these statements in turn. Notice that the statement, "That which is red is colored," is always true, for its denial, "That which is red is *not* colored," is a self-contradiction, granting that as we ordinarily use the color word "red," to say that something is red is to say that it is colored. For the same reason, of course, the self-contradictory statement, "Red objects are *not* colored," will always be false.

Now consider the Pythagorean Theorem, which I wish to discuss because it exemplifies those matter-of-logic statements which are part of a logical system of statements, as that theorem is a part of Euclidean geometry. It is the case that this sort of matter-of-logic statement is also always true; indeed it is this characteristic which leads us to classify these statements, too, as matter-of-logic statements. However, these statements are not said to be always true because their denials are self-contradictory, as is the case with "That which is red is colored." A longer explanation is required. We say that the Pythagorean Theorem is true because we can prove it within the context of Euclidean geometry. We appeal to the relevant definitions, postulates, and axioms laid down in the beginning, and to any relevant theorems that were proved earlier, and our claim is that all of these taken together imply the truth of the Pythagorean Theorem. The principle of our proof is that we can show the Pythagorean Theorem to be consistent with the rest of Euclidean geometry. If we then counted it as false, we should be contradicting ourselves, in the light of our adherence to the rest of Euclidean geometry. Valuing self-consistency, we therefore count the Pythagorean Theorem as true and its denial as false. Could its denial ever be true? Yes, if we invented an alternative geometry into which it could fit; and that such a geometry is conceivable is what makes us refrain from calling the denial of the Pythagorean Theorem a self-contradiction. We only say that within Euclidean geometry it cannot be true.

There is another way to bring out the reason for classifying both "Red objects are colored" and the Pythagorean Theorem as matter-of-logic statements. It is that we disallow the denial of each for a logical reason: in the first case because it is a self-contradiction and in the second because of inconsistency with our original principles. We may then formulate rules for detecting each of the different sorts of matter-of-logic statement. The first is that if a statement's denial is a self-contradiction, then it is a matter-of-logic statement. The second is that if the assertion of a statement's denial is disallowed because of its inconsistency with the logical system of statements into which the statement itself fits, then it is a matter-of-logic statement. Notice that if the application of one rule is inconclusive, the other must be applied before one can be satisfied about whether a given statement belongs in the matter-of-logic category.

We may now notice another characteristic of matter-of-logic statements. They do not describe the world. Consider, for example, "That which is red is colored." The statement makes no claim that there is anything red in the world. It is only an assertion that if there are red things in the world, then they are colored. But even though matter-of-logic statements do not describe the world, they may have a great deal to do with the way in which we look at the world. Consider, for example, the usefulness of "The whole is equal to the sum of its parts," a matter-of-logic statement I have already discussed. We do not want to say that this statement describes the world in the sense that it can be confirmed or disproved by experience. But in our use of the statement it is clearly not unrelated to experience, for we do order appropriate parts of our experiences in accordance with it. This is not to say, however, that all matter-of-logic statements are, or need to be, useful in the ordering of experience. For instance, many geometries have been invented simply because of the charm which their elegant self-consistency has exercised on the minds of their inventors; and no thought is given to the question of whether they describe any discoverable space.

MATTERS OF FACT AND LOGIC

From what I have written thus far, my readers may suppose that all statements come neatly labeled "matter-of-fact" or "matter-of-logic," and there can be no trouble in deciding into which basket a given statement should be sorted. Unfortunately this orderly picture is inaccurate, and the kind of puzzle about which a philosopher is most likely to work his head to the bone is one generated by the ins and outs of classifying some statement. There are, however, ways of testing statements that help to decide whether they are to be classified as matter-of-fact or matter-of-logic. I have already described the rules for testing for matter-of-logic statements. I want now to show how points made earlier provide a test for identifying matter-of-fact statements.

Consider the statement, "My collar button is on the bureau." Now even though my collar button is on the bureau, and thus the statement is true, I know what it would be like for its denial, "My collar button is *not* on the bureau," to be true. As I have described things, the denial is, of course, false; but notice that if I did not know how to find out the truth of both statements, I could not find out the truth of either. To find that my collar button is on the bureau, I must also know what it would be like for it not to be on the bureau, or else how could I start looking for it? Should the reader doubt what I have said, he may set himself the task of finding out the truth of the statement, "There is a xonygl in the next room." His first question must be, "What is a xonygl?" If he does not know how to tell the difference between xonygls and everything else in the next room, he is in no position to check on the presence of xonygls. Philosophers like to speak of this as knowing the difference between xonygls and non-xonygls. When someone knows this difference, he will be able to find out the truth of either "There is a xonygl in the next room" or "There is *not* a xonygl in the next room."

The denials of matter-of-fact statements, then, may be either true or false, and a look at the world is required in order to decide whether a given matter-of-fact statement or its denial is true. Here, then, is our test for matter-of-fact statements: Their denials are as conceivable as the original statements, and we can decide which is true only by an appeal to experience. Here too is a basis for our distinction between matter-of-fact and matter-of-logic statements. The denial of the first sort of matter-of-logic statement we noticed is inconceivable because it is a self-contradiction; and the denial of the second sort is not to be allowed because it is inconsistent with the logical system of statements into which the original statement fits.

These distinctions are neatly stated; but they are not the end of the matter. The tangle of fact and logic is such that there are some statements which we sometimes allow to be matter-of-fact and at other times count as matter-of-logic. It would seem that our distinctions depend not only on the outcome of our tests, but also on which test we want to make. It remains to make this state of affairs as clear as it can be made in a small space and without long practice on the reader's part.

Is "My orange is segmented" a matter-of-fact or a matter-of-logic statement? Orange segments are those pieces into which the inner membrane naturally divides the pulp. Now, is its denial, "My orange is *not* segmented," conceivable? Can we say what we should have to find, in order to say that the statement is true? I think so. A non-segmented orange would have no inner membrane, so that the pulp would be undifferentiated, as in peaches. Notice that it does seem that if we did not know how to tell the difference between being segmented and being nonsegmented, we could not discover the truth of either "My orange is segmented" or its denial. Since we can conceive its denial, we must put this statement in the matter-of-fact basket.

But at this point, someone might ask this puzzling question: "Would you call that object you are eating an orange if it were not segmented?" I am being squeezed to decide whether "My orange is segmented" *must* be either matter-of-fact or matter-of-logic. If I answer "Yes," then the statement could be true or false and it is matter-of-fact. If I answer "No," the statement is being made to work like a definition. It is, therefore, always true, and must be counted as a matter-of-logic statement. Let us consider this "No" answer a little more.

When I say that I would not consider the object I am eating an orange if it were not segmented, I am agreeing to a rule for defining oranges: "If it is an orange, then it is segmented." Having agreed to such a rule, I must say either, "My orange is segmented," or nothing at all. Clearly I cannot say, "My orange is not segmented," for that is a self-contradictory statement. How do these considerations help me to decide whether my statement is matter-of-fact or matter-of-logic? It should now be clear that my decision depends on how I decide that I am using the statement. This is what I meant earlier when I said that we must not only apply the tests for distinguishing matter-of-fact and matter-of-logic statements, we must also decide what test is to be made. If I say that I am describing my orange when I say, "My orange is segmented," then the test can be applied to discover that the statement is matter-of-fact. If I say that I am speaking in accordance with the botanical definition of "orange" when I say, "My orange is segmented," then the test can be applied to discover that the statement is matter-of-logic.

We may finish by noticing what the classification of statements has to do with the limits of human knowledge. Philosophers have claimed that whatever is knowledge is expressible in either a matter-of-fact or a matter-of-logic statement. It must be admitted that this claim is open to challenge; but it is such a fundamental characteristic of philosophy that it is seldom challenged. Indeed, it is extremely difficult to imagine the terms in which a challenge could be stated. To carry the argument, one would have to convince a philosopher either that he has a cognitive power beyond the usual ones of perception and conception, or at the very least that there are people who have this new power and that he can be convinced of its existence as certainly as he can be convinced of the difference between blind and sighted persons. But convincing a philosopher that a hitherto unknown human power exists, when it is the case both that to appreciate the power he would have to exercise it or perceive it exercised, and that he denies that it is present to be exercised, appears to be an insuperable task. The little more that I can say on this point is that radical disagreement with the claim that whatever is knowledge is expressible in either matter-of-fact or matter-of-logic statements is most apt to occur when someone is caught in a violent disagreement over how the principle is to be applied, and no other way of saving his knowledge claim appears open to him except the invention of new ways of knowing and of new kinds of knowledge.

Within the limits of knowledge recognized by philosophy, then, philosophers' debates are over whether a given matter is a matter of fact or a matter of logic; and these are the debates which we shall overhear as we consider what philosophers tell us that we can know about the world, gods, human freedom, morals, and politics.

What is at stake in these debates? Most philosophers are ready to distinguish between what is in the world and what is in my mind. If something counts as a matter of fact, it exists in the world. If something counts as a matter of logic, it exists in a mind as a concept or, as I should prefer to say, as someone's knowing how to use a word. But in the history of philosophy a premium has been put on showing that something is a matter of fact, that it affects us because it is in the world and not just a concept in the mind. Thus, philosophical debates are hottest between those philosophers who want to make certain entries in the list of what there is in the world and other philosophers who do not want to let them get away with it.

For Further Study

Austin, J. L. *Sense and Sensibilia*. New York: Oxford U. Press, 1964. (Galaxy Book GB108.)

Ayer, A. J. *Language, Truth and Logic*. London: Gollancz, 1946, Ch. 4, "The A Priori." (Also Dover paperback.)

Bacon, Francis. *Novum Organum*, 1620, Aphorisms 38–62.

Bergson, Henri. *The Creative Mind*. Trans. by Mabelle L. Andison. New York: Philosophical Library, 1946, Ch. 4, "Philosophical Intuition."

Boas, George. *The Limits of Reason*. New York: Harper, 1961, Ch. 1, "Reason and Experience."

Chisholm, Roderick M. *Theory of Knowledge*. Englewood Cliffs: Prentice-Hall, 1966. (Foundations of Philosophy Series.)

Descartes, René. *Meditations*, 1641, esp. Meditation 1.

Ewing, A. C. *Fundamental Questions of Philosophy*. London: Routledge & Kegan Paul, 1951, Ch. 2, "The 'A Priori' and the Empirical," esp. pp. 26–36. (Also Collier Book AS250V.)

Garnett, A. Campbell. *The Perceptual Process*. Madison: U. of Wisconsin Press, 1965.

Locke, John. *An Essay Concerning Human Understanding*, 1690, Book 2, Ch. 1, "Of Ideas in General, and Their Original."

Peirce, Charles Sanders. *Collected Papers*. Ed. by Charles Hartshorne and Paul Weiss. Cambridge: Belknap Press of Harvard U. Press, 1962, Vol. 5, "The Fixation of Belief."

3 The Nature of Knowledge

GEORGE BERKELEY / To Be Is To Be Perceived *

George Berkeley (1685–1753), along with Locke and Hume, developed British empiricism. He attacked the concept of material substance and defended an idealistic immaterialism.

IT IS EVIDENT to anyone who takes a survey of the *objects* of human knowledge that they are either ideas actually imprinted on the senses, or else such as are perceived by attending to the passions and operations of the mind, or lastly, ideas formed by help of memory and imagination—either compounding, dividing, or barely representing those originally perceived in the aforesaid ways. By sight I have the ideas of light and colors, with their several degrees and variations. By touch I perceive, for example, hard and soft, heat and cold, motion and resistance, and of all these more and less either as to quantity or degree. Smelling furnishes me with odors, the palate with tastes, and hearing conveys sounds to the mind in all their variety of tone and composition. And as several of these are observed to accompany each other, they come to be marked by one name, and so to be reputed as one thing. Thus, for example, a certain color, taste, smell, figure, and consistence having been observed to go together, are accounted one distinct thing signified by the name "*apple*"; other collections of ideas constitute a stone, a tree, a book, and the like sensible things—which as they

* George Berkeley, from A *Treatise Concerning the Principles of Human Knowledge* (1710), Secs. 1–4, 6–7, 9, 15, 25–30, 33.

are pleasing or disagreeable excite the passions of love, hatred, joy, grief, and so forth.

2. But, besides all that endless variety of ideas or objects of knowledge, there is likewise something which knows or perceives them and exercises divers operations, as willing, imagining, remembering, about them. This perceiving, active being is what I call *mind, spirit, soul,* or *myself.* By which words I do not denote any one of my ideas, but a thing entirely distinct from them, wherein they exist or, which is the same thing, whereby they are perceived—for the existence of an idea consists in being perceived.

3. That neither our thoughts, nor passions, nor ideas formed by the imagination exist without the mind is what everybody will allow. And it seems no less evident that the various sensations or ideas imprinted on the sense, however blended or combined together (that is, whatever objects they compose), cannot exist otherwise than in a mind perceiving them.—I think an intuitive knowledge may be obtained of this by anyone that shall attend to what is meant by the term *exist* when applied to sensible things. The table I write on I say exists, that is, I see and feel it; and if I were out of my study I should say it existed—meaning thereby that if I was in my study I might perceive it, or that some other spirit actually does perceive it. There was an odor, that is, it was smelled; there was a sound, that is to say, it was heard; a color or figure, and it was perceived by sight or touch. This is all that I can understand by these and the like expressions. For as to what is said of the absolute existence of unthinking things without any re- lation to their being perceived, that seems perfectly unintelligible. Their *esse* is *percipi,* nor is it possible they should have any existence out of the minds or thinking things which perceive them.

4. It is indeed an opinion strangely prevailing amongst men that houses, mountains, rivers, and, in a word, all sensible objects have an existence, natural or real, distinct from their being perceived by the understanding. But with how great an assurance and acquiescence soever this principle may be entertained in the world, yet whoever shall find in his heart to call it in question may, if I mistake not, perceive it to involve a manifest con- tradiction. For what are the forementioned objects but the things we per- ceive by sense? And what do we perceive besides our own ideas or sensa- tions? And is it not plainly repugnant that any one of these, or any com- bination of them, should exist unperceived? . . .

6. Some truths then are so near and obvious to the mind that a man need only open his eyes to see them. Such I take this important one to be, to wit, that all the choir of heaven and furniture of the earth, in a word, all those bodies which compose the mighty frame of the world, have not any subsistence without a mind—that their *being* is to be perceived or known, that, consequently, so long as they are not actually perceived by me or do not exist in my mind or that of any other created spirit, they must either

have no existence at all or else subsist in the mind of some eternal spirit—it being perfectly unintelligible, and involving all the absurdity of abstraction, to attribute to any single part of them an existence independent of a spirit. [To be convinced of which, the reader need only reflect, and try to separate in his own thoughts, the *being* of a sensible thing from its *being perceived.*]

7. From what has been said it follows there is not any other substance than *Spirit*, or that which perceives. But, for the fuller proof of this point, let it be considered the sensible qualities are color, figure, motion, smell, taste, and such like—that is, the ideas perceived by sense. Now, for an idea to exist in an unperceiving thing is a manifest contradiction, for to have an idea is all one has to perceive; that, therefore, wherein color, figure, and the like qualities exist must perceive them; hence it is clear there can be no unthinking substance or *substratum* of those ideas. . . .

9. Some there are who make a distinction betwixt *primary* and *secondary* qualities. By the former they mean extension, figure, motion, rest, solidity or impenetrability, and number; by the latter they denote all other sensible qualities, as colors, sounds, tastes, and so forth. The ideas we have of these they acknowledge not to be the resemblances of anything existing without the mind, or unperceived, but they will have our ideas of the primary qualities to be patterns or images of things which exist without the mind, in an unthinking substance which they call "matter." By "matter," therefore, we are to understand an inert, senseless substance, in which extension, figure, and motion do actually subsist. But it is evident from what we have already shown that extension, figure, and motion are only ideas existing in the mind, and that an idea can be like nothing but another idea, and that consequently neither they nor their archetypes can exist in an unperceiving substance. Hence it is plain that the very notion of what is called *matter* or *corporeal substance* involves a contradiction in it. . . .

15. In short, let anyone consider those arguments which are thought manifestly to prove that colors and taste exist only in the mind, and he shall find they may with equal force be brought to prove the same thing of extension, figure, and motion. Though it must be confessed this method of arguing does not so much prove that there is no extension or color in an outward object as that we do not know by sense which is the true extension or color of the object. But the arguments foregoing plainly show it to be impossible that any color or extension at all, or other sensible quality whatsoever, should exist in an unthinking subject without the mind, or, in truth, that there should be any such thing as an outward object. . . .

25. All our ideas, sensations, or the things which we perceive, by whatsoever names they may be distinguished, are visibly inactive—there is nothing of power or agency included in them. So that one idea or object of thought cannot produce or make any alteration in another. To be satisfied

of the truth of this, there is nothing else requisite but a bare observation of our ideas. For since they and every part of them exist only in the mind, it follows that there is nothing in them but what is perceived; but whoever shall attend to his ideas, whether of sense or reflection, will not perceive in them any power or activity; there is, therefore, no such thing contained in them. A little attention will discover to us that the very being of an idea implies passiveness and inertness in it, insomuch that it is impossible for an idea to do anything or, strictly speaking, to be the cause of anything; neither can it be the resemblance or pattern of any active being. . . . Whence it plainly follows that extension, figure, and motion cannot be the cause of our sensations. To say, therefore, that these are the effects of powers resulting from the configuration, number, motion, and size of corpuscles must certainly be false.

26. We perceive a continual succession of ideas, some are anew excited, others are changed or totally disappear. There is, therefore, some cause of these ideas, whereon they depend and which produces and changes them. That this cause cannot be any quality or idea or combination of ideas is clear from the preceding section. It must therefore be a substance; but it has been shown that there is no corporeal or material substance: it remains, therefore, that the cause of ideas is an incorporeal, active substance or spirit.

27. A spirit is one simple, undivided, active being—as it perceives ideas it is called the *understanding*, and as it produces or otherwise operates about them it is called the *will*. Hence there can be no *idea* formed of a soul or spirit; for all ideas whatever, being passive and inert (*vide* sect. 25), they cannot represent unto us, by way of image or likeness, that which acts. A little attention will make it plain to anyone that to have an idea which shall be like that active principle of motion and change of ideas is absolutely impossible. Such is the nature of *spirit*, or that which acts, that it cannot be of itself perceived, but only by the effects which it produces. If any man shall doubt of the truth of what is here delivered, let him but reflect and try if he can frame the idea of any power or active being, and whether he has ideas of two principal powers marked by the names *will* and *understanding*, distinct from each other as well as from a third idea of substance or being in general, with a relative notion of its supporting or being the subject of the aforesaid powers—which is signified by the name *soul* or *spirit*. This is what some hold; but, so far as I can see, the words *will, soul, spirit* do not stand for different ideas or, in truth, for any idea at all, but for something which is very different from ideas, and which, being an agent, cannot be like unto, or represented by, any idea whatsoever. [Though it must be owned at the same time that we have some notion of soul, spirit, and the operations of the mind, such as willing, loving, hating —in as much as we know or understand the meaning of those words.]

28. I find I can excite ideas in my mind at pleasure, and vary and shift the scene as oft as I think fit. It is no more than willing, and straightway this or that idea arises in my fancy; and by the same power it is obliterated and makes way for another. This making and unmaking of ideas does very properly denominate the mind active. Thus much is certain and grounded on experience; but when we talk of unthinking agents or of exciting ideas exclusive of volition, we only amuse ourselves with words.

29. But, whatever power I may have over my own thoughts, I find the ideas actually perceived by sense have not a like dependence on my will. When in broad daylight I open my eyes, it is not in my power to choose whether I shall see or no, or to determine what particular objects shall present themselves to my view; and so likewise as to the hearing and other senses; the ideas imprinted on them are not creatures of my will. There is therefore some *other* will or spirit that produces them.

30. The ideas of sense are more strong, lively, and distinct than those of the imagination; they have likewise a steadiness, order, and coherence, and are not excited at random, as those which are the effects of human wills often are, but in a regular train or series, the admirable connection whereof sufficiently testifies the wisdom and benevolence of its Author. Now the set rules or established methods wherein the mind we depend on excites in us the ideas of sense are called the *laws of nature*; and these we learn by experience, which teaches us that such and such ideas are attended with such and such other ideas in the ordinary course of things. . . .

33. The ideas imprinted on the senses by the Author of Nature are called *real things*; and those excited in the imagination, being less regular, vivid, and constant, are more properly termed *ideas* or *images of things* which they copy and represent. But then our sensations, be they never so vivid and distinct, are nevertheless ideas, that is, they exist in the mind, or are perceived by it, as truly as the ideas of its own framing. The ideas of sense are allowed to have more reality in them, that is, to be more strong, orderly, and coherent than the creatures of the mind; but this is no argument that they exist without the mind. They are also less dependent on the spirit, or thinking substance which perceives them, in that they are excited by the will of another and more powerful spirit; yet still they are *ideas*; and certainly no idea, whether faint or strong, can exist otherwise than in a mind perceiving it.

BERTRAND RUSSELL / A Critique of Berkeley *

Bertrand Russell (1872–   ) is a British mathematician, logician, and philosopher who, with G. E. Moore, was largely responsible for the rise of realistic and analytic philosophy in England in the early decades of this century. His many books cover a wide range of topics both within and beyond the field of philosophy.

. . . Berkeley . . . proved first, by arguments which were largely valid, that our sense-data cannot be supposed to have an existence independent of us, but must be, in part at least, "in" the mind, in the sense that their existence would not continue if there were no seeing or hearing or touching or smelling or tasting. So far, his contention was almost certainly valid, even if some of his arguments were not so. But he went on to argue that sense-data were the only things of whose existence our perceptions could assure us, and that to be known is to be "in" a mind, and therefore to be mental. Hence he concluded that nothing can ever be known except what is in some mind, and that whatever is known without being in my mind must be in some other mind.

In order to understand his argument, it is necessary to understand his use of the word "idea." He gives the name "idea" to anything which is *immediately* known, as, for example, sense-data are known. Thus a particular colour which we see is an idea; so is a voice which we hear, and so on. But the term is not wholly confined to sense-data. There will also be things remembered or imagined, for with such things also we have immediate acquaintance at the moment of remembering or imagining. All such immediate data he calls "ideas."

He then proceeds to consider common objects, such as a tree, for instance. He shows that all we know immediately when we "perceive" the tree consists of ideas in his sense of the word, and he argues that there is not the slightest ground for supposing that there is anything real about the tree except what is perceived. Its being, he says, consists in being perceived: in the Latin of the schoolmen its *"esse"* is *"percipi."* He fully admits that the tree must continue to exist even when we shut our eyes or

* Bertrand Russell, from "Idealism," in *The Problems of Philosophy* (New York: Oxford University Press, Inc., 1912), pp. 38–43. Used by permission of the publisher.

when no human being is near it. But this continued existence, he says, is due to the fact that God continues to perceive it; the "real" tree, which corresponds to what we called the physical object, consists of ideas in the mind of God, ideas more or less like those we have when we see the tree, but differing in the fact that they are permanent in God's mind so long as the tree continues to exist. All our perceptions, according to him, consist in a partial participation in God's perceptions, and it is because of this participation that different people see more or less the same tree. Thus apart from minds and their ideas there is nothing in the world, nor is it possible that anything else should ever be known, since whatever is known is necessarily an idea.

There are in this argument a good many fallacies which have been important in the history of philosophy, and which it will be as well to bring to light. In the first place, there is a confusion engendered by the use of the word "idea." We think of an idea as essentially something *in* somebody's mind, and thus when we are told that a tree consists entirely of ideas, it is natural to suppose that, if so, the tree must be entirely in minds. But the notion of being "in" the mind is ambiguous. We speak of bearing a person in mind, not meaning that the person is in our minds, but that a thought of him is in our minds. When a man says that some business he had to arrange went clean out of his mind, he does not mean to imply that the business itself was ever in his mind, but only that a thought of the business was formerly in his mind, but afterwards ceased to be in his mind. And so when Berkeley says that the tree must be in our minds if we can know it, all that he really has a right to say is that a thought of the tree must be in our minds. To argue that the tree itself must be in our minds is like arguing that a person whom we bear in mind is himself in our minds. This confusion may seem too gross to have been really committed by any competent philosopher, but various attendant circumstances rendered it possible. In order to see how it was possible, we must go more deeply into the question as to the nature of ideas.

Before taking up the general question of the nature of ideas, we must disentangle two entirely separate questions which arise concerning sense-data and physical objects. We saw that, for various reasons of detail, Berkeley was right in treating the sense-data which constitute our perception of the tree as more or less subjective, in the sense that they depend upon us as much as upon the tree, and would not exist if the tree were not being perceived. But this is an entirely different point from the one by which Berkeley seeks to prove that whatever can be immediately known *must* be in a mind. For this purpose arguments of detail as to the dependence of sense-data upon us are useless. It is necessary to prove, generally, that by being known, things are shown to be mental. This is what Berkeley believes himself to have done. It is this question, and not our previous question as to the difference between sense-data and the physical object, that must now concern us.

Taking the word "idea" in Berkeley's sense, there are two quite distinct things to be considered whenever an idea is before the mind. There is on the one hand the thing of which we are aware—say the colour of my table—and on the other hand the actual awareness itself, the mental act of apprehending the thing. The mental act is undoubtedly mental, but is there any reason to suppose that the thing apprehended is in any sense mental? Our previous arguments concerning the colour did not prove it to be mental; they only proved that its existence depends upon the relation of our sense organs to the physical object—in our case, the table. That is to say, they proved that a certain colour will exist, in a certain light, if a normal eye is placed at a certain point relatively to the table. They did not prove that the colour is in the mind of the percipient.

Berkeley's view, that obviously the colour *must* be in the mind, seems to depend for its plausibility upon confusing the thing apprehended with the act of apprehension. Either of these might be called an "idea"; probably either would have been called an idea by Berkeley. The act is undoubtedly in the mind; hence, when we are thinking of the act, we readily assent to the view that ideas must be in the mind. Then, forgetting that this was only true when ideas were taken as acts of apprehension, we transfer the proposition that "ideas are in the mind" to ideas in the other sense, i.e. to the things apprehended by our acts of apprehension. Thus, by an unconscious equivocation, we arrive at the conclusion that whatever we can apprehend must be in our minds. This seems to be the true analysis of Berkeley's argument, and the ultimate fallacy upon which it rests.

This question of the distinction between act and object in our apprehending of things is vitally important, since our whole power of acquiring knowledge is bound up with it. The faculty of being acquainted with things other than itself is the main characteristic of a mind. Acquaintance with objects essentially consists in a relation between the mind and something other than the mind; it is this that constitutes the mind's power of knowing things. If we say that the things known must be in the mind, we are either unduly limiting the mind's power of knowing, or we are uttering a mere tautology. We are uttering a mere tautology if we mean by "*in* the mind" the same as by "*before* the mind," i.e. if we mean merely being apprehended by the mind. But if we mean this, we shall have to admit that what, *in this sense*, is in the mind, may nevertheless be not mental. Thus when we realize the nature of knowledge, Berkeley's argument is seen to be wrong in substance as well as in form, and his grounds for supposing that "ideas"—i.e. the objects apprehended—must be mental, are found to have no validity whatever. . . .

For Further Study

Ewing, A. E. *Reason and Intuition*. New York: Oxford U. Press, 1942. (A lecture.)

Farber, Marvin. *Naturalism and Subjectivism*. Springfield: Charles C. Thomas, 1959, Ch. 1, "Experience and Basic Fact"; Ch. 7, "The Limits of Subjectivism."

Grene, Marjorie. *The Knower and the Known*. New York: Basic Books, 1966.

Hendel, Charles W. "The Subjective as a Problem: An Essay in Criticism of Naturalistic and Existential Philosophies," *Philosophical Review*, 62 (1953): 327–354.

Locke, Don. *Perception and Our Knowledge of the External World*. New York: Humanities Press, 1967.

Plato. *Theaetetus*. (Various editions.)

Russell, Bertrand. *Human Knowledge: Its Scope and Limits*. New York: Simon and Schuster, 1948, Part 6, Ch. 1, "Kinds of Knowledge."

———. *The Problems of Philosophy*. New York: Oxford U. Press, 1912, Ch. 1, "Appearance and Reality."

Sellars, W. F. *Science, Perception, and Reality*. New York: Humanities Press, 1963.

Yolton, John W., ed. *Theory of Knowledge*. New York: Macmillan, 1965. (Sources in Philosophy Series.)

4 The Validity of Knowledge

A. C. EWING / Criteria of Truth *

A. C. Ewing (1899–   ) is a Fellow of the British Academy and has
taught for many years at Cambridge University. He has written widely
in the fields of moral philosophy and metaphysics.

WE SHALL now turn to the question of the criterion or criteria of truth.
This question has not always been carefully separated from the question of
the definition of truth, but I think it ought to be. The question, what
truth is, is in itself different from the question how we are to find out
whether a proposition is true. If we know that truth is to be defined as A,
it may be thought that this at once gives us also the criterion of truth, because we could then always look for the characteristic A in order to decide
whether a proposition was true. But it might well be the case that A was
something which we could not thus directly discover but must determine
by indirect means. For instance, only at the best in a minority of cases
could we claim to see by direct inspection whether a proposition corresponded to the real, since to do so we should have to have an immediate
awareness of the latter, whereas most of the propositions which we believe
are established by inference and not thus immediately seen to be true. Yet
this admission would not necessarily contradict the view that correspondence constituted the definition of truth. So we had better handle separately the question of the criterion and the question of the definition of
truth. The only way of determining the criterion or criteria is to investigate

* Reprinted with permission of The Macmillan Company from *The Fundamental
Questions of Philosophy* by A. C. Ewing. First published in 1951. From "Criteria of
Truth," pp. 59–67.

the different kinds of well-authenticated knowledge and belief we have and see what the criteria are that convince us of their truth. There is no means of proving *a priori* what the criteria should be apart from such an investigation of what we find we must actually believe in ordinary cases.

We might well speak of "correspondence" as the criterion of truth in cases of straightforward sense-experience or introspection. We can then observe the fact in question immediately and see whether our judgment corresponds. But, as we shall discover later, it is difficult to hold that we ever directly sense external physical objects; and in any case most of our judgments about them certainly go beyond anything we experience immediately.

What is to be the criterion of these? It may be contended that the best single word to describe it is "coherence." Certainly something that we may describe as a coherence test is needed to decide between rival scientific theories or even to distinguish illusion from genuine perception. Many of our sense-perceptions are unhesitatingly rejected just because they do not fit into a coherent system. That is the case with dreams. Why do we not believe our dreams when awake? Because they do not cohere with the perceptions of waking life. A dreamt that he was hanged last night, but that does not agree (cohere) with the fact that he is still alive. I sometimes dream that I am in a place hundreds or thousands of miles away from where I am when I wake, though no known means of locomotion can have transported me from there. The lack of coherence with waking life would be still more obvious if somebody else were in the room at the time I dreamt and could observe my presence. Again, if we always believed in the sense-perceptions even of waking life, we should have to suppose that the same physical thing had all manner of different shapes, since the shape varies with the position of the observer, and rather than do this we reject very many of our perceptions as illusory. In water an oar appears bent, but to assume that it is really bent would not agree (cohere) well with the fact that we can use it to row effectively. All this can be cited to show the very important part which coherence plays in our actual thinking as a test of truth. It may be said to be the sole criterion by which we distinguish illusions and correct perceptions.

A great deal of stress has rightly been laid on the supreme importance for science of observation, but it may be doubted whether there is a single accepted proposition of science which could be established by observation alone, and I do not think this is altered when we add to observation deductive logic and mathematics. An obstinate person could always adopt the course of the opponents of Galileo when the latter claimed to have discovered the satellites of Jupiter. When they denied the existence of these bodies, Galileo challenged them to look through the newly invented telescope and see them for themselves. They replied that they knew already there were no such satellites and would not look through the telescope because, if they did, the devil might make them see them although they were not there. This is ridiculous enough, but it must be admitted both that the view is logically possible and that a similar course is adopted by all of us in regard to the objects of dreams and other appearances condemned as illusory (except that we do not attribute the deception to the devil but to our sense-organs). These objects do not conform to our intellectual standards of coherence, and so we just say they were not really there, though we have seen them perfectly well. (Of course we do not mean they are not real at all. We give them reality as sort of mental images, but not as physical things.) Even without resorting to such heroic expedients as Galileo's opponents, most physical theories that have been held at any time could avoid outright refutation if a sufficient number of arbitrary *ad hoc* assumptions were made. Take the Ptolemaic theory, for instance. If we relied on observation primarily, the right reply to Copernicus's suggestion would be that put by Bernard Shaw in the mouth of a medieval soldier: "The utter fool! Why could not he use his eyes?" It may be retorted that the Ptolemaic theory, although in accordance with experiences such as that of seeing the sun rise, was logically incompatible with observations of a more recondite order, so that these latter refuted it. But this is not the case: it would be possible to maintain the Ptolemaic system compatibly with the evidence of the senses provided we made sufficient arbitrary *ad hoc* assumptions unconnected by any principle. This was what was done in face of the first criticisms of Copernicans, but eventually as the number of such assumptions became greater the Ptolemaic theory became less and less plausible until it was quite dead, although never strictly refuted, and this is what happens with most discarded theories of science.

Advocates of the coherence theory are well aware that complete coherence must be regarded as an unattainable ideal, but views may still be judged according to their greater or less distance from it. The nearest approach to it is to be found in mathematics. Here the different propositions are so connected that each follows necessarily from others and that you could not deny any one without contradicting a vast number of others. If we assumed that $2 + 2$ was equal to 5 we could, I think, without making any further mistake draw conclusions which contradicted every arithmetical truth there is about any number. Other sciences cannot attain to this degree of coherence, but in any science we assume that of two theories, equally compatible with observed facts, the one which brings us nearer to this ideal is the more likely to be true. To be successful a theory must not be inconsistent with empirical facts, but coherence must not be interpreted in terms of mere consistency. Two truths might be quite compatible and yet quite independent and logically unconnected, e.g. that Washington is the capital of the United States and that I have a pain in my big toe. A successful theory must not just enumerate logically compatible facts without connecting them or causally explaining them. It must, if possible, bring them under laws, and the only evidence for the laws may be said to be their coherence with experience. We bring together into a coherent system what previously appeared unconnected by deducing different facts from the same set of laws, e.g. the fall of apples in an orchard and the movements of the stars. We may have no insight into the causal laws governing nature, but nevertheless in deciding what these laws are we can be swayed only by two considerations. Either we must see the laws accepted to be those which can easiest be reconciled with our experience, i.e. cohere best with it. Or we must see that they increase the coherence of our experience by bringing different elements of it together under the same law, instead of two separate unconnected laws. It is difficult to see what other criteria there could be for a scientific law, and these certainly can be brought under the heading of the principle of coherence. In our psychological interpretation of people's actions and testimony we similarly apply the coherence test, accepting the explanation which we say "makes the best sense" of their actions. We presuppose it even in a detective story, for the correct theory as to the origin of the crime will be the one which accounts for the facts and fits them into a coherent system. The fundamental principles of logic themselves can be justified by this criterion on the ground that there could be no coherent system at all without these principles. But the argument does not in any way support the view that coherence by itself is the sole criterion, but rather *coherence with experience*. This would probably be admitted by most advocates of the coherence theory, but it may then be urged that "coherence with experience" really means "coherence with propositions based on experience," so that we have now admitted a second set of propositions not themselves based on coherence but on the mere fact that we can see them to correspond to our experience. The coherence criterion cannot without being thus supplemented by the correspondence criterion ever do justice to the empirical element in our knowledge. Only we must not think of the empirical data as known completely quite apart from the use of the coherence test and thus serving as an altogether independent starting-point already there in its entirety. In order really to know the empirical data, we must have already fitted them into some rough kind of system. We cannot know them, still less communicate our knowledge, without classifying them and bringing them under universal concepts, and this already presupposes a conceptual system in the light of which we make all our judgments and which is tested by its ability to give a coherent interpretation of our empirical data. We must remember that with the exception of proper names almost every word we use stands for a universal concept of one sort or other, and this means that it is part of a conceptual system which men have gradually built up in order to describe their experiences to each other and interpret them to themselves.

There are other gaps in a purely coherence theory of truth besides its inability to deal with empirical data. It is true that the coherence theory cannot get on without admitting immediate empirical cognitions not just based on coherence. But it is true also that it cannot get on without immediate cognitions of a different sort. The advocates of the coherence theory reject the view that any propositions are self-evident in their own right. They would say that the fundamental logical propositions, like the law of contradiction, which seem self-evident, are validated not by their self-evidence, but by the fact that they are presupposed if there is to be any knowledge or any coherent system at all. Of subordinate principles they would say that they must be accepted as true because, although these are not themselves necessary presuppositions of knowledge, they follow from general principles which are. But I find it hard to believe that we only know the law of contradiction because we see that without it we could have no knowledge or that we only know that numbers can be summed because we see that otherwise we could have no arithmetic or no consistent arithmetic. But, however that may be, there is in any case a definite proof that the coherence theory cannot dispense altogether with the notion of self-evidence or intuition. Suppose a belief is accepted or a proposition known because it coheres with the system. But how do we see that it coheres with the system? We might see it as the result of a process of mediate inference, but that could not go on *ad infinitum*. Sooner or later we should have to come to a proposition of which we could only say that it is evident that it coheres with the others or that we just see immediately that it coheres. . . .

Again, I do not see how, if we were never immediately aware of the presence of goodness or badness, rightness or wrongness in any particular instance, we could ever establish any ethical proposition by the coherence test. Ethical propositions cannot be proved by argument from non-ethical, so some ethical propositions must be known immediately if we are to know any at all. Finally, I do not see how the coherence theory can give a satisfactory account of memory judgments. These are clearly not inferences, they are not established, though they may be confirmed, by coherence; they are as much given as the data of sense-perception. They represent still another kind, and a very important and all-pervasive kind of immediate cognitions.

It seems to me therefore that "coherence with experience" is not a formula adequate to cover the whole of knowledge and justified belief. There are other immediate cognitions besides those of objects of our present introspection and sense-experience. But a parallel formula might be found to cover all cases. We might say that the criterion is "coherence with direct cognitions in general." By an "immediate cognition" or "direct awareness" I mean a "cognition otherwise than by inference," thus covering alike sense-perception, introspection, memory, intuition of the logically self-evident and of immediately apprehended ethical propositions. To say that correspondence was the sole criterion would be to try to bring all criteria under the heading of this direct awareness, but the correspondence theory has to admit that we are able to make inferences beyond our immediate experience or memory. Similarly, the coherence theory has to admit that coherence by itself is not the sole criterion, but at least coherence with experience, and, I should say, "coherence with immediate cognitions in general." When this has been admitted, either theory has left a place for the other, and the difference between them has become one of relative emphasis.

It is clear in any case that we cannot do with just one criterion of truth. Neither sense-experience nor coherence can fulfil this role for all truths, if only because there are both *a priori* and empirical propositions. Intuition we have to introduce as a third criterion, if only because all inference presupposes intuitions by which we see that a stage in the inference follows from the preceding one. Since intuitions are usually concerned with facts of a kind that could not be confirmed or refuted by sense-experience or memory, coherence provides a specially valuable test for them; but coherence is also absolutely essential for building up our ordinary conception of the physical world and of human minds. Nor can we dispense with memory as a fourth means of attaining knowledge and justified belief. Memory is not sense-perception or present introspection, nor is it inference, and it can rightly claim to be its own adequate guarantee in a vast multitude of cases. Memory, introspection and perception of the immediate object of sense may perhaps be all appropriately brought under the correspondence formula as cases where we just see immediately that the propositions believed or known correspond to the facts, but it seems less appropriate to apply this formula to knowledge by inference.

The discussion has brought out the fact that there are two elements in knowledge and true belief to both of which it is essential to give an adequate place in our philosophy, (1) active construction and systematizing by the mind, (2) an objectively given basis independent of the first element and the foundation of its work. Extreme empiricism neglects the former element, most forms of the coherence and pragmatist theories the latter.

Are we to add to the other criteria the pragmatic test of which so much is said nowadays? Now no doubt a belief in a true proposition will usually (though not always) work well and a belief in a false proposition badly, and therefore practical success may commonly serve as a criterion which will at least make it likely that the proposition in question is true. But I cannot regard this criterion as an ultimate one. How are we to know that a belief works badly? Because the consequences which should follow if the belief were true do not in fact occur? But this is a direct theoretical refutation which every theory recognizes. The point which shows the belief false is not its practical bearing, i.e. that it injures somebody, but the fact that it conflicts with experience. A false belief might be refuted by a conflict with experience of a kind which was highly agreeable to the believer, as when he has a pleasant surprise. And it may be urged that we know by perception and inference a great many propositions without seeing how they work at all. To this it may be retorted that, since we do not assume all our perceptions to be correct and do not see the canons of at least inductive arguments to be logically self-evident, we must in judging what we perceive and making inductive inferences at any rate presuppose certain general principles which can only be justified by their working. The question is not whether a particular proposition works, but whether it is a consistent deduction from the application of principles of inference which have worked in dealing with experience and are justified by their working. But we may reply that this is a vicious circle. What the pragmatist is trying to justify is the belief in induction, i.e. the argument from what we have observed to the unobserved, and the argument offered to justify it is that the belief has worked in the past. But this is no argument that it will work in the future unless he already assumes the principles of induction which he is trying to justify. And, since he has not yet shown that they will work, these principles must be assumed independently of any test by their working. We may of course interpret "working" as "systematizing empirical facts," but then we shall be falling back on the coherence test. The question is: Can the mere fact that some belief produces good consequences, apart from any further argument which shows that the belief in question would not be likely to produce good consequences if it were not true, itself supply a criterion of truth? I am not clear why it should. If we were perfectly adjusted to the real, true beliefs would perhaps always work better than false, but then nobody can claim that we are perfectly adjusted.

WILLIAM JAMES / Pragmatism's Conception of Truth *

William James (1842–1910), after receiving an M.D. and teaching physiology at Harvard, turned to psychology and then to philosophy. In psychology he founded the first experimental laboratory in the United States and wrote an important two-volume text. Through his lectures and writings in philosophy he popularized pragmatic ideas and established pragmatism as a distinctive philosophical movement in America.

TRUTH, as any dictionary will tell you, is a property of certain of our ideas. It means their "agreement," as falsity means their disagreement, with "reality." Pragmatists and intellectualists both accept this definition as a matter of course. They begin to quarrel only after the question is raised as to what may precisely be meant by the term "agreement," and what by the term "reality," when reality is taken as something for our ideas to agree with.

In answering these questions the pragmatists are more analytic and painstaking, the intellectualists more offhand and irreflective. The popular notion is that a true idea must copy its reality. Like other popular views, this one follows the analogy of the most usual experience. Our true ideas of sensible things do indeed copy them. Shut your eyes and think of yonder clock on the wall, and you get just such a true picture or copy of its dial. But your idea of its "works" (unless you are a clockmaker) is much less of a copy, yet it passes muster, for it in no way clashes with the reality. Even though it should shrink to the mere word "works," that word still serves you truly; and when you speak of the "timekeeping function" of the clock, or of its spring's "elasticity," it is hard to see exactly what your ideas can copy.

You perceive that there is a problem here. Where our ideas cannot copy definitely their object, what does agreement with that object mean? Some idealists seem to say that they are true whenever they are what God means that we ought to think about that object. Others hold the copy-view all through, and speak as if our ideas possessed truth just in proportion as they approach to being copies of the Absolute's eternal way of thinking.

These views, you see, invite pragmatistic discussion. But the great as-

* William James, from "Pragmatism's Conception of Truth," in *Pragmatism* (New York: Longmans, Green, 1907), pp. 198–202, 205–206, 212–213, 222–223.

sumption of the intellectualists is that truth means essentially an inert static relation. When you've got your true idea of anything, there's an end of the matter. You're in possession; you *know*; you have fulfilled your thinking destiny. You are where you ought to be mentally; you have obeyed your categorical imperative; and nothing more need follow on that climax of your rational destiny. Epistemologically you are in stable equilibrium.

Pragmatism, on the other hand, asks its usual question. "Grant an idea or belief to be true," it says, "what concrete difference will its being true make in any one's actual life? How will the truth be realized? What experiences will be different from those which would obtain if the belief were false? What, in short, is the truth's cash-value in experiential terms?"

The moment pragmatism asks this question, it sees the answer: *True ideas are those that we can assimilate, validate, corroborate and verify. False ideas are those that we can not.* That is the practical difference it makes to us to have true ideas; that, therefore, is the meaning of truth, for it is all that truth is known as.

This thesis is what I have to defend. The truth of an idea is not a stagnant property inherent in it. Truth *happens* to an idea. It *becomes* true, is *made* true by events. Its verity *is* in fact an event, a process: the process namely of its verifying itself, its veri-*fication*. Its validity is the process of its valid-*ation*.

But what do the words verification and validation themselves pragmatically mean? They again signify certain practical consequences of the verified and validated idea. It is hard to find any one phrase that characterizes these consequences better than the ordinary agreement-formula—just such consequences being what we have in mind whenever we say that our ideas "agree" with reality. They lead us, namely, through the acts and other ideas which they instigate, into or up to, or towards, other parts of experience with which we feel all the while—such feeling being among our potentialities—that the original ideas remain in agreement. The connexions and transitions come to us from point to point as being progressive, harmonious, satisfactory. This function of agreeable leading is what we mean by an idea's verification. . . .

Our experience meanwhile is all shot through with regularities. One bit of it can warn us to get ready for another bit, can "intend" or be "significant of" that remoter object. The object's advent is the significance's verification. Truth, in these cases, meaning nothing but eventual verification, is manifestly incompatible with waywardness on our part. Woe to him whose beliefs play fast and loose with the order which realities follow in his experience; they will lead him nowhere or else make false connexions.

By "realities" or "objects" here, we mean either things of common sense, sensibly present, or else common-sense relations, such as dates, places, distances, kinds, activities. . . .

Realities mean, then, either concrete facts, or abstract kinds of things and relations perceived intuitively between them. They furthermore and thirdly mean, as things that new ideas of ours must no less take account of, the whole body of other truths already in our possession. But what now does "agreement" with such threefold realities mean?—to use again the definition that is current. . . .

To "agree" in the widest sense with a reality *can only mean to be guided either straight up to it or into its surroundings, or to be put into such working touch with it as to handle either it or something connected with it better than if we disagreed.* Better either intellectually or practically! And often agreement will only mean the negative fact that nothing contradictory from the quarter of that reality comes to interfere with the way in which our ideas guide us elsewhere. To copy a reality is, indeed, one very important way of agreeing with it, but it is far from being essential. The essential thing is the process of being guided. Any idea that helps us to *deal,* whether practically or intellectually, with either the reality or its belongings, that doesn't entangle our progress in frustrations, that *fits,* in fact, and adapts our life to the reality's whole setting, will agree sufficiently to meet the requirement. It will hold true of that reality. . . .

"The true," to put it very briefly, *is only the expedient in the way of our thinking, just as "the right" is only the expedient in the way of our behaving.* Expedient in almost any fashion; and expedient in the long run and on the whole of course; for what meets expediently all the experience in sight won't necessarily meet all farther experiences equally satisfactorily. Experience, as we know, has ways of *boiling over,* and making us correct our present formulas.

The "absolutely" true, meaning what no farther experience will ever alter, is that ideal vanishing-point towards which we imagine that all our temporary truths will some day converge. It runs on all fours with the perfectly wise man, and with the absolutely complete experience; and, if these ideals are ever realized, they will all be realized together. Meanwhile we have to live to-day by what truth we can get to-day, and be ready to-morrow to call it falsehood. . . .

For Further Study

Adler, Mortimer I. *The Conditions of Philosophy.* New York: Dell Publishing Co., 1967, Ch. 9, "Tests of Truth in Philosophy." (Delta Book 1451.)

Blanshard, Brand. *The Nature of Thought.* 2 vols.; New York: Macmillan, 1939, II, Ch. 25, "The Tests of Truth"; Ch. 26, "Coherence as the Nature of Truth."

Brunner, Emil. *Christianity and Civilisation*. New York: Scribner's, 1949, Part 1, Ch. 3, "The Problem of Truth."

Ehman, Robert R. "Subjectivity and Solipsism," *Review of Metaphysics*, 20 (September, 1966): 3–24.

Murphy, Arthur E. *The Uses of Reason*. New York: Macmillan, 1943, pp. 85–95, "The Pragmatic Theory of Truth."

Pepper, Stephen. *World Hypotheses: A Study in Evidence*. Berkeley and Los Angeles: U. of California Press, 1942, Ch. 1, "The Utter Skeptic," esp. pp. 3–10; Ch. 2, "Dogmatists."

Polanyi, Michael. *Personal Knowledge*. Chicago: U. of Chicago Press, 1958, Part One, "The Art of Knowing."

Russell, Bertrand. *Human Knowledge: Its Scope and Limits*. New York: Simon and Schuster, 1948, Part 2, Ch. 11, "Fact, Belief, Truth, and Knowledge."

Schmitt, Richard. "Two Senses of Knowing," *Review of Metaphysics*, 18 (June, 1965): 657–677.

Weiss, Paul. "Our Knowledge of What is Real," *Review of Metaphysics*, 18 (September, 1964): 3–22.

5 Scientific Methods of Inquiry

MORRIS R. COHEN & ERNEST NAGEL
/ The Nature, Limits, and Value of
Scientific Method *

Morris R. Cohen (1880–1947) taught philosophy for many years at the
College of the City of New York. Among his outstanding works are
Reason and Nature; A Preface to Logic; and *The Meaning of Human
History.*

Ernest Nagel (1901–   ) has taught philosophy at Columbia University since 1931. He has been an editor of the *Journal of Philosophy* and
the *Journal of Symbolic Logic.* Among his books are *Principles of the
Theory of Probability; Sovereign Reason;* and *The Structure of Science.*
He gave the Carus Lectures in 1963.

§ 1. What Is Scientific Method?

. . . [We have] asserted that the method of science is free from the limitations and willfulness of the alternative methods for settling doubt which
we . . . rejected. Scientific method, we declared, is the most assured technique man has yet devised for controlling the flux of things and establishing stable beliefs. What are the fundamental features of this method? . . .

* Morris R. Cohen and Ernest Nagel, from *An Introduction to Logic and Scientific
Method* (New York: Harcourt, Brace, 1934), pp. 391–403. Used by permission of
the publisher.

FACTS AND SCIENTIFIC METHOD

The method of science does not seek to impose the desires and hopes of men upon the flux of things in a capricious manner. It may indeed be employed to satisfy the desires of men. But its successful use depends upon seeking, in a deliberate manner, and irrespective of what men's desires are, to recognize, as well as to take advantage of, the structure which the flux possesses.

1. Consequently, scientific method aims to discover what the facts truly are, and the use of the method must be guided by the discovered facts. But, as we have repeatedly pointed out, what the facts are cannot be equated to the brute immediacy of our sensations. When our skin comes into contact with objects having high temperatures or with liquid air, the immediate experiences may be similar. We cannot, however, conclude without error that the temperatures of the substances touched are the same. Sensory experience sets the problem for knowledge, and just because such experience is immediate and final it must become informed by reflective analysis before knowledge can be said to take place.

2. Every inquiry arises from some felt problem, so that no inquiry can even get under way unless some selection or sifting of the subject matter has taken place. Such selection requires . . . some hypothesis, preconception, prejudice, which guides the research as well as delimits the subject matter of inquiry. Every inquiry is specific in the sense that it has a definite problem to solve, and such solution terminates the inquiry. It is idle to collect "facts" unless there is a problem upon which they are supposed to bear.

3. The ability to formulate problems whose solution may also help solve other problems is a rare gift, requiring extraordinary genius. The problems which meet us in daily life can be solved, if they can be solved at all, by the application of scientific method. But such problems do not, as a rule, raise far-reaching issues. The most striking applications of scientific method are to be found in the various natural and social sciences.

4. The "facts" for which every inquiry reaches out are propositions for whose truth there is considerable evidence. Consequently what the "facts" are must be determined by inquiry, and cannot be determined antecedently to inquiry. Moreover, what we believe to be the facts clearly depends upon the stage of our inquiry. There is therefore no sharp line dividing facts from guesses or hypotheses. During any inquiry the status of a proposition may change from that of hypothesis to that of fact, or from that of fact to that of hypothesis. Every so-called fact, therefore, may be challenged for the evidence upon which it is asserted to be a fact, even though no such challenge is actually made.

HYPOTHESES AND SCIENTIFIC METHOD

The method of science would be impossible if the hypotheses which are suggested as solutions could not be elaborated to reveal what they imply. The full meaning of a hypothesis is to be discovered in its implications.

1. Hypotheses are suggested to an inquirer by something in the subject matter under investigation, and by his previous knowledge of other subject matters. No rules can be offered for obtaining fruitful hypotheses, any more than rules can be given for discovering significant problems.

2. Hypotheses are required at every stage of an inquiry. It must not be forgotten that what are called general principles or laws (which may have been confirmed in a previous inquiry) can be applied to a present, still unterminated inquiry only with some risk. For they may not in fact be applicable. The general laws of any science function as hypotheses, which guide the inquiry in all its phases.

3. Hypotheses can be regarded as suggestions of possible connections between actual facts or imagined ones. The question of the truth of hypotheses need not, therefore, always be raised. The necessary feature of a hypotheses, from this point of view, is that it should be statable in a determinate form, so that its implications can be discovered by logical means.

4. The number of hypotheses which may occur to an inquirer is without limit, and is a function of the character of his imagination. There is a need, therefore, for a technique to choose between the alternative suggestions, and to make sure that the alternatives are in fact, and not only in appearance, *different* theories. Perhaps the most important and best explored part of such a technique is the technique of formal inference. . . .

5. It is convenient to have on hand—in storage, so to speak—different hypotheses whose consequences have been carefully explored. It is the task of mathematics to provide and explore alternative hypotheses. Mathematics receives hints concerning what hypotheses to study from the natural sciences; and the natural sciences are indebted to mathematics for suggestions concerning the type of order which their subject matter embodies.

6. The deductive elaboration of hypotheses is not the sole task of scientific method. Since there is a plurality of possible hypotheses, it is the task of inquiry to determine which of the possible explanations or solutions of the problem is in best agreement with the facts. Formal considerations are therefore never sufficient to establish the material truth of any theory.

7. No hypothesis which states a general proposition can be demonstrated as absolutely true. We have seen that all inquiry which deals with matters of fact employs probable inference. The task of such investigations is to select that hypothesis which is the most probable on the factual evi-

dence; and it is the task of further inquiry to find other factual evidence which will increase or decrease the probability of such a theory.

EVIDENCE AND SCIENTIFIC METHOD

Scientific method pursues the road of systematic doubt. It does not doubt *all* things, for this is clearly impossible. But it does question whatever lacks adequate evidence in its support.

1. Science is not satisfied with psychological certitude, for the mere intensity with which a belief is held is no guarantee of its truth. Science demands and looks for logically adequate grounds for the propositions it advances.

2. No single proposition dealing with matters of fact is beyond every significant doubt. No proposition is so well supported by evidence that other evidence may not increase or decrease its probability. However, while no single proposition is indubitable, the body of knowledge which supports it, and of which it is itself a part, is better grounded than any alternative body of knowledge.

3. Science is thus always ready to abandon a theory when the facts so demand. But the facts must really demand it. It is not unusual for a theory to be modified so that it may be retained in substance even though "facts" contradicted an earlier formulation of it. Scientific procedure is therefore a mixture of a willingness to change, and an obstinacy in holding on to, theories apparently incompatible with facts.

4. The verification of theories is only approximate. Verification simply shows that, within the margin of experimental error, the experiment is *compatible* with the verified hypothesis.

SYSTEM IN THE IDEAL OF SCIENCE

The ideal of science is to achieve a systematic interconnection of facts. Isolated propositions do not constitute a science. Such propositions serve merely as an opportunity to find the logical connection between them and other propositions.

1. "Common sense" is content with a miscellaneous collection of information. As a consequence, the propositions it asserts are frequently vague, the range of their application is unknown, and their mutual compatibility is generally very questionable. The advantages of discovering a system among facts are therefore obvious. A condition for achieving a system is the introduction of accuracy in the assertions made. The limit within which propositions are true is then clearly defined. Moreover, inconsisten-

cies between propositions asserted become eliminated gradually because propositions which are part of a system must support and correct one another. The extent and accuracy of our information is thus increased. In fact scientific method differs from other methods in the accuracy and number of facts it studies.

2. When, as frequently happens, a science abandons one theory for another, it is a mistake to suppose that science has become "bankrupt" and that it is incapable of discovering the structure of the subject matter it studies. Such changes indicate rather that the science is progressively realizing its ideal. For such changes arise from correcting previous observations or reasoning, and such correction means that we are in possession of more reliable facts.

3. The ideal of system requires that the propositions asserted to be true should be connected without the introduction of further propositions for which the evidence is small or nonexistent. In a system the number of unconnected propositions and the number of propositions for which there is no evidence are at a minimum. Consequently, in a system the requirements of simplicity, as expressed in the principle of Occam's razor, are satisfied in a high degree. For that principle declares that entities should not be multiplied beyond necessity. This may be interpreted as a demand that whatever is capable of proof should be proved. But the ideal of system requires just that.

The evidence for propositions which are elements in a system accumulates more rapidly than that for isolated propositions. The evidence for a proposition may come from its own verifying instances, or from the verifying instances of *other* propositions which are connected with the first in a system. It is this systematic character of scientific theories which gives such high probabilities to the various individual propositions of a science.

THE SELF-CORRECTIVE NATURE OF SCIENTIFIC METHOD

Science does not desire to obtain conviction for its propositions in *any* manner and at *any* price. Propositions must be supported by logically acceptable evidence, which must be weighed carefully and tested by the well-known canons of necessary and probable inference. It follows that the *method* of science is more stable, and more important to men of science, than any particular result achieved by its means.

1. In virtue of its method, the enterprise of science is a self-corrective process. It appeals to no special revelation or authority whose deliverances are indubitable and final. It claims no infallibility, but relies upon the methods of developing and testing hypotheses for assured conclusions. The canons of inquiry are themselves discovered in the process of reflection,

and may themselves become modified in the course of study. The method makes possible the noting and correction of errors by continued application of itself.

2. General propositions can be established only by the method of repeated sampling. Consequently, the propositions which a science puts forward for study are either confirmed in all possible experiments or modified in accordance with the evidence. It is this self-corrective nature of the method which allows us to challenge any proposition, but which also assures us that the theories which science accepts are more probable than any alternative theories. By not claiming more certainty than the evidence warrants, scientific method succeeds in obtaining more logical certainty than any other method yet devised.

3. In the process of gathering and weighing evidence, there is a continuous appeal from facts to theories or principles, and from principles to facts. For there is nothing intrinsically indubitable, there are no absolutely first principles, in the sense of principles which are self-evident or which must be known prior to everything else.

4. The method of science is thus essentially circular. We obtain evidence for principles by appealing to empirical material, to what is alleged to be "fact"; and we select, analyze, and interpret empirical material on the basis of principles. In virtue of such give and take between facts and principles, everything that is dubitable falls under careful scrutiny at one time or another.

THE ABSTRACT NATURE OF SCIENTIFIC THEORIES

No theory asserts *everything* that can possibly be asserted about a subject matter. Every theory selects certain aspects of it and excludes others. Unless it were possible to do this—either because such other aspects are irrelevant or because their influence on those selected is very minute—science as we know it would be impossible.

1. All theories involve abstraction from concrete subject matter. No rule can be given as to which aspects of a subject matter should be abstracted and so studied independently of other aspects. But in virtue of the goal of science—the achievement of a systematic interconnection of phenomena—in general those aspects will be abstracted which make a realization of this goal possible. Certain common elements in the phenomenon studied must be found, so that the endless variety of phenomena may be viewed as a system in which their structure is exhibited.

2. Because of the abstractness of theories, science often seems in patent contradiction with "common sense." In "common sense" the unique character and the pervasive character of things are not distinguished, so that

the attempt by science to disclose the invariant features often gives the appearance of artificiality. Theories are then frequently regarded as "convenient fictions" or as "unreal." However, such criticisms overlook the fact that it is just certain *selected invariant relations* of things in which science is interested, so that many familiar properties of things are necessarily neglected by the sciences. Moreover, they forget that "common sense" itself operates in terms of abstractions, which are familiar and often confused, and which are inadequate to express the complex structure of the flux of things.

TYPES OF SCIENTIFIC THEORIES

Scientific explanation consists in subsuming under some rule or law which expresses an invariant character of a group of events, the particular events it is said to explain. Laws themselves may be explained, and in the same manner, by showing that they are consequences of more comprehensive theories. The effect of such progressive explanation of events by laws, laws by wider laws or theories, is to reveal the interconnection of many apparently isolated propositions.

1. It is clear, however, that the process of explanation must come to a halt at some point. Theories which cannot be shown to be special consequences from a wider connection of facts must be left unexplained, and accepted as a part of the brute fact of existence. Material considerations, in the form of contingent matters of fact, must be recognized in at least two places. There is contingency at the level of sense: just *this* and not *that* is given in sense experience. And there is contingency at the level of explanation: a definite system, although not the only possible one from the point of view of formal logic, is found to be exemplified in the flux of things.

2. In a previous chapter we have enumerated several kinds of "laws" which frequently serve as explanations of phenomena. There is, however, another interesting distinction between theories. Some theories appeal to an easily imagined *hidden mechanism* which will explain the observable phenomena; other theories eschew all reference to such hidden mechanisms, and make use of *relations* abstracted from the phenomena actually observable. The former are called *physical* theories; the latter are called *mathematical* or *abstractive* theories.

It is important to be aware of the difference between these two kinds of theories, and to understand that some minds are especially attracted to one kind, while others are comfortable only with the other kind. But it is also essential not to suppose that either kind of theory is more fundamental or more valid than the other. In the history of science there is a constant oscillation between theories of these two types; sometimes both types of theories are used successfully on the same subject matter. Let us, however, make clear the difference between them.

The English physicist Rankine explained the distinction as follows: There are two methods of framing a theory. In a mathematical or abstractive theory, "a class of objects or phenomena is defined . . . by describing . . . that assemblage of properties which is common to all the objects or phenomena composing the class, as perceived by the senses, without introducing anything hypothetical." In a physical theory "a class of objects is defined . . . as being constituted, in a manner not apparent to the senses, by a modification of some other class of objects or phenomena whose laws are already known." [1]

In the second kind of theory, some visualizable model is made the pattern for a mechanism hidden from the senses. Some physicists, like Kelvin, cannot be satisfied with anything less than a mechanical explanation of observable phenomena, no matter how complex such a mechanism may be. Examples of this kind of theory are the atomic theory of chemistry, the kinetic theory of matter as developed in thermodynamics and the behavior of gases, the theory of the gene in studies on heredity, the theory of lines of force in electrostatics, and the recent Bohr model of the atom in spectroscopy.

In the mathematical type of theory, the appeal to hidden mechanisms is eliminated, or at any rate is at a minimum. How this may be done is graphically described by Henri Poincaré: "Suppose we have before us any machine; the initial wheel work and the final wheel work alone are visible, but the transmission, the intermediary machinery by which the movement is communicated from one to the other, is hidden in the interior and escapes our view; we do not know whether the communication is made by gearing or by belts, by connecting-rods or by other contrivances. Do we say that it is impossible for us to understand anything about this machine so long as we are not permitted to take it to pieces? You know well we do not, and that the principle of the conservation of energy suffices to determine for us the most interesting point. We easily ascertain that the final wheel turns ten times less quickly than the initial wheel, since these two wheels are visible; we are able thence to conclude that a couple applied to the one will be balanced by a couple ten times greater applied to the other. For that there is no need to penetrate the mechanism of this equilibrium and to know how the forces compensate each other in the interior of the machine." [2] Examples of such theories are the theory of gravitation, Galileo's laws of falling bodies, the theory of the flow of heat, the theory of organic evolution, and the theory of relativity.

As we suggested, it is useless to quarrel as to which type of theory is the

[1] W. J. M. Rankine, *Miscellaneous Scientific Papers*, 1881, p. 210.
[2] *Ibid.*, pp. 290–91.

more fundamental and which type should be universally adopted. Both kinds of theories have been successful in coordinating vast domains of phenomena, and fertile in making discoveries of the most important kind. At some periods in the history of a science, there is a tendency to mechanical models and atomicity; at others, to general principles connecting characteristics abstracted from directly observable phenomena; at still others, to a fusion or synthesis of these two points of view. Some scientists, like Kelvin, Faraday, Lodge, Maxwell, show an exclusive preference for "model" theories; other scientists, like Rankine, Ostwald, Duhem, can work best with the abstractive theories; and still others, like Einstein, have the unusual gift of being equally at home with both kinds.

§ 2. The Limits and the Value of Scientific Method

The desire for knowledge for its own sake is more widespread than is generally recognized by anti-intellectualists. It has its roots in the animal curiosity which shows itself in the cosmological questions of children and in the gossip of adults. No ulterior utilitarian motive makes people want to know about the private lives of their neighbors, the great, or the notorious. There is also a certain zest which makes people engage in various intellectual games or exercises in which one is required to find out something. But while the desire to know is wide, it is seldom strong enough to overcome the more powerful organic desires, and few indeed have both the inclination and the ability to face the arduous difficulties of scientific method in more than one special field. The desire to know is not often strong enough to sustain critical inquiry. Men generally are interested in the results, in the story or romance of science, not in the technical methods whereby these results are obtained and their truth continually is tested and qualified. Our first impulse is to accept the plausible as true and to reject the uncongenial as false. We have not the time, inclination, or energy to investigate everything. Indeed, the call to do so is often felt as irksome and joy-killing. And when we are asked to treat our cherished beliefs as mere hypotheses, we rebel as violently as when those dear to us are insulted. This provides the ground for various movements that are hostile to rational scientific procedure (though their promoters do not often admit that it is science to which they are hostile).

Mystics, intuitionists, authoritarians, voluntarists, and fictionalists are all trying to undermine respect for the rational methods of science. These attacks have always met with wide acclaim and are bound to continue to do so, for they strike a responsive note in human nature. Unfortunately they do not offer any reliable alternative method for obtaining verifiable knowledge. The great French writer Pascal opposed to logic the spirit of subtlety or finesse (*esprit géometrique* and *esprit de finesse*) and urged that the heart has its reasons as well as the mind, reasons that cannot be accurately formulated but which subtle spirits apprehend none the less. Men as diverse as James Russell Lowell and George Santayana are agreed that:

The soul is oracular still,

and

It is wisdom to trust the heart . . .
To trust the soul's invincible surmise.

Now it is true that in the absence of omniscience we must trust our soul's surmise; and great men are those whose surmises or intuitions are deep or penetrating. It is only by acting on our surmise that we can procure the evidence in its favor. But only havoc can result from confusing a surmise with a proposition for which there is already evidence. Are all the reasons of the heart sound? Do all oracles tell the truth? The sad history of human experience is distinctly discouraging to any such claim. Mystic intuition may give men absolute subjective certainty, but can give no proof that contrary intuitions are erroneous. It is obvious that when authorities conflict we must weigh the evidence in their favor logically if we are to make a rational choice. Certainly, when a truth is questioned it is no answer to say, "I am convinced," or, "I prefer to rely on this rather than on another authority." The view that physical science is no guide to proof, but is a mere fiction, fails to explain why it has enabled us to anticipate phenomena of nature and to control them. These attacks on scientific method receive a certain color of plausibility because of some indefensible claims made by uncritical enthusiasts. But it is of the essence of scientific method to limit its own pretension. Recognizing that we do not know everything, it does not claim the ability to solve all of our practical problems. It is an error to suppose, as is often done, that science denies the truth of all unverified propositions. For that which is unverified today may be verified tomorrow. We may get at truth by guessing or in other ways. Scientific method, however, is concerned with verification. Admittedly the wisdom of those engaged in this process has not been popularly ranked as high as that of the sage, the prophet, or the poet. Admittedly, also, we know of no way of supplying creative intelligence to those who lack it. Scientists, like all other human beings, may get into ruts and apply their techniques regardless of varying circumstances. There will always be formal procedures which are fruitless. Definitions and formal distinctions may be a sharpening of tools without the wit to use them properly, and statistical information may conform to the highest technical standards and yet be irrelevant and inconclusive. Nevertheless, scientific method is the only way to increase the general body of tested and verified truth and to eliminate arbitrary opinion. It is well to clarify our ideas by asking for the precise meaning of our words, and to try to check our favorite ideas by applying them to accurately formulated propositions.

In raising the question as to the social need for scientific method, it is well to recognize that the suspension of judgment which is essential to that method is difficult or impossible when we are pressed by the demands of immediate action. When my house is on fire, I must act quickly and promptly—I cannot stop to consider the possible causes, nor even to estimate the exact probabilities involved in the various alternative ways of reacting. For this reason, those who are bent upon some specific course of action often despise those devoted to reflection; and certain ultramodernists seem to argue as if the need for action guaranteed the truth of our decision. But the fact that I must either vote for candidate X or refrain from doing so does not of itself give me adequate knowledge. The frequency of our regrets makes this obvious. Wisely ordered society is therefore provided with means for deliberation and reflection *before* the pressure of action becomes irresistible. In order to assure the most thorough investigation, all possible views must be canvassed, and this means toleration of views that are *prima facie* most repugnant to us.

In general the chief social condition of scientific method is a widespread desire for truth that is strong enough to withstand the powerful forces which make us cling tenaciously to old views or else embrace every novelty because it is a change. Those who are engaged in scientific work need not only leisure for reflection and material for their experiments, but also a community that respects the pursuit of truth and allows freedom for the expression of intellectual doubt as to its most sacred or established institutions. Fear of offending established dogmas has been an obstacle to the growth of astronomy and geology and other physical sciences; and the fear of offending patriotic or respected sentiment is perhaps one of the strongest hindrances to scholarly history and social science. On the other hand, when a community indiscriminately acclaims every new doctrine the love of truth becomes subordinated to the desire for novel formulations.

On the whole it may be said that the safety of science depends on there being men who care more for the justice of their methods than for any results obtained by their use. For this reason it is unfortunate when scientific research in the social field is largely in the hands of those not in a favorable position to oppose established or popular opinion.

We may put it the other way by saying that the physical sciences can be more liberal because we are sure that foolish opinions will be readily eliminated by the shock of facts. In the social field, however, no one can tell what harm may come of foolish ideas before the foolishness is finally, if ever, demonstrated. None of the precautions of scientific method can prevent human life from being an adventure, and no scientific investigator knows whether he will reach his goal. But scientific method does enable large numbers to walk with surer step. By analyzing the possibilities of any step or plan, it becomes possible to anticipate the future and adjust ourselves to it in advance. Scientific method thus minimizes the shock of novelty and the uncertainty of life. It enables us to frame policies of action and of moral judgment fit for a wider outlook than those of immediate physical stimulus or organic response.

Scientific method is the only effective way of strengthening the love of truth. It develops the intellectual courage to face difficulties and to overcome illusions that are pleasant temporarily but destructive ultimately. It settles differences without any external force by appealing to our common rational nature. The way of science, even if it is up a steep mountain, is open to all. Hence, while sectarian and partisan faiths are based on personal choice or temperament and divide men, scientific procedure unites men in something nobly devoid of all pettiness. Because it requires detachment, disinterestedness, it is the finest flower and test of a liberal civilization.

For Further Study

Benjamin, A. Cornelius. *Science, Technology, and Human Values*. Columbia: U. of Missouri Press, 1965.

Campbell, Norman. *What Is Science?* New York: Dover, 1952, Ch. 3, "The Laws of Science."

Kemeny, John G. *A Philosopher Looks at Science*. Princeton: Van Nostrand, 1959, Ch. 5, "The Method."

Platt, John Rader. *The Excitement of Science*. Boston: Houghton Mifflin, 1962.

Rapport, Samuel and Wright, Helen. *Science: Method and Meaning*. New York: New York U. Press, 1963. (The New York U. Library of Science.)

Stebbing, L. S. *A Modern Introduction to Logic*. New York: Harper, 1961, Ch. 13, "The Nature of Scientific Inquiry." (Torchbook TB 538.)

Toulmin, Stephen. *Foresight and Understanding: An Enquiry into the Aims of Science*. Bloomington: Indiana U. Press, 1961. (Also Harper Torchbook TB 564.)

Werkmeister, W. H. *A Philosophy of Science*. Lincoln: U. of Nebraska Press, 1965, Ch. 2, "The Method of Science."

6 Science and Philosophy

WILLIAM A. EARLE / Science and Philosophy *

William A. Earle (1919–   ) is professor of philosophy at Northwestern University. He has taught at Stanford and has been a visiting
lecturer at Yale and Harvard. His writings include *Objectivity* and he
has translated Karl Jasper's *Reason and Existenz*.

WE HAVE all heard the story once too often: science is knowledge about
what is; the scientific method is self-correcting, its results cumulative, and
is in fact the only way in which we can achieve publicly warrantable assertions about things in the world. If in the popular phrase, "Science says it
is," then it *is*; and if Science says it isn't, then it isn't. Science therefore is
knowledge. But philosophy also claims to be knowledge; and yet it obviously isn't any experimental or observational science at all. Philosophy will
therefore be *analytic*; it will analyze the synthetic conceptual compositions
of science, render clear the method of science, its language, how it forms
concepts, how it verifies them, etc. In short, we are already on that particular toboggan which carries philosophy downhill until it reaches dead rest in
the form of the philosophy of science, art, religion, history, namely, the
philosophy of something which is already in operation, living its own life;
and I should suppose in no need whatever of our own snooping over its
shoulder to correct or analyze its method. Are we not dangerously near that

* William Earle from "Science and Philosophy" in *Science, Philosophy and our
Educational Tasks*, ed. John P. Anton and George Kimball Plochmann, *Buffalo
Studies*: 2. (July, 1966): 59–67. Published jointly by The University Council for
Educational Administration and The School of Education, State University of New
York at Buffalo. Used by permission of the author and the editors.

particular phase where philosophers have become the somewhat meddle-some handmaidens of everybody else? Part and parcel of this view is the notion that there may still be some role for philosophy, namely that of throwing off brilliant but as yet untested hypotheses, or suggesting new sci-ences. In a word, it is conceived as "speculative" in the worst, not best sense of that term, something akin to armchair science, or dreaming, an activity which again might help those too close to their own work in the laboratory, but which has no serious right to be called knowledge until tested in that laboratory. Estheticians are thus "proud" to be of help to artists; and some artists have been known to accept that help in clearing up their own esthetics, but it is doubtful if any painting was better painted as a result. Unquestionably, some philosopher of science has found something gone astray in the work of his scientist cousins, and been useful to them, much as they might be useful to one another on occasions. But is it not time that we examine the question whether philosophy must inherently be the analysis and reflection upon the ongoing activities of others, or whether in fact it has not always had another aim, another method, if it has any at all, and its *own* proud independence from *science* and also all other forms of mind. Our question, then, is what can philosophy do that nothing else can do; and secondly, whether science, as well as the philosophy of science, should not always inherently be a derived, and secondary theme for philos-ophy? I am here arguing that philosophy is the king of the humanities, not a handmaiden of the sciences.

Heidegger says at the outset of *Sein und Zeit* that to define philosophy as the philosophy of *life* is as pleonastic as to speak of the "botany of plants." Perhaps there are other legitimate concerns of philosophy than life, but, for all that, it has as one of its *central* concerns life, and not every form and mode of life but *human* life, namely, our own; and further, not our own lives as seen from any and every possible perspective, such as the biological, sociological, psychological, but our lives seen from the point of view of the very men living them, ourselves, as we live them, in our own living present. Speaking in and about life so considered is a possible mode of expression; the truth is, that it is what lies closest to us as living human beings. It is, if you like, a possible "subject-matter," it has its own aims, its own forms of excellence, and it is essential, I believe to recognize that it is inherently not a subject-matter for science, nor is its excellence that of scientific method, and its goal is certainly not that of publicly warrantable assertions. It is least of all the analysis of sentences uttered by scientists. But human life so con-sidered is that which is closest to us in every way: since it is our life, we are speaking about ourselves, and speaking about not so much what we may or may not know about nature, but about what we have done and are about to do, what we choose, what consent to, what revolt against; instead of a purportedly value-free discourse in "law-like" sentences about what is inherently not ourselves, it is at least in effort, the attempt to gain whatever clarification might be gained about a certain perpetual problem: how to live. The clarification is not of something called "humanity," but remains personal; it is not a clarification of its problem through laws or generalities, but rather through a rendering explicit of the existing singular; its utility is not in predicting the future but in rendering evident the problem and alternatives of the perpetual present. It hardly aspires to neutral, value-free observations or descriptions, but is expressive and hortatory—if we can deprive the latter term of its empty politico-religious connotations. Now, if such an effort at articulation, exhortation, clarification of ultimate horizons in life, is not warrantable public assertion, then with *that* stipulation for "knowledge," philosophy is not knowledge. It might even aspire to be wisdom. But the capturing of the term "knowledge" by science does have the disastrous effect of leaving us with no term to characterize that philosophy which is not science except as empty emotion, attitude, or posturing. But if philosophy has always sought wisdom, whatever wisdom is, it has something to do with knowing, and if the knowing in question is not scientific knowing, then it is knowing of another sort. The wise man can hardly be regarded as a fool.

I have been trying to point to a domain which I should maintain (following Karl Jaspers) is absolutely not a province to be explored by any science, since its very character is inherently not subject to either observation or experiment. Further it is not some curious corner, left over from science, of merely private or personal concern; a somewhat messy corner, where anything can be said, so long as it is said in an urgent tone. This particular domain, I believe, happens to be nothing short of our lives, and far from being undisciplined, merely emotional, a matter of guesses and hunches, is in fact the sole domain of the arts and of philosophy, when that discourse understands itself. If it is not explorable by any natural science, and if it touches precisely what we are, then the natural sciences and philosophy conceived as an analysis of the work of natural scientists, both recede into the somewhat secondary curiosities which I believe they inherently are. It is all a question of principle, and not the "present state" of science; it is not possible in principle for psychology, sociology, or cybernetics to clarify this domain, and thereupon render its philosophical clarification either superfluous, or scientifically false or true. The domains are kept distinct; and the remainder of my remarks will be an effort to make plausible this distinctness of domain, of method, and of goal. Science has virtually nothing to do with life as it is lived, its methods and attitudes. Observation, experiment, impersonal materiality transferred to life would amount to a destruction of the appropriate attitudes we entertain towards one another, and its goal of prediction through law utterly irrelevant. Yet, this domain is where we are so long as we exist. Meanwhile, although in contrast to science, it is sometimes thought that the humanistic-philosophical clarification of existence lags behind the sciences, makes no dramatic "breakthroughs," is in effect something rather apologetic and retrospective, defining itself only negatively against the brilliance of modern physics, I should like to give some evidence that the domain of life has in fact been explored with a nuance and precision not merely unattained but wholly unattainable in the natural sciences, and that its expression in poetry and philosophy represents the *clearest* form of knowledge we do or could possess. But it is not publicly warrantable assertion, additive or cumulative.

The natural sciences, first of all, must gather data, pertinent to whatever problem they wish to pose. These data obviously must be experienceable; imagined or dreamed-of experiences, or experiences which in principle only a single man could have, would hardly supply a very firm foundation for publicly warrantable assertions. And so with experiments. Both observation and experiment must be experiences of something; they must, secondly, be repeatable experiences, repeatable by a "standard observer." As we all know, the aim of the repeatable experience is to settle some problem, and the problem is, typically, to answer the question of either how things work or why they work this particular way, in a word, a law which will describe or explain the experienced; and that law again is for the purpose of predicting the character of future experiences under similar circumstances. Some such thing I would suppose to be the method of the natural sciences, and no doubt it is remarkably successful for its proper domain, nature. But its success there is a correlate to its absolute failure elsewhere, namely, in the domain of our living existence. For, first of all, it needs experienceable data of some sort. But now, if we turn that same experiencing mode of consciousness *within*, the first thing we find is that there is *nothing* there to be experienced; secondly, that my *awareness* of my present existence is not an *experience* of it at all, but rather a *reflexive consciousness* of it. The essential characteristic of anything that should be called experience is that it is a mediated awareness of an *independent object*; my perception of the stone is not the stone itself, but rather a perception of it from where I am, with my organs of perception, operating through their own appropriate media and distances. It is precisely due to this mediated character of the perceived thing, that one and the same thing could in principle simultaneously be perceived by another, and therefore supply us with a something or other which in principle could be public and repeatable, hence a fit object for scientific observation. For if anything is clear it is that my *perceptions* can not be perceived by another, are not themselves perceivable objects, and therefore my awareness of my own perceptions is not itself another perception but a reflexive awareness in which I am *immediately* aware of my own perceptions. Hence it is false to say that we experience our experiences or that we perceive our perceptions; we are indeed *aware* of performing these acts, but not by either experience or perception, whichever term is preferred. Accordingly, acts of consciousness *as* they are enacted by the consciousness, are not fit objects for either observation or experiment. This hardly implies that we are unconscious of them; but rather that our consciousness of them is immediate, and reflexive. And, since they are given immediately to consciousness itself, there is no possibility of repeatability. Another act may be performed very much like the first; but since these acts do not have a thing-like character, the only witness to the similarity would have to be the consciousness immediately having them; and in any event, similarity between two singular acts is radically distinct from the simultaneous perspectives which a plurality of observers can take on a single, perceived thing or event.

The first reason, then, why our existence as we exist in it is not a fit object for science is that it is *wholly* inaccessible to observation and experiment. It will be at once objected that this is not strictly true; we can by observing the behavior of the *body* from the outside make perfectly legitimate inferences as to what the consciousness is conscious of. In common experience, if I see a man's face contorted, I surely am safe in concluding that he is in pain. And we are told by physiologists that inferences can be drawn from measurable brain waves to the consciousness belonging to that brain. I, for one, would be the last to deny these facts. But I think their bearing on our question is different from what might seem to be the case at first sight. What are in these instances publicly observable are faces and meter-readings. What is *not* publicly observable is the pain or the dream. The line of inference, then, is not from one publicly observable to another, but from a publicly observable to a private consciousness, *never* publicly observable. The inference then rests for its plausibility on private reports by that consciousness of its own acts, which are then correlated with the public data. Further, observation directed wholly to the observable and possessing no private reflexive awareness of itself as consciousness, if such a thing were possible, could never have the slightest inkling of what it was trying to conclude *to;* unaware of the immediate sense of its own consciousness, it would run along concluding from what was observable to another thing observable, from brain states to muscle twitches, and would never have the slightest motivation for associating these observables with any private consciousness. The very sense of consciousness would be lost. We are driven to the conclusion that consciousness as it is lived may make public manifestations, but in itself it is inherently private; it must report what it is like out of its reflection, and these reflexive reports or descriptions or expressions are not based upon experience but upon immediate reflection. Further, although private, they are communicable through expression; expression has a public vehicle, like sound, or the body, but its *sense* is not equally a perceptible public object. It demands consciousness for its interpretation. Human existence as it is lived can be reported, expressed, clarified; but any observational-experimental inference to it presupposes it; if philosophy could articulate and clarify human existence, it would not be by way of inferences or supposed laws connecting observable data to the inner lived sense of that existence.

Now if we turn our reflexive consciousness to our own living present, what do we find? I said before that we find nothing. We certainly do not find something called a mind, namely our own, painted over with certain *states* or *qualities* like "pain", "pleasure", colors, shapes, etc.; instead we find ourselves *in act*; we have just come from somewhere and are going somewhere; consciousness is as it were in flight, always aimed at something which is not the flight itself, but something in its own future. We are, in this sense, always about to become something; but we never can settle into being that thing. Sartre has described this aspect of consciousness in great detail. Consciousness is inherently intentional, and projective. And so no wonder if we find nothing there but a restlessness. This supplies another very good reason why there can be no natural science of consciousness; so long as we exist, we never *are* anything to be observed. We can certainly recall what we have done; and we can imagine what we are about to do; but the present is torn between the two, a flight from one *to* the other, hence not a thing with thing-like properties, Hence even our reflexive awareness of our lives is nothing like staring within at a datum, but is an awareness of an inner projection toward what we are about to become, our possible alternatives. Or, since existence in this sense is not a collective or public project, a projection toward what *I* am about to become. But what I am *about* to do, I have *not yet* done; I must choose it, decide it, affirm it, consent to it. And, since it appears to me in the light of a *possible* act, and not already *necessarily* implicated by my present, it is of such a sort that it could either be or not; I can always say yes or no to it. I remain free, I choose what inherently depends upon my choice for its existence; and my choice of this rather than that is identical with conferring "value" upon it. The predictability from the outside of my choice has no bearing on this internal lived freedom whatsoever; if I invariably keep my promises, in short, if I am a man of character, "reliable," then indeed I can be depended upon, I act "predictably"; but I am hardly less free for choosing consistently than in being erratic, undependable. Hence, if natural science seeks a law governing experienceables according to which the future can be predicted, nothing would prevent it, so far as I can see, from finding such a law for us. But it hardly means that it has thereby disproven our freedom; it would have established nothing more than that freedom can choose coherently and consistently, and it most frequently does that when it is satisfied with its values, and can see no reason for change. Further, if natural science now turned into psychology and sociology, should find the law, it had better keep this a well-hidden secret; knowing what it was, what would prevent any of us from violating it out of spite?

To bring these remarks together: There is a domain in which the methods of the natural sciences are inapplicable, the domain of our own lives so long as we are alive, and alive for us, not for an external observer. This domain is accessible to us in the form of reflection and not observation or experiment. And our most immediate reflection upon it uncovers it as inherently characterized by singularity, freedom, projectedness, choice, and value. Summed up, our existence is a perpetual *problem* of how to exist; there can be inherently no solution which extinguishes the problem as such except the extinction of life itself. Under these circumstances, our knowledge of ourselves is not in the least publicly warrantable assertion, but far more of the character of expression, clarification, confession, and finally valuation. But this is already within the realm of the arts. The man who speaks best of how human existence is, what it can be, what it has been, is the poet, and he gives us not an "explanation" or "general law," but rather a story and a metaphor. He makes no contribution to a general science of man but rather to our own imaginative awareness of possibilities of choice, what men have chosen, what they might choose; his dependence for this upon the imagination is notorious; neither he nor the philosopher conducts observations repeatable by others or experiments. As Husserl showed, for these purposes imagination is a far superior faculty than experience. And, unless he gets led astray into allegories, he always speaks of himself, or of other singular and unique men in singular circumstances, with singular destinies. Is this "knowledge"? But if it is only the clarification and articulation of the possibilities before us, and remains an awareness of the concrete and singular *possible*, precisely what *existent* thing does he know? Man? But man, as we take him here, is but a projection into the possible; he is not finished off in the present. And yet it is awareness. If Freud as theoretician of his science knew some generalizations about men, and therefore perhaps approached something like a natural science of certain types of man, are we simply to hold Shakespeare in contrast ignorant? Or did he, too, have knowledge, or if that term is infected with scientific implications, then at least the most extended, and subtle awareness of the possibilities latent in man?

In the domain we are trying to explore, the essential thing is singularity, uniqueness, the individual, *not* the law, the principle, the general. In Hegelian terminology we are in the domain of spirit, and that is the domain of the concrete universal, not the vacuous abstractions of science but the intelligible singularities of human existence.

If the arts in general *present* or *show* us how we are, were or could be, what is left for philosophy? But the answer is, I believe, to be drawn from Hegel. To *show* man, or rather this and that man in his singular historical circumstances, is not quite the same thing as to *think* this or that life in its singularity. But philosophy thinks; it thinks then about what art wishes to show. This of course does not mean that it is now to be the philosophy of art, esthetics, but rather it tries to think that same spirit which the arts try to show. Nor, if we reintroduce the term "thought" at this point, is the thought in question to be that almost unavoidable tendency to skim off the general from the individual, and arrive back at some universal theory of man, in which all singularities are considered only as cases of a type; and our thought, abstracting from historical singularity, contents itself with the vacuous again. The singular can be made intelligible in its singularity, and not by way of cancelling that singularity, on the supposition, utterly misled in my opinion, that only the universal in and for itself is intelligible. The artist already shows us intelligible singularities. Shakespeare exhibits Hamlet, and not Man, and Hamlet is intelligible to us not by subsuming him under supposed general psychological laws, unknown to both Shakespeare as well as Hamlet, but in his singular circumstances where everything pertinent is shown; the play is a *whole*, and that means we are shown all that, and only that, which needs to be shown to render Hamlet's unique choice intelligible. This is certainly not "explanation" but rather presupposes at every step the freedom, that is, the humanity of Hamlet.

If philosophy then tries to *think* life, rather than exhibit it in the imagination or on the stage, that thinking must be conceived not as explanation through general principles, but as a phenomenological clarification of singular human existence; and not the existence of everyone, which is the same as the existence of no one in particular, but the existence of the thinker. Gertrude Stein wrote something she called *Everybody's Autobiography*, and had the serious project of talking about everybody; but interesting as the work is, she succeeds in writing, in the end, only her own life.

Why, then, is it outrageous if a philosopher attempts to think through to the bottom his own life, in its depth and in its singularity, and bring us something which might elucidate possibilities in our own existence—in short, write an ontological autobiography? If someone should ask, Why should anyone else be interested in the merely autobiographical, what contribution would it make to the universal science of man, the appropriate reply, I suppose, would be: Why should anyone be interested in *anything else* but a singular man who is or was, who is not mankind but only himself, and perhaps, if he is or was wise enough could elucidate some possibilities of our own, so that he could help by having been there before? Considered in this light, both the natural sciences and the philosophy of science must be considered interesting curiosities but existentially irrelevant; philosophy itself is rather a passionate attempt to explore the passionate possibilities which offer themselves to passionate men. It is autobiographical, inseparable from values and urgencies, provided with its own distinctive clarity, and for these reasons above all inherently *closest* to us.

KARL JASPERS / *Philosophy and Science* *

Karl Jaspers (1883–1969) was a German existentialist who worked in the fields of medicine and psychology before he turned to a career in philosophy and became professor of philosophy at Basel in 1948. Among his translated works are *Man in the Modern Age, The Perennial Scope of Philosophy, The Origin and Goal of History,* and *The Great Philosophers.*

PHILOSOPHY HAS FROM its very beginnings looked upon itself as science, indeed as science par excellence. To achieve the highest and most certain knowledge is the goal that has always animated its devotees.

How its scientific character came to be questioned can be understood only in the light of the development of the specifically modern sciences. These sciences made their greatest strides in the nineteenth century, largely outside philosophy, often in opposition to philosophy, and finally in an atmosphere of indifference to it. If philosophy was still expected to be a science, it was in a different sense than before; it was now expected to be a science in the same sense as those modern sciences that convince by virtue of their accomplishments. If it were unable to do so, it was argued, it had become pointless and might just as well die out.

Some decades ago the opinion was widespread that philosophy had had its place up to the moment when all the sciences had become independent of it, the original universal science. Now that all possible fields of research have been marked off, the days of philosophy are over. Now that we know how science obtains its universal validity, it has become evident that phi-

* Karl Jaspers, from "Philosophy and Science," trans. Ralph Manheim, *The Partisan Review,* 16 (September, 1949): 871–884 with omissions. Used by permission of the publisher and the estate of Karl Jaspers.

losophy cannot stand up against judgment by these criteria. It deals in empty ideas because it sets up undemonstrable hypotheses, it disregards experience, it seduces by illusions, it takes possession of energies needed for genuine investigation and squanders them in empty talk about the whole.

This was the picture of philosophy as seen against science conceived as methodical, cogent, universally valid insight. Under such circumstances could any philosophy legitimately claim to be scientific? To this situation philosophy reacted in two ways:

1) The attack was regarded as justified. Philosophers withdrew to limited tasks. If philosophy is at an end because the sciences have taken over all its subject matter, there remains nevertheless the knowledge of its history, first as a factor in the history of the sciences themselves, then as a phenomenon in the history of thought, the history of the errors, the anticipated insights, the process of liberation by which philosophy has made itself superfluous. Finally, the history of philosophy must preserve the knowledge of the philosophical texts, if only for their aesthetic interest. Although these texts do not make any serious contribution to scientific truth, they are nevertheless worth reading for the sake of their style and the intellectual attitude they reflect.

Others paid tribute to the modern scientific trend by rejecting all previous philosophy and striving to give philosophy an exact scientific foundation. They seized upon questions which, they claimed, were reserved for philosophy because they concern all the sciences; namely, logic, epistemology, phenomenology. In an effort to refurbish its reputation, philosophy became a servile imitator, a handmaiden to the sciences. It proceeded to establish in theory the validity of scientific knowledge, which was not questioned anyhow. But in the field of logic it developed a specialized science which because of the universality of its purpose, i.e., to define the form of all true thinking, to provide a *mathesis universalis*, seemed capable of replacing all previous philosophy. Today many thinkers regard symbolic logic as the whole of philosophy.

This first reaction seems today to have given rise to the view that philosophy is a science among other sciences, a discipline among other disciplines. And like the others, it is carried on by specialists, it has its narrow circle of experts, its congresses, and its learned periodicals.

2) In opposition to this infatuation with science there has been a second reaction. Philosophy attempted to save itself from destruction by dropping its claim to scientific knowledge. Philosophy—according to this view—is not a science at all. It is based on feeling and intuition, on imagination and genius. It is conceptual magic, not knowledge. It is *élan vital* or resolute acceptance of death. Indeed, some went further and said: It does not behoove philosophy to concern itself with science since it is aware that all scientific truth is questionable. The modern sciences are altogether in

error, witness the ruinous consequences for the soul and for life in general of the rational attitude. Philosophy itself is not a science, and for that very reason its element is authentic truth.

Both reactions—submission to science and rejection of science conceived as cogent, methodical, and universally valid knowledge—seem to spell the end of philosophy. Whether it is the slave of science or whether it denies all science, it has in either case ceased to be philosophy.

The seeming triumph of the sciences over philosophy has for some decades created a situation in which philosophers go back to various sources in search of true philosophy. If such a thing is found, the question of the relation between philosophy and science will be answered, both in a theoretical and in a concrete sense. It is a practical question of the utmost urgency.

We shall appreciate the full weight of this problem if we consider its historical origin. It developed from three complexly intertwined factors. These are a) the spirit of modern science; b) the ancient and ever recurrent attempt to achieve universal philosophical knowledge; c) the philosophical concept of truth, as it was first and for all time elucidated in Plato.

Ad a) The modern sciences, developed only in the last few centuries, have brought into the world a new scientific attitude which existed neither in Asia nor in antiquity nor in the Middle Ages.

Even the Greeks, to be sure, conceived of science as methodical, cogently certain, and universally valid knowledge. But the modern sciences not only have brought out these basic attributes of science with greater purity (a task which has not yet been completed), they have also given new form and new foundation to the purpose, scope, and unity of their fields of inquiry. I shall indicate certain of their fundamental characteristics:

1) To modern science *nothing is indifferent*. In its eyes every fact, even the smallest and ugliest, the most distant and most alien, is a legitimate object of inquiry for the very reason that it exists. Science has become truly universal. There is nothing that can evade it. Nothing must be hidden or passed over in silence; nothing must remain a mystery.

2) Modern science is by definition unfinished, because it progresses toward the infinite, whereas ancient science in every one of its forms presented itself as finished; its actual development was in every case short lived, and it never set its own development as its conscious goal. Modern scientists have understood that an all-embracing world-system, which deduces everything that exists from one or a few principles, is impossible. A world-system has other sources and can only claim universal validity if scientific critique is relaxed and particulars are mistaken for absolutes. Such

unprecedented systematizations as those achieved by modern physics cover only one aspect of reality. Through them reality as a whole has become more split up and deprived of foundations than it ever before seemed to the human mind. Hence the incompleteness of the modern world as compared to the Greek cosmos.

3) The ancient sciences remained *scattered*, unrelated to one another. They did not aim at constituting an all-embracing body of specific knowledge, whereas the modern sciences strive to be integrated into a universal frame of reference. Though a true world-system is no longer possible for them, a cosmos of the sciences is still conceivable. Our sense of the inadequacy of each special branch of knowledge demands that each science be connected with knowledge as a whole.

4) The modern sciences attach little value to the *possibilities* of thought; they recognize the idea only in definite and concrete knowledge, after it has proved its worth as an instrument of discovery and been subjected to infinite modifications in the process of investigation. True, there is a certain similarity between ancient and modern atomic theory, in so far as the general pattern is concerned. But the ancient theory was merely an intrinsically finished interpretation of possibilities, based on plausible explanations of available experience, while the modern theory, in constant association with experience, undergoes perpetual change by confirmation and disproof and is itself an implement of investigation.

5) Today a scientific attitude has become possible, an attitude of inquiry toward all phenomena; today the scientist can know certain things clearly and definitely, he can distinguish between what he knows and what he does not know; and he has amassed an unprecedented abundance of knowledge (how very little the Greek physician or the Greek technician knew by comparison!). The moral imperative of modern science is to search for reliable knowledge on the basis of unprejudiced inquiry and critique, without any preconceived ideas. When we enter into its sphere, we have the sensation of breathing clean air, of leaving behind us all vague talk, all plausible opinions, all stubborn prejudice and blind faith.

Ad b) Modern science shares the age-old striving for total philosophical knowledge. Philosophy had from the first set itself up as the science that knows the whole—not as infinitely progressing, factual knowledge but as self-contained doctrine. Now modern philosophy since Descartes has identified itself with modern science but in such a way that it still retained the philosophical concept of a total knowledge. It can be shown, however, that for this very reason Descartes did not understand modern science, the investigations of Galileo for example, and that his own work had in spirit little to do with modern science, although as a creative mathematician he helped to advance this science. The ensuing philosophers, even to a certain extent Kant, were still caught in this totalist conception of science. Hegel once again believed that he was achieving the construction of an authentic total science and that he possessed all the sciences in his cosmos of the mind.

This identification of modern science and modern philosophy with their old aspiration to total knowledge was catastrophic for both of them. The modern sciences which, by a self-deception common to all of them, looked on those great philosophies of the seventeenth century and on some later philosophies as pillars of their own edifice were tainted by their aspirations to absolute knowledge. Modern philosophy has done its greatest work only "in spite of" all this, or one might say, by a constant misunderstanding.

Ad c) Neither the modern concept of science nor science in the sense of a total philosophical system coincides with the strictly philosophical conception of science which Plato formulated in a way that has never been surpassed. How far removed is the truth, the knowledge of which Plato interprets in his parable of the cave and touches on in his dialectic, this truth that applies to being and to that which is above all being—how fundamentally different it is from the truth of the sciences, which move only amid the manifestations of being without ever attaining to being itself, and how different from the truth of the dogmatic system which holds itself to be in possession of the whole of being. What a distance between the truth which can nowhere be set down in writing but which, according to Plato's seventh epistle, though it can only be attained by thought, is kindled in a favourable moment of communication among men of understanding, and the truth which is written, universally cogent and intelligible, distinct and available to all thinking creatures!

Three so different conceptions of scientific knowledge—the first patterned on the method of modern science, the second derived from the idea of a total philosophical system, and the third related to faith in a truth which is directly apprehended by the intellect (Plato's truth being an example)—all contribute to the present confusion. . . .

At a time when confusion prevails regarding the meaning of science, three tasks are imperative, corresponding to the three tendencies discussed above.

First, the idea that total philosophical knowledge is scientific knowledge must be exposed as false. The sciences themselves critically explode this false total knowledge. It is here that the opposition to philosophy has its root, and in this respect contempt of it is justifiable.

Second, the sciences must be made pure. This can be accomplished through constant struggle and awareness in the course of our scientific activity itself. By and large, the need for basic clarity concerning science and its limits is readily admitted even by those who sin against such clarity in practice. But the essential is to achieve this purity within the specific sciences. This must be done largely through the critical work of the scientists themselves. But the philosopher who wishes to test the truth-meaning of scientific knowledge, to auscultate it, so to speak, must participate in the actual work of these scientists.

Third, a pure philosophy must be worked out in the new conditions that have been created by the modern sciences. This is indispensable for the sake of the sciences themselves. For philosophy is always alive in the sciences and so inseparable from them that the purity of both can be achieved only jointly. The rejection of philosophy usually leads to the unwitting development of a bad philosophy. The concrete work of the scientist is guided by his conscious or unconscious philosophy, and this philosophy cannot be the object of scientific method.

For example: It is impossible to prove scientifically that there should be such a thing as science. Or: The choice of an object of science that is made from among an infinite number of existing objects on the basis of this object itself is a choice that cannot be justified scientifically. Or: The ideas that guide us are tested in the systematic process of investigation, but they themselves do not become an object of direct investigation.

Science left to itself as mere science becomes homeless. The intellect is a whore, said Nicholas of Cusa, for it can prostitute itself to anything. Science is a whore, said Lenin, for it sells itself to any class interest. For Nicholas of Cusa it is Reason, and ultimately the knowledge of God, that gives meaning, certainty, and truth to intellectual knowledge; for Lenin, it is the classless society that promotes pure science. Be that as it may, awareness of all this is the business of philosophical reflection. Philosophy is inherent in the actual sciences themselves; it is their inner meaning that provides the scientist with sustenance and guides his methodical work. He who consolidates this guidance through reflection and becomes conscious of it has reached the stage of explicit philosophizing. If this guidance fails, science falls into gratuitous convention, meaningless correctness, aimless busy-ness, and spineless servitude.

A pure science requires a pure philosophy.

. . . [P]hilosophy turns against those who despise the sciences, against the sham prophets who deprecate scientific inquiry, who mistake the errors of science for science itself, and who would even hold science, "modern science," responsible for the evils and the inhumanity of our era.

Rejecting superstitious belief in science as well as contempt of science, philosophy grants its unconditional recognition to modern science. In its eyes science is a marvellous thing which can be relied upon more than anything else, the most significant achievement of man in his history, an achievement that is the source of great dangers but of even greater opportunities and that from now on must be regarded as a prerequisite of all human dignity. Without science, the philosopher knows, his own pursuits eventuate in nothing. . . .

The one philosophy is the *philosophia perennis* around which all philosophies revolve, which no one possesses, in which every genuine philosopher shares, and which nevertheless can never achieve the form of an intellectual edifice valid for all and exclusively true.

Thus philosophy is not only less but also more than science, namely, as the source of a truth that is inaccessible to scientifically binding knowledge. It is this philosophy that is meant in such definitions as: To philosophize is to learn how to die or to rise to godhead—or to know being qua being. The meaning of such definitions is: Philosophical thought is inward action; it appeals to freedom; it is a summons to transcendence. Or the same thing can be formulated differently: Philosophy is the act of becoming conscious of genuine being—or is the thinking of a faith in man that must be infinitely elucidated—or is the way of man's self-assertion through thinking. . . .

For Further Study

Burtt, E. A. "The Value Presuppositions of Science," in *The New Scientist: Essays on the Methods and Values of Modern Science*, eds. Paul C. Obler and Herman A. Estrin. New York: Doubleday, 1962. (Anchor Book A 319.)

Conant, James B. *Modern Science and Modern Man*. Garden City: Doubleday, 1953. (Anchor Book, 187 pp.)

Frank, Philipp. *Philosophy of Science: The Link Between Science and Philosophy*. Englewood Cliffs: Prentice-Hall, 1957, Ch. 1, "The Chain That Links Science with Philosophy."

McCarthy, Harold E. "Science and Its Critics," in *Readings in Philosophy of Science*, ed. Philip P. Wiener. New York: Scribner's, 1953, Ch. 35.

Morgenbesser, Sidney (ed.). *Philosophy of Science Today*. New York: Basic Books, 1967.

Smart, J. J. C. *Between Science and Philosophy*. New York: Random House, 1968, Ch. 1.

Whitehead, Alfred North. *Adventures of Ideas*. New York: Macmillan, 1933, Ch. 9, "Science and Philosophy."

PART 2

Man and His Place
in the World

7 Scientific Progress and Philosophical Problems

WERNER HEISENBERG / From Plato to Max Planck *

Werner Heisenberg (1901–   ) is a distinguished scientist who was awarded a Nobel Prize (1932) for his work in quantum theory. He is well known for his Principle of Indeterminacy and his Unified Field Theory.

SURROUNDED as we are by hundreds of projects aimed at putting the discoveries of atomic physics to fruitful economic use, all too easily we forget that we are simultaneously struggling with questions which men have been asking themselves for a long, long time. The present-day preoccupations of the human spirit are, in fact, closely related to intellectual efforts first undertaken by men thousands of years ago. These links with the past are doubtless more interesting to the historian than to the physicist, but even the physicist can gain valuable insights into his own current problems by considering certain of the fundamental patterns that the history of the atom reveals.

Modern physics, and particularly the quantum theory—the discovery of Max Planck, the centennial of whose birth was celebrated in 1958—has raised a series of very general questions, dealing not only with the narrow

* Werner Heisenberg, *The Atlantic Monthly*, 204 (November, 1959): 109–113. Used by permission of the author.

problems of physics as such but also with the nature of matter and with the method of the exact sciences. These questions have forced physicists to wrestle once more with philosophical problems which seemed already to have found a definitive answer within the framework of classical physics.

Two questions, in particular, have been reopened by Planck's discoveries. The first concerns the nature of matter, or, to put it more precisely, the old question that troubled the Greek philosophers: How can the manifold diversity of material phenomena be reduced to simple principles and thus rendered intelligible? The other has to do with the epistemological question which has cropped up with particular insistence since Kant's time: the question of the extent to which it is possible to objectify scientific or any sensory experiences—the extent, in other words, to which one can go from observed phenomena to an objective conclusion independent of the observer.

Let us consider the first of these questions. When the Greek philosophers came to examine the unity of observable phenomena, they encountered the problem of the smallest units of matter. Two opposing points of view emerged from this period of human thought which were to have a profound influence on the subsequent evolution of philosophy. They have been given the names of materialism and idealism.

The atomic theory propounded by Leucippus and Democritus regarded the smallest particles of matter as existing in the most literal sense. These tiniest particles were thought to be indivisible and unchangeable; they were eternal, ultimate units, and as such they were called atoms, and could neither provide nor require further explanation. The only properties that fitted them were geometric. They were thought by the philosophers to possess form, to be separate from each other in empty space, and by virtue of their different spatial positions and movements to be capable of bringing about the manifold variety of phenomena. But they did not have color, smell, or taste, nor did they have a temperature or any other physical properties. The qualities of the things we apprehend in life were indirectly governed by the different rearrangements and movements of the atoms. Just as tragedy or comedy can be written with the same letters of the alphabet, so, according to Democritus' theory, can very different happenings in the world be produced by the same atoms. Atoms were therefore the true, objectively real kernels of matter, and thus of phenomena. They were what existed in the truest sense, whereas the diverse multiplicity of phenomena was merely an indirect and subsidiary product of them. This view of things was therefore given the name of materialism. . . .

For Plato, in contrast to Democritus, the smallest particles were not unchangeable or indestructible; they could be reduced to triangles, and out of triangles built up again. The triangles themselves would no longer be matter, for they would have no spatial extension. Thus, at the end of this series of material concepts we encounter something which is no longer material but simply a mathematical form—or, if you prefer, an intellectual construction. The ultimate root concept capable of rendering the world intelligible was for Plato the mathematical pattern, the picture, the idea. This view of things was therefore called idealism.

The old controversy between materialism and idealism has, oddly enough, been revived recently in a quite specific way by modern atomic physics, and especially by the quantum theory. The exact sciences—physics and chemistry—of modern times were, until the discovery of the Planck quantum, materialistically oriented. In nineteenth-century chemistry, the atoms and their composite particles were thought to be the only real things, the real substratum of all matter. Atoms appeared incapable of furnishing or of demanding further explanation.

Planck, however, discovered in the phenomena of radiation a feature of discontinuity, which seemed surprisingly linked to the existence of the atom but which could not be explained in terms of it. This aspect of discontinuity revealed by the quantum gave birth to the suspicion that not only this discontinuity but the very existence of the atom might stem from some fundamental law of nature. There might be a mathematical structure in nature the formulation of which would provide that unified understanding of the structure of matter which the Greek philosophers had looked for. The existence of the atom, far from being a final, irreducible fact, might, as Plato had thought, be traced back to the operation of mathematically conceivable laws of nature—to the effect of mathematical symmetries. . . .

. . . [A] great deal of the earlier intuitive physics has gone by the board —not only the applicability of its concepts and laws but the entire notion of reality which underlay the exact sciences until our present-day atomic physics. By "notion of reality" I mean the idea that there are objective occurrences which somehow take place in time and space quite independently of whether or not they are observed. Observations in atomic physics can no longer be objectified in this simple manner; they can no longer be related to an objective, describable interval in time and space.

Here again we are brought up sharply before the rock-bottom truth that in science we are not dealing with nature itself but with the science of nature—that is, with a nature which has been thought through and described by man. This is not to introduce an element of subjectivity into science, for it is in no way asserted that events in the world of nature depend on our observation of them; it is simply to say that science stands between man and nature and that we cannot renounce the application of concepts that have been intuitively given to or are inborn in man.

This aspect of the quantum theory has made it difficult to adhere absolutely to the program of materialistic philosophy and to designate the smallest particles of matter as being "truly real." For if the quantum theory is correct, these elemental particles are not real in the same sense as the things in our daily lives—for example, trees or stones—are real; they appear as abstractions derived from observed material which in a literal sense is real. Now, if it is impossible to ascribe existence in the strictest sense to these elemental particles, it is difficult to regard matter as truly real. This explains why, in recent years, reservations have been expressed in the camp of dialectical materialism about the now generally accepted implications of the quantum theory.

We cannot escape the conclusions that our earlier notions of reality are no longer applicable in the field of the atom and that we are dealing with weighty abstractions when we set out to define the atom as what is truly real. Modern physics, in the final analysis, has already discredited the concept of the truly real, so that it is at the very starting point that the materialistic philosophy must be modified.

The development of atomic physics in the last two decades has led it even further away from the basic assumptions of the materialistic philosophy of the ancients. Experiments have shown that the elemental particles, which we assume to be the smallest units of nature, are not eternal and immutable, as Democritus supposed, but can be transmuted into one another. Now, there must be some reason for our considering these subatomic particles as being the smallest particles of matter. It could, nonetheless, be true that the elemental particles are made up of still smaller ones, themselves eternal and unchangeable. How can the physicist exclude the possibility that these still smaller units have so far eluded our powers of observation?

The answer which present-day physics gives to this question brings out clearly the nonintuitive character of modern atomic physics. If someone wants to decide experimentally whether an elemental particle is simple or compound, he clearly must set out to shatter it with the most powerful means available. The huge atomic accelerators which are today being used, or being built, in various parts of the world serve precisely this purpose. With such machines one can accelerate elemental particles—usually protons—to extremely high velocities, have them intercepted by other tiny particles of matter, and then make a detailed study of what happens in the subsequent collisions. Although a great deal of experimental material on the details of such collisions still must be collected before we can have a truly clear picture of this area of physics, we are already in a position to describe roughly what takes place. What has been discovered is that a shattering of the elemental particles can certainly take place. Sometimes a great many particles are produced by such collisions, but the surprising and supreme paradox is this: the particles resulting from these collisions are not smaller than the shattered particles they spring from. They are themselves elemental particles all over again.

The paradox is explained by the theory of relativity, according to which energy can be converted into mass. The elemental particles, which are given a huge kinetic energy with the aid of accelerators, can with the use of this energy, which is convertible into matter, produce new elemental particles. The elemental particles are therefore the ultimate units of matter—precisely those units into which matter decomposes under the impact of external forces.

This state of affairs can be summed up thus: All elemental particles are made of the same stuff—namely, energy. They are the various forms which energy must assume in order to become matter. Here once again we encounter that old pair of concepts—content and form or matter and form—which has come down to us from Aristotle's philosophy. Energy is not only the force which keeps everything in motion; it is also, like fire in Heraclitus' philosophy, the basic stuff of which the world is made. Matter exists because energy assumes the form of the elemental particle. We now know that there are no less than twenty-five different kinds of subatomic particles and we have good grounds for supposing that all these forms are patterned on fundamental mathematical constructions. They are, therefore, the consequence of a fundamental law that can be expressed in mathematical language and from which the subatomic particles can logically be derived in much the same way as the different energy states of the hydrogen atom could be deduced from Schrödinger's differential equation.

This fundamental law, which present-day physics is seeking, must fulfill two conditions, both of them stemming from experimental evidence. The investigations that have been made on elemental particles with the aid of huge accelerators have produced certain rules of selection for the transformations occurring from collisions or in radioactive fall-out. These rules of selection can be formulated mathematically on the basis of collected quantum figures, and they are the immediate expression of properties of symmetry bound up with the fundamental equation of matter. The fundamental law must in one way or another embrace these observed symmetries; it must represent them mathematically.

In the second place, the fundamental equation of matter, assuming that such a simple formulation exists, must contain at least another constant of measurement similar to the one for the velocity of light and to the Planck quantum. Observations of the atomic nucleus and of the atomic particles lead us to believe that this constant can be represented as a universal length, whose magnitude should be around ten centimeters.

The real conceptual core of this fundamental law, however, must be based on the mathematical symmetries exhibited in it. The most important of these symmetries are already empirically known to us (the Lorenz group, describing the properties of time and space needed by the special theory of relativity; the quantum number, derived from twenty years of observation, that allows us to differentiate between neutrons and protons and which is now generally known as isotopic spin; mirror symmetries of time and space; and so forth).

One proposal for such a fundamental equation of matter which satisfies the above requirements has already been made. This is a most simple and highly symmetrical equation of nonlinear waves for a field operator known as a spinor. Whether or not this is the correct formulation of the fundamental law of nature will be known only after searching mathematical analysis.

One can already say that, irrespective of the exact nature of this evidence, the final answer will more closely approximate the views expressed in Plato's *Timaeus* than those of the ancient materialists. This realization should not be misunderstood as an all-too-facile rejection of the modern materialistic thinking of the nineteenth century, which contributed many important elements of knowledge that were lacking in ancient science. But it is true that the elemental particles of present-day physics are more closely related to the Platonic bodies than they are to the atoms of Democritus.

The elemental particles of modern physics, like the regular bodies of Plato's philosophy, are defined by the requirements of mathematical symmetry. They are not eternal and unchanging, and they can hardly, therefore, strictly be termed real. Rather, they are simple expressions of fundamental mathematical constructions which one comes upon in striving to break down matter ever further, and which provide the content for the underlying laws of nature. In the beginning, therefore, for modern science, was the form, the mathematical pattern, not the material thing. And since the mathematical pattern is, in the final analysis, an intellectual concept, one can say in the words of Faust, "Am Anfang war der Sinn"—"In the beginning was the meaning."

The task of present-day atomic physics is to explore this meaning in all its details and with all the complex apparatus at our command. It seems to me fascinating to reflect that today, in the most varied parts of the earth and with the most powerful instruments available, men are seeking to wrest solutions from problems posed by the Greek philosophers more than two thousand years ago; and it is exhilarating to think that we may know the answer in a few years, perhaps—or, at the latest, in a couple of decades.

JOHN DEWEY / The Influence of Darwinism
on Philosophy *

John Dewey (1859–1952), one of the most eminent of American
philosophers, over a long life produced many books and articles that
have had a continuing influence in the fields of education, social and
political philosophy, ethics, logic, and aesthetics. He called his version
of pragmatism "instrumentalism."

I

THAT THE PUBLICATION of the "Origin of Species" marked an epoch in the
development of the natural sciences is well known to the layman. That the
combination of the very words origin and species embodied an intellectual
revolt and introduced a new intellectual temper is easily overlooked by the
expert. The conceptions that had reigned in the philosophy of nature and
knowledge for two thousand years, the conceptions that had become the
familiar furniture of the mind, rested on the assumption of the superiority
of the fixed and final; they rested upon treating change and origin as signs
of defect and unreality. In laying hands upon the sacred ark of absolute
permanency, in treating the forms that had been regarded as types of fixity
and perfection as originating and passing away, the "Origin of Species" introduced a mode of thinking that in the end was bound to transform the
logic of knowledge, and hence the treatment of morals, politics, and religion. . . .

II

Few words in our language foreshorten intellectual history as much as does
the word species. The Greeks, in initiating the intellectual life of Europe,
were impressed by characteristic traits of the life of plants and animals; so
impressed indeed that they made these traits the key to defining nature
and to explaining mind and society. And truly, life is so wonderful that a
seemingly successful reading of its mystery might well lead men to believe
that the key to the secrets of heaven and earth was in their hands. The
Greek rendering of this mystery, the Greek formulation of the aim and

* John Dewey, The Influence of Darwin on Philosophy, Copyright 1910, 1938 Holt,
Rinehart and Winston, Inc. Reprinted by permission. Pp. 1–19 with omissions.

standard of knowledge, was in the course of time embodied in the word species, and it controlled philosophy for two thousand years. To understand the intellectual face-about expressed in the phrase "Origin of Species," we must, then, understand the long dominant idea against which it is a protest.

Consider how men were impressed by the facts of life. Their eyes fell upon certain things slight in bulk, and frail in structure. To every appearance, these perceived things were inert and passive. Suddenly, under certain circumstances, these things—henceforth known as seeds or eggs or germs—begin to change, to change rapidly in size, form, and qualities. Rapid and extensive changes occur, however, in many things—as when wood is touched by fire. But the changes in the living thing are orderly; they are cumulative; they tend constantly in one direction; they do not, like other changes, destroy or consume, or pass fruitless into wandering flux; they realize and fulfil. Each successive stage, no matter how unlike its predecessor, preserves its net effect and also prepares the way for a fuller activity on the part of its successor. In living beings, changes do not happen as they seem to happen elsewhere, any which way; the earlier changes are regulated in view of later results. This progressive organization does not cease till there is achieved a true final term, a *telos*, a completed, perfected end. This final form exercises in turn a plenitude of functions, not the least noteworthy of which is production of germs like those from which it took its own origin, germs capable of the same cycle of self-fulfilling activity.

But the whole miraculous tale is not yet told. The same drama is enacted to the same destiny in countless myriads of individuals so sundered in time, so severed in space, that they have no opportunity for mutual consultation and no means of interaction. As an old writer quaintly said, "things of the same kind go through the same formalities"—celebrate, as it were, the same ceremonial rites.

This formal activity which operates throughout a series of changes and holds them to a single course; which subordinates their aimless flux to its own perfect manifestation; which, leaping the boundaries of space and time, keeps individuals distant in space and remote in time to a uniform type of structure and function: this principle seemed to give insight into the very nature of reality itself. To it Aristotle gave the name, *eidos*. This term the scholastics translated as *species*.

The force of this term was deepened by its application to everything in the universe that observes order in flux and manifests constancy through change. From the casual drift of daily weather, through the uneven recurrence of seasons and unequal return of seed time and harvest, up to the majestic sweep of the heavens—the image of eternity in time—and from this to the unchanging pure and contemplative intelligence beyond nature lies one unbroken fulfilment of ends. Nature as a whole is a progressive realization of purpose strictly comparable to the realization of purpose in any single plant or animal. . . .

The influence of Darwin upon philosophy resides in his having conquered the phenomena of life for the principle of transition, and thereby freed the new logic for application to mind and morals and life. When he said of species what Galileo had said of the earth, *e pur se muove*, he emancipated, once for all, genetic and experimental ideas as an organon of asking questions and looking for explanations.

III

The exact bearings upon philosophy of the new logical outlook are, of course, as yet, uncertain and inchoate. We live in the twilight of intellectual transition. One must add the rashness of the prophet to the stubbornness of the partizan to venture a systematic exposition of the influence upon philosophy of the Darwinian method. At best, we can but inquire as to its general bearing—the effect upon mental temper and complexion, upon that body of half-conscious, half-instinctive intellectual aversions and preferences which determine, after all, our more deliberate intellectual enterprises. In this vague inquiry there happens to exist as a kind of touchstone a problem of long historic currency that has also been much discussed in Darwinian literature. I refer to the old problem of design *versus* chance, mind *versus* matter, as the causal explanation, first or final, of things.

As we have already seen, the classic notion of species carried with it the idea of purpose. In all living forms, a specific type is present directing the earlier stages of growth to the realization of its own perfection. Since this purposive regulative principle is not visible to the senses, it follows that it must be an ideal or rational force. Since, however, the perfect form is gradually approximated through the sensible changes, it also follows that in and through a sensible realm a rational ideal force is working out its own ultimate manifestation. These inferences were extended to nature: (a) She does nothing in vain; but all for an ulterior purpose. (b) Within natural sensible events there is therefore contained a spiritual causal force, which as spiritual escapes perception, but is apprehended by an enlightened reason. (c) The manifestation of this principle brings about a subordination of matter and sense to its own realization, and this ultimate fulfilment is the goal of nature and of man. The design argument thus operated in two directions. Purposefulness accounted for the intelligibility of nature and the possibility of science, while the absolute or cosmic character of this purposefulness gave sanction and worth to the moral and religious endeavors of man. Science was underpinned and morals authorized by one and the same principle, and their mutual agreement was eternally guaranteed.

This philosophy remained, in spite of sceptical and polemic outbursts, the official and the regnant philosophy of Europe for over two thousand years. The expulsion of fixed first and final causes from astronomy, physics, and chemistry had indeed given the doctrine something of a shock. But, on the other hand, increased acquaintance with the details of plant and animal life operated as a counterbalance and perhaps even strengthened the argument from design. The marvelous adaptations of organisms to their environment, of organs to the organism, of unlike parts of a complex organ —like the eye—to the organ itself; the foreshadowing by lower forms of the higher; the preparation in earlier stages of growth for organs that only later had their functioning—these things were increasingly recognized with the progress of botany, zoology, paleontology, and embryology. Together, they added such prestige to the design argument that by the late eighteenth century it was, as approved by the sciences of organic life, the central point of theistic and idealistic philosophy.

The Darwinian principle of natural selection cut straight under this philosophy. If all organic adaptations are due simply to constant variation and the elimination of those variations which are harmful in the struggle for existence that is brought about by excessive reproduction, there is no call for a prior intelligent causal force to plan and preordain them. Hostile critics charged Darwin with materialism and with making chance the cause of the universe. . . .

IV

So much for some of the more obvious facts of the discussion of design *versus* chance, as causal principles of nature and of life as a whole. We brought up this discussion, you recall, as a crucial instance. What does our touchstone indicate as to the bearing of Darwinian ideas upon philosophy? In the first place, the new logic outlaws, flanks, dismisses—what you will— one type of problem and substitutes for it another type. Philosophy forswears inquiry after absolute origins and absolute finalities in order to explore specific values and the specific conditions that generate them.

Darwin concluded that the impossibility of assigning the world to chance as a whole and to design in its parts indicated the insolubility of the question. Two radically different reasons, however, may be given as to why a problem is insoluble. One reason is that the problem is too high for intelligence; the other is that the question in its very asking makes assumptions that render the question meaningless. The latter alternative is unerringly pointed to in the celebrated case of design *versus* chance. Once admit that the sole verifiable or fruitful object of knowledge is the particular set of changes that generate the object of study together with the consequences that then flow from it, and no intelligible question can be asked about what, by assumption, lies outside. To assert—as is often asserted—that specific values of particular truth, social bonds and forms of beauty, if they can be shown to be generated by concretely knowable conditions, are meaningless and in vain; to assert that they are justified only when they and their particular causes and effects have all at once been gathered up into some inclusive first cause and some exhaustive final goal, is intellectual atavism. Such argumentation is reversion to the logic that explained the extinction of fire by water through the formal essence of aqueousness and the quenching of thirst by water through the final cause of aqueousness. Whether used in the case of the special event or that of life as a whole, such logic only abstracts some aspect of the existing course of events in order to re-duplicate it as a petrified eternal principle by which to explain the very changes of which it is the formalization.

When Henry Sidgwick casually remarked in a letter that as he grew older his interest in what or who made the world was altered into interest in what kind of a world it is anyway, his voicing of a common experience of our own day illustrates also the nature of that intellectual transformation effected by the Darwinian logic. Interest shifts from the wholesale essence back of special changes to the question of how special changes serve and defeat concrete purposes; shifts from an intelligence that shaped things once for all to the particular intelligences which things are even now shaping; shifts from an ultimate goal of good to the direct increments of justice and happiness that intelligent administration of existent conditions may beget and that present carelessness or stupidity will destroy or forego.

In the second place, the classic type of logic inevitably set philosophy upon proving that life *must* have certain qualities and values—no matter how experience presents the matter—because of some remote cause and eventual goal. The duty of wholesale justification inevitably accompanies all thinking that makes the meaning of special occurrences depend upon something that once and for all lies behind them. The habit of derogating from present meanings and uses prevents our looking the facts of experience in the face; it prevents serious acknowledgment of the evils they present and serious concern with the goods they promise but do not as yet fulfil. It turns thought to the business of finding a wholesale transcendent remedy for the one and guarantee for the other. One is reminded of the way many moralists and theologians greeted Herbert Spencer's recognition of an unknowable energy from which welled up the phenomenal physical process without and the conscious operations within. Merely because Spencer labeled his unknowable energy "God," this faded piece of metaphysical goods was greeted as an important and grateful concession to the reality of the spiritual realm. Were it not for the deep hold of the habit of seeking justification for ideal values in the remote and transcendent, surely this reference of them to an unknowable absolute would be despised in comparison with the demonstrations of experience that knowable energies are daily generating about us precious values.

The displacing of this wholesale type of philosophy will doubtless not arrive by sheer logical disproof, but rather by growing recognition of its futility. Were it a thousand times true that opium produces sleep because of its dormitive energy, yet the inducing of sleep in the tired, and the recovery to waking life of the poisoned, would not be thereby one least step forwarded. And were it a thousand times dialectically demonstrated that life as a whole is regulated by a transcendent principle to a final inclusive goal, none the less truth and error, health and disease, good and evil, hope and fear in the concrete, would remain just what and where they now are. To improve our education, to ameliorate our manners, to advance our politics, we must have recourse to specific conditions of generation.

Finally, the new logic introduces responsibility into the intellectual life. To idealize and rationalize the universe at large is after all a confession of inability to master the courses of things that specifically concern us. As long as mankind suffered from this impotency, it naturally shifted a burden of responsibility that it could not carry over to the more competent shoulders of the transcendent cause. But if insight into specific conditions of value and into specific consequences of ideas is possible, philosophy must in time become a method of locating and interpreting the more serious of the conflicts that occur in life, and a method of projecting ways for dealing with them: a method of moral and political diagnosis and prognosis.

The claim to formulate *a priori* the legislative constitution of the universe is by its nature a claim that may lead to elaborate dialectic developments. But it is also one that removes these very conclusions from subjection to experimental test, for, by definition, these results make no differences in the detailed course of events. But a philosophy that humbles its pretensions to the work of projecting hypotheses for the education and conduct of mind, individual and social, is thereby subjected to test by the way in which the ideas it propounds work out in practice. In having modesty forced upon it, philosophy also acquires responsibility.

Doubtless I seem to have violated the implied promise of my earlier remarks and to have turned both prophet and partizan. But in anticipating the direction of the transformations in philosophy to be wrought by the Darwinian genetic and experimental logic, I do not profess to speak for any save those who yield themselves consciously or unconsciously to this logic. No one can fairly deny that at present there are two effects of the Darwinian mode of thinking. On the one hand, there are making many sincere and vital efforts to revise our traditional philosophic conceptions in accordance with its demands. On the other hand, there is as definitely a recrudescence of absolutistic philosophies; an assertion of a type of philosophic knowing distinct from that of the sciences, one which opens to us another kind of reality from that to which the sciences give access; an appeal through experience to something that essentially goes beyond experience. This reaction affects popular creeds and religious movements as well as technical philosophies. The very conquest of the biological sciences by the new ideas has led many to proclaim an explicit and rigid separation of philosophy from science.

Old ideas give way slowly; for they are more than abstract logical forms and categories. They are habits, predispositions, deeply engrained attitudes of aversion and preference. Moreover, the conviction persists—though history shows it to be a hallucination—that all the questions that the human mind has asked are questions that can be answered in terms of the alternatives that the questions themselves present. But in fact intellectual progress usually occurs through sheer abandonment of questions together with both of the alternatives they assume—an abandonment that results from their decreasing vitality and a change of urgent interest. We do not solve them: we get over them. Old questions are solved by disappearing, evaporating, while new questions corresponding to the changed attitude of endeavor and preference take their place. Doubtless the greatest dissolvent in contemporary thought of old questions, the greatest precipitant of new methods, new intentions, new problems, is the one effected by the scientific revolution that found its climax in the "Origin of Species."

For Further Study

Boas, George. *The Challenge of Science.* Seattle: U. of Washington Press, 1965.

Bondi, Hermann. "Astronomy and Cosmology," in *What Is Science?* ed. James R. Newman. New York: Simon and Schuster, 1955.

Heisenberg, Werner. *Physics and Philosophy: The Revolution in Modern Science.* New York: Harper, 1962, esp. Ch. 11, "The Role of Modern Physics in the Present Development of Human Thinking." (Torchbook TB 549.)

Hempel, Carl G. *Philosophy of Natural Science.* Englewood Cliffs: Prentice-Hall, 1966. (Foundations of Philosophy Series.)

Lehman, Hugh. "Are Biological Species Real?" *Philosophy of Science,* 34 (June, 1967): 157–167.

Manser, A. R. "The Concept of Evolution," *Philosophy,* 40 (January, 1965): 18–34.

Mirsky, Alfred E. "The Discovery of DNA," *Scientific American,* 218 (June, 1968): 78–88.

Munitz, Milton. *Space, Time, and Creation: Philosophical Aspects of Scientific Cosmology.* Glencoe: Free Press and Falcon's Wing Press, 1957, Ch. 2, "The Development of Cosmology from Myth to Science."

Schrödinger, Erwin. *What Is Life? and Other Scientific Essays.* New York: Doubleday, 1956, "On the Peculiarity of the Scientific World-View." (Anchor Book A 88.)

Shapere, Dudley, ed. *Philosophical Problems of Natural Science.* New York: Macmillan, 1965. (Sources in Philosophy Series.)

Shapley, Harlow. *Men and Stars.* Boston: Beacon, 1958. (Also Washington Square Press paperback W 601.)

8 The Nature of Man

PAUL WEISS / Man as a Human Being *

Paul Weiss (1901–   ) is Sterling professor of philosophy at Yale University. His interest led to the founding of the Metaphysical Society and the *Review of Metaphysics*, which he edited 1947–1963. His many books include *Modes of Being* and *The Making of Man*.

IT DOES NOT seem worth while to dispute the contention that man has an animal ancestry and came to be in the course of history. The view is supported by the independent investigations of geologists, archeologists and anthropologists. It is opposed only by the theory that man has always existed in his present form or that he is a special creation inserted within the frame of nature. It would be a mistake, however, to suppose that if it be granted that man had an animal origin it is also granted that he is nothing but an animal. Just as it is possible for a child to surpass its parents, so it is possible for an animal to pass beyond the limits within which its ancestors dwelt, and to arrive at the stage where it becomes a radically distinct type of being. It would then attain and exercise powers which it did not have before and which have no animal mode of expression. In short, it is possible for an animal to become a man, though a man is not and cannot become an animal.

* Paul Weiss, from *Nature and Man* (Carbondale and Edwardsville: Southern Illinois U. Press, 1965. Copyright 1947 by Paul Weiss), pp. 124–267 with omissions. Used by permission of the author and the publisher.

DARWIN'S THESIS

To show that man is an animal, one must show that every trait of man, bodily or nonbodily in nature, is a developed, complex or variant form of some animal character, differing from it in degree and not in kind. An attempt to do this has been made a number of times in the course of history, notably by Montaigne, La Mettrie and Condillac. The most persuasive presentation of the thesis, however, is I think to be found in Darwin's *Descent of Man*.

Darwin maintained that man's capacity for happiness and sorrow, love and hate, his sense of beauty and of right and wrong, as well as his ability to remember, imagine and reason, were either duplicated in other animals or were present in them in a rudimentary form. Dogs impressed Darwin as not only having intelligence, but self-consciousness; he thought birds had a sense of beauty, monkeys an ability to make tools, and dogs, birds and monkeys some form of speech and moral sense. He could find nothing in man which was not duplicated, at least in embryonic form, elsewhere in the animal kingdom. As he quaintly put it, "If man had not been his own classifier, he would never have thought of founding a separate order for his reception."

Darwin erred, however, in supposing that every human characteristic is duplicated somewhere and to some degree in the animal kingdom.

Man is sometimes religious. No animal ever is. It is not to the point to say, as Darwin does, that there are men who have no religion, for one kind of being is not to be distinguished from another by virtue of an *activity* in which all the members of one group engage and all the members of the other do not. One type of being differs from another by virtue of a *capacity* which all its members and no other beings have. What Darwin should have shown is that there are types of men who *cannot* be religious or that there are animals which are or can be religious, if only in a minor way. But this he fails to do.

Animals decorate and occasionally show sensitivity in color and design. But an artist reproduces in his art the meaning of another thing, and this no mere manipulation of color or design begins to approach. The sense of beauty of an animal, and the art of which it is capable, differ not in degree but in kind from that open to a man.

Man, too, alone has science, philosophy and history—speculative inquiries into the nature of realities he never directly encounters through the senses. What animals know is what they learn from sense experience. No multiplication of such experiences could ever sum up to a knowledge of that which lies outside the reach of any sense.

And then there is man's speech, his use of symbols, his ability to pledge himself to do something in the future, his ability to cook and his ability to engage in sexual acts for pleasure rather than for the sake of reproduction.

There is no evidence that animals engage in such acts even to a slight degree. On behalf of Darwin's thesis, it could however be maintained that, though animals have the ability to engage in such acts, they do not exercise it. But we ought to say that animals are unable to do what no one of them in fact ever does, because in that way we suppose nothing beyond what the evidence warrants. It is arbitrary to assert that a dog is a man or angel in disguise, unfortunately limited by an inadequate body or a sluggish will. A sound method and a sure sense of values dictate that things be taken in the shape they appear until we are forced to view them in a different light.

It is possible to hold that dogs do not speak because they do not have the requisite equipment or inclination. But it would be more reasonable to assert that they do not speak because they do not have the ability. Similarly, it would be possible to maintain that there are no animal scientists or philosophers, either because the animals have not been properly educated or because they are not interested. But it would be more reasonable to say that animals do not pursue these subjects because they cannot. Animals present themselves as animals and nothing more. We have no reason for supposing that the evidence is insufficient.

But, on the other hand, there are also men who are dumb, insensitive and irrational. It would seem reasonable, then, to conclude that they too are without a capacity for speech, religion, art, science, philosophy and history. The practitioners of these various subjects protest. They deny that any man is completely devoid of the ability to practice them. It is a rare artist indeed who does not believe that every man has some artistic ability; theologians affirm that atheists are not only capable of religion but are actually engaged in practising it in some aberrant form; it is a commonplace with many philosophers that all men speculate to some extent. One must yield to these protests or give up the idea that these different abilities, although possible only to men, are essential to them. We ought not, I think, yield to these protests. Found in all mature, normal men, these abilities are not in the rest.

If these abilities were essential to men, they would be present in every human being. Unfortunately there are idiots, and fortunately there are infants in the world. If these are human—and human they seem to be—they must already have these various abilities, or these abilities are not essential. But we term the one an idiot and the other a child precisely because they lack the abilities which mature and normal men possess. They can be termed human, not because they have these various abilities, but only because they possess a power which, in favorable circumstances, may become expressed in these diverse forms.

Because there are idiots and children, we are forced by a different route to come to the same conclusion that Darwin does: religion, reason, speculation and art do not suffice to define men as beings of a radically distinct type from animals. Darwin obtained his conclusion by minimizing the kind of ability some men possess. We obtained it by affirming that these were abilities possible only to men, and then remarking that there were human beings who could not rightly be said to possess them. Such abilities can not therefore serve to distinguish all men from animals.

THE NECESSITY FOR THE BODY

What is essential and common to men is not a set of specific abilities to think or cook—for then idiots and children would not be human—but a single power which is the source of these diverse abilities. Though an infant and an idiot neither understand more nor deliberate better than a dog or a horse, mankind has rightly refused to equate infants and idiots with dogs and horses. There is a great difference in one's attitude towards those who desire to vivisect the former and those who desire to vivisect the latter. Everyone has at least a dim awareness of the fact that the child is merely too young and the idiot too unfortunate to be able to bring their singularly human power to adequate expression. Even the most highly developed of men are only occasionally rational or deliberate, religious or artistic. And they lose nothing of their humanity when they put their reason and skills aside under the pressure of affection, sentiment and misfortune. Men are human, not because some of them do things animals cannot, but because all of them have a power all animals lack—though to be sure only some of the men use that power to do things animals cannot.

If we can affirm that there is a singularly human power which is the source of all man's abilities, an important neglected truth is within our grasp: man cannot be an animal in whole or in part. Even his body, despite the many features which it shares with animals must, if quickened by a single human power, be nonanimal in nature.

A single power characteristic of man must be either separable or inseparable from his body. If separable, his definition will involve a consideration only of his "soul"; if inseparable, the nature of his power cannot be grasped without taking into account the fact that he has a body. The first of these alternatives is accepted by Plato. According to him, who here echoes something of the views of the East, and is echoed in turn by Descartes, Christian Scientists and Spiritualists, "what makes each one of us what we are is only the soul." The body, on this view, is unessential and the soul "never voluntarily has connection with it." But, theorize as much as we like, the fact is that men sit and run, eat and drink, laugh and cry, and this no mere soul or spirit could do. To deny that the body is an essential part of a man is to deny that a man can be ruined by cutting his throat, or that a man ought to have food and shelter in order to remain human.

The objections are obvious and pressing. It is no surprise therefore to find that those who try to view the body as an unessential part of man, change without apology to the view that the body is an essential but unwanted and impoverishing part of him. The main tenor of Plato's views is in this direction, particularly in such dialogues as the *Republic*, where gymnastics, the training of the body, is defined as an indispensable part of every man's education.

But this view, too, will not do. It plays havoc with the truth that a man who merely thinks about the good is not good enough, and that to be truly good he must be able to realize his ideals in fact to some degree. To bring the good about, a man needs a body; if that body is necessary for the good to be achieved, it is so far not undesirable or unwanted, but desirable and necessary. Ascetics have discovered a way by which they can avoid the evils which the body makes possible; but that way unfortunately is also one that makes them give up the goods which the body helps achieve. The nature of man involves a reference to the body as an indispensable avenue through which his power is to be at least partly expressed and his promise at least partly fulfilled.

For a desperate problem sometimes a desperate remedy must be found. To save the view that man's body is an undesirable part of him, one would have to deny that any body or bodily act could possibly be good. The good in man, we are then bound to say, dwells solely in his soul. But that denial cannot be maintained. If a body is in someone's way, it must be a good thing to take it away. Since a body is no hindrance once it is dead, we ought to be able to help a man by shortening his days. This we can do, not by retreating inside ourselves, but by using our body in gross bodily ways. Our body will then prove itself to be a good, if not to us, then to our fellows. Only because we have a body, can we perform the charitable act of helping our neighbors free themselves from the evils which their bodies entrain. . . .

THE HUMAN CONSTANT

A man is not a body. He has a body, and that body is necessary and desirable. This conclusion is so obvious and inevitable that it would be hard to find anyone who consistently and explicitly denies it. Even those who underscore other interpretations of the nature of man, constantly shift their emphases and assert this last as well. . . .

The problem of the nature of man is one of our most neglected problems. One clue is to be found in the fact that he is, in some sense, the self-same being from birth to death. He is not, of course, self-identical as a body. He grows vertically and horizontally in the course of his career. As an adult his appearance often differs so greatly from the appearance he presented as a child that it would be hazardous to assert that anyone could see a similarity. Even more important is the physiologically substantiated fact that his body contains hardly any of the cells that were present a dozen years or so before. So far as size, shape, skill, strength and appearance are concerned, a man becomes considerably transformed over the years, while so far as the constituent cells of his body are in question, he is almost entirely changed. Yet there is a deep and undeniable sense in which it is the same man who is adult and who was embryo or child. Unless a man is to be designated as a new being every time he loses or adds a cell, changes in strength, skill or appearance, it is necessary to affirm that there is something in him which is of his essence and which remains constant throughout his days. Despite the fact that he changes, he remains self-same, a being with a single essence and career. . . .

There are men; the men change. But to be that which changes, a man must also be that which is constant. Otherwise what was before and what was later would not characterize *him*. But if he is constant he cannot be a new substance at each moment.

We know it is ourselves who change. That is why we know it is ourselves who are constant. And because we know that we are constant, we know it is ourselves who change. Because we know we are constant and because we know we change, we know we are neither momentary nor nontemporal substances.

A man is guilty of a crime he committed a year ago. His guilt is not decreased but in fact increased if he changes his face and fingerprints in the meantime. He is guilty all the while, and this whether or not he is conscious of the fact. We want him to be conscious of his guilt before we punish him so that the full meaning of the punishment will be clear. We await his awakening, not his recovery of identity. He does not lose his identity by forgetting who he is; he does not become a renewed man by remembering who he was. He is self-same all the while, in sleep and waking, but the latter alone is the appropriate time to let him know the nature of the crimes he committed. If he changes his face and fingerprints he is different in appearance from what he was. But throughout he is the self-same being. The differences characterize him; they are changes *of* him, not changes *to* and *from* or *in* him.

A man has a single, constant essence. It is tempting to suppose that this essence is the life which quickens his body. The embryo does not have a life which passes away as soon as the embryo assumes the shape of a child. The child does not die in order to become a youth. It is the same life which vitalizes the embryo and the developed body. Only one life is allotted to a man. That life relates, permeates and vitalizes every part of the body; it is sensitive to the adventures these parts undergo. One life suffuses the whole and suffuses it from birth to death.

The life of a being, however, varies in intensity, force, mode of expression and bent from the beginning to the end of his days. The vitality of an embryo is different in nature and stress from that of a man. The life in the body is a continuous rather than a constant thing. There is more to a man, too, than the life that happens to be exhibited in his body. He is equally himself when he is passive as when he is active, when asleep as when awake, though the degree of life exhibited in the body varies considerably at these different times. Only part of him is immersed in the form of a life in the body, and this seems to ebb and flow in the course of the day. A part of man's nature might be said to be expressed as the life of his body but there must be a part existing outside his bodily frame.

The life that is immersed in the body is a persistent but flickering flame. A man cannot be identified with it, for he remains self-same even while it fluctuates. Nor can he be identified with that life as together with the body which it quickens, for two changing things do not add to a constant unless their variations balance one another. The body and the life within it vary in the same direction, and to somewhat the same degree. The life in the body, no less than the body, is something which a man has rather than is.

All changes presuppose something constant. Either, then, men are but passing shadows across the face of some more constant thing, or there is within them a constant factor which is expressed as a fluctuating life in a changing body. But men act on their own and are self-same throughout their careers. There must be something in them which is neither body, the life which animates it, nor the changing composite of the two. We must look elsewhere for the secret of man's identity.

Were men merely unified bodies, everything they did would be a function of those bodies. Yet all seem to have a reason of their own. Though that reason expresses, responds and reports the things the body does and undergoes, it frequently concerns itself with other things as well. While the body feeds and grows, it thinks of mathematical truths or the scent of the rose. Though it does not operate until the brain is developed, and though it often reflects the state of the glands and the general health of the body, it is often vigorous though the body is weak, and feeble though the body is strong. The greatest intellects do not necessarily have the largest or most convoluted brains, the best physiques or the most stable and perfect bodily health.

One could then make out a strong case for the identification of oneself with one's reason. Despite the fact that the body constantly changes in shape, size and accomplishment, the reason seems to have a rather constant cast. Men seem to retain the same mental qualities and intellectual bents throughout their lives. No matter how they vary the nature of their bodies they do not seem to be able to change themselves from engineers into poets, or from poets into mathematicians. The body also distorts and limits their intentions, but the reason seems to allow them full play.

Yet the reason cannot be what we seek. The reason is a late achievement, not present in the embryo. It has a different cargo and a different destination at different times. The statement that a man is a rational being expresses the character of a hope rather than the nature of a fact, unless experience deceives us most grievously.

Nor is it the memory, as Locke suggests, which is at the end of our search. The memory splits into multiple unrelated fragments as one develops, embraces only part of what one is, does not encompass the present moment, and has little, if any, existence at the moment of birth. But what is constant in man is unitary and all-embracing, exists at the very beginning of his life, and encompasses the present moment.

The human constant might more reasonably be identified with the will than with the memory or the reason. One can will to act, to think or to remember, and so far as this is true the will must be more fundamental than these others. The will, too, seems to remain constant for quite a while. Future deliberations run along the same course as past ones, and men hold themselves responsible for those past promises and acts they willingly performed. Yet despite all this, the will cannot be that of which we are in search. The will waxes and wanes in strength and direction from time to time. It is not a constant. It is not possessed by all human beings, nor by any all the time. Infants and those asleep and unconscious seem to be without a will of any kind. A will exists only when one is willing; the rest of the time it disappears into the recesses of one's being, appearing once again with somewhat the same, though not necessarily the identical, bent it had before.

The constant factor characteristic of a man lies beneath his life, memory, mind and will. It is not the whole of him, for the life and the body, the memory, mind and will are part of him as well. Nor is it separated off from these, for he is one being and not many. A man is both a constant and a changing being. He can be both and still be a unity because his changes are determinations, because they are the possessions of a single undetermined factor which is unchanged throughout his days. That constant, undetermined unit is his *self*.

To know oneself it is necessary to know something of one's self. That self is what a psyche becomes when it is concerned with realizing not only its own good or that of its kind but also a good pertinent to others. Baby or idiot, immature or ill, a human, by virtue of his self, is concerned with some goods that do good neither to him nor even to mankind. This of course must be shown, but for the time being it will perhaps suffice to remark that the self is partly expressed from the very beginning as a life in the body and soon becomes expressed as well in the form of a will and a mind, to make man an embodied self which may eventually will and think.

The self is a constant, enabling a man to be self-same throughout his career. But because that self, from the very beginning, is expressed in and through his body, a man can change in acts, structure and powers in the course of time.

MAN'S FOURFOLD BOND

Like the rest of the beings in nature all of us are held captive by our pasts, our bodies, our fellows and the world about. These form a fourfold barrier, standing perpetually in our way. They limit what we could possibly and actually be, have and do.

We are creatures of experiences already lived through. What we did days ago plays a part in our acts today. The past keeps us moving within narrow grooves, turning us into biased beings who concentrate on one prospect rather than another, sometimes even to our detriment. It forces some tendencies to the fore and keeps others repressed, though our needs may require a different stress. The shape of our tomorrow we molded all yesterday.

Our bodies have requirements, drives and modes of acting which can be controlled at times, but never entirely defied. Possessing their own structures and habits, those bodies have rhythms and make demands to which we must submit whether we will or no. Those who have often exhibited fear by running, find it hard to avoid a frightened run even when they would prefer to be at rest. Before a timid man has a chance to say what he would like to do, his legs are on the move, precipitately carrying him from the scene. Anyone else, in the same circumstances, might also have been frightened. But some would have had their bodies so well keyed that it would be hard to discern a move. If we demand of the brave that they do not budge when startled—a common, though not easily satisfied demand—only those can be brave whose bodies have been properly trained. Whatever praise they deserve is earned then and there by their bodies alone, though credit is also due them, as distinct from their bodies, for past practice and control. Whether trained or untrained, the body leaves its mark on whatever we do.

All of us have been shaped by our societies. We act as social beings even in solitude. The lives of other human beings constantly interplay with and intersect our own. From birth on, our neighbors drive us subtly but surely along paths we never chose. They provoke certain acts and the repression of others; they stand in the way of our efforts and of the effects which those efforts would otherwise produce; they force us to occupy ourselves with problems we would have preferred to ignore, and then they compete with us and force us to forego resolving the issues they raised. Our attempts and our achievements bear unmistakable signs of the pressure exerted by our fellow men.

We are parts of a universe, beings in nature, as well as members of a society. No matter how aloof we try to be, we always yield somewhat to the demands and force imposed by nonhuman beings. At every moment, we are compelled to take account of them as having natures and careers not in harmony with our own, and we constantly shift our emphases in the endeavor to subject them to some control. They help fix the boundaries of our future; they alter the shape our acts assume in fact. The world that lies ahead is structured primarily by what lies alongside.

There is no real escape from our fourfold bond, struggle as we may. If a man could free himself from his past, his body, his fellows or the world, he would be without roots, a language or a home: in the world and yet not part of it. He would be alone and ignorant, untaught and untrained.

Something can be said, in fact, for those who recommend that we passively submit to all our bonds. The more a man yields to the conditions which hem him in, the more secure and stable he often is, the more definite is his future, the more routine and easy is his life. Those who persist in battering their heads against a wall are caught as surely as are those who passively yield. And in addition they lose the peace that comes from the acceptance of the conditions that prevail. They also soon batter according to a pattern, thereby revealing how much they are under the influence of habit, the demands of the body, the pressure of their fellows and the character of the wall. Professional rebels are conservatives in disguise, breaking the fixtures of thought and existence in a somewhat steady and tedious way. They are trapped as surely as others are; their judgments and acts are no less dated and are no less predictable than are those of the quietest conservative. The heresies of today are the prelude to the dogmas of tomorrow. Rebellion at bondage is but a preparation for being bound again, sometimes even more firmly than before.

Yet each man does and must avoid being a creature of any one of these four bonds. Otherwise he would be dead in spirit and in body. He would do nothing, but would have everything done to and for him. Those who pride themselves on being stable steadily recede into the background. The defenders of the *status quo* are now in the process of becoming part of the *status ante*. "I am a man of my times," is the birthcry of an antiquarian. To be alive is to master the fourfold ring of conditions in a manner all one's own. And this every man does to some degree. None is wholly passive. All subject their bonds to some control. We differ from one another primarily in the extent to which we master our bonds while we submit to them.

We are never completely bound by the past. Nor do we ever free ourselves from it entirely. To be sure, we can reform. Yet we cannot reform ourselves completely at one fell swoop. A complete reform would take a lifetime to perform. By the time it was completed, the earlier stages of the reform through which we had gone would be solidified into constraints as effective as those from which we had escaped. The most radical reform touches but facets of a man's nature. Though he change the bent of his interests, forget what he has learned, defy the lessons of his experience, develop virtues where he before encouraged vice, he will continue to act somewhat as he did before. There is a common signature signed to all acts before and after a reform. In opposing the demands of his past, a man inevitably yields to it in other ways.

Nor is anyone completely under the dominance or completely in control of his body. We can master the body's rhythm, break its habits, enliven and constrain it despite its demands. We can, to some degree, even change its tone and structure through drugs, exercise and surgery. All but the most drastic changes are quickly caught and absorbed within the body as a whole, which continues with almost the same strength, insistence and direction it had before. Like a surging sea which may be successfully fought at every moment but never defeated, the body reasserts itself no matter how often it has been denied. No man can rightly claim that he is the master of his body, but only that he has mastered it at various times. The way to escape from the thrall of the body is to control it again and again. And since men must eat and sleep, drink and breathe, each must constantly submit to his body in some respects in order to be able to resist it at all. To control the body we must yield to it, if not in one way then in some other. And every gain that is made must be recovered the next day.

Nor need men quietly submit to the pressure of their fellows. There have been and there undoubtedly always will be a number who resist beyond any assigned degree. Social defiance, however, is but another way of expressing a submission at the same time. Men do not change their societies; the most they can do is introduce changes within them. They cannot cut themselves off completely from their fellow men, but must act in terms of what their fellows produce and intend. Revolutionaries and criminals work inside the frame of an established social whole, differing from others and from one another in the way they treat the good and evil others have made possible. Both opposition and conformity to society presuppose a social field which determines what is respectable or criminal, conservative or revolutionary, reasonable or foolish, promoting security or disorder.

Finally, men do not quietly submit to or really try to escape from nature. They struggle with her, yielding to her in one way while mastering her in another. Men have always struggled with nature, but only in our age has the struggle been buttressed with strategy and accompanied with an acute awareness that we will yield in the end, though not without having made some gain. Our scientists and engineers force nature along unaccustomed routes by following her at the same time. They made the airplane possible, not by ignoring but by yielding to the fact of gravitation. They conquered nature by infecting her with their own demands, which she then proceeded to carry out without their aid or encouragement.

All four barriers are forever in our way. We are always trying to subject them to some control. As a result of our efforts they take on the contours of our intentions and we, though still trapped, often do what we want. We are in fact free beings, for we can and do initiate acts, and can and do assert ourselves—sometimes with considerable success—while firmly bound.

MAN'S THREEFOLD FREEDOM

No barrier can come so close that it can prevent our being free. If it could it would destroy us as independent beings and would as a consequence have nothing to constrain. We are able to be trapped only because we stand over against any possible bond.

We are free—independent beings who act on our own—in a threefold way. Each of us independently initiates acts in the endeavor to realize some privately isolated objective. And when those acts encounter the opposition they inevitably must, we freely call upon unused reserves in the effort to achieve the result we were on the verge of losing. Finally, when the opposition is too great for us, we freely occupy ourselves with new objectives in terms of which we may be able to act and struggle with more effect. Our freedom is a triply employed power by which we endeavor to realize objectives, initially regardless of, then in the face of, and finally tangentially to the opposition we happen to encounter. It turns our barriers firstly into fields of operation, then into more or less effective means for the realization of our ends, and finally into occasions for acting in new ways.

Freedom is a power by which the indeterminate is made determinate, the general specific, the abstract concrete, the possible actual. It is most perfectly expressed when we initiate actions designed to convert a result intended into a result attained. Each of us has a characteristic way of focussing on the future, of interpreting it from his own perspective, of treating it as an objective, as a possible good to be made into a good that is real. As intended, the objective is more determinate than it was, but it is not yet entirely determinate. Action is required to make it fully determinate, to give it definiteness and substance.

In origin our acts are means for re-forming ourselves and perhaps other beings so as to make concrete and present what is now abstract and future. Produced from within, they are free sources of the determinations by which we attempt to convert possibilities into realities. When they encounter the opposition they inevitably do, we must, if we are to realize our objectives, express ourselves spontaneously, thereby exerting additional effort. Though none of us can break through any of our barriers, all of us can and do vitalize them, shape them anew, spontaneously reply to the opposition which they offer to the realization of our objectives. We thereby master the past, the body, fellow beings and the world to some degree.

Sometimes our barriers are too much for us. They effectively prevent us from realizing our objectives. We are then prompted to make an effort to isolate and realize new objectives. Only if there were—as there is—an ultimate objective, an end to whose realization we are necessarily pledged, would we, despite every defeat and regardless of all appearance to the contrary, always strive to realize it.

Because only men have ultimate objectives, only they are unable to change into superior types of being when they encounter insuperable obstacles to the expression of their human concerns. When they encounter resistance which effectively prevents the expression of a concern for their ultimate objectives, they try to change the nature of their acts. Like other beings they are, despite an inability to change in nature, always free to meet defeat with a new adventure, feeble and unsuccessful though this may prove to be.

Each of us initiates acts. Each of us struggles with all four barriers. Each of us spontaneously shifts his emphasis in the face of defeat. Most of us concentrate our energies, however, on only one of these three enterprises, and are inclined to struggle more with some barriers than with others. But a man is somewhat less than a man should be, unless he employs his freedom fully in all three ways and takes adequate account of all the obstacles he confronts. . . .

THE TASK OF MAN

No matter how insignificant, servile, impotent or vicious a man, he has a unique value, unduplicatable, unrepeatable and irreplaceable. He may look like, behave like and think like others, his power may be weak and his productions trivial. His character may be contemptible. He may be less good than he ought to be; yet he has a value that cannot be reproduced or replaced and which is greater than that possessed by any other type of being. . . .

No man is a mere creature of circumstances. He molds them in a characteristic way. Changes in his cells or organs, or the conditions which hem him in from without, make possible new acts and enterprises otherwise beyond his reach, enabling him to develop and exercise new talents, and prompting him occasionally to undergo a radical reform. Yet everything he does bears the self-same signature, written though it is on different things, at different times and in different ways. Each makes and mars in his own individual way.

Given equal health, fortune and opportunity, each man, it would seem, should be able to achieve what every other can. Men begin to diverge, however, from the very start, for as embryos they already live in different environments, are fed by different foods, and inevitably lay the ground for patterns of expression and activity which cannot readily be dislodged or radically changed. Not all can be professional athletes, mathematicians, or political leaders, for as embryos they have already set individual limits to what they can attain as mature technicians of mind and body. No change in health, opportunity or determination will suffice to turn one into a violinist of distinction if his gifts do not lie in that direction. Free and unlimited though a man's promise is and always remains, it is yet bound irrevocably at the beginning of his life, for the individual works in new contexts from the standpoint and with the equipment of the old. Though there is nothing which is not in principle open to everyone equally, from the first much that a man might do is excluded beyond recall, and as he grows, more and more is outside his possible reach.

Each man can, to some degree, control the activities of most of his organs, individually and together, for the good of his body. He can also interrelate them for an end beyond. His problem is to move from the state of living in and through his body to the state of living by means of it in order to benefit others as well as himself. It is his task to remake the world, to realize to a maximum the good with which he is concerned. Only so far as he succeeds, does he fulfill his duty. Only then does he exhibit himself as one not bound by things as they are. Only then does he do what he ought —improve the world by making it the embodiment of the absolute good.

Man is a natural being with a fixed core, directed towards a good which is pertinent to all that exists. And he has a responsibility from which he can never escape. It is the primary function of his body, mind and will to help him live up to this responsibility. Trapped though he is by the bonds of past, body, society and the world, he is free to act and thus is accountable for his every failure to realize the good fully in fact. Even if he could not possibly master those bonds, he would still be responsible. He has infinite value because he has an infinite responsibility, and conversely. To deny him the one is to deny him the other.

A man's fundamental right is the right to be good. This requires him to realize the good. Whether or not, and to what degree it can be realized is therefore a vital problem. It is in fact a central problem of ethics. A man, because he is responsible, owes it to himself to plumb the foundations of ethics and make evident to himself what he ought to do. Only then can he make himself the man he ought to be.

For Further Study

Fromm, Erich. *The Heart of Man: Its Genius for Good and Evil*. New York: Harper & Row, 1964.

Heschel, Abraham J. *Who Is Man?* Stanford: Stanford U. Press, 1965. (Stanford Paperback SP 64.)

Kahler, Erich. *Man the Measure*. New York: Pantheon, 1943, pp. 603–640.

Mascall, E. L. *The Importance of Being Human*. New York: Columbia U. Press, 1958, Ch. 1, "The Uniqueness of Man."

Phenix, Philip H. *Man and His Becoming*. New Brunswick, N. J.: Rutgers U. Press, 1964.

Platt, John R., ed. *New Views of the Nature of Man*. Chicago: U. of Chicago Press, 1965.

Polanyi, Michael. *The Study of Man*. Chicago: U. of Chicago Press, 1959, 102 pp.

Scheler, Max. *Man's Place in Nature*. New York: The Noonday Press, 1962. (Noonday paperback N 231.)

9   What Is the Self?

DAVID HUME / *The Self as Fleeting Perceptions* *

David Hume (1711–1776) is the eminent philosophical skeptic in the British empirical tradition. His thoughts are still vigorously debated by philosophers. His writings are in the fields of epistemology, psychology, morals, religion, and history.

OF THE ORIGIN OF OUR IDEAS

ALL THE PERCEPTIONS of the human mind resolve themselves into two distinct kinds, which I shall call *impressions* and *ideas*. The difference betwixt these consists in the degrees of force and liveliness, with which they strike upon the mind, and make their way into our thought or consciousness. Those perceptions which enter with most force and violence, we may name *impressions*; and under this name I comprehend all our sensations, passions, and emotions, as they make their first appearance in the soul. By *ideas* I mean the faint images of these in thinking and reasoning; such as, for instance, are all the perceptions excited by the present discourse, excepting only those which arise from the sight and touch, and excepting the immediate pleasure or uneasiness it may occasion. I believe it will not be very necessary to employ many words in explaining this distinction. . . .

* David Hume, from A *Treatise of Human Nature* (1738), Book I, Part 1, Secs. 1, 6, and Appendix.

. . . We shall here content ourselves with establishing one general proposition, *That all our simple ideas in their first appearance are derived from simple impressions, which are correspondent to them, and which they exactly represent.* . . .

OF PERSONAL IDENTITY

There are some philosophers who imagine we are every moment intimately conscious of what we call our *self*; that we feel its existence and its continuance in existence; and are certain, beyond the evidence of a demonstration, both of its perfect identity and simplicity. The strongest sensation, the most violent passion, say they, instead of distracting us from this view, only fix it the more intensely and make us consider their influence on *self* either by their pain or pleasure. To attempt a further proof of this were to weaken its evidence; since no proof can be derived from any fact of which we are so intimately conscious; nor is there anything of which we can be certain if we doubt of this.

Unluckily all these positive assertions are contrary to that very experience which is pleaded for them; nor have we any idea of *self*, after the manner it is here explained. For from what impression could this idea be derived? This question it is impossible to answer without a manifest contradiction and absurdity; and yet it is a question which must necessarily be answered, if we would have the idea of self pass for clear and intelligible. It must be some one impression that gives rise to every real idea. But self or person is not any one impression, but that to which our several impressions and ideas are supposed to have a reference. If any impression gives rise to the idea of self, that impression must continue invariably the same, through the whole course of our lives; since self is supposed to exist after that manner. But there is no impression constant and invariable. Pain and pleasure, grief and joy, passions and sensations succeed each other, and never all exist at the same time. It cannot therefore be from any of these impressions, or from any other, that the idea of self is derived; and consequently there is no such idea.

But further, what must become of all our particular perceptions upon this hypothesis? All these are different, and distinguishable, and separable from each other, and may be separately considered, and may exist separately, and have no need of anything to support their existence. After what manner therefore do they belong to self, and how are they connected with it? For my part, when I enter most intimately into what I call *myself*, I always stumble on some particular perception or other, of heat or cold, light or shade, love or hatred, pain or pleasure. I never can catch *myself* at any time without a perception, and never can observe anything but the perception. When my perceptions are removed for any time, as by sound sleep, so long am I insensible of *myself*, and may truly be said not to exist. And were all my perceptions removed by death, and could I neither think, nor feel, nor see, nor love, nor hate, after the dissolution of my body, I should be entirely annihilated, nor do I conceive what is further requisite to make me a perfect nonentity. If any one, upon serious and unprejudiced reflection, thinks he has a different notion of *himself*, I must confess I can reason no longer with him. All I can allow him is, that he may be in the right as well as I, and that we are essentially different in this particular. He may, perhaps, perceive something simple and continued, which he calls *himself*; though I am certain there is no such principle in me.

But setting aside some metaphysicians of this kind, I may venture to affirm of the rest of mankind, that they are nothing but a bundle or collection of different perceptions, which succeed each other with an inconceivable rapidity, and are in a perpetual flux and movement. Our eyes cannot turn in their sockets without varying our perceptions. Our thought is still more variable than our sight; and all our other senses and faculties contribute to this change; nor is there any single power of the soul, which remains unalterably the same, perhaps for one moment. The mind is a kind of theatre, where several perceptions successively make their appearance; pass, repass, glide away, and mingle in an infinite variety of postures and situations. There is properly no *simplicity* in it at one time, nor *identity* in different, whatever natural propension we may have to imagine that simplicity and identity. The comparison of the theatre must not mislead us. They are the successive perceptions only, that constitute the mind; nor have we the most distant notion of the place where these scenes are represented, or of the materials of which it is composed. . . .

We now proceed to explain the nature of *personal identity*, which has become so great a question in philosophy, especially of late years in England, where all the abstruser sciences are studied with a peculiar ardour and application. And here it is evident the same method of reasoning must be continued which has so successfully explained the identity of plants, and animals, and ships, and houses, and of all compounded and changeable productions either of art or nature. The identity which we ascribe to the mind of man is only a fictitious one, and of a like kind with that which we ascribe to vegetable and animal bodies. It cannot therefore have a different origin, but must proceed from a like operation of the imagination upon like objects.

But lest this argument should not convince the reader, though in my opinion perfectly decisive, let him weigh the following reasoning, which is still closer and more immediate. It is evident, that the identity which we attribute to the human mind, however perfect we may imagine it to be, is not able to run the several different perceptions into one, and make them lose their characters of distinction and difference, which are essential to them. It is still true that every distinct perception which enters into the composition of the mind, is a distinct existence, and is different, and distinguishable, and separable from every other perception, either contemporary or successive. But as, notwithstanding this distinction and separability, we suppose the whole train of perceptions to be united by identity, a question naturally arises concerning this relation of identity, whether it be something that really binds our several perceptions together, or only associates their ideas in the imagination; that is, in other words, whether in pronouncing concerning the identity of a person, we observe some real bond among his perceptions, or only feel one among the ideas we form of them. This question we might easily decide, if we would recollect what has been already proved at large, that the understanding never observes any real connection among objects, and that even the union of cause and effect, when strictly examined, resolves itself into a customary association of ideas. For from thence it evidently follows, that identity is nothing really belonging to these different perceptions, and uniting them together, but is merely a quality which we attribute to them, because of the union of their ideas in the imagination when we reflect upon them. Now, the only qualities which can give ideas a union in the imagination, are the three relations below mentioned. These are the uniting principles in the ideal world, and without them every distinct object is separable by the mind, and may be separately considered, and appears not to have any more connection with any other object than if disjointed by the greatest difference and remoteness. It is therefore on some of these three relations of resemblance, contiguity, and causation, that identity depends; and as the very essence of these relations consists in their producing an easy transition of ideas, it follows that our notions of personal identity proceed entirely from the smooth and uninterrupted progress of the thought along a train of connected ideas, according to the principles above explained. . . .

I had entertained some hopes, that however deficient our theory of the intellectual world might be, it would be free from those contradictions and absurdities which seem to attend every explication that human reason can give of the material world. But upon a more strict review of the section concerning *personal identity*, I find myself involved in such a labyrinth that, I must confess, I neither know how to correct my former opinions, nor how to render them consistent. If this be not a good *general* reason for scepticism, it is at least a sufficient one (if I were not already abundantly supplied) for me to entertain a diffidence and modesty in all my decisions.

When we talk of *self* or *substance*, we must have an idea annexed to these terms, otherwise they are altogether unintelligible. Every idea is derived from preceding impressions; and we have no impression of self or substance, as something simple and individual. We have, therefore, no idea of them in that sense. . . .

Appendix

Whatever is distinct is distinguishable, and whatever is distinguishable is separable by the thought or imagination. All perceptions are distinct. They are, therefore, distinguishable, and separable, and may be conceived as separately existent, and may exist separately, without any contradiction or absurdity.

When I view this table and that chimney, nothing is present to me but particular perceptions, which are of a like nature with all the other perceptions. This is the doctrine of philosophers. But this table, which is present to me, and that chimney, may, and do exist separately. This is the doctrine of the vulgar, and implies no contradiction. There is no contradiction, therefore, in extending the same doctrine to all the perceptions.

In general, the following reasoning seems satisfactory. All ideas are borrowed from preceding perceptions. Our ideas of objects, therefore, are derived from that source. Consequently no proposition can be intelligible or consistent with regard to objects, which is not so with regard to perceptions. But it is intelligible and consistent to say, that objects exist distinct and independent, without any common *simple* substance or subject of inhesion. This proposition, therefore, can never be absurd with regard to perceptions.

When I turn my reflection on *myself*, I never can perceive this *self* without some one or more perceptions; nor can I ever perceive anything but the perceptions. It is the composition of these, therefore, which forms the self.

We can conceive a thinking being to have either many or few perceptions. Suppose the mind to be reduced even below the life of an oyster. Suppose it to have only one perception, as of thirst or hunger. Consider it in that situation. Do you conceive anything but merely that perception? Have you any notion of *self* or *substance*? If not, the addition of other perceptions can never give you that notion.

The annihilation which some people suppose to follow upon death, and which entirely destroys this self, is nothing but an extinction of all particular perceptions; love and hatred, pain and pleasure, thought and sensation. These, therefore, must be the same with self, since the one cannot survive the other.

Is *self* the same with *substance?* If it be, how can that question have place, concerning the subsistence of self, under a change of substance? If they be distinct, what is the difference betwixt them? For my part, I have a notion of neither, when conceived distinct from particular perceptions.

Philosophers begin to be reconciled to the principle, *that we have no idea of external substance, distinct from the ideas of particular qualities.*

This must pave the way for a like principle with regard to the mind, *that we have no notion of it, distinct from the particular perception.*

So far I seem to be attended with sufficient evidence. But having thus loosened all our particular perceptions, when I proceed to explain the principle of connection, which binds them together, and makes us attribute to them a real simplicity and identity, I am sensible that my account is very defective, and that nothing but the seeming evidence of the precedent reasonings could have induced me to receive it. If perceptions are distinct existences, they form a whole only by being connected together. But no connections among distinct existences are ever discoverable by human understanding. We only *feel* a connection or determination of the thought to pass from one object to another. It follows, therefore, that the thought alone feels personal identity, when reflecting on the train of past perceptions that compose a mind, the ideas of them are felt to be connected together, and naturally introduce each other. However extraordinary this conclusion may seem, it need not surprise us. Most philosophers seem inclined to think that personal identity *arises* from consciousness, and consciousness is nothing but a reflected thought or perception. The present philosophy, therefore, has so far a promising aspect. But all my hopes vanish when I come to explain the principles that unite our successive perceptions in our thought or consciousness. I cannot discover any theory which gives me satisfaction on this head.

In short, there are two principles which I cannot render consistent, nor is it in my power to renounce either of them, viz. *that all our distinct perceptions are distinct existences,* and *that the mind never perceives any real connection among distinct existences.* Did our perceptions either inhere in something simple and individual, or did the mind perceive some real connection among them, there would be no difficulty in the case. For my part, I must plead the privilege of a sceptic, and confess that this difficulty is too hard for my understanding. I pretend not, however, to pronounce it absolutely insuperable. Others, perhaps, or myself, upon more mature reflections, may discover some hypothesis that will reconcile those contradictions.

JAMES BISSETT PRATT / The Self as Substance *

James Bissett Pratt (1875–1944) was professor of philosophy at Williams College. He was a member of the group known as critical realists, but preferred the name *personal realism* for his own philosophy. He had wide interests in the psychology and philosophy of religion, as well as in epistemology and metaphysics.

FROM THE BEGINNING I have maintained that the self is a substance; and that means an existent being possessing qualities. But there are many grades and many kinds of substance and a self is a substance of its own kind. It is *sui generis*. I cannot make this too emphatic. One of the chief reasons why the self is so persistently misunderstood, so very hard to understand, is because we naturally seek to form an image of it, even to visualize it, and naturally construct our image on the outline of the spatial things we see and handle. This is a costly mistake, but it is a natural one. Both in the individual and in the race, theory or understanding follows action, and is in all men first produced, and in many men only produced, for the sake of action. Now action, the vital needs of life, the necessities that dominate our activities as living beings in a spatial world of dangerous and useful, tangible and visible things, force us to center most of our attention on the spatial, tangible, and visible. Hence it has come about that the very notion of an entity or real being is associated in our minds with spatial characters, and even when we come to realize that there are, or may be, real beings which are not spatial, our inveterate tendency is still to think of them by means of visual images and to interpret them in spatial terms. . . . And so it has come about that every word one can discover when used to express the meaning of the self tends to betray one, and to lead the hearer, and often the speaker, into materialistic pictures the very reverse of what one really wishes to convey.

Hence, let me repeat, the necessity of realizing that by the self one means something essentially unique and *sui generis*. It is a substance, but this does not mean that it is either tangible or visible. And since it is not visible, all efforts to visualize it must be misleading. We must, therefore, not expect that the self will be a substance of the same sort as material things. . . .

. . . We must remember that by substance one does not mean an abstract core of being taken by itself, but an entity with characters. There is no substance without attributes and no characterless self without qualities or acts. As well ask for an existent form completely divorced from matter. The self is therefore full of variety. In it variety and unity are harmonized. That this can be is no miracle, except as all existence is miraculous. . . .

Of course questions may be asked about the self which it will be hard to answer. If the self is more than a stream of consciousness, more than a collection, it may well be asked, what is this *more*? A partial answer, and one which at least points in a hopeful direction, will be that the self is the doer of certain acts. It is the sort of being that does the acts we find it doing. This may not be a complete answer, but it is at least as much of an answer as we can give concerning other things. Things are known by what they do: so is the self. If, then, the question be raised: What is the self aside from all its attributes and all its acts? the answer is that the self is never without attributes and that if it were it would be just nothing at all. It is *that which* has certain characters and acts in certain ways. . . .

THE UNITY OF THE SELF

The self is *sui generis* in possessing a unity of an inherent sort which no other substance possesses. Non-living material things have, indeed, relations, but no inherent unity. Many of them possess only so much unity as we read into them. The Great Bear, or Dipper, is a unity because we choose to regard it as such. My watch is a unity because of its relation to my purposes. But without relation to conscious purpose or thought it would have no unity. The unities of the physical and nonliving world depend upon living and conscious beings. Living organisms have a certain degree of inherent unity. But in so far as this unity is unconscious, unrealized, it is of a potential sort. It is true that the root and the leaves of the rose plant co-operate, and that we justly find in them together a unity in variety. But it is just as true that they are *two* as that they are one. The only being that is *essentially* one is a self.

The unity-in-variety which uniquely characterizes a self is seen in each of its three most noticeable characters or functions. The first of these is its role as subject in feeling and cognition. The second is its agency as the actor, the doer of deeds, the one who wills in volition, the efficient cause in its achievements. Finally the self is not only the unity that lies behind each mental state and the grasper that unites and compares: it is also the unity and the unifier in successive states, the identical being that endures in the midst of its changing acts and states. As Professor Wilson has admirably put it, the self is "that which maintains itself through its experiences."

CAN THE SELF BE KNOWN?

. . . Knowledge is a notoriously ambiguous word. To know *about* an object is one thing: to be directly aware of it, to have it as one's immediate experience, is another. Plainly it is only this second and direct kind of knowledge of the self, "knowledge of acquaintance," which is denied by both Yajnavalkya and Hume. It is conceivable that though we lack this, it still may be possible for us to have knowledge about the self. How, one may ask, do we know *physical* things? I do not mean, How do we know our own sensations and percepts, but how do we know the physical things all men except idealistic philosophers in their few official moments believe in? The answer to this question given by the form of Realism I have advocated in this volume is the following: We do not perceive or know physical things "directly," *i.e.*, not in the direct fashion in which we know our own sensations. But we have a strong and native impulse to believe there are physical things corresponding to and causing our percepts, and our reflective thought discovers that we can make sense of our experience only by supposing that this native impulse is justified. Our knowledge of the physical world is indirect: it is *knowledge about*, not *acquaintance with*. We have at least this same kind of knowledge of the self. We do not find it as we do its feelings and percepts; but everyone has a natural impulse to believe in it, and our experience is such that no theory is satisfactory which fails to recognize self as the actor and knower, the inner unity and the inner unifier of our multiform lives. We know *that* the self is, and we know *what* it is by observing what it does. And this we know because every theory of the inner life which fails to recognize a knower and actor does violence to the facts of experience. If this is the case, and I believe I have shown that it is the case, the fact that the self cannot be directly found is irrelevant: in fact it is exactly what, upon our theory, we should expect to be true. "How couldst thou know the knower?"

But it would be only a partial presentation of the truth should we stop here. I think we do have the same kind of evidence for the existence of the self that we have for the existence of physical things; but I think we have also a kind of knowledge concerning the self that we do not have concerning any physical thing. . . . The self is not part of the conscious content found directly as feelings and sensa are. But in every case of knowledge we are directly aware of the "datum" not merely as a thing but as *a datum*, *i.e.*, as something given. The givenness is given. The datum is something given to us, it is an object of our awareness or of our thought.

All experience contains the implications of a subject. The subject-object relation is one of the characters which we find or feel whenever we are aware of anything. It is like the stick illustration—the stick which, no matter how often one cuts it, has two ends. The self, indeed, cannot be found in the way Hume sought to find it, but the reason is that it is too near to be seen. It is, of course, the very finder, and we can never get away from it. "When me they fly, I am the wings." . . .

CHARACTERISTICS OF THE SELF

. . . The self is a substance. We have considerable knowledge about it, and a certain immediate realization of it. It is not a blank and abstract substance nor a blank unity, but a substance with qualities, a unity that possesses rich variety. These qualities or characters and this variety are seen in the conscious states of the self and in its activities. It is characterized by its passing sensa—a relatively unimportant matter—by its memories, its tendencies, its activities, its powers or potentialities for action, its efforts of attention and will, its reasoning power, its sentiments, its purposes. From the point of view of the social and ethical life, the purposes of the self are perhaps its most important characteristic. . . .

The self is to be discerned in every act and moment of our conscious living. But it is probably in the free act of will that it makes itself most vividly plain. In attention with effort, in sticking to the distasteful mental task in spite of monotony, in spite of weariness, in spite of pain, we are often most obvious to ourselves. And in those crises in which the will acts against instinctive tendency, even against the biological interests of the organism, the self shines with its own light, in its essential superiority to the merely physical and physiological and psychological. Asceticism has often been carried to utterly irrational limits, but the fact that asceticism is possible, that the soul can so triumph over the flesh as the great ascetics East and West have shown us that it can, throws a new light upon human nature. The martyrs of all time, the Irish and Indian patriots of a few years ago refusing to allow their hungry bodies to taste of food until they die of starvation for the sake of an ideal—things like these make almost ludicrous any attempt to explain human nature out of stimuli and reflexes and associations. Nor need we turn to martyrs for striking cases of the self in unmistakable action. The steady drive of the will against the choice of the weary body *most* of us have known. And in many a case where we outsiders see no sign of effort, the self may be struggling with and dominating the great mass of native psycho-physical tendencies, and its victory be all the greater, all the surer token of its own reality, because quite hidden. . . .

For Further Study

Blanshard, Brand and Skinner, B. F. "The Problem of Consciousness— A Debate," *Philosophy and Phenomenological Research,* 27 (March 1967): 317–337.

Bukala, C. R., S. J. "The Existential Structure of Person," *The Personalist,* 49 (Spring, 1968): 215–226.

Castell, Alburey. *The Self in Philosophy.* New York: Macmillan, 1965.

de Laguna, Grace. *On Existence and the Human World.* New Haven: Yale U. Press, 1966, Ch. 4, "The Person."

Johnstone, Henry W., Jr. "Persons and Selves," *Philosophy and Phenomenological Research,* 28 (December 1967): 205–212.

King, Robert H. "The Concept of the Person," *Journal of Religion,* 46 (January, 1966): 37–44.

Kolenda, Konstantin. "The Crisis of the Self," *Personalist,* 48 (Winter, 1967): 129–143.

Penelhum, Terence. "Hume on Personal Identity," *Philosophical Review,* 64 (1955): 571–589.

Shaffer, Jerome. "Persons and Their Bodies," *Philosophical Review,* 75 (January, 1966): 59–77.

Strawson, P. F. *Individuals: An Essay in Descriptive Metaphysics.* Garden City: Doubleday, 1963, Ch. 3, "Persons." (Anchor Book A 364.)

10 What Is the Mind?

RENÉ DESCARTES / A Thinking Thing *

René Descartes (1596–1650) is often called the "Father of Modern Philosophy" because of his criticism of earlier thought and his advocacy of methodical doubt as a first step in the discovery of truth. He also made important contributions to the development of mathematics.

THE MEDITATION of yesterday has filled my mind with so many doubts, that it is no longer in my power to forget them. Nor do I see, meanwhile, any principle on which they can be resolved; and, just as if I had fallen all of a sudden into very deep water, I am so greatly disconcerted as to be unable either to plant my feet firmly on the bottom or sustain myself by swimming on the surface. I will, nevertheless, make an effort, and try anew the same path on which I had entered yesterday, that is, proceed by casting aside all that admits of the slightest doubt, not less than if I had discovered it to be absolutely false; and I will continue always in this track until I shall find something that is certain, or at least, if I can do nothing more, until I shall know with certainty that there is nothing certain. Archimedes, that he might transport the entire globe from the place it occupied to another, demanded only a point that was firm and immovable; so, also, I shall be entitled to entertain the highest expectations, if I am fortunate enough to discover only one thing that is certain and indubitable.

* René Descartes, from "Meditations," in *The Method, Meditations and Philosophy,* trans. John Veitch (Washington: Dunne, 1901), Meditation II, pp. 224–229, 232–233.

I suppose, accordingly, that all the things which I see are false (fictitious); I believe that none of those objects which my fallacious memory
represents ever existed; I suppose that I possess no senses; I believe that
body, figure, extension, motion, and place are merely fictions of my mind.
What is there, then, that can be esteemed true? Perhaps this only, that
there is absolutely nothing certain.

But how do I know that there is not something different altogether from
the objects I have now enumerated, of which it is impossible to entertain
the slightest doubt? Is there not a God, or some being, by whatever name I
may designate him, who causes these thoughts to arise in my mind? But
why suppose such a being, for it may be I myself am capable of producing
them? Am I, then, at least not something? But I before denied that I possessed senses or a body; I hesitate, however, for what follows from that?
Am I so dependent on the body and the senses that without these I cannot
exist? But I had the persuasion that there was absolutely nothing in the
world, that there was no sky and no earth, neither minds nor bodies; was I
not, therefore, at the same time, persuaded that I did not exist? Far from
it; I assuredly existed, since I was persuaded. But there is I know not what
being, who is possessed at once of the highest power and the deepest cunning, who is constantly employing all his ingenuity in deceiving me.
Doubtless, then, I exist, since I am deceived; and, let him deceive me as he
may, he can never bring it about that I am nothing, so long as I shall be
conscious that I am something. So that it must, in fine, be maintained, all
things being maturely and carefully considered, that this proposition (*pro-
nunciatum*) I am, I exist, is necessarily true each time it is expressed by
me, or conceived in my mind.

But I do not yet know with sufficient clearness what I am, though
assured that I am; and hence, in the next place, I must take care, lest per-
chance I inconsiderately substitute some other object in place of what is
properly myself, and thus wander from truth, even in that knowledge (cognition) which I hold to be of all others the most certain and evident. For
this reason, I will now consider anew what I formerly believed myself to
be, before I entered on the present train of thought; and of my previous
opinion I will retrench all that can in the least be invalidated by the
grounds of doubt I have adduced, in order that there may at length remain
nothing but what is certain and indubitable. What then did I formerly
think I was? Undoubtedly I judged that I was a man. But what is a man?
Shall I say a rational animal? Assuredly not; for it would be necessary
forthwith to inquire into what is meant by animal, and what by rational,
and thus, from a single question, I should insensibly glide into others, and
these more difficult than the first; nor do I now possess enough of leisure
to warrant me in wasting my time amid subtleties of this sort. I prefer here
to attend to the thoughts that sprung up of themselves in my mind, and

were inspired by my own nature alone, when I applied myself to the consideration of what I was. In the first place, then, I thought that I possessed a countenance, hands, arms, and all the fabric of members that appears in a corpse, and which I called by the name of body. It further occurred to me that I was nourished, that I walked, perceived, and thought, and all those actions I referred to the soul; but what the soul itself was I either did not stay to consider, or, if I did, I imagined that it was something extremely rare and subtile, like wind, or flame, or ether, spread through my grosser parts. As regarded the body, I did not even doubt of its nature, but thought I distinctly knew it, and if I had wished to describe it according to the notions I then entertained, I should have explained myself in this manner: By body I understand all that can be terminated by a certain figure; that can be comprised in a certain place, and so fill a certain space as therefrom to exclude every other body; that can be perceived either by touch, sight, hearing, taste, or smell; that can be moved in different ways, not indeed of itself, but by something foreign to it by which it is touched [and from which it receives the impression]; for the power of self-motion, as likewise that of perceiving and thinking, I held as by no means pertaining to the nature of body; on the contrary, I was somewhat astonished to find such faculties existing in some bodies.

But [as to myself, what can I now say that I am], since I suppose there exists an extremely powerful, and, if I may so speak, malignant being, whose whole endeavors are directed toward deceiving me? Can I affirm that I possess any one of all those attributes of which I have lately spoken as belonging to the nature of body? After attentively considering them in my own mind, I find none of them that can properly be said to belong to myself. To recount them were idle and tedious. Let us pass, then, to the attributes of the soul. The first mentioned were the powers of nutrition and walking; but, if it be true that I have no body, it is true likewise that I am capable neither of walking nor of being nourished. Perception is another attribute of the soul; but perception too is impossible without the body; besides, I have frequently, during sleep, believed that I perceived objects which I afterward observed I did not in reality perceive. Thinking is another attribute of the soul; and here I discover what properly belongs to myself. This alone is inseparable from me. I am—I exist: this is certain; but how often? As often as I think; for perhaps it would even happen, if I should wholly cease to think, that I should at the same time altogether cease to be. I now admit nothing that is not necessarily true. I am therefore, precisely speaking, only a thinking thing, that is, a mind (*mens sive animus*), understanding, or reason, terms whose signification was before unknown to me. I am, however, a real thing, and really existent; but what thing? The answer was, a thinking thing. The question now arises, am I aught besides? I will stimulate my imagination with a view to discover whether I am not still something more than a thinking being. Now it is plain I am not the assemblage of members called the human body; I am not a thin and penetrating air diffused through all these members, or wind, or flame, or vapor, or breath, or any of all the things I can imagine; for I supposed that all these were not, and, without changing the supposition, I find that I still feel assured of my existence.

But it is true, perhaps, that those very things which I suppose to be non-existent, because they are unknown to me, are not in truth different from myself whom I know. This is a point I cannot determine, and do not now enter into any dispute regarding it. I can only judge of things that are known to me: I am conscious that I exist, and I who know that I exist inquire into what I am. It is, however, perfectly certain that the knowledge of my existence, thus precisely taken, is not dependent on things, the existence of which is as yet unknown to me: and consequently it is not dependent on any of the things I can feign in imagination. Moreover, the phrase itself, I frame an image (*effingo*), reminds me of my error; for I should in truth frame one if I were to imagine myself to be anything, since to imagine is nothing more than to contemplate the figure or image of a corporeal thing; but I already know that I exist, and that it is possible at the same time that all those images, and in general all that relates to the nature of body, are merely dreams [or chimeras]. From this I discover that it is not more reasonable to say, I will excite my imagination that I may know more distinctly what I am, than to express myself as follows: I am now awake, and perceive something real; but because my perception is not sufficiently clear, I will of express purpose go to sleep that my dreams may represent to me the object of my perception with more truth and clearness. And, therefore, I know that nothing of all that I can embrace in imagination belongs to the knowledge which I have of myself, and that there is need to recall with the utmost care the mind from this mode of thinking, that it may be able to know its own nature with perfect distinctness.

But what, then, am I? A thinking thing, it has been said. But what is a thinking thing? It is a thing that doubts, understands [conceives], affirms, denies, wills, refuses; that imagines also, and perceives. Assuredly it is not little, if all these properties belong to my nature. But why should they not belong to it? Am I not that very being who now doubts of almost everything; who, for all that, understands and conceives certain things; who affirms one alone as true, and denies the others; who desires to know more of them, and does not wish to be deceived; who imagines many things, sometimes even despite his will; and is likewise percipient of many, as if through the medium of the senses. Is there nothing of all this as true as that I am, even although I should be always dreaming, and although he who gave me being employed all his ingenuity to deceive me? Is there also any one of these attributes that can be properly distinguished from my thought, or that can be said to be separate from myself? For it is of itself so evident that it is I who doubt, I who understand, and I who desire, that it is here unnecessary to add anything by way of rendering it more clear. And I am as certainly the same being who imagines; for although it may be (as I before supposed) that nothing I imagine is true, still the power of imagination does not cease really to exist in me and to form part of my thought. In fine, I am the same being who perceives, that is, who apprehends certain objects as by the organs of sense, since, in truth, I see light, hear a noise, and feel heat. But it will be said that these presentations are false, and that I am dreaming. Let it be so. At all events it is certain that I seem to see light, hear a noise, and feel heat; this cannot be false, and this is what in me is properly called perceiving (*sentire*), which is nothing else than thinking. From this I begin to know what I am with somewhat greater clearness and distinctness than heretofore. . . .

But, finally, what shall I say of the mind itself, that is, of myself? for as yet I do not admit that I am anything but mind. What, then! I who seem to possess so distinct an apprehension of the piece of wax, do I not know myself, both with greater truth and certitude, and also much more distinctly and clearly? For if I judge that the wax exists because I see it, it assuredly follows, much more evidently, that I myself am or exist, for the same reason: for it is possible that what I see may not in truth be wax, and that I do not even possess eyes with which to see anything; but it cannot be that when I see, or, which comes to the same thing, when I think I see, I myself who think am nothing. So likewise, if I judge that the wax exists because I touch it, it will still also follow that I am; and if I determine that my imagination, or any other cause, whatever it be, persuades me of the existence of the wax, I will still draw the same conclusion. And what is here remarked of the piece of wax, is applicable to all the other things that are external to me. And further, if the [notion or] perception of wax appeared to me more precise and distinct, after . . . not only sight and touch, but many other causes besides, rendered it manifest to my apprehension, with how much greater distinctness must I now know myself, since all the reasons that contribute to the knowledge of the nature of wax, or of any body whatever, manifest still better the nature of my mind? And there are besides so many other things in the mind itself that contribute to the illustration of its nature, that those dependent on the body, to which I have here referred, scarcely merit to be taken into account.

But, in conclusion, I find I have insensibly reverted to the point I desired; for, since it is now manifest to me that bodies themselves are not properly perceived by the senses nor by the faculty of imagination, but by the intellect alone; and since they are not perceived because they are seen and touched, but only because they are understood [or rightly comprehended by thought], I readily discover that there is nothing more easily or clearly apprehended than my own mind. But because it is difficult to rid one's self so promptly of an opinion to which one has been long accustomed, it will be desirable to tarry for some time at this stage, that, by long continued meditation, I may more deeply impress upon my memory this new knowledge.

GILBERT RYLE / Descartes' Myth *

Gilbert Ryle (1900–   ) is a leading member of the Oxford University group of philosophers who emphasize the analysis of ordinary language as a clue to the solution of philosophical puzzles.

(1) THE OFFICIAL DOCTRINE

THERE IS A DOCTRINE about the nature and place of minds which is so prevalent among theorists and even among laymen that it deserves to be described as the official theory. Most philosophers, psychologists and religious teachers subscribe, with minor reservations, to its main articles and, although they admit certain theoretical difficulties in it, they tend to assume that these can be overcome without serious modifications being made to the architecture of the theory. It will be argued here that the central principles of the doctrine are unsound and conflict with the whole body of what we know about minds when we are not speculating about them.

The official doctrine, which hails chiefly from Descartes, is something like this. With the doubtful exceptions of idiots and infants in arms every human being has both a body and a mind. Some would prefer to say that every human being is both a body and a mind. His body and his mind are ordinarily harnessed together, but after the death of the body his mind may continue to exist and function.

Human bodies are in space and are subject to the mechanical laws which govern all other bodies in space. Bodily processes and states can be inspected by external observers. So a man's bodily life is as much a public affair as are the lives of animals and reptiles and even as the careers of trees, crystals and planets.

---

* Gilbert Ryle, from "Descartes' Myth," in *The Concept of Mind* (London: Hutchinson, 1949), pp. 11–18, 22–23. Used by permission of the publisher.

But minds are not in space, nor are their operations subject to mechanical laws. The workings of one mind are not witnessable by other observers; its career is private. Only I can take direct cognisance of the states and processes of my own mind. A person therefore lives through two collateral histories, one consisting of what happens in and to his body, the other consisting of what happens in and to his mind. The first is public, the second private. The events in the first history are events in the physical world, those in the second are events in the mental world.

It has been disputed whether a person does or can directly monitor all or only some of the episodes of his own private history; but, according to the official doctrine, of at least some of these episodes he has direct and unchallengeable cognisance. In consciousness, self-consciousness and introspection he is directly and authentically apprised of the present states and operations of his mind. He may have great or small uncertainties about concurrent and adjacent episodes in the physical world, but he can have none about at least part of what is momentarily occupying his mind.

It is customary to express this bifurcation of his two lives and of his two worlds by saying that the things and events which belong to the physical world, including his own body, are external, while the workings of his own mind are internal. This antithesis of outer and inner is of course meant to be construed as a metaphor, since minds, not being in space, could not be described as being spatially inside anything else, or as having things going on spatially inside themselves. But relapses from this good intention are common and theorists are found speculating how stimuli, the physical sources of which are yards or miles outside a person's skin, can generate mental responses inside his skull, or how decisions framed inside his cranium can set going movements of his extremities.

Even when "inner" and "outer" are construed as metaphors, the problem how a person's mind and body influence one another is notoriously charged with theoretical difficulties. What the mind wills, the legs, arms and the tongue execute; what affects the ear and the eye has something to do with what the mind perceives; grimaces and smiles betray the mind's moods and bodily castigations lead, it is hoped, to moral improvement. But the actual transactions between the episodes of the private history and those of the public history remain mysterious, since by definition they can belong to neither series. They could not be reported among the happenings described in a person's autobiography of his inner life, but nor could they be reported among those described in some one else's biography of that person's overt career. They can be inspected neither by introspection nor by laboratory experiment. They are theoretical shuttlecocks which are forever being bandied from the physiologist back to the psychologist and from the psychologist back to the physiologist.

Underlying this partly metaphorical representation of the bifurcation of a person's two lives there is a seemingly more profound and philosophical assumption. It is assumed that there are two different kinds of existence or status. What exists or happens may have the status of physical existence, or it may have the status of mental existence. Somewhat as the faces of coins are either heads or tails, or somewhat as living creatures are either male or female, so, it is supposed, some existing is physical existing, other existing is mental existing. It is a necessary feature of what has physical existence that it is in space and time; it is a necessary feature of what has mental existence that it is in time but not in space. What has physical existence is composed of matter, or else is a function of matter; what has mental existence consists of consciousness, or else is a function of consciousness.

There is thus a polar opposition between mind and matter, an opposition which is often brought out as follows. Material objects are situated in a common field, known as "space," and what happens to one body in one part of space is mechanically connected with what happens to other bodies in other parts of space. But mental happenings occur in insulated fields, known as "minds," and there is, apart maybe from telepathy, no direct causal connection between what happens in one mind and what happens in another. Only through the medium of the public physical world can the mind of one person make a difference to the mind of another. The mind is its own place and in his inner life each of us lives the life of a ghostly Robinson Crusoe. People can see, hear and jolt one another's bodies, but they are irremediably blind and deaf to the workings of one another's minds and inoperative upon them.

What sort of knowledge can be secured of the workings of a mind? On the one side, according to the official theory, a person has direct knowledge of the best imaginable kind of the workings of his own mind. Mental states and processes are (or are normally) conscious states and processes, and the consciousness which irradiates them can engender no illusions and leaves the door open for no doubts. A person's present thinkings, feelings and willings, his perceivings, rememberings and imaginings are intrinsically "phosphorescent"; their existence and their nature are inevitably betrayed to their owner. The inner life is a stream of consciousness of such a sort that it would be absurd to suggest that the mind whose life is that stream might be unaware of what is passing down it.

True, the evidence adduced recently by Freud seems to show that there exist channels tributary to this stream, which run hidden from their owner. People are actuated by impulses the existence of which they vigorously disavow; some of their thoughts differ from the thoughts which they acknowledge; and some of the actions which they think they will to perform they do not really will. They are thoroughly gulled by some of their own hypocrisies and they successfully ignore facts about their mental lives which on the official theory ought to be patent to them. Holders of the official theory tend, however, to maintain that anyhow in normal circumstances a person must be directly and authentically seized of the present state and workings of his own mind.

Besides being currently supplied with these alleged immediate data of consciousness, a person is also generally supposed to be able to exercise from time to time a special kind of perception, namely inner perception, or introspection. He can take a (non-optical) "look" at what is passing in his mind. Not only can he view and scrutinize a flower through his sense of sight and listen to and discriminate the notes of a bell through his sense of hearing; he can also reflectively or introspectively watch, without any bodily organ of sense, the current episodes of his inner life. This self-observation is also commonly supposed to be immune from illusion, confusion or doubt. A mind's reports of its own affairs have a certainty superior to the best that is possessed by its reports of matters in the physical world. Sense-perceptions can, but consciousness and introspection cannot, be mistaken or confused.

On the other side, one person has no direct access of any sort to the events of the inner life of another. He cannot do better than make problematic inferences from the observed behaviour of the other person's body to the states of mind which, by analogy from his own conduct, he supposes to be signalised by that behaviour. Direct access to the workings of a mind is the privilege of that mind itself; in default of such privileged access, the workings of one mind are inevitably occult to everyone else. For the supposed arguments from bodily movements similar to their own to mental workings similar to their own would lack any possibility of observational corroboration. Not unnaturally, therefore, an adherent of the official theory finds it difficult to resist this consequence of his premises, that he has no good reason to believe that there do exist minds other than his own. Even if he prefers to believe that to other human bodies there are harnessed minds not unlike his own, he cannot claim to be able to discover their individual characteristics, or the particular things that they undergo and do. Absolute solitude is on this showing the ineluctable destiny of the soul. Only our bodies can meet.

As a necessary corollary of this general scheme there is implicitly prescribed a special way of construing our ordinary concepts of mental powers and operations. The verbs, nouns and adjectives, with which in ordinary life we describe the wits, characters and higher-grade performances of the people with whom we have to do, are required to be construed as signifying special episodes in their secret histories, or else as signifying tendencies for such episodes to occur. When someone is described as knowing, believing or guessing something, as hoping, dreading, intending or shirking something, as designing this or being amused at that, these verbs are supposed to denote the occurrence of specific modifications in his (to us) occult stream of consciousness. Only his own privileged access to this stream in direct awareness and introspection could provide authentic testimony that these mental-conduct verbs were correctly or incorrectly applied. The onlooker, be he teacher, critic, biographer or friend, can never assure himself that his comments have any vestige of truth. Yet it was just because we do in fact all know how to make such comments, make them with general correctness and correct them when they turn out to be confused or mistaken, that philosophers found it necessary to construct their theories of the nature and place of minds. Finding mental-conduct concepts being regularly and effectively used, they properly sought to fix their logical geography. But the logical geography officially recommended would entail that there could be no regular or effective use of these mental-conduct concepts in our descriptions of, and prescriptions for, other people's minds.

(2) THE ABSURDITY OF THE OFFICIAL DOCTRINE

Such in outline is the official theory. I shall often speak of it, with deliberate abusiveness, as "the dogma of the Ghost in the Machine." I hope to prove that it is entirely false, and false not in detail but in principle. It is not merely an assemblage of particular mistakes. It is one big mistake and a mistake of a special kind. It is, namely, a category-mistake. It represents the facts of mental life as if they belonged to one logical type or category (or range of types or categories), when they actually belong to another. The dogma is therefore a philosopher's myth. In attempting to explode the myth I shall probably be taken to be denying well-known facts about the mental life of human beings, and my plea that I aim at concepts will probably be disallowed as mere subterfuge.

I must first indicate what is meant by the phrase "Category-mistake." This I do in a series of illustrations.

A foreigner visiting Oxford or Cambridge for the first time is shown a number of colleges, libraries, playing fields, museums, scientific departments and administrative offices. He then asks "But where is the University? I have seen where the members of the Colleges live, where the Registrar works, where the scientists experiment and the rest. But I have not yet seen the University in which reside and work the members of your University." It has then to be explained to him that the University is not another collateral institution, some ulterior counterpart to the colleges, laboratories and offices which he has seen. The University is just the way in which all that he has already seen is organized. When they are seen and when their co-ordination is understood, the University has been seen. His mistake lay in his innocent assumption that it was correct to speak of Christ Church, the Bodleian Library, the Ashmolean Museum *and* the University, to speak, that is, as if "the University" stood for an extra member of the class of which these other units are members. He was mistakenly allocating the University to the same category as that to which the other institutions belong.

The same mistake would be made by a child witnessing the march-past of a division, who, having had pointed out to him such and such battalions, batteries, squadrons, etc., asked when the division was going to appear. He would be supposing that a division was a counterpart to the units already seen, partly similar to them and partly unlike them. He would be shown his mistake by being told that in watching the battalions, batteries and squadrons marching past he had been watching the division marching past. The march-past was not a parade of battalions, batteries, squadrons *and* a division; it was a parade of the battalions, batteries and squadrons *of* a division.

One more illustration. A foreigner watching his first game of cricket learns what are the functions of the bowlers, the batsmen, the fielders, the umpires and the scorers. He then says "But there is no one left on the field to contribute the famous element of team-spirit. I see who does the bowling, the batting and the wicket-keeping; but I do not see whose role it is to exercise *esprit de corps*." Once more, it would have to be explained that he was looking for the wrong type of thing. Team-spirit is not another cricketing-operation supplementary to all of the other special tasks. It is, roughly, the keenness with which each of the special tasks is performed, and performing a task keenly is not performing two tasks. Certainly exhibiting team-spirit is not the same thing as bowling or catching, but nor is it a third thing such that we can say that the bowler first bowls *and* then exhibits team-spirit or that a fielder is at a given moment *either* catching *or* displaying *esprit de corps*.

These illustrations of category-mistakes have a common feature which must be noticed. The mistakes were made by people who did not know how to wield the concepts *University*, *division* and *team-spirit*. Their puzzles arose from inability to use certain items in the English vocabulary. . . .

My destructive purpose is to show that a family of radical category-mistakes is the source of the double-life theory. The representation of a person as a ghost mysteriously ensconced in a machine derives from this argument. Because, as is true, a person's thinking, feeling and purposive doing cannot be described solely in the idioms of physics, chemistry and physiology, therefore they must be described in counterpart idioms. As the human body is a complex organised unit, so the human mind must be another complex organised unit, though one made of a different sort of stuff and with a different sort of structure. Or, again, as the human body, like any other parcel of matter, is a field of causes and effects, so the mind must be another field of causes and effects, though not (Heaven be praised) mechanical causes and effects. . . .

When two terms belong to the same category, it is proper to construct conjunctive propositions embodying them. Thus a purchaser may say that he bought a left-hand glove and a right-hand glove, but not that he bought a left-hand glove, a right-hand glove and a pair of gloves. "She came home in a flood of tears and a sedan-chair" is a well-known joke based on the absurdity of conjoining terms of different types. It would have been equally ridiculous to construct the disjunction "She came home either in a flood of tears or else in a sedan-chair." Now the dogma of the Ghost in the Machine does just this. It maintains that there exist both bodies and minds; that there occur physical processes and mental processes; that there are mechanical causes of corporeal movements and mental causes of corporeal movements. I shall argue that these and other analogous conjunctions are absurd; but, it must be noticed, the argument will not show that either of the illegitimately conjoined propositions is absurd in itself. I am not, for example, denying that there occur mental processes. Doing long division is a mental process and so is making a joke. But I am saying that the phrase "there occur mental processes" does not mean the same sort of thing as "there occur physical processes," and, therefore, that it makes no sense to conjoin or disjoin the two.

If my argument is successful, there will follow some interesting consequences. First, the hallowed contrast between Mind and Matter will be dissipated, but dissipated not by either of the equally hallowed absorptions of Mind by Matter or of Matter by Mind, but in quite a different way. For the seeming contrast of the two will be shown to be as illegitimate as would be the contrast of "she came home in a flood of tears" and "she came home in a sedan-chair." The belief that there is a polar opposition between Mind and Matter is the belief that they are terms of the same logical type.

It will also follow that both Idealism and Materialism are answers to an improper question. The "reduction" of the material world to mental states and processes, as well as the "reduction" of mental states and processes to physical states and processes, presuppose the legitimacy of the disjunction "either there exist minds or there exist bodies (but not both)." It would be like saying, "Either she bought a left-hand and a right-hand glove or she bought a pair of gloves (but not both)."

It is perfectly proper to say, in one logical tone of voice, that there exist minds and to say, in another logical tone of voice, that there exist bodies. But these expressions do not indicate two different species of existence, for "existence" is not a generic word like "coloured" or "sexed." They indicate two different senses of "exist," somewhat as "rising" has different senses in "the tide is rising," "hopes are rising," and "the average age of death is rising." A man would be thought to be making a poor joke who said that three things are now rising, namely the tide, hopes and the average age of death. It would be just as good or bad a joke to say that there exist prime numbers and Wednesdays and public opinions and navies; or that there exist both minds and bodies. . . .

C. J. DUCASSE / In Defense of Dualism *

C. J. Ducasse (1881–1969) taught philosophy at Brown University for over thirty-five years. His writings include *Philosophy as a Science*; *Philosophy of Art*; *Nature, Mind, and Death* (The Carus Lectures); and A *Philosophical Scrutiny of Religion*.

NEITHER in the section of this symposium on "The Mind-Body Problem" nor in that on "The Brain and the Machine" is much, if any, attention given to the dualist-interactionist conception of the relation between mind and brain. A summary presentation of the case for it and against its rivals may therefore be appropriate here.

The first point to which attention must be called is that, beyond question, there are things—events, substances, processes, relations, etc.— denominated "material," or "physical," that there are also certain others denominated instead "mental," or "psychical," and that no thing is denominated both "physical" and "psychical," or both "material" and "mental." Rocks, trees, water, air, animal and human bodies and the processes occurring among them or within them, are examples of the things called "material" or "physical"; emotions, desires, moods, sensations, cravings, images, thoughts, etc., are examples of the things called "mental" or "psychical."

To question whether the first *really* are physical or the second *really* are psychical would be absurd, as it would be absurd to question whether a certain boy whom his parents named "George" really was George. For just as "George" is a name, so "physical" or "material," and "psychical" or "mental," are names; and a name is essentially a *pointer*, which does point

* C. J. Ducasse, from "In Defense of Dualism," in *Dimensions of Mind*, Sidney Hook (ed.) (New York: New York U. Press, 1960), pp. 85–90 with omissions. Used by permission of the publisher.

at—designates, indicates, denotes, directs attention to—whatever it actually is employed to point at. . . .

In the case of the things called "physical," the patent characteristic common to and peculiar to them, which determined their being all denoted by one and the same name, was simply that all of them were, or were capable of being, *perceptually public*—the same tree, the same thunderclap, the same wind, the same dog, the same man, etc., can be perceived by every member of a human public suitably located in space and in time. To be material or physical, then, *basically* means to be, or to be capable of being, perceptually public. And the unperceivable, recondite things physicists discover—electrons, protons, etc., and the processes that occur among them—only have title at all to be also called physical *derivatively*—in virtue, namely, (and *only* in virtue) of their being *constituents* of the things that are perceptually public.

On the other hand, the patent characteristic which functioned as a basis for the application of one identical name to all the things called "psychical" or "mental" was their *inherently private* character, attention to them, as distinguished from attention to what they may signify, being accordingly termed "introspection," not "perception." . . .

Psychical events *themselves* are never *public* and never can be made so. That, for example, I *now remember* having dreamed of a Siamese cat last night is something which I can *publish* by means of perceptually public words, spoken or written. Other persons are then *informed of it*. But to be informed *that I remember* having so dreamed is one thing, and to *remember* having so dreamed is altogether another thing, and one *inherently private*. The dreaming itself was not, and the remembering itself is not, a *public* event at all and cannot possibly be made so in the way in which my *statement* that I remember that I so dreamed is or can be made public. . . .

. . . [C]ontrary to what is sometimes alleged, causation of a physical by a psychical event, or of a psychical event by stimulation of a physical sense organ, is not in the least paradoxical. The causality relation—whether defined in terms of regularity of succession, or (preferably) in terms of single antecedent difference—does not presuppose at all that its cause-term and its effect-term both belong to the same ontological category, but only that both of them be *events*.

Moreover, the objection that we cannot understand how a psychical event could cause a physical one (or vice versa) has no basis other than blindness to the fact that the "how" of causation is capable at all of being either mysterious or understood only in cases of *remote* causation, never in cases of *proximate* causation. For the question as to the "how" of causation of a given event by a given other event never has any other sense than *through what intermediary causal steps* does the one cause the other.

Hence, to ask it in a case of proximate causation is to be guilty of what Professor Ryle has called a "category mistake"—a mistake, incidentally, of which he is himself guilty when he alleges that the "how" of psychophysical causation would be mysterious. . . .

Interactionism, then, as presented in what precedes, though not as presented by Descartes, is a perfectly tenable conception of the relation between some mental events and some brain events, allowing as it does also that some brain events have bodily causes, and that some mental events directly cause some other mental events. It conceives minds as consisting, like material substances, of sets of systematically interrelated dispositions, i.e., of capacities, abilities, powers, and susceptibilities, each of which can be analyzed as a causal connection, more or less enduring, between any event of some particular kind—C, occurring in a state of affairs of some particular kind—S, and a sequent event in it, of some particular kind—E. The series of *exercises* of the different dispositions (which together define the *nature* of a given mind) constitutes the *history* of that particular mind, i.e., its *existence* as distinguished from only its *description*.

For Further Study

Blanshard, Brand. "The Nature of Mind," *Journal of Philosophy*, 38 (1941): 207–216.

Feigl, Herbert. "Mind-Body, *Not* a Pseudoproblem," in *Dimensions of Mind*, ed. Sidney Hook. New York: New York U. Press, 1960. (Also Collier Book BS38, 1961.)

Flew, Antony G. N., ed. *Body, Mind, and Death*. New York: Macmillan, 1964 (Macmillan Paperback 166.)

Heinemann, F. H. "Man Without Mind?" *The Hibbert Journal*, 49 (October, 1950): 54–61.

Landesman, Charles. "The New Dualism in the Philosophy of Mind," *Review of Metaphysics*, 19 (December, 1965): 329–345.

Mace, C. A. "The 'Body-Mind Problem' in Philosophy, Psychology and Medicine," *Philosophy*, 41 (April, 1966): 153–164.

Price, H. H. "Some Objections to Behaviorism," in *Dimensions of Mind*, ed. Sidney Hook. New York: New York U. Press, 1960. (Also Collier Book BS38, 1961.)

Rorty, Richard. "Mind-Body Identity, Privacy, and Categories," *Review of Metaphysics*, 19 (September, 1965): 24–54.

White, Alan R. *The Philosophy of Mind*. New York: Random House, 1967.

11 How Free Is Man?

BRAND BLANSHARD / The Case for Determinism *

Brand Blanshard (1892–   ) has taught philosophy at a number of schools and was professor of philosophy at Yale University for nearly two decades. He has written many books and articles, and he delivered the Gifford Lectures at the University of St. Andrews, Scotland, in 1952–1953.

I AM a determinist. None of the arguments offered on the other side seem of much weight except one form of the moral argument, and that itself is far from decisive. Perhaps the most useful thing I can do in this paper is explain why the commoner arguments for indeterminism do not, to my mind, carry conviction. In the course of this explanation the brand of determinism to which I am inclined should become gradually apparent.

But first a definition or two. Determinism is easier to define than indeterminism, and at first glance there seems to be no difficulty in saying what one means by it. It is the view that all events are caused. But unless one also says what one means by "event" and "caused," there is likely to be trouble later. Do I include among events not only changes but the lack of change, not only the fall of the water over the cataract's edge, but the persistence of ice in the frozen river? The answer is "Yes." By an event I mean any change or persistence of state or position. And what is meant by saying

* Brand Blanshard, from "The Case for Determinism," in Determinism and Freedom, Sidney Hook (ed.) (New York: New York U. Press, 1958), pp. 3–7, 10–15. Used by permission of the publisher.

that an event is caused? The natural answer is that the event is so connected with some preceding event that unless the latter had occurred the former would not have occurred. Indeterminism means the denial of this. And the denial of this is the statement that there is at least one event to which no preceding event is necessary. But that gets us into trouble at once, for it is doubtful if any indeterminist would want to make such an assertion. What he wants to say is that his decision to tell the truth is undetermined, not that there is no preceding event necessary to it. He would not contend, for example, that he could tell the truth if he had never been born. No, the causal statement to which the indeterminist takes exception is a different one. He is not saying that there is any event to which some namable antecedents are not necessary; he is saying that there are some events whose antecedents do not make them necessary. He is not denying that all consequents have necessary antecedents; he is denying that all antecedents have necessary consequents. He is saying that the state of things just before he decided to tell the truth might have been exactly what it was and yet he might have decided to tell a lie.

By determinism, then, I mean the view that every event A is so connected with a later event B that, given A, B must occur. By indeterminism I mean the view that there is some event B that is not so connected with any previous event A that, given A, it must occur. Now, what is meant here by "must"? We cannot in the end evade that question, but I hope you will not take it as an evasion if at this point I am content to let you fill in the blank in any way you wish. Make it a logical "must," if you care to, or a physical or metaphysical "must," or even the watered-down "must" that means "A is always in fact followed by B." We can discuss the issue usefully though we leave ourselves some latitude on this point.

With these definitions in mind, let us ask what are the most important grounds for indeterminism. This is not the same as asking what commonly moves people to be indeterminists; the answer to that seems to me all too easy. Everyone vaguely knows that to be undetermined is to be free, and everyone wants to be free. My question is rather, When reflective people accept the indeterminist view nowadays, what considerations seem most cogent to them? It seems to me that there are three: first, the stubborn feeling of freedom, which seems to resist all dialectical solvents; second, the conviction that natural science itself has now gone over to the indeterminist side; and, third, that determinism would make nonsense of moral responsibility. The third of these seems to me the most important, but I must try to explain why none of them seem to me conclusive.

One of the clearest heads that ever devoted itself to this old issue was Henry Sidgwick. Sidgwick noted that, if at any given moment we stop to think about it, we always feel as if more than one course were open to us, that we could speak or be silent, lift our hand or not lift it. If the determinist is right, this must be an illusion, of course, for whatever we might have done, there must have been a cause, given which we had to do what we did. Now, a mere intuitive assurance about ourselves may be a very weak ground for belief; Freud has shown us that we may be profoundly deceived about how we really feel or why we act as we do. But the curious point is that, though a man who hates his father without knowing it can usually be shown that he does and can often be cured of his feeling, no amount of dialectic seems to shake our feeling of being free to perform either of two proposed acts. By this feeling of being free I do not mean merely the freedom to do what we choose. No one on either side questions that we have that sort of freedom, but it is obviously not the sort of freedom that the indeterminist wants, since it is consistent with determinism of the most rigid sort. The real issue, so far as the will is concerned, is not whether we can do what we choose to do, but whether we can choose our own choice, whether the choice itself issues in accordance with law from some antecedent. And the feeling of freedom that is relevant as evidence is the feeling of an open future as regards the choice itself. After the noise of argument has died down, a sort of intuition stubbornly remains that we can not only lift our hand if we choose, but that the choice itself is open to us. Is this not an impressive fact?

No, I do not think it is. The first reason is that when we are making a choice our faces are always turned toward the future, toward the consequences that one act or the other will bring us, never toward the past with its possible sources of constraint. Hence these sources are not noticed. Hence we remain unaware that we are under constraint at all. Hence we feel free from such constraint. The case is almost as simple as that. When you consider buying a new typewriter your thought is fixed on the pleasure and advantage you would gain from it, or the drain it would make on your budget. You are not delving into the causes that led to your taking pleasure in the prospect of owning a typewriter or to your having a complex about expenditure. You are too much preoccupied with the ends to which the choice would be a means to give any attention to the causes of which your choice may be an effect. But that is no reason for thinking that if you did preoccupy yourself with these causes you would not find them at work. You may remember that Sir Francis Galton was so much impressed with this possibility that for some time he kept account in a notebook of the occasions on which he made important choices with a full measure of this feeling of freedom; then shortly after each choice he turned his eye backward in search of constraints that might have been acting on him stealthily. He found it so easy to bring such constraining factors to light that he surrendered to the determinist view.

But this, you may say, is not enough. Our preoccupation with the future may show why we are not aware of the constraints acting on us, and hence why we do not feel bound by them; it does not explain why our sense of freedom persists after the constraints are disclosed to us. By disclosing the causes of some fear, for example, psychoanalytic therapy can remove the fear, and when these causes are brought to light, the fear commonly does go. How is it, then, that when the causes of our volition are brought to light volition continues to feel as free as before? Does this not show that it is really independent of those causes?

No again. The two cases are not parallel. The man with the panic fear of dogs is investing all dogs with the qualities remembered, though in disguised form—of the monster that frightened him as a child. When this monster and his relation to it are brought to light, so that they can be dissociated from the Fidos and Towsers around him, the fear goes, because its appropriate object has gone. It is quite different with our feeling of freedom. We feel free, it was suggested, because we are not aware of the forces acting on us. Now, in spite of the determinist's conviction that when a choice is made there are always causal influences at work, he does not pretend to reveal the influences at work in our present choice. The chooser's face is always turned forward; his present choice is always unique; and no matter how much he knows about the will and the laws, his present choice always emerges out of deep shadow. The determinist who buys a typewriter is as little interested at the moment in the strings that may be pulling at him from his physiological or subconscious cellars as his indeterminist colleague, and hence feels just as free. Thus, whereas the new knowledge gained through psychoanalysis does remove the grounds of fear, the knowledge gained by the determinist is not at all of the sort that would remove the grounds for the feeling of freedom. To make the persistence of this feeling in the determinist an argument against his case is therefore a confusion.

The second reason, I suggested, why so many thoughtful persons remain indeterminists is that they are convinced that science has gone indeterminist. Well, has it? If you follow Heisenberg, Eddington, and Born, it has. If you follow Russell, Planck, and Einstein, it has not. When such experts disagree it is no doubt folly for the layman to rush in. But since I am discussing the main reasons why people stick to indeterminism, and have admitted that the new physics is one of them, I cannot afford to be quite prudent. Let me say, then, with much hesitation that, as far as I can follow the argument, it provides no good evidence for indeterminism even in the physical world, and that, if it did, it would provide no good evidence for indeterminism in the realm of will. . . .

We come now to the third of the reasons commonly advanced in support of indeterminism. This is that determinism makes a mess of morality. The charge has taken many forms. We are told that determinism makes praise and blame meaningless, punishment brutal, remorse pointless, amendment hopeless, duty a deceit. All these allegations have been effectively answered except the one about duty, where I admit I am not quite satisfied. But none of them are in the form in which determinism most troubles the plain man. What most affronts him, I think, is the suggestion that he is only a machine, a big foolish clock that seems to itself to be acting freely but whose movements are controlled completely by the wheels and weights inside, a Punch-and-Judy show whose appearance of doing things because they are right or reasonable is a sham because everything is mechanically regulated by wires from below. He has no objections to determinism as applied by physicists to atoms, by himself to machines, or by his doctor to his body. He has an emphatic objection to determinism as applied by anyone to his reflection and his will, for this seems to make him a gigantic mechanical toy, or worse, a sort of Frankenstein monster.

In this objection I think we must agree with the plain man. If anyone were to show me that determinism involved either materialism or mechanism, I would renounce it at once, for that would be equivalent, in my opinion, to reducing it to absurdity. The "physicalism" once proposed by Neurath and Carnap as a basis for the scientific study of behavior I could not accept for a moment, because it is so dogmatically anti-empirical. To use empirical methods means, for me, not to approach nature with a preconceived notion as to what facts must be like, but to be ready to consider all kinds of alleged facts on their merits. Among these the introspectively observable fact of reflective choice, and the inference to its existence in others, are particularly plain, however different from anything that occurs in the realm of the material or the publicly observable or the mechanically controlled.

Now, what can be meant by saying that such choice, though not determined mechanically, is still determined? Are you suggesting, it will be asked, that in the realm of reflection and choice there operates a different kind of causality from any we know in the realm of bodies? My answer is: Yes, just that. To put it more particularly, I am suggesting (1) that even within the psychical realm there are different causal levels, (2) that a causality of higher level may supervene on one of lower level, and (3) that when causality of the highest level is at work, we have precisely what the indeterminists, without knowing it, want.

1. First, then, as to causal levels. I am assuming that even the indeterminist would admit that most mental events are causally governed. No one would want to deny that his stepping on a tack had something to do with his feeling pain, or that his touching a flame had something to do with his getting burned, or that his later thought of the flame had something to do with his experience of its hotness. A law of association is a causal law of mental events. In one respect it is like a law of physical events: in neither case have we any light as to *why* the consequent follows on the antecedent.

Hume was right about the billiard balls. He was right about the flame and the heat; we do not see why something bright and yellow should also be hot. He was right about association; we do not understand how one idea calls up another; we only know that it does. Causality in all such cases means to us little if anything more than a routine of regular sequence.

Is all mental causation like that? Surely not. Consider a musician composing a piece or a logician making a deduction. Let us make our musician a philosopher also, who after adding a bar pauses to ask himself, "Why did I add just that?" Can we believe he would answer, "Because whenever in the past I have had the preceding bars in mind, they have always been followed by this bar"? What makes this suggestion so inept is partly that he may never have thought of the preceding bars before, partly that, if he had, the repetition of an old sequence would be precisely what he would avoid. No, his answer, I think, would be something like this: "I wrote what I did because it seemed the right thing to do. I developed my theme in the manner demanded to carry it through in an aesthetically satisfactory way." In other words, the constraint that was really at work in him was not that of association; it was something that worked distinctly against association; it was the constraint of an aesthetic ideal. And, if so, there is a causality of a different level. It is idle to say that the musician is wholly in the dark about it. He can see not only *that* B succeeded A; as he looks back, he can see in large measure *why* it did.

It is the same with logical inference, only more clearly so. The thinker starts, let us say, with the idea of a regular solid whose faces are squares, and proceeds to develop in thought the further characteristics that such a solid must possess. He constructs it in imagination and then sees that it must have six faces, eight vertices, and twelve edges. Is this association merely? It may be. It is, for example, if he merely does in imagination what a child does when it counts the edges on a lump of sugar. This is not inference and does not feel like it. When a person, starting with the thought of a solid with square faces, deduces that it must have eight vertices, and then asks why he should have thought of that, the natural answer is, Because the first property entails the second. Of course this is not the only condition, but it seems to me contrary to introspectively plain fact to say that it had nothing to do with the movement of thought. It is easy to put this in such a way as to invite attack. If we say that the condition of our thinking of B is the observed necessity between A and B, we are assuming that B is already thought of as a means of explaining how it comes to be thought of. But that is not what I am saying. I am saying that in thinking at its best thought comes under the constraint of necessities in its object, so that the objective fact that A necessitates B partially determines our passing in thought from A to B. Even when the explanation is put in this form, the objection has been raised that necessity is a timeless link between concepts, while causality is a temporal bond between events, and that the two must be kept sharply apart. To which the answer is: Distinct, yes; but always apart, no. A timeless relation may serve perfectly well as the condition of a temporal passage. I hold that in the course of our thinking we can easily verify this fact, and, because I do, I am not put off by pronouncements about what we should and should not be able to see.

2. My second point about the causal levels is that our mental processes seldom move on one level alone. The higher is always supervening on the lower and taking over partial control. Though brokenly and imperfectly rational, rational creatures we still are. It must be admitted that most of our so-called thinking moves by association, and is hardly thinking at all. But even in the dullest of us "bright shoots of everlastingness," strands of necessity, aesthetic or logical, from time to time appear. "The quarto and folio editions of mankind" can follow the argument with fewer lapses than most of us; in the texts of the greatest of all dramas, we are told, there was seldom a blot or erasure; but Ben Jonson added, and no doubt rightly, that there ought to have been a thousand. The effort of both thought and art is to escape the arbitrary, the merely personal, everything that, causal and capricious, is irrelevant, and to keep to lines appointed by the whole that one is constructing. I do not suggest that logical and aesthetic necessity are the same. I do say that they are both to be distinguished from association or habit as representing a different level of control. That control is never complete; all creation in thought or art is successful in degree only. It is successful in the degree to which it ceases to be an expression of merely personal impulses and becomes the instrument of a necessity lying in its own subject matter.

3. This brings us to our last point. Since moral choice, like thought and art, moves on different causal levels, it achieves freedom, just as they do, only when it is determined by its own appropriate necessity. Most of our so-called choices are so clearly brought about by association, impulse, and feeling that the judicious indeterminist will raise no issue about them. When we decide to get a drink of water, to take another nibble of chocolate, to go to bed at the usual hour, the forces at work are too plain to be denied. It is not acts like these on which the indeterminist takes his stand. It is rather on those where, with habit, impulse, and association prompting us powerfully to do X, we see that we ought to do Y and therefore do it. To suppose that in such cases we are still the puppets of habit and impulse seems to the indeterminist palpably false.

So it does to us. Surely about this the indeterminist is right. Action impelled by the sense of duty, as Kant perceived, is action on a different level from anything mechanical or associative. But Kant was mistaken in supposing that when we were determined by reason we were not determined at all. This supposition seems to me wholly unwarranted. The determination is still there, but, since it is a determination by the moral necessities of the case, it is just what the moral man wants and thus is the equivalent of freedom. For the moral man, like the logician and the artist, is really seeking self-surrender. Through him as through the others an impersonal ideal is working, and to the extent that this ideal takes possession of him and molds him according to its pattern, he feels free and is free.

The logician is most fully himself when the wind gets into his sails and carries him effortlessly along the line of his calculations. Many an artist and musician have left it on record that their best work was done when the whole they were creating took the brush or pen away from them and completed the work itself. It determined them, but they were free, because to be determined by this whole was at once the secret of their craft and the end of their desire. This is the condition of the moral man also. He has caught a vision, dimmer perhaps than that of the logician or the artist, but equally objective and compelling. It is a vision of the good. This good necessitates certain things, not as means to ends merely, for that is not usually a necessary link, but as integral parts of itself. It requires that he should put love above hate, that he should regard his neighbor's good as of like value with his own, that he should repair injuries, and express gratitude, and respect promises, and revere truth. Of course it does not guide him infallibly. On the values of a particular case he may easily be mistaken. But that no more shows that there are no values present to be estimated, and no ideal demanding a special mode of action, than the fact that we make a mistake in adding figures shows that there are no figures to be added, or no right way of adding them. In both instances what we want is control by the objective requirements of the case. The saint, like the thinker and the artist, has often said this in so many words. I feel most free, said St. Paul, precisely when I am most a slave.

We have now dealt, as best we can in a restricted space, with the three commonest objections to determinism. They all seem to admit of answers. To the objection that we always feel free, we answer that it is natural to feel so, even if we are determined, since our faces are set toward results and not toward causes, and the causes of present action always elude us. To the objection that science has gone indeterminist, we answer that that is only one interpretation of recent discoveries, and not the most plausible one, and that, even if it were true, it would not carry with it indeterminism for human choice. To the objection that determinism would reduce us to the level of mechanical puppets, we answer that though we are puppets in part we live, as Aristotle said, on various levels. And so far as causality in reflection, art, and moral choice involves control by immanent ideal, mechanism has passed over into that rational determinism that is the best kind of freedom.

C. A. CAMPBELL / The Defence of Free Will *

C. A. Campbell (1897–   ) was Professor of Logic and Rhetoric at Glasgow University, 1938–1961. Among his writings are *Scepticism and Construction*, and *On Selfhood and Godhead* (the Gifford Lectures 1953–1955).

IN CASTING ABOUT for a suitable topic upon which to address you to-day, I have naturally borne in mind that an inaugural lecture of this sort should be devoted to some theme of much more than merely esoteric import: to some theme, for preference, sufficiently central in character to have challenged the attention of all who possess a speculative interest in the nature of the universe and man's place within it. That is a principal reason why I have chosen to-day to speak on free will. Mighty issues turn, and turn directly, on the solution of the free will problem. It is in no way surprising that for centuries past it has exercised a fascination for thinkers both within and without the ranks of the professional philosophers that is probably not paralleled in the case of any of the other great problems of metaphysics. . . .

Let us begin by noting that the problem of free will gets its urgency for the ordinary educated man by reason of its close connection with the conception of moral responsibility. When we regard a man as morally responsible for an act, we regard him as a legitimate object of moral praise or blame in respect of it. But it seems plain that a man cannot be a legitimate object of moral praise or blame for an act unless in willing the act he is in some important sense a 'free' agent. Evidently free will in some sense, therefore, is a pre-condition of moral responsibility. Without doubt it is the realization that any threat to freedom is thus a threat to moral responsibility—with all that that implies—combined with the knowledge that there are a variety of considerations, philosophic, scientific, and theological, tending to place freedom in jeopardy, that gives to the problem of free will its perennial and universal appeal. And it is therefore in close connection with the question of the conditions of moral responsibility that any discus-

---

* C. A. Campbell, from "In Defence of Free Will," in *In Defence of Free Will, with Other Philosophical Essays* (London: George Allen and Unwin Ltd.; New York: Humanities Press, 1967), pp. 35–49 with omissions. Used by permission of the publisher.

sion of the problem must proceed, if it is not to be academic in the worst sense of the term.

We raise the question at once, therefore, what are the conditions, in respect of freedom, which must attach to an act in order to make it a morally responsible act? It seems to me that the fundamental conditions are two. . . .

The first condition is the universally recognised one that the act must be *self*-caused, *self*-determined. But it is important to accept this condition in its full rigour. The agent must be not merely *a* cause but the *sole* cause of that for which he is deemed morally responsible. If entities other than the self have also a causal influence upon an act, then that act is not one for which we can say without qualification that the *self* is morally responsible. If in respect of it we hold the self responsible at all, it can only be for some feature of the act—assuming the possibility of disengaging such a feature— of which the self *is* the sole cause. I do not see how this conclusion can be evaded. But it has awkward implications which have led not a few people to abandon the notion of individual moral responsibility altogether.

This first condition, however, is quite clearly not sufficient. It is possible to conceive an act of which the agent is the sole cause, but which is at the same time an act *necessitated* by the agent's nature. Some philosophers have contended, for example, that the act of Divine creation is an act which issues necessarily from the Divine nature. In the case of such an act, where the agent could not do otherwise than he did, we must all agree, I think, that it would be inept to say that he *ought* to have done otherwise and is thus morally blameworthy, or *ought not* to have done otherwise and is thus morally praiseworthy. It is perfectly true that we do sometimes hold a person morally responsible for an act, even when we believe that he, being what he now is, virtually could not do otherwise. But underlying that judgment is always the assumption that the person has *come* to be what he now is in virtue of past acts of will in which he *was* confronted by real alternatives, by genuinely open possibilities: and, strictly speaking, it is in respect of these *past* acts of his that we praise or blame the agent *now*. For ultimate analysis, the agent's power of alternative action would seem to be an inexpugnable condition of his liability to moral praise or blame, i.e. of his moral responsibility.

We may lay down, therefore, that an act is a 'free' act in the sense required for moral responsibility only if the agent (*a*) is the sole cause of the act; and (*b*) could exert his causality in alternative ways. And it may be pointed out in passing that the acceptance of condition (*b*) implies the recognition of the inadequacy for moral freedom of mere 'self-determination'. The doctrine called 'Self-determinism' is often contrasted by its advocates with mere Determinism on the one hand and Indeterminism on the other, and pronounced to be the one true gospel. I must insist, however, that if 'Self-determinism' rejects condition (*b*), it cannot claim to be a doctrine of free will in the sense required to vindicate moral responsibility. The doctrine which demands, and asserts, the fulfilment of both conditions is the doctrine we call 'Libertarianism'. And it would in my opinion minister greatly to clarity if it were more widely recognized that for any doctrine which is not a species of Libertarianism to pose as a doctrine of 'free will' is mere masquerade.

And now, the conditions of free will being defined in these general terms, we have to ask whether human beings are in fact capable of performing free acts; and if so, where precisely such acts are to be found. In order to prepare the way for an answer, it is desirable, I think, that we should get clear at once about the significance of a certain very familiar, but none the less formidable, criticism of free will which the Self-determinist as well as the Libertarian has to meet. This is the criticism which bases itself upon the facts of heredity on the one hand and of environment on the other. I may briefly summarize the criticism as follows.

Every historic self has an hereditary nature consisting of a group of inborn propensities, in range more or less common to the race, but specific to the individual in their respective strengths. With this equipment the self just *happens* to be born. Strictly speaking, it antedates the existence of the self proper, i.e. the existence of the self-conscious subject, and it is itself the effect of a series of causes leading back to indefinitely remote antiquity. It follows, therefore, that any of the self's choices that manifests the influence of his hereditary nature is not a choice of which *he*, the actual historic self, is the sole cause. The choice is determined, at least in part, by factors external to the self. The same thing holds good of 'environment'. Every self is born and bred in a particular physical and social environment, not of his own choosing, which plays upon him in innumerable ways, encouraging this propensity, discouraging that, and so on. Clearly any of the self's choices that manifests the influence of environmental factors is likewise a choice which is determined, at least in part, by factors external to the self. But if we thus grant, as seems inevitable, that heredity and environment are external influences, where shall we find a choice in the whole history of a self that is not subject to external influence? Surely we must admit that every particular act of choice bears the marks of the agent's hereditary nature and environmental nurture; in which case a free act, in the sense of an act determined solely by the self, must be dismissed as a mere chimaera. . . .

The externality of these influences is taken for granted in our reflective practical judgments upon persons. On those occasions when we are in real earnest about giving a critical and considered estimate of a man's moral calibre—as, e.g., in any serious biographical study—we impose upon ourselves as a matter of course the duty of enquiring with scrupulous care into his hereditary propensities and environmental circumstances, with a view to discovering how far his conduct is influenced by these factors. And having traced these influences, we certainly do not regard the result as having no bearing on the question of the man's moral responsibility for his conduct. On the contrary, the very purpose of the enquiry is to enable us, by due appreciation of the *external* influences that affect his conduct, to gain as accurate a view as possible of that which can justly be attributed to the man's own *self*-determination. The allowances that we all of us do in practice make for hereditary and environmental influences in passing judgment on our fellows would be meaningless if we did not suppose these influences to be in a real sense 'external' to the self. . . .

We know now that condition (*a*) is not fulfilled by any act in respect of which inheritance or environment exerts a causal influence. For that type of influence has been shown to be in a real sense external to the self. The free act of which we are in search has therefore got to be one into which influences of this kind do not enter at all.

Moreover, one encouraging portent has emerged in the course of our brief discussion. For we noticed that our reflective practical judgments on persons, while fully recognizing the externality of the influence of heredity and environment, do nevertheless presuppose throughout that there *is* *something* in conduct which is genuinely self-determined; something which the agent contributes solely on his own initiative, unaffected by external influences; something for which, accordingly, he may justly be held morally responsible. That conviction may, of course, be a false one. But the fact of its widespread existence can hardly be without significance for our problem.

Let us proceed, then, by following up this clue. Let us ask, why do human beings so obstinately persist in believing that there is an indissoluble core of purely *self*-originated activity which even heredity and environment are powerless to affect? There can be little doubt, I think, of the answer in general terms. They do so, at bottom, because they feel certain of the existence of such activity from their immediate practical experience of themselves. Nor can there be in the end much doubt, I think, in what function of the self that activity is to be located. There seems to me to be one, and only one, function of the self with respect to which the agent can even pretend to have an assurance of that absolute self-origination which is here at issue. But to render precise the nature of that function is obviously of quite paramount importance: and we can do so, I think, only by way of a somewhat thorough analysis—which I now propose to attempt—of the experiential situation in which it occurs, viz., the situation of 'moral temptation'.

It is characteristic of that situation that in it I am aware of an end A which I believe to be morally right, and also of an end B, incompatible with A, towards which, in virtue of that system of conative dispositions which constitutes my 'character' as so far formed, I entertain a strong desire. There may be, and perhaps must be, desiring elements in my nature which are directed to A also. But what gives to the situation its specific character as one of moral temptation is that the urge of our desiring nature towards the right end, A, is felt to be *relatively* weak. We are sure that if our desiring nature is permitted to issue directly in action, it is end B that we shall choose. That is what is meant by saying, as William James does, that end B is 'in the line of least resistance' relatively to our conative dispositions. The expression is, of course, a metaphorical one, but it serves to describe, graphically enough, a situation of which we all have frequent experience, viz., where we recognize a specific end as that towards which the 'set' of our desiring nature most strongly inclines us, and which we shall indubitably choose if no inhibiting factor intervenes.

But inhibiting factors, we should most of us say, *may* intervene: and that in two totally different ways which it is vital to distinguish clearly. The inhibiting factor may be of the nature of another desire (or aversion), which operates by changing the balance of the desiring situation. Though at one stage I desire B, which I believe to be wrong, more strongly than I desire A, which I believe to be right, it may happen that before action is taken I become aware of certain hitherto undiscerned consequences of A which I strongly desire, and the result may be that now not B but A presents itself to me as the end in the line of least resistance. Moral temptation is here overcome by the simple process of ceasing to be a moral temptation.

That is one way, and probably by far the commoner way, in which an inhibiting factor intervenes. But it is certainly not regarded by the self who is confronted by moral temptation as the *only* way. In such situations we all believe, rightly or wrongly, that even although B *continues* to be in the line of least resistance, even although, in other words, the situation remains one with the characteristic marks of moral temptation, we *can* nevertheless align ourselves with A. We can do so, we believe, because we have the power to introduce a new energy, to make what we call an 'effort of will', whereby we are able to act contrary to the felt balance of mere desire, and to achieve the higher end despite the fact that it continues to be in the line of greater resistance relatively to our desiring nature. The self in practice believes that it has this power; and believes, moreover, that the decision rests solely with its self, here and now, whether this power be exerted or not.

Now the objective validity or otherwise of this belief is not at the moment in question. I am here merely pointing to its existence as a psychological fact. No amount of introspective analysis, so far as I can see, even tends to disprove that we do as a matter of fact believe, in situations of moral temptation, that it rests with our self absolutely to decide whether we exert the effort of will which will enable us to rise to duty, or whether we shall allow our desiring nature to take its course.

I have now to point out, further, how this act of moral decision, at least in the significance which it has for the agent himself, fulfils in full the two conditions which we found it necessary to lay down at the beginning for the kind of 'free' act which moral responsibility presupposes.

For obviously it is, in the first place, an act which the agent believes he could perform in alternative ways. He believes that it is genuinely open to him to put forth effort—in varying degrees, if the situation admits of that —or withhold it altogether. And when he *has* decided—in whatever way— he remains convinced that these alternative courses were really open to him.

It is perhaps a little less obvious, but, I think, equally certain, that the agent believes the second condition to be fulfilled likewise, i.e. that the act of decision is determined *solely* by his self. It appears less obvious, because we all realize that formed character has a great deal to do with the choices that we make; and formed character is, without a doubt, partly dependent on the external factors of heredity and environment. But it is crucial here that we should not misunderstand the precise nature of the influence which formed character brings to bear upon the choices that constitute conduct. No one denies that it determines, at least largely, what things we desire, and again how greatly we desire them. It may thus fairly be said to determine the felt balance of desires in the situation of moral temptation. But all that that amounts to is that formed character prescribes the nature of the situation *within* which the act of moral decision takes place. It does not in the least follow that it has any influence whatsoever in determining the act of decision itself—the decision as to whether we shall exert effort or take the easy course of following the bent of our desiring nature: take, that is to say, the course which, in virtue of the determining influence of our character as so far formed, we feel to be in the line of least resistance.

When one appreciates this, one is perhaps better prepared to recognize the fact that the agent himself in the situation of moral temptation does not, and indeed could not, regard his formed character as having any influence whatever upon his act of decision as such. For the very nature of that decision, as it presents itself to him, is as to whether he will or will not permit his formed character to dictate his action. In other words, the agent distinguishes sharply between the self which makes the decision, and the self which, as formed character, determines not the decision but the situation within which the decision takes place. Rightly or wrongly, the agent believes that through his act of decision he can oppose and transcend his own formed character in the interest of duty. We are therefore obliged to say, I think, that the agent *cannot* regard his formed character as in any sense a determinant of the act of decision as such. The act is felt to be a genuinely creative act, originated by the self *ad hoc*, and by the self alone.

Here then, if my analysis is correct, in the function of moral decision in situations of moral temptation, we have an act of the self which at least *appears to the agent* to satisfy both of the conditions of freedom which we laid down at the beginning. The vital question now is, is this 'appearance' true or false? Is the act of decision really what it appears to the agent to be, determined solely by the self, and capable of alternative forms of expression? If it is, then we have here a free act which serves as an adequate basis for moral responsibility. . . . If, on the other hand, there is good reason to believe that the agent is the victim of illusion in supposing his act of decision to bear this character, then in my opinion the whole conception of moral responsibility must be jettisoned altogether. For it seems to me certain that there is no other function of the self that even looks as though it satisfied the required conditions of the free act. . . .

The charge made is that the Libertarian view is incompatible with the *predictability* of human conduct. For we do make rough predictions of people's conduct, on the basis of what we know of their character, every day of our lives, and there can be no doubt that the practice, within certain limits, is amply justified by results. Indeed if it were not so, social life would be reduced to sheer chaos. The close relationship between character and conduct which prediction postulates really seems to be about as certain as anything can be. But the Libertarian view, it is urged, by ascribing to the self a mysterious power of decision uncontrolled by character, and capable of issuing in acts inconsistent with character, denies that continuity between character and conduct upon which prediction depends. If Libertarianism is true, prediction is impossible. But prediction *is* possible, therefore Libertarianism is untrue.

My answer is that the Libertarian view is perfectly compatible with prediction within certain limits, and that there is no empirical evidence at all that prediction is in fact possible beyond these limits. . . .

Let us pass on then to consider a much more interesting and, I think, more plausible criticism. It is constantly objected against the Libertarian doctrine that it is fundamentally *unintelligible*. Libertarianism holds that the act of moral decision is the *self's* act, and yet insists at the same time that it is not influenced by any of those determinate features in the self's nature which go to constitute its 'character'. But, it is asked, do not these two propositions contradict one another? Surely a *self*-determination which is determination by something other than the self's *character* is a contradiction in terms? What meaning is there in the conception of a 'self' in abstraction from its 'character'? If you really wish to maintain, it is urged, that the act of decision is not determined by the self's character, you ought to admit frankly that it is not determined by the *self* at all. But in that case, of course, you will not be advocating a freedom which lends any kind of support to moral responsibility; indeed very much the reverse.

Now this criticism, and all of its kind, seem to me to be the product of a simple, but extraordinarily pervasive, error: the error of confining one's self to the categories of the external observer in dealing with the actions of human agents. . . .

I conclude, therefore, that those who find the Libertarian doctrine of the self's causality in moral decision inherently unintelligible find it so simply because they restrict themselves, quite arbitrarily, to an inadequate standpoint: a standpoint from which, indeed, a genuinely creative activity, if it existed, never *could* be apprehended.

For Further Study

Aquinas, St. Thomas. *Summa Theologica,* Part I, Question 82, Articles 1–4; Question 83, Articles 1–4.

Compton, Arthur H. "Science and Man's Freedom," *The Atlantic Monthly,* 200 (October, 1957): 71–74.

Emmet, E. R. *Learning to Philosophise.* New York: Philosophical Library, 1965, Ch. 7, "Free Will and Determinism."

Hobart, Charles W. "Freedom, A Neglected Area for Social Research," *Ethics,* 75 (April, 1965): 153–165.

Hook, Sidney (ed.). *Determinism and Freedom.* New York: New York U. Press, 1958, 237 pp. (Also Collier Book BS37, 1961.)

Hume, David. *An Inquiry Concerning Human Understanding,* 1748, Section 8, "Of Liberty and Necessity."

James, William. *The Will to Believe and Other Essays in Popular Philosophy.* New York: Longmans, Green, 1897, pp. 145–183, "The Dilemma of Determinism."

Kenner, Lionel. "Causality, Determinism and Freedom of the Will," *Philosophy,* 39 (July, 1964): 233–248.

Rose, Mary C. "The Free Will Hypothesis," *Personalist,* 47 (Winter, 1966): 29–42.

Somerville, John. "Marxist Ethics, Determinism, and Freedom," *Philosophy and Phenomenological Research,* 28 (September, 1967): 17–23.

Zimmerman, Marvin. "Is Free Will Incompatible With Determinism?" *Philosophy and Phenomenological Research,* 26 (March, 1966): 415–420.

PART 3

The Types of Philosophy

12 Some Forms of Naturalism

ERNEST NAGEL / Naturalism Reconsidered *

See the biographical note on p. 51.

THE PAST QUARTER CENTURY has been for philosophy in many parts of the world a period of acute self-questioning, engendered in no small measure by developments in scientific and logical thought, and in part no doubt by fundamental changes in the social order. In any event, there has come about a general loss of confidence in the competence of philosophy to provide by way of a distinctive intellectual method a basic ground-plan of the cosmos, or for that matter to contribute to knowledge of any primary subject-matter except by becoming a specialized positive science and subjecting itself to the discipline of empirical inquiry. Although the abysses of human ignorance are undeniably profound, it has also become apparent that ignorance, like actual knowledge, is of many special and heterogeneous things; and we have come to think, like the fox and unlike the hedgehog of whom Mr. Isaiah Berlin has recently reminded us, that there are a great many things which are already known or remain to be discovered, but that there is no one "big thing" which, if known, would make everything else coherent and unlock the mystery of creation. In consequence, many of us have ceased to emulate the great system-builders in the history of philosophy. In partial imitation of the strategy of modern sci-

* Reprinted with permission of the publisher from *Logic Without Metaphysics* by Ernest Nagel. Copyright 1956 by The Free Press, A Corporation. From "Naturalism Reconsidered," pp. 3–18.

ence, and in the hope of achieving responsibly held conclusions about matters concerning which we could acquire genuine competence, we have tended to become specialists in our professional activities. We have come to direct our best energies to the resolution of limited problems and puzzles that emerge in the analysis of scientific and ordinary discourse, in the evaluation of claims to knowledge, in the interpretation and validation of ethical and esthetic judgments, and in the assessment of types of human experience. . . .

Some of us, I know, are distressed by the widespread scepticism of the traditional claims for a *philosophia perennis*, and have dismissed as utterly trivial most if not all the products of various current forms of analytical philosophy. I do not share this distress, nor do I think the dismissal is uniformly perspicacious and warranted. For in my judgment, the scepticism which many deplore is well-founded. Even though a fair-sized portion of recent analytical literature seems inconsequential also to me, analytical philosophy in our own day is the continuation of a major philosophic tradition, and can count substantial feats of clarification among its assets. Concentration on limited and determinate problems has yielded valuable fruits, not least in the form of an increased and refreshing sensitivity to the demands of responsible discourse.

On the other hand, philosophers like other men conduct their lives within the framework of certain comprehensive if not always explicit assumptions about the world they inhabit. These assumptions color evaluations of major ideals and proposed policies. I also suspect that the directions taken by analyses of specific intellectual problems are frequently if subtly controlled by the expressed or tacit beliefs philosophers hold concerning the over-all nature of things, by their views on human destiny, and by their conceptions of the scope of human reason. But conversely, resolutions of special problems made plausible by recent philosophical analysis, as well as by the findings of various positive sciences, seem to me to support certain broad generalizations about the cosmos and to disconfirm others. It is clearly desirable that such basic intellectual commitments, which are at once the matrix and the outcome of inquiries into specific problems, be made as explicit as possible. A philosopher who is a reflective man by profession, certainly owes it to himself to articulate, if only occasionally, what sort of world he thinks he inhabits, and to make clear to himself where approximately lies the center of his convictions.

The discharge of the important obligation which is mine this evening, seems to me an appropriate occasion for stating as simply and as succinctly as I can the substance of those intellectual commitments I like to call "naturalism." The label itself is of no importance, but I use it partly because of its historical associations, and partly because it is a reminder that the doctrines for which it is a name are neither new nor untried. With

Santayana, I prefer not to accept in philosophic debate what I do not believe when I am not arguing; and naturalism as I construe it merely formulates what centuries of human experience have repeatedly confirmed. At any rate, naturalism seems to me a sound generalized account of the world encountered in practice and in critical reflection, and a just perspective upon the human scene. I wish to state briefly and hence with little supporting argument what I take to be its major tenets, and to defend it against some recent criticisms.

Claims to knowledge cannot ultimately be divorced from an evaluation of the intellectual methods used to support those claims. It is nevertheless unfortunate that in recent years naturalists in philosophy have so frequently permitted their allegiance to a dependable method of inquiry to obscure their substantive views on things in general. For it is the inclusive intellectual image of nature and man which naturalism supplies that sets it off from other comprehensive philosophies. In my conception of it, at any rate, naturalism embraces a generalized account of the cosmic scheme and of man's place in it, as well as a logic of inquiry.

I hasten to add, however, that naturalism does not offer a theory of nature in the sense that Newtonian mechanics, for example, provides a theory of motion. Naturalism does not, like the latter, specify a set of substantive principles with the help of which the detailed course of concrete happenings can be explained or understood. Moreover, the principles affirmed by naturalism are not proposed as competitors or underpinnings for any of the special theories which the positive sciences assert. Nor, finally, does naturalism offer its general view of nature and man as the product of some special philosophical mode of knowing. The account of things proposed by naturalism is a distillation from knowledge acquired in the usual way in daily encounters with the world or in specialized scientific inquiry. Naturalism articulates features of the world which, because they have become so obvious, are rarely mentioned in discussions of special subject-matter, but which distinguish our actual world from other conceivable worlds. The major affirmations of naturalism are accordingly meager in content; but the principles affirmed are nevertheless effective guides in responsible criticism and evaluation.

Two theses seem to me central to naturalism as I conceive it. The first is the existential and causal primacy of organized matter in the executive order of nature. This is the assumption that the occurrence of events, qualities and processes, and the characteristic behaviors of various individuals, are contingent on the organization of spatio-temporally located bodies, whose internal structures and external relations determine and limit the appearance and disappearance of everything that happens. That this is so, is one of the best-tested conclusions of experience. We are frequently ignorant of the special conditions under which things come into being or pass away; but we have also found repeatedly that when we look closely, we eventually ascertain at least the approximate and gross conditions under which events occur, and we discover that those conditions invariably consist of some more or less complex organization of material substances. Naturalism does not maintain that only what is material exists, since many things noted in experience, for example, modes of action, relations of meaning, dreams, joys, plans, aspirations, are not as such material bodies or organizations of material bodies. What naturalism does assert as a truth about nature is that though *forms* of behavior or *functions* of material systems are indefeasibly parts of nature, forms and functions are not themselves agents in their own realization or in the realization of anything else. In the conception of nature's processes which naturalism affirms, there is no place for the operation of disembodied forces, no place for an immaterial spirit directing the course of events, no place for the survival of personality after the corruption of the body which exhibits it.

The second major contention of naturalism is that the manifest plurality and variety of things, of their qualities and their functions, are an irreducible feature of the cosmos, not a deceptive appearance cloaking some more homogeneous "ultimate reality" or transempirical substance, and that the sequential orders in which events occur or the manifold relations of dependence in which things exist are *contingent* connections, not the embodiments of a fixed and unified pattern of logically necessary links. The existential primacy of organized matter does not make illusory either the relatively permanent or the comparatively transient characters and forms which special configurations of bodies may possess. In particular, although the continued existence of the human scene is precarious and is dependent on a balance of forces that doubtless will not endure indefinitely, and even though its distinctive traits are not pervasive throughout space, it is nonetheless as much a part of the "ultimate" furniture of the world, and is as genuine a sample of what "really" exists, as are atoms and stars. There undoubtedly occur integrated systems of bodies, such as biological organisms, which have the capacity because of their material organization to maintain themselves and the direction of their characteristic activities. But there is no positive evidence, and much negative evidence, for the supposition that all existential structures are teleological systems in this sense, or for the view that whatever occurs is a phase in a unitary, teleologically organized, and all-inclusive process or system. Modern physical cosmology does indeed supply some evidence for definite patterns of evolutionary development of stars, galactic systems, and even of the entire physical universe; and it is quite possible that the stage of cosmic evolution reached at any given time causally limits the types of things which can occur during that period. On the other hand, the patterns of change investigated in physical cosmogony are not patterns that are exhaustive of everything that happens; and nothing in these current physical speculations requires the conclusion that changes in one star or galaxy are related by inherent necessity to every action of biological organisms in some remote planet. Even admittedly teleological systems contain parts and processes which are causally irrelevant to some of the activities maintained by those systems; and the causal dependencies known to hold between the parts of any system, teleological or not, have never been successfully established as forms of logically necessary relations. In brief, if naturalism is true, irreducible variety and logical contingency are fundamental traits of the world we actually inhabit. The orders and connections of things are all accessible to rational inquiry; but these orders and connections are not all derivable by deductive methods from any set of premises that deductive reason can certify.

It is in this framework of general ideas that naturalism envisages the career and destiny of man. Naturalism views the emergence and the continuance of human society as dependent on physical and physiological conditions that have not always obtained, and that will not permanently endure. But it does not in consequence regard man and his works as intrusions into nature, any more than it construes as intrusions the presence of heavenly bodies or of terrestrial protozoa. The stars are no more foreign to the cosmos than are men, even if the conditions for the existence of both stars and men are realized only occasionally or only in a few regions. Indeed, the conception of human life as a war with nature, as a struggle with an implacable foe that has doomed man to extinction, is but an inverted theology, with a malicious Devil in the seat of Omnipotence. It is a conception that is immodest as well as anthropomorphic in the importance it imputes to man in the scheme of things.

On the other hand, the affirmation that nature is man's "home" as much as it is the "home" of anything else, and the denial that cosmic forces are *intent* on destroying the human scene, do not warrant the interpretation that every sector of nature is explicable in terms of traits known to characterize only human individuals and human actions. Man undoubtedly possesses characteristics which are shared by everything that exists; but he also manifests traits and capacities that appear to be distinctive of him. Is anything gained but confusion when all forms of dependence between things, whether animate or inanimate, and all types of behaviors they display, are subsumed under distinctions that have an identifiable content only in reference to the human psyche? Measured by the illumination they bring, there is nothing to differentiate the thesis that human traits are nothing but the properties of bodies which can be formulated exclusively in the language of current physical theory, from the view that every change and every mode of operation, in whatever sector of the cosmos it may be encountered, is simply an illustration of some category pertinent to the description of human behavior.

Indeed, even some professed naturalists sometimes appear to promote the confusion when they make a fetish of continuity. Naturalists usually stress the emergence of novel forms in physical and biological evolution, thereby emphasizing the fact that human traits are not identical with the traits from which they emerge. Nevertheless, some distinguished contemporary naturalists also insist, occasionally with overtones of anxiety, that there is a "continuity" between the typically human on the one hand, and the physical and biological on the other. But is man's foothold in the scheme of things really made more secure by showing that his distinctive traits are in some sense "continuous" with features pervasive in nature, and would man's place in nature be less secure if such continuity did not obtain? The actual evidence for a continuity of development is conclusive in some instances of human traits, however it may be in others. But I sometimes suspect that the cardinal importance philosophers assign to the alleged universality of such continuity is a lingering survival of that ancient conception, according to which things are intelligible only when seen as teleological systems producing definite ends, so that nature itself is properly understood only when construed as the habitat of human society. In any event, a naturalism that is not provincial in its outlook will not accept the intellectual incorporation of man into nature at the price of reading into all the processes of the cosmos the passions, the strivings, the defeats and the glories of human life, and then exhibiting man as the most adequate, because most representative, expression of nature's inherent constitution. No, a mature naturalism seeks to understand what man is, not in terms of a discovered or postulated continuity between what is distinctive of him and what is pervasive in all things. Without denying that even the most distinctive human traits are dependent on things which are non-human, a mature naturalism attempts to assess man's nature in the light of *his* actions and achievements, *his* aspirations and capacities, *his* limitations and tragic failures, and *his* splendid works of ingenuity and imagination.

Human nature and history, in short, are *human* nature and history, not the history and nature of anything else, however much knowledge of other things contributes to a just appraisal of what man is. In particular, the adequacy of proposed ideals for human life must be judged, not in terms of their causes and origins, but in reference to how the pursuit and possible realization of ideals contribute to the organization and release of *human* energies. Men are animated by many springs of action, no one of which is intrinsically good or evil; and a moral ideal is the imagined satisfaction of some complex of impulses, desires, and needs. When ideals are handled responsibly, they therefore function as hypotheses for achieving a balanced exercise of human powers. Moral ideals are not self-certifying, any more than are the theories of the physical sciences; and evidence drawn from experienced satisfactions is required to validate them, however difficult may be the process of sifting and weighing the available data. Moral problems arise from a conflict of specific impulses and interests. They cannot, however, be effectively resolved by invoking standards derived from the study of non-human nature, or of what is allegedly beyond nature. If moral problems can be resolved at all, they can be resolved only in the light of specific human capacities, historical circumstance and acquired skills, and the opportunities (revealed by an imagination disciplined by knowledge) for altering the physical and social environment and for redirecting habitual behaviors. Moreover, since human virtues are in part the products of the society in which human powers are matured, a naturalistic moral theory is at the same time a critique of civilization, that is, a critique of the institutions that channel human energies, so as to exhibit the possibilities and limitations of various forms and arrangements of society for bringing enduring satisfactions to individual human careers.

These are the central tenets of what I take to be philosophical naturalism. They are tenets which are supported by compelling empirical evidence, rather than dicta based on dogmatic preference. In my view of it, naturalism does not dismiss every other differing conception of the scheme of things as logically impossible; and it does not rule out all alternatives to itself on a priori grounds. It is possible, I think, to conceive without logical inconsistency a world in which disembodied forces are dynamic agents, or in which whatever happens is a manifestation of an unfolding logical pattern. In such possible worlds it would be an error to be a naturalist. But philosophy is not identical with pure mathematics, and its ultimate concern is with the actual world, even though philosophy must take cognizance of the fact that the actual world contains creatures who can envisage possible worlds and who employ different logical procedures for deciding which hypothetical world is the actual one. It is partly for this reason that contemporary naturalists devote so much attention to methods of evaluating evidence. When naturalists give their allegiance to the method of intelligence commonly designated as the method of modern empirical science, they do so because that method appears to be the most assured way of achieving reliable knowledge.

As judged by that method, the evidence in my opinion is at present conclusive for the truth of naturalism, and it is tempting to suppose that no one familiar with the evidence can fail to acknowledge that philosophy. Indeed, some commentators there are who assert that all philosophies are at bottom only expressions in different idioms of the same conceptions about the nature of things, so that the strife of philosophic systems is mainly a conflict over essentially linguistic matters. Yet many thinkers for whom I have a profound respect explicitly reject naturalism, and their espousal of contrary views seems to me incompatible with the irenic claim that we really are in agreement on fundamentals.

Although I do not have the time this evening to consider systematically the criticisms currently made of naturalism, I do wish to examine briefly two repeatedly voiced objections which, if valid, would in my opinion seriously jeopardize the integrity and adequacy of naturalism as a philosophy. Stated summarily, the first objection is that in relying exclusively on the logico-empirical method of modern science for establishing cognitive claims, naturalists are in effect stacking the cards in their own favor, since thereby all alternative philosophies are antecedently disqualified. It is maintained, for example, that naturalism rejects any hypothesis about trans-empirical causes or time-transcending spiritual substances as factors in the order of things, not because such hypotheses are actually shown to be false, but simply because the logic of proof adopted dismisses as irrelevant any evidence which might establish them.

This criticism does not seem to me to have merit: the logico-empirical method of evaluating cognitive claims to which naturalists subscribe does not eliminate by fiat any hypothesis about existence for which evidence can be procured, that is, evidence that in the last resort can be obtained through sensory or introspective observation. Thus, anyone who asserts a hypothesis postulating a trans-empirical ground for all existence, presumably seeks to understand in terms of that ground the actual occurrences in nature, and to account thereby for what actually happens as distinct from what is merely imagined to happen. There must therefore be some connection between the postulated character of the hypothetical trans-empirical ground, and the empirically observable traits in the world around us; for otherwise the hypothesis is otiose, and not relevant to the spatio-temporal processes of nature. This does not mean, as some critics of naturalism suppose the latter to maintain, that the hypothetical trans-empirical ground must be characterized exclusively in terms of the observable properties of the world, any more than that the sub-microscopic particles and processes which current physical theory postulates must be logical constructions out of the observable traits of macroscopic objects. But it does mean that unless the hypothesis implies, even if only by a circuitous route, some statements about empirical data, it is not adequate to the task for which it is proposed. If naturalists reject hypotheses about trans-empirical substances, they do not do so arbitrarily. They reject such hypotheses either because their relevance to the going concerns of nature is not established, or because, though their relevance is not in question, the actual evidence does not support them.

Nor does naturalism dismiss as unimportant and without consideration experiences such as of the holy, of divine illumination, or of mystical ecstasy, experiences which are of the greatest moment in the lives of many men, and which are often taken to signify the presence and operation of some purely spiritual reality. Such experiences have dimensions of meaning for those who have undergone them, that are admittedly not on par with the import of more common experiences like those of physical hunger, general well-being, or feelings of remorse and guilt. Yet such experiences are nonetheless events among other events; and though they may be evidence for something, their sheer occurrence does not certify *what* they are evidence for, any more than the sheer occurrence of dreams, hopes, and delusions authenticates the actual existence of their ostensible objects. In particular, whether the experience labelled as an experience of divine illumination is evidence for the existence of a divinity, is a question to be settled by inquiry, not by dogmatic affirmations or denials. When naturalists refuse to acknowledge, merely on the strength of such experiences, the operation or presence of a divine power, they do so not because their commitment to a logical method prevents them from treating it seriously, but because independent inquiry fails to confirm it. Knowledge is knowledge, and cannot without confusion be identified with intuitive insight or with the vivid immediacy of profoundly moving experiences. Claims to knowledge must be capable of being tested; and the testing must be conducted by eventual reference to such evidence as counts in the responsible conduct of everyday affairs as well as of systematic inquiry in the sciences. Naturalists are therefore not engaged in question-begging when, through the use of the logic of scientific intelligence, they judge non-naturalistic accounts of the order of things to be unfounded.

There is, however, a further objection to naturalism, to the effect that in committing itself to the logic of scientific proof, it is quite analogous to religious belief in resting on unsupported and indemonstrable faith. For that logic allegedly involves assumptions like the uniformity of nature or similar principles which transcend experience, cannot be justified empirically, and yet provide the premises that constitute the ultimate warrant for the conclusions of empirical inquiry. But if naturalism is thus based on unprovable articles of faith, on what cogent grounds can it reject a different conception of the true order of governance of events which rests on a different faith?

I cannot here deal adequately with the complex issues raised by this objection. Its point is not satisfactorily turned by claiming, as some have done, that instead of being articles of faith, the alleged indemonstrable postulates of scientific method are simply rules of the scientific game which *define* what in that game is to be understood by the words "knowledge" and "evidence." As I see it, however, the objection has force only for those whose ideal of reason is demonstration, and who therefore refuse to dignify anything as genuine knowledge unless it is demonstrable from self-luminous and self-evident premises. But if, as I also think, that ideal is not universally appropriate, and if, furthermore, a *wholesale* justification for knowledge and its methods is an unreasonable demand and a misplaced effort, the objection appears as quite pointless. The warrant for a proposition about some specific inter-relations of events does not derive from a faith in the uniformity of nature or in other principles with a cosmic scope. The warrant derives exclusively from the specific evidence available for that proposition, and from the contingent historical fact that the special ways employed in obtaining and appraising the evidence have been generally effective in yielding reliable knowledge. Subsequent inquiry may show that we were mistaken in accepting a proposition on the evidence available earlier; and further inquiry may also reveal that a given inductive policy, despite a record of successful past performance, requires correction if not total rejection. Fortunately, however, we are not always mistaken in accepting various propositions or in employing certain inductive policies, even though we are unable to demonstrate that we shall never fall into error. Accordingly, though many of our hopes for the stability of beliefs in the face of fresh experience may turn out to be baseless, and though no guarantees can be given that our most assured claims to knowledge may not eventually need revision, in adopting scientific method as the instrument for evaluating claims to knowledge, naturalists are not subscribing to an indemonstrable faith.

The bitter years of cataclysmic wars and social upheavals through which our generation has been passing have also witnessed a general decline of earlier hopes in the possibilities of modern science for achieving a liberal and humane civilization. Indeed, as is well known, many men have become convinced that the progress and spread of science, and the consequent secularization of society, are the prime sources of our present ills; and a not inconsiderable number of thinkers have made widely popular various revived forms of older religious and irrationalistic philosophies as guides to human salvation. Moreover, since naturalists have not abandoned their firm adherence to the method of scientific intelligence, naturalism has been repeatedly charged with insensitivity toward spiritual values, with a shallow optimism toward science as an instrument for ennobling the human estate, and with a philistine blindness toward the ineradicable miseries of human existence. I want to conclude with a few brief comments on these allegations.

It is almost painful to have to make a point of the elementary fact that whatever may happen to be the range of special interests and sensibilities of individual naturalists, there is no incompatibility, whether logical or psychological, between maintaining that warranted knowledge is secured only through the use of a definite logical method, and recognizing that the world can be experienced in many other ways than by knowing it. It is a matter of record that outstanding exponents of naturalism, in our own time as well as in the past, have exhibited an unequaled and tender sensitivity to the esthetic and moral dimensions of human experience; and they have been not only movingly eloquent celebrants of the role of moral idealism and of intellectual and esthetic contemplation in human life, but also vigorous defenders of the distinctive character of these values against facile attempts to reduce them to something else.

It seems to me singularly inept, moreover, to indict naturalism as a philosophy without a sense for the tragic aspects of life. For unlike many world-views, naturalism offers no cosmic consolation for the unmerited defeats and undeserved sufferings which all men experience in one form or another. It has never sought to conceal its view of human destiny as an episode between two oblivions. To be sure, naturalism is not a philosophy of despair. For one facet in its radical pluralism is the truth that a human good is nonetheless a good, despite its transitory existence. There doubtless are foolish optimists among those professing naturalism, though naturalism has no monopoly in this respect, and it is from other quarters that one usually receives glad tidings of a universal nostrum. But in any event, neither the pluralism so central to naturalism, nor its cultivation of scientific reason, is compatible with any dogmatic assumption to the effect that men can be liberated from *all* the sorrows and evils to which they are now heirs, through the eventual advances of science and the institution of appropriate physical and social innovations. Indeed, why suppose that a philosophy which is wedded to the use of the sober logic of scientific intelligence, should thereby be committed to the dogma that there are no irremediable evils? On the contrary, human reason is potent only against evils that are *remediable*. At the same time, since it is impossible to decide responsibly, *antecedent* to inquiry, *which* of the many human ills can be mitigated if not eradicated by extending the operations of scientific reason into human affairs, naturalism is not a philosophy of *general* renunciation, even though it recognizes that it is the better part of wisdom to be equably resigned to what, in the light of available evidence, cannot be avoided. Human reason is not an omnipotent instrument for the achievement of human goods; but it is the only instrument we do possess, and it is not a contemptible one. Although naturalism is acutely sensitive to the actual limitations of rational effort, those limitations do not warrant a romantic philosophy of general despair, and they do not blind naturalism to the possibilities implicit in the exercise of disciplined reason for realizing human excellence.

JOSEPH STALIN / *Dialectical and Historical Materialism* *

Joseph Stalin (1879–1953) was the leader in the U.S.S.R. and the most powerful figure in the communist world in the era between Lenin and Khrushchev.

DIALECTICAL materialism is the world outlook of the Marxist-Leninist party. It is called dialectical materialism because its approach to the phenomena of nature, its method of studying and apprehending them, is *dialectical*, while its interpretation of the phenomena of nature, its conception of these phenomena, its theory, is *materialistic*.

Historical materialism is the extension of the principles of dialectical materialism to the study of social life, an application of the principles of dialectical materialism to the phenomena of the life of society, to the study of society and its history.

When describing their dialectical method, Marx and Engels usually refer to Hegel as the philosopher who formulated the main features of dialectics. This, however, does not mean that the dialectics of Marx and Engels is identical with the dialectics of Hegel. As a matter of fact, Marx and Engels took from the Hegelian dialectics only its "rational kernel," casting aside its idealistic shell, and developed it further so as to lend it a modern scientific form. . . .

1. The principal features of the Marxist *dialectical method* are as follows:

(a) Contrary to metaphysics, dialectics does not regard nature as an accidental agglomeration of things, of phenomena, unconnected with, isolated from, and independent of, each other, but as a connected and integral whole, in which things, phenomena, are organically connected with, dependent on, and determined by, each other.

The dialectical method therefore holds that no phenomenon in nature can be understood if taken by itself, isolated from surrounding phenomena, inasmuch as any phenomenon in any realm of nature may become meaningless to us if it is not considered in connection with the surround-

---

* Joseph Stalin, from *Dialectical and Historical Materialism* (New York: International Publishers, 1940), pp. 5, 7–8, 11–16.

ing conditions, but divorced from them; and that, vice versa, any phenomenon can be understood and explained if considered in its inseparable connection with surrounding phenomena, as one conditioned by surrounding phenomena.

(b) Contrary to metaphysics, dialectics holds that nature is not a state of rest and immobility, stagnation and immutability, but a state of continuous movement and change, of continuous renewal and development, where something is always arising and developing, and something always disintegrating and dying away.

The dialectical method therefore requires that phenomena should be considered not only from the standpoint of their interconnection and interdependence, but also from the standpoint of their movement, their change, their development, their coming into being and going out of being. . . .

(c) Contrary to metaphysics, dialectics does not regard the process of development as a simple process of growth, where quantitative changes do not lead to qualitative changes, but as a development which passes from insignificant and imperceptible quantitative changes to open, fundamental changes, to qualitative changes; a development in which the qualitative changes occur not gradually, but rapidly and abruptly, taking the form of a leap from one state to another; they occur not accidentally but as the natural result of an accumulation of imperceptible and gradual quantitative changes. . . .

(d) Contrary to metaphysics, dialectics holds that internal contradictions are inherent in all things and phenomena of nature, for they all have their negative and positive sides, a past and a future, something dying away and something developing; and that the struggle between these opposites, the struggle between the old and the new, between that which is dying away and that which is being born, between that which is disappearing and that which is developing, constitutes the internal content of the process of development, the internal content of the transformation of quantitative changes into qualitative changes.

The dialectical method therefore holds that the process of development from the lower to the higher takes place not as a harmonious unfolding of phenomena, but as a disclosure of the contradictions inherent in things and phenomena, as a "struggle" of opposite tendencies which operate on the basis of these contradictions. . . .

Such, in brief, are the principal features of the Marxist dialectical method.

It is easy to understand how immensely important is the extension of the principles of the dialectical method to the study of social life and the history of society, and how immensely important is the application of these principles to the history of society and to the practical activities of the party of the proletariat.

If there are no isolated phenomena in the world, if all phenomena are interconnected and interdependent, then it is clear that every social system and every social movement in history must be evaluated not from the standpoint of "eternal justice" or some other preconceived idea, as is not infrequently done by historians, but from the standpoint of the conditions which gave rise to that system or that social movement and with which they are connected.

The slave system would be senseless, stupid and unnatural under modern conditions. But under the conditions of a disintegrating primitive communal system, the slave system is a quite understandable and natural phenomenon, since it represents an advance on the primitive communal system.

The demand for a bourgeois-democratic republic when tsardom and bourgeois society existed, as, let us say, in Russia in 1905, was a quite understandable, proper and revolutionary demand, for at that time a bourgeois republic would have meant a step forward. But now, under the conditions of the U.S.S.R., the demand for a bourgeois-democratic republic would be a meaningless and counter-revolutionary demand, for a bourgeois republic would be a retrograde step compared with the Soviet republic.

Everything depends on the conditions, time and place.

It is clear that without such a *historical* approach to social phenomena, the existence and development of the science of history is impossible, for only such an approach saves the science of history from becoming a jumble of accidents and an agglomeration of most absurd mistakes.

Further, if the world is in a state of constant movement and development, if the dying away of the old and the upgrowth of the new is a law of development, then it is clear that there can be no "immutable" social systems, no "eternal principles" of private property and exploitation, no "eternal ideas" of the subjugation of the peasant to the landlord, of the worker to the capitalist.

Hence the capitalist system can be replaced by the socialist system, just as at one time the feudal system was replaced by the capitalist system.

Hence we must not base our orientation on the strata of society which are no longer developing, even though they at present constitute the predominant force, but on those strata which are developing and have a future before them, even though they at present do not constitute the predominant force. . . .

Hence, in order not to err in policy, one must look forward, not backward.

Further, if the passing of slow quantitative changes into rapid and abrupt qualitative changes is a law of development, then it is clear that revolutions made by oppressed classes are a quite natural and inevitable phenomenon.

Hence the transition from capitalism to socialism and the liberation of the working class from the yoke of capitalism cannot be effected by slow changes, by reforms, but only by a qualitative change of the capitalist system, by revolution.

Hence, in order not to err in policy, one must be a revolutionary, not a reformist.

Further, if development proceeds by way of the disclosure of internal contradictions, by way of collisions between opposite forces on the basis of these contradictions and so as to overcome these contradictions, then it is clear that the class struggle of the proletariat is a quite natural and inevitable phenomenon.

Hence we must not cover up the contradictions of the capitalist system, but disclose and unravel them; we must not try to check the class struggle but carry it to its conclusion.

Hence, in order not to err in policy, one must pursue an uncompromising proletarian class policy, not a reformist policy of harmony of the interests of the proletariat and the bourgeoisie, not a compromisers' policy of "the growing of capitalism into socialism."

Such is the Marxist dialectical method when applied to social life, to the history of society.

As to Marxist philosophical materialism, it is fundamentally the direct opposite of philosophical idealism.

2. The principal features of Marxist philosophical *materialism* are as follows:

(a) Contrary to idealism, which regards the world as the embodiment of an "absolute idea," a "universal spirit," "consciousness," Marx's philosophical materialism holds that the world is by its very nature *material*, that the multifold phenomena of the world constitute different forms of matter in motion, that interconnection and interdependence of phenomena, as established by the dialectical method, are a law of the development of moving matter, and that the world develops in accordance with the laws of movement of matter and stands in no need of a "universal spirit." . . .

(b) Contrary to idealism, which asserts that only our mind really exists, and that the material world, being, nature, exists only in our mind, in our sensations, ideas and perceptions, the Marxist materialist philosophy holds that matter, nature, being, is an objective reality existing outside and independent of our mind; that matter is primary, since it is the source of sensations, ideas, mind, and that mind is secondary, derivative, since it is a reflection of matter, a reflection of being; that thought is a product of matter which in its development has reached a high degree of perfection, namely, of the brain, and the brain is the organ of thought; and that therefore one cannot separate thought from matter without committing a grave error. Engels says:

> The question of the relation of thinking to being, the relation of spirit to nature is the paramount question of the whole of philosophy. . . . The answers which the philosophers gave to this question split them into two great camps. Those who asserted the primacy of spirit to nature . . . comprised the camp of *idealism*. The others, who regarded nature as primary, belong to the various schools of *materialism*. (*Ludwig Feuerbach*.)

PAUL KURTZ / A Definition of Humanism *

Paul Kurtz (1925–   ) teaches philosophy at the State University of New York at Buffalo, and edits *The Humanist*. He is author of *Decision and the Condition of Man* and editor of several other books.

HUMANISTS have been debating for years the proper definition of humanism. It is clear that humanism is not a dogma or creed, and that there are many varieties and meanings to humanism. Nevertheless, one may suggest at least four characteristics that contemporary humanists emphasize.

First, humanists have some confidence in man and they believe that the only basis for morality is human experience and human needs. Second, many or most humanists are opposed to all forms of super-naturalistic and authoritarian religion. Third, many humanists believe that critical reason and scientific intelligence can assist in reconstructing our moral values. And fourth, humanism is humanitarian in that it is concerned with the good life and social justice as moral ideals. It is committed to democracy, social equality, freedom and peace.

Humanism as a movement is wide enough to include many people who will agree with some of the above points, but not all. It is clear that one can be a humanist in the first and second senses above, that is, affirm the dignity of man and deny the reality of God, yet not accept humanism in its third sense; that is, one may be sceptic about the use of reason in life. What characterizes an increasing number of people is dedication to *humanitarianism* and a commitment to a moral point of view in which

---

* Paul Kurtz, "A Definition of Humanism," *The Humanist*, 28 (May/June 1968): 1. Used by permission of the author and editor.

mankind is viewed as a whole. Humanists may honestly disagree about their political beliefs, about Vietnam, sexual morality, drugs and any number of social questions. There is no humanist party line. What humanists today share in common, however, is a concern for humanity, a belief that moral values must be removed from the mantle of theological dogma, and a conviction that our moral ideals must be constantly reexamined and revised in the light of present needs and social demands.

For Further Study

Blanshard, Brand. "Reflections on Economic Determinism," *Journal of Philosophy*, 63 (March 31, 1966): 169–178.

Hocutt, Max. "In Defense of Materialism," *Philosophy and Phenomenological Research*, 27 (March, 1967): 366–385.

Hook, Sidney. *Reason, Social Myths, and Democracy*. New York: John Day, 1940, Ch. 9, "Dialectic and Nature." (Reprinted by Humanities Press, 1950.)

Huxley, Julian. "The Humanist Frame," in *The Humanist Frame*, ed. Julian Huxley. London: Allen & Unwin, 1961.

Manicas, Peter T. "Men, Machines, Materialism, and Morality," *Philosophy and Phenomenological Research*, 27 (December, 1966): 238–246.

Odajnyk, Walter. *Marxism and Existentialism*. Garden City: Doubleday, 1965. (Anchor Book A 443.)

Randall, John Herman, Jr. "Epilogue: The Nature of Naturalism," in *Naturalism and the Human Spirit*, ed. Yervant H. Krikorian. New York: Columbia U. Press, 1944, Ch. 15.

Reiser, Oliver L. *Cosmic Humanism*. Cambridge, Mass.: Schenkman, 1966.

Sellars, Roy Wood. "The New Materialism," in *A History of Philosophical Systems*, ed. Vergilius Ferm. New York: Philosophical Library, 1950.

Somerville, John. *The Philosophy of Marxism: An Exposition*. New York: Random House, 1967.

Tucker, Robert C. *Philosophy and Myth in Karl Marx*. London: Cambridge U. Press, 1961, Part 4, "Mature Marxism."

13 Idealism and Its Implications

JOSIAH ROYCE / Reality and Idealism *

Josiah Royce (1855–1916) was a leading American idealistic philosopher who taught at Harvard, where he was a colleague of James and Santayana. His books include *The World and the Individual; The Philosophy of Loyalty;* and *The Problem of Christianity.*

. . . I MUST REMIND you that idealism has two aspects. It is, for the first, a kind of analysis of the world, an analysis which so far has no absolute character about it, but which undertakes, in a fashion that might be acceptable to any skeptic, to examine what you mean by all the things, whatever they are, that you believe in or experience. This idealistic analysis consists merely in a pointing out, by various devices, that the world of your knowledge, whatever it contains, is through and through such stuff as ideas are made of, that you never in your life believed in anything definable *but* ideas, that, as Berkeley put it, "this whole choir of heaven and furniture of earth" is nothing for any of us but a system of ideas which govern our belief and our conduct. Such idealism has numerous statements, interpretations, embodiments: forms part of the most various systems and experiences, is consistent with Berkeley's theism, with Fichte's ethical absolutism, with Professor Huxley's agnostic empiricism, with Clifford's mind-stuff theory, with countless other theories that have used such idealism as a part of their scheme. In this aspect idealism is already a little puzzling to our natural consciousness, but it becomes quickly familiar, in fact almost

* Josiah Royce, from "Reality and Idealism," in *The Spirit of Modern Philosophy* (Boston: Houghton Mifflin, 1892), pp. 350–361, 364, 366–368, 370, 373, 379.

commonplace, and seems after all to alter our practical faith or to solve our deeper problems very little.

The other aspect of idealism is the one which gives us our notion of the absolute Self. To it the first is only preparatory. This second aspect is the one which from Kant, until the present time, has formed the deeper problem of thought. Whenever the world has become more conscious of its significance, the work of human philosophy will be, not nearly ended (Heaven forbid an end!), but for the first time fairly begun. For then, in critically estimating our passions, we shall have some truer sense of whose passions they are.

I begin with the first and the less significant aspect of idealism. Our world, I say, whatever it may contain, is such stuff as ideas are made of. This preparatory sort of idealism is the one that, as I just suggested, Berkeley made prominent, and after a fashion familiar. I must state it in my own way, although one in vain seeks to attain novelty in illustrating so frequently described a view.

Here, then, is our so real world of the senses, full of light and warmth and sound. If anything could be solid and external, surely, one at first will say, it is this world. Hard facts, not mere ideas, meet us on every hand. Ideas any one can mould as he wishes. Not so facts. In idea socialists can dream out Utopias, disappointed lovers can imagine themselves successful, beggars can ride horses, wanderers can enjoy the fireside at home. In the realm of facts, society organizes itself as it must, rejected lovers stand for the time defeated, beggars are alone with their wishes, oceans roll drearily between home and the wanderer. Yet this world of fact is, after all, not entirely stubborn, not merely hard. The strenuous will can mould facts. We can form our world, in part, according to our ideas. Statesmen influence the social order, lovers woo afresh, wanderers find the way home. But thus to alter the world we must work, and just because the laborer is worthy of his hire, it is well that the real world should thus have such fixity of things as enables us to anticipate what facts will prove lasting, and to see of the travail of our souls when it is once done. This, then, is the presupposition of life, that we work in a real world, where house-walls do not melt away as in dreams, but stand firm against the winds of many winters, and can be felt as real. We do not wish to find facts wholly plastic; we want them to be stubborn, if only the stubbornness be not altogether unmerciful. Our will makes constantly a sort of agreement with the world, whereby, if the world will continually show some respect to the will, the will shall consent to be strenuous in its industry. Interfere with the reality of my world, and you therefore take the very life and heart out of my will.

The reality of the world, however, when thus defined in terms of its stubbornness, its firmness as against the will that has not conformed to its laws, its kindly rigidity in preserving for us the fruits of our labors,—such reality, I say, is still something wholly unanalyzed. In what does this stubbornness consist? Surely, many different sorts of reality, as it would seem, may be stubborn. Matter is stubborn when it stands in hard walls against us, or rises in vast mountain ranges before the path-finding explorer. But minds can be stubborn also. The lonely wanderer, who watches by the seashore the waves that roll between him and his home, talks of cruel facts, material barriers that, just because they *are* material, and not ideal, shall be the irresistible foes of his longing heart. "In wish," he says, "I am with my dear ones, but alas, wishes cannot cross oceans! Oceans are material facts, in the cold outer world. Would that the world of the heart were all!" But alas! to the rejected lover the world of the heart *is* all, and that is just his woe. Were the barrier between him and his beloved only made of those stubborn material facts, only of walls or of oceans, how lightly might his will erelong transcend them all! Matter stubborn! Outer nature cruelly the foe of ideas! Nay, it is just an idea that now opposes him,—just an idea, and that, too, in the mind of the maiden he loves. But in vain does he call this stubborn bit of disdain a merely ideal fact. No flint was ever more definite in preserving its identity and its edge than this disdain may be. Place me for a moment, then, in an external world that shall consist wholly of ideas,—the ideas, namely, of other people about me, a world of maidens who shall scorn me, of old friends who shall have learned to hate me, of angels who shall condemn me, of God who shall judge me. In what piercing north winds, amidst what fields of ice, in the labyrinths of what tangled forests, in the depths of what thick-walled dungeons, on the edges of what tremendous precipices, should I be more genuinely in the presence of stubborn and unyielding facts than in that conceived world of ideas! So, as one sees, I by no means deprive my world of stubborn reality, if I merely call it a world of ideas. On the contrary, as every teacher knows, the ideas of the people are often the most difficult of facts to influence. We were wrong, then, when we said that whilst matter was stubborn, ideas could be moulded at pleasure. Ideas are often the most implacable of facts. Even my own ideas, the facts of my own inner life, may cruelly decline to be plastic to my wish. . . .

No, here are barriers worse than any material chains. The world of ideas has its own horrible dungeons and chasms. Let those who have refuted Bishop Berkeley's idealism by the wonder why he did not walk over every precipice or into every fire if these things existed only in his idea, let such, I say, first try some of the fires and the precipices of the inner life, ere they decide that dangers cease to be dangers as soon as they are called ideal, or even subjectively ideal in me.

Many sorts of reality, then, may be existent at the heart of any world of facts. But this bright and beautiful sense-world of ours,—what, amongst these many possible sorts of reality, does that embody? . . . Evidently here we shall have no question. So far as the sense-world is beautiful, is majestic, is sublime, this beauty and dignity exist only for the appreciative observer. If they exist beyond him, they exist only for some other mind, or as the thought and embodied purpose of some universal soul of nature. . . . But let us look a little deeper. Surely, if the objects yonder are unideal and outer, odors and tastes and temperatures do not exist in these objects in just the way in which they exist in us. Part of the being of these properties, at least, if not all of it, is ideal and exists for us, or at best is once more the embodiment of the thought or purpose of some world-mind. About tastes you cannot dispute, because they are not only ideal but personal. For the benumbed tongue and palate of diseased bodily conditions, all things are tasteless. As for temperatures, a well-known experiment will show how the same water may seem cold to one hand and warm to the other. But even so, colors and sounds are at least in part ideal. Their causes may have some other sort of reality; but colors themselves are not in the things, since they change with the light that falls on the things, vanish in the dark (whilst the things remained unchanged), and differ for different eyes. And as for sounds, both the pitch and the quality of tones depend for us upon certain interesting peculiarities of our hearing organs, and exist in nature only as voiceless sound-waves trembling through the air. All such sense qualities, then, are ideal. . . .

. . . [T]hat real world (to repeat one of the commonplaces of modern popular science) is in itself, apart from somebody's eyes and tongue and ears and touch, neither colored nor tasteful, neither cool nor warm, neither light nor dark, neither musical nor silent. All these qualities belong to our ideas, being indeed none the less genuine facts for that, but being in so far ideal facts. . . .

But now, at this point, the Berkeleyan idealist goes one step further. The real outside world that is still left unexplained and unanalyzed after its beauty, its warmth, its odors, its tastes, its colors, and its tones, have been relegated to the realm of ideal truths, what do you now *mean* by calling it real? No doubt it *is* known as somehow real, but *what* is this reality *known as* being? . . . What I mean by saying that the things yonder have shape and size and trembling molecules, and that there is air with sound-waves, and ether with light-waves in it,—what I *mean* by all this is that experience forces upon me, directly or indirectly, a vast system of ideas, which may indeed be founded in truth beyond me, which in fact *must* be founded in such truth if my experience has any sense, but which, like my ideas of color and of warmth, are simply expressions of how the world's order must appear to me, and to anybody constituted like me. . . .

Thus, all the reality that *we* attribute to our world, in so far as *we* know and can tell what we mean thereby, becomes ideal. There is, in fact, a certain system of ideas, forced upon us by experience, which we have to use as the guide of our conduct. This system of ideas we can't change by our wish; it is for us as overwhelming a fact as guilt, or as the bearing of our fellows towards us, but we know it only *as* such a system of ideas. And we call it the world of matter. John Stuart Mill very well expressed the puzzle of the whole thing, as we have now reached the statement of this puzzle, when he called matter a mass of "permanent possibilities of experience" for each of us. Mill's definition has its faults, but it is a very fair beginning. You know matter as something that either now gives you this idea or experience, or that would give you some other idea or experience under other circumstances. . . .

. . . The closer I come to the truth about the things, the more ideas I get. Isn't it plain, then, that *if* my world yonder is anything knowable at all, it must be in and for itself essentially a mental world? Are my ideas to *resemble* in any way the world? Is the truth of my thought to consist in its *agreement* with reality? And am I thus capable, as common sense supposes, of *conforming* my ideas to things? Then reflect. What can, after all, so well agree with an idea as another idea? To what can things that go on in my mind conform unless it be to another mind? If the more my mind grows in mental clearness, the nearer it gets to the nature of reality, then surely the reality that my mind thus resembles must be in itself mental.

After all, then, would it deprive the world here about me of reality, nay, would it not rather save and assure the reality and the knowableness of my world of experience, if I said that this world, as it exists outside of my mind, and of any other human minds, exists in and for a standard, an universal mind, whose system of ideas simply constitutes the world? Even if I fail to prove that there is such a mind, do I not at least thus make plausible that, as I said, our world of common sense has no fact in it which we cannot interpret in terms of ideas, so that this world is throughout such stuff as ideas are made of? . . .

Note the point we have reached. *Either,* as you see, your real world yonder is through and through a world of ideas, an outer mind that you are more or less comprehending through your experience, *or else,* in so far as it is real and outer it is unknowable, an inscrutable *x*, an absolute mystery. The dilemma is perfect. There is no third alternative. Either a mind yonder, or else the unknowable; that is your choice. . . . Surely one must choose the former alternative. The real world may be unknown; it can't be essentially unknowable. . . .

. . . For any fair and statable problem admits of an answer. If the world exists yonder, its essence is then already capable of being known by some mind. If capable of being known by a mind, this essence is then already essentially ideal and mental. A mind that knew the real world would, for instance, find it a something possessing qualities. But qualities are ideal existences, just as much as are the particular qualities called odors or tones or colors. A mind knowing the real world would again find in it relations, such as equality and inequality, attraction and repulsion, likeness and unlikeness. But such relations have no meaning except as objects of a mind. In brief, then, the world as known would be found to be a world that had all the while been ideal and mental, even before it became known to the particular mind that we are to conceive as coming into connection with it. . . . The real world must be a mind, or else a group of minds.

But with this result we come in presence of a final problem. All this, you say, depends upon my assurance that there is after all a real and therefore an essentially knowable and rational world yonder. Such a world would have to be in essence a mind, or a world of minds. But after all, how does one ever escape from the prison of the inner life? Am I not in all this merely wandering amidst the realm of my own ideas? . . . My world is thus a world of ideas, but alas! how do I then ever reach those ideas of the minds beyond me?

The answer is a simple, but in one sense a very problematic one. You, in one sense, namely, never *do* or can get beyond your own ideas, nor ought you to wish to do so, because in truth all those other minds that constitute your outer and real world are in essence one with your own self. This whole world of ideas is essentially *one* world, and so it is essentially the world of one self and *That art Thou.* . . .

. . . In order to think *about* a thing, it is *not* enough that I should have an idea in me that merely resembles that thing. This last is a very important observation. I repeat, it is *not* enough that I should merely have an idea in me that resembles the thing whereof I think. I have, for instance, in me the idea of a pain. Another man has a pain just like mine. Say we both have toothache; or have both burned our finger-tips in the same way. Now my idea of pain is just like the pain in him, but I am not on that account necessarily thinking about *his* pain, merely because what I am thinking about, namely my own pain, resembles his pain. No; to think about an object you must not merely have an idea that resembles the object, but you must *mean* to have your idea resemble that object. Stated in other form, to think of an object you must consciously aim at that object, you must pick out that object, you must already in some measure possess that object enough, namely, to identify it as what you mean. But how can you *mean*, how can you *aim at*, how can you *possess*, how can you *pick out*, how can you *identify* what is not already present in essence to your own hidden self? Here is surely a deep question. When you aim at yonder object, be it the mountains in the moon or the day of your death, you really say, "I, as my real self, as my larger self, as my complete consciousness, already in deepest truth possess that object, have it, own it, identify it. And that, and that alone, makes it possible for me in my transient, my individual, my momentary personality, to mean yonder object, to inquire about it, to be partly aware of it and partly ignorant of it." You can't mean what is utterly foreign to you. You mean an object, you assert about it, you talk about it, yes, you doubt or wonder about it, you admit your private and individual ignorance about it, only in so far as your larger self, your deeper personality, your total of normal consciousness already *has* that object. . . .

. . . The relation of my thought to its object has, I insist, this curious character, that *unless* the thought and its object are parts of one larger thought, I can't even be *meaning* that object yonder, can't even be in error about it, can't even doubt its existence. You, for instance, are part of one larger self with me, or else I can't even be meaning to address you as outer beings. You are part of one larger self along with the most mysterious or most remote fact of nature, along with the moon, and all the hosts of heaven, along with all truth and all beauty. Else could you not even intend to speak of such objects beyond you. For whatever you speak of you will find that your world is meant by you as just your world. Talk of the unknowable, and it forthwith becomes your unknowable, your problem, whose solution, unless the problem be a mere nonsense question, your larger self must own and be aware of. The deepest problem of life is, "What is this deeper self?" And the only answer is, *It is the self that knows in unity all truth.* This, I insist, is no hypothesis. It is actually the presupposition of your deepest doubt. And that is why I say: Everything finite is more or less obscure, dark, doubtful. Only the Infinite Self, the problem-solver, the complete thinker, the one who knows what we mean even when we are most confused and ignorant, the one who includes us, who has the world present to himself in unity, before whom all past and future truth, all distant and dark truth is clear in one eternal moment, to whom far and forgot is near, who thinks the whole of nature, and in whom are all things, the Logos, the world-possessor,—only his existence, I say, is perfectly sure. . . .

Flee where we will, then, the net of the larger Self ensnares us. We are lost and imprisoned in the thickets of its tangled labyrinth. The moments are not at all in themselves, for as moments they have no meaning; they exist only in relation to the beyond. The larger Self alone is, and they are by reason of it, organic parts of it. They perish, but it remains; they have truth or error only in its overshadowing presence.

And now, as to the unity of this Self. Can there be many such organic selves, mutually separate unities of moments and of the objects that these moments mean? Nay, were there *many* such, would not their manifoldness be a truth? Their relations, would not these be real? Their distinct places in the world-order, would not these things be objects of possible true or false thoughts? If so, must not there be once more the inclusive real Self for whom these truths were true, these separate selves interrelated, and their variety absorbed in the organism of its rational meaning?

There is, then, at last, but one Self, organically, reflectively, consciously inclusive of all the selves, and so of all truth. . . .

BRAND BLANSHARD / The Heritage of Idealism *

See the biographical note on p. 136.

TWENTIETH-CENTURY philosophy in America begins with idealism. At the turn of the century it was in the ascendant everywhere. Royce and Palmer at Harvard, Bowne at Boston, Ladd and Bakewell at Yale, Butler at Columbia, Ormond and Hibben at Princeton, Fullerton at Pennsylvania, Garman at Amherst, Everett at Brown, Creighton and Thilly at Cornell, Wenley and Lloyd at Michigan, Bascom at Wisconsin, Howison at California—they all spoke the same high language though with somewhat varying accents. . . .

. . . Whatever their technical deficiencies, these idealists were wise men, wiser than many of their successors. Wisdom is of course a large word. What I mean is that they were more than learned men—though apart from science their learning was considerable—and more than clever reasoners—though they knew how to state a case. . . . Philosophy for these idealists was not an avocation or a specialty but a way of life and the breath of life; it was a passionate pursuit of reasonableness in action and feeling as well as in thought. . . .

I have suggested that they stood for moral as well as philosophical idealism. But it is with their philosophy that we are concerned, and we must try at once to see what that philosophy was. For what we want to do is to learn what has happened in American thought in the last fifty years, and the fact is that all its main developments have come as reactions against

* Brand Blanshard, from "The Heritage of Idealism," in *Changing Patterns in American Civilization*, Dixon Wecter, *et al.* (Philadelphia: U. of Pennsylvania Press, 1949), pp. 82, 83–90. Used by permission of the publisher.

the great system that held the field at the turn of the century. We must know what that system was if we are to catch the point or the reason of the passionate protests against it. Very well, what is idealism?

The idealism of the turn of the century was a fusion of two streams of thought. One of these, subjective idealism, took its rise in the ingenious mind of Bishop Berkeley and flowed down through Hume and Mill. The other, objective idealism, is as old as Plato and comes down through the Germany of Hegel, and the England of Green and Bradley, to Josiah Royce in Harvard Yard. The first of these idealisms stands for the thesis, "All that is real is experience." The second stands for the thesis, "All that is real is rational." To see what American absolute idealism meant, we must see the meaning of both these theses.

There are few excitements in philosophy to compare with reading for the first time the argument for subjective idealism and feeling how powerful it is. Take any common thing, say an apple, and let it stand for nature as a whole. The argument of the idealist is an act of intellectual prestidigitation by which he undertakes to make the apple vanish as a physical thing and reappear as a bit of consciousness. The first step is to get you to admit that the apple, as you know it, is a set of sensed qualities. If you were to remove from the apple its redness and roundness, sweetness and hardness, coldness and smoothness, would there be any apple left? No. The perceived apple then is composed of these qualities? Yes. Where do these qualities reside? The idealist answers, "In consciousness," and he offers two main arguments.

First, the causal argument. Assume, as everyone does, that there is a physical apple out there. Clearly enough its existence is only a hypothesis; we never see or feel *it*. What we do see and feel is these sense data, but they apparently arise at the end of a long causal chain. Light rays strike our retinas and start nervous pulses there; these, when they reach our brains, give rise in some mysterious way to sensations of red and green. But these sensations come at the end of the chain, not at the beginning; responsible physicists would not hold that the red and green we see are out there in the source from which the light rays come; they are effects that arise in us. They have their independent causes, but to say this is already to admit the case, for then it becomes perfectly clear that you cannot identify the inner or conscious effect, the sensation of red for example, with the outward cause, which is separated from this effect by at least several feet in space and perhaps half a second in time. If this is true of the color, it is true equally of the other qualities. But if true of these, it is true of the apple as you know it, for you have admitted that it consists of these. And in that case what you have done is to shift this apple into consciousness. Indeed you have done a great deal more. You have done what Archimedes wanted to do; you have put a lever under experienced nature as a whole and heaved it across the boundary into mind. Rocks and rivers, clouds and mountains, the whole "choir of heaven and furniture of earth" as Berkeley called them, are seen to be "such stuff as dreams are made on." They arise and flourish and die within the realm of conscious experience.

The second argument for subjective idealism is as follows: Assume that qualities as we know them do really belong to physical things, and you end by contradicting yourself. The classic illustration is Locke's. You believe, do you, that the qualities given in sense really belong to the physical thing? Good; then, for example, the hots and colds you feel belong to the physical thing. But consider what follows. One of your hands has been resting on a hot-water bottle and the other on a block of ice; you plunge them both into a basin of water; the water feels cold to one hand and hot to the other. On your assumption, the water is both hot and cold, and that does not make sense. The idealist says that the most plausible way out is to admit that the hot and cold are not in the physical thing at all, but in our experience, for while it is incredible that the water is in any straightforward sense both hot and cold, there is no trouble at all in saying that at one time we can sense both hot and cold. And what is true of hots and colds is true of shapes and sizes. To say that all the shapes we see as we walk round a table, all the sizes that we see as our friend walks away from us down the street, belong out there in the thing is impossible in the ordinary sense of "belonging"; to hold that they are all appearances in our consciousness is a perfectly plausible belief. That is what the idealist did say. What did he take these arguments to show? Not, if he was self-critical, that there was nothing in nature but consciousness; they clearly do not prove that there is nothing "out there" at all to *cause* these appearances in our minds. Jeans and Eddington thought that the protons and electrons were mental also. Whether they were right or not it is immensely difficult to say. But as for the rocks and rivers, the hills and clouds, the frame of nature generally *as we directly know it*, the case of subjective idealism seems to me to have a higher plausibility than any alternative realism that has yet been offered.

Now what is *absolute* idealism? It is a philosophy, as we have said, whose principle is that the real is the rational. How does it reach that belief? It does so through two steps, one of self-inspection and one of faith. Josiah Royce looked into his mind as he was philosophizing and asked himself what he was trying to do. The answer seemed clear enough; he was trying to understand the world. But what do you mean by understanding? You mean explaining to yourself. Yes, but when is a thing explained? It is explained, Royce answered, when you see not only *that* it is, but *why* it is, when you see that, given the conditions, it had to be what it is. When is the Pythagorean theorem explained? It is explained when you see that, given the postulates of Euclid, it follows with such necessity that if it were denied, the postulates and indeed the whole system would have to go with it. This, said Royce, is what you do when you try to understand anything; you place it in a system, and when you see that within that system it has to be what it is, you are satisfied. Now that, he said, is what philosophy tries to do for our whole world of common experience; it tries to find the system to which things belong and within which they are necessary and therefore intelligible. I have a philosopher-friend with a small daughter. She fell into discussion one day with a neighbor's boy about the relative merits of their fathers. "What does your father do?" said the boy, with a hoity-toity air. She had never thought about this, but after a moment's reflection she came up with, "His business is words." "What words?" said the boy scornfully. "He says Why?" was her reply. That is philosophy in three letters. Philosophy, as James said, is a peculiarly stubborn effort to think clearly; it is an insistent raising of the question why; and nothing short of a single intelligible system will set that question finally at rest. To see that is the first step in absolute idealism.

The second step is an act of faith. Suppose that by superhuman exertion and ability you did arrive at a system in which everything was apparently included and seen to be necessary; your intellectual ideal would be realized. But what surety have you that when you have reached what satisfies your own mind, you have also reached what is outwardly true? Is it not possible, as Kant believed, that we are all little metaphysical spiders, spinning webs which are much alike but bear no resemblance to the outward nature of things? Here is where faith comes in. The idealist does not, if he knows his business, try to juggle from his own hat a proof that the world is rational. What he says is more modest and more plausible. He says that philosophy is the attempt to understand the world—that is, to render it intelligible—that, unless the world really is so, the attempt must be defeated, and that it would be silly to accept defeat before it comes. The rationality of the world is not for him a proved conclusion but rather a postulate on which his enterprise proceeds and on whose truth its success depends.

This, then, is idealism. It holds that the world of colors, shapes, and sounds that each of us lives in is really the world of his own mind. But our minds are islands, "finite centers" as Bradley called them, in a larger world, and since the idealist believes this larger world to be rational through and through, he is inclined to think it too is mental or spiritual. For him the prime business of life is to escape his fragmentariness, to bring his own little spirit into closer approximation to the world spirit both in extent and in inward order. Like Marcus Aurelius, St. Paul, and Spinoza, his rationalism has usually run out into mysticism; and he has conceived the best hope for himself as lying in self-surrender to the reason that animates the nature of things. Only through becoming the servant of that reason could he become in the best sense free.

For Further Study

Brightman, Edgar Sheffield. *An Introduction to Philosophy*. Revised by Robert N. Beck. 3rd ed.; New York: Holt, Rinehart and Winston, 1963, Ch. 11, "What Are the Merits and Defects of Idealisms?" Ch. 12, "What Is Personal Idealism (Personalism)?"

Hocking, William Ernest. *Types of Philosophy*. With the collaboration of Richard Boyle O'Reilly Hocking. 3rd ed.; New York: Scribner's, 1959, Type 5, "Idealism."

Radhakrishnan, S. *An Idealist View of Life*. 2nd ed.; London: Allen and Unwin, 1937, pp. 13–51, 262–345.

Randall, John Herman, Jr. "Josiah Royce and American Idealism," *Journal of Philosophy*, 63 (February 3, 1966): 57–83.

Robinson, Daniel S. *Royce and Hocking, American Idealists*. Boston: Christopher Publishing House, 1968.

Royce, Josiah. *Lectures on Modern Idealism*. New Haven: Yale U. Press, 1919, Lecture 10, "Later Problems of Idealism and Its Present Position."

Shimer, William Allison. *Conscious Clay*. New York: Scribner's, 1948, Chs. 1–5.

Steinkraus, Warren E. "Is Berkeley a Subjective Idealist?" *Personalist*, 48 (Winter, 1967): 103–117.

14 Realism and Its Implications

DURANT DRAKE / The Grounds of Realism *

Durant Drake (1878–1933) was professor of philosophy and education at Vassar College 1915–1933. He was the author of various books
including *Problems of Conduct, Essays in Critical Realism* (with
others), *Mind and Its Place in Nature*, and *The New Morality*.

EVERYONE, except a few philosophers and their disciples, believes in the
realistic world; the belief is implied in all our science and all our ordinary
discourse. There is considerable variation of opinion among reflective
thinkers as to the fundamental stuff of which things consist, but there is an
almost complete agreement that the physical world is made up of electrons
and protons (whatever they may be) combining in complicated structures
to form atoms, chemical compounds, biological organisms, and astronomical bodies. Causal interactions are going on in this intricately patterned world, quite independently of our experience; indeed, to a great
extent, these processes are not yet known by any human observer, or even
imagined. External as these physical things are to our bodies, and to our
minds, we can, somehow, know a good deal *about* them. And other people
can know about them; they are objects of common, public knowledge. We
can also know a good deal about one another's *minds*. And we can see that
these things which physics studies are *different* from minds, that minds

* Durant Drake, from "The Grounds of Realism," in *Invitation to Philosophy*
(Boston: Houghton Mifflin, 1933), pp. 152–160. Used by permission of the publisher.

(i.e., such minds as we quite definitely discover about us) are immersed, so to speak, in a great sea of what is quite different from mind. Such is the world of common sense, the familiar world of mind *and* matter.

The subjectivist is right, however, in protesting that we have no *guaranty* of the existence of this world. It is conceivable that our supposed knowledge of it is illusion and our experience but a coherent dream. As cautious thinkers we must beware of trusting common sense; we must see whether we can *justify* our instinctive realism—just as we have insisted that the idealist justify his idealism. Belief in *any* sort of universe, belief, for that matter, in anything whatever beyond the passing data of experience, is, in the nature of the case, *hypothesis*, and not unquestionable *datum*.

Well, how do we set out to justify any hypothesis? If we use the empirical method, we accept an hypothesis when it seems to cover the facts of experience more adequately than any other hypothesis that we can frame. And our belief in realism rests, in the end, upon our discovery that it fits, it explains, the peculiarities of experience better than any form of idealism. In fact, there is no scientific hypothesis which serves to tie together and explain so many otherwise inexplicable facts as this hypothesis of realism. The following paragraphs will summarize the most notable peculiarities of our experience which serve in this way as the *evidence* for realism—in the same sense as that in which the sense-data accumulated by the astronomer are evidence for the truth of the Copernican hypothesis, which covers and explains them.

1. THE DIFFERENCE BETWEEN PERCEPTUAL AND
NON-PERCEPTUAL EXPERIENCE

Within our experience itself there is an observable difference between our sensa and the images which appear to us in our dreaming, thinking, imagining. There is, indeed, a borderland where it is difficult to distinguish the two types of data, but in general they are clearly distinguishable. Sensa are relatively vivid, clear, steady, coherent, whereas these other images are, by contrast, faint, blurred, flickering. If realism is true, this difference is easily intelligible. Sensa are produced in our experience by causal processes coming from the outer world, they are sharply defined by the definite nature of the messages that reach us from without, and are as stable as those processes—which, in turn, reflect the stability of the outer objects which initiate them. Our non-perceptual experience is engendered from within the organism, lacks the shock-effect of the experience provoked from without, and lacks its steadiness, since it is not subject to this outer control. This suggests, with force, that physical things are not mere "potentialities of perception," but are *realities*, of a very definite nature, capable of affecting our experience in definite ways, pretty clearly distinguishable from the ways in which our non-perceptual experience develops.

2. THE MECHANISM OF PERCEPTION

Sensa are obtained in a different way from that in which non-perceptual experience is obtained. The latter can be had with eyes shut and all the other sense-organs slumbering. To get sensa we have to have sense-organs functioning, and a whole series of events proceeding from the outer object to the brain. If any link in this chain of events is broken, the perceptual experience will not be had. Now it is conceivable that our experience of this complicated series of events is merely one kind of *experience,* not actually revealing a series of real events *preceding* the appearance of our sensa. But if so, the question insistently arises, Why do we find, so regularly, this particular series of experiences obtainable, whenever we have sensa of each particular sort? The whole business *looks* as if these experiences (our knowledge of light-waves, eye-events, and optical-nerve-events, for example) reveal to us a real series of events going on outside our minds and necessarily preceding the appearance in our field of consciousness of each definite sort of sensum. If there *are* no physical things, if there are only minds, why this constant illusion of a complicated inter-mental medium? If there is, in reality, only One Mind, why should one part of it affect another part in this roundabout way, instead of in the way one part of my mind affects another part, without the complicated mechanism of sense-perception? Is not realism the most sensible hypothesis to cover these facts?

3. THE CONTINUITY OF THE PHYSICAL ORDER

Our sense-experience is very fragmentary. But the pieces strongly suggest a continuous, coherent set of processes back of them, giving them their precise nature. For example, I start a fire on the hearth and then leave the room. Ten minutes later I return and find the wood partly consumed. An hour later I return and find nothing but hot ashes. It *looks* as if a continuous process was going on during that hour of which my sensa reveal definite phases, whenever I put myself in a position to receive effects from it. I can construct in my imagination such a series of physical events, external to me, the events making up the fire itself. My sensa invariably report the stage due at each moment of that series of events. When I enter the room they jump into my conscious field, unrelated to anything antecedently there; they apparently obey, not laws of my mind, primarily, but the laws of that external series of events which I have imagined. That external order is a changing order. Relatively few of its changes are reflected in my direct experience, but they serve nevertheless as controls of the experience which I actually have. After dreamless sleep, my experience picks up the pattern, so to speak—the pattern of processes which apparently have been going on while I slept. Are not these facts *explicanda?* And what explanation of them can we give half as plausible as the explanation that the processes we have imagined really *are* going on in the world about us, even when we are not aware of them?

4. THE CONVERGING TESTIMONY OF DIFFERING SENSES

Physical objects are usually perceived by several senses. I can see my table, I can feel of it, push against it, lift it, hear the sound I make when I hit it. In subjectivistic language, I have groups of very different sorts of sensa, which, in spite of their differences, fit together to form my concept of this table. Why should our experience be thus analyzable into groups of sensa which combine to form the picture of a physical *thing?* Various other people have somewhat similar groups of sensa, which seem, as we describe and utilize them, to reveal this same table. What meaning can these facts have, if not that there *is* a single physical table, which affects several of my senses, thus producing several differing groups of sensa, and similarly affects other people's senses, producing in their experience more or less similar groups of sensa?

5. THE TIME-GAP WHEN MIND AFFECTS MIND

When I speak to you, *my* experience-of-speaking occurs at a certain time. Then an interval of time elapses. Then you hear my voice. The time-gap varies exactly with our distance apart. Now, if only minds exist, why should there be this interval between the event-in-me, the cause, and the event-in-you, the effect? What happens during that interval? And what is the real meaning of what we call distance? If Space is only a form of experience, something *within* minds, not something existing *between* minds, and separating them, why should it take longer for my mind to influence yours when we are, as we commonly say, farther apart than when we are nearer? If the reality is One Mind, and nothing else, the matter becomes, if possible, still stranger. Why should one part of the Divine Mind require half a second to influence another part, and two seconds to influence another part? And what happens during the interval, when neither part is conscious of speaking or hearing, when apparently *no* (relevant) conscious experience is taking place? Surely it *looks* as if distance were real, and a real series of events were taking place *between* the two minds, requiring time to occur, in proportion to the distance.

6. THE DEPENDENCE OF MINDS UPON MATTER

Our ideational-volitional life—our thinking, dreaming, planning, willing—is, to some degree, self-contained. Our ideas follow one another along the lines of traceable associations; they are, in part, modifiable at will, and depend upon the state of our mind at a given time. But with sensa it is quite different. We are *confronted* by them. They appear suddenly in our field of experience, often quite unrelated to anything antecedently there. We cannot banish them by effort of will. They evidently obey other laws than those of our minds. And we are at their mercy. A cold wind blows on me (i.e., I have sensa thus described in realistic language), and I suffer, perhaps become ill. The sensa implied by saying that a bullet has hit me are followed, perhaps, by the complete and permanent cessation of my consciousness. Is it not clear that we are in the grip of a world of realities vastly greater than ourselves? To see a man freezing to death, or dying of a bullet wound, is, inevitably, to be a realist, at least *pro tem.*

These extreme experiences—which come to us all, in some form sooner or later—make us realize that even our ideational and volitional experience is at the mercy of this environing world. A bottle of whiskey alters the whole tone of my mental life, a whiff of chloroform brings it to an abrupt end for the time being, a clotting of blood may drive me insane. Specifically, . . . our whole mental life is dependent, point by point, upon the functioning of our *brains*. But if our brains are but a name for a certain group of potentialities of experience, or even if they are a certain specific group of images in a Universal Mind, it seems curious that our whole mental life should be dependent upon them.

7. THE FACTS OF COSMIC HISTORY

It is generally agreed that the universe existed for long ages before any minds appeared on this earth, or, so far as we know, anywhere. The events of this cosmic history are known by astronomers and geologists, in considerable detail. But what *meaning* is there in this long story, on idealistic premises, if there were no experiencers present to experience these events? It will be said that we have here the story of the unfolding of the Divine Experience. And this is conceivable. But when one reads the story in detail—the evolution of stars from nebulæ (a monotonous process consuming trillions of years), the (apparently accidental) formation of our solar system, the laborious laying-down of rocks, the slow development of chemical compounds, the seething of currents of wind and water, the breeding of endless varieties of microbes, worms, reptiles, and all the strange profusion of vegetable and animal life, one creature warring upon and devouring another creature, with volcanic eruptions, floods, droughts wiping out countless millions at a sweep—the story surely sounds far more like a realistic story of separate *things* and organisms, than like the unfolding of the story of a Divine consciousness.

It is quite evident that our fragmentary and evanescent data of experience can never be *understood* except as an *enclave* within a far greater, independent reality, which we call Nature; and that this Nature is, in detail, just what the sciences report it to be. Our experience is not only fragmentary, it is, by itself, a jumble, a chaos. Only by constructing, with infinite patience, this picture of a vast environing Nature, can we replace this chaos with order, predict future experiences, and learn, in increasing measure, to control them. The belief in a Universal Mind inspires and consoles some people; but it does not help us to predict and control experience. Thus realism is, at least, pragmatically justified.

And what more *could* we have in the way of proof? As we saw in studying the empirical method, there is no such thing as guaranteed proof, of the Q.E.D. sort, except in the purely hypothetical realms of logic and mathematics. An independently existing physical world is proved to exist in the same sense, and with as great certainty, as *anything* can be proved to exist. The idealist accepts as proved the facts of human history. But these facts, and indeed the facts of the idealist's own earlier life, can be proved to be actual facts by no other method, and with no greater certainty, than the facts of the life of the physical world.

C. H. WHITELEY / Physical Objects *

C. H. Whiteley (1911–   ) is Reader in philosophy at the University of Birmingham, England. He is the author of *Introduction to Metaphysics* and articles in *Mind, Philosophy, Analysis,* and other journals.

THE PROBLEM I shall discuss is What reason have we for believing that there are physical objects? My purpose is not either to raise or to dispel doubts as to the existence of physical objects; this doubt constitutes a medical rather than a philosophical problem. The point of asking the question is that, while there can be no reasonable difference of opinion as to whether there are physical objects, there can be and is reasonable difference of opinion as to how the notion of a physical object is to be analysed; and if we are clear as to what grounds there are for believing in physical objects, we shall also be clearer as to what sort of physical objects we have grounds for believing in. Also, it is worth while to inquire which other beliefs are logically connected with, and which are logically independent of, the belief in physical objects.

I make one important assumption at the outset: namely, that by a physical object or process we mean something that exists or occurs apart from and independently of our perceptions, and of our experiences of other kinds. The distinction between the physical or "real" world and the "subjective" or "imaginary"—illusions, hallucinations, after-images, shadows, rainbows, mental pictures, what we merely suppose, imagine or expect —is a distinction between things and events which exist or occur whether anybody is aware of them or not, and things and events which have their being only as and when somebody is aware of them. A belief in physical objects is a belief in things which are sometimes at least unobserved by the believer.

It is obvious that the existence of such things is not a question to be settled by sense-perception alone. That there is a material world cannot be established or even made plausible merely by looking, listening, touching; it is not *given* in the way in which the existence of something red and something round, of sounds, smells, aches, feelings of sadness, can be given. I do not mean that the something red or round cannot be a physical

* C. H. Whiteley, "Physical Objects," *Philosophy,* 34 (1959), 142–149. Used by permission of the author and the publisher.

object; I mean that it cannot be known to be a physical object just by looking at it or otherwise perceiving it. For I cannot, simply by perceiving something, tell whether that something continues to exist when I cease to perceive it. This logical necessity is not evaded by naïve realism which holds that the something red or round which appears to sight is (usually at least) identical with a physical object; for though this may be so, we cannot know it just by looking. Nor is it evaded by phenomenalism; for no phenomenalist does or plausibly could analyse statements about physical objects into statements asserting the *actual* occurrence of sense-data; he must add statements about what sense-data *would* be sensed if certain conditions were fulfilled; and this fact is not given by sense-perception, but reasons for it are required. That there are physical objects is not something we observe or perceive, but something we suppose or assume (to call it a "hypothesis" or "postulate" is to suggest something rather too deliberate and self-conscious). In old-fashioned language, it is a transcendent belief; it goes beyond the evidence.

Thus there is no logical absurdity in denying or refusing to admit the existence of a material world. To say that there are no physical objects, while doubtless very foolish, does not involve a man in any logical contradiction, nor does it force him to shut his eyes to any patent and indisputable facts. An intellectually indolent percipient, whose few wants were supplied independently of his own efforts, might well abstain from supposing that there was a physical world. There is some evidence that young babies, who are more or less in this situation, do not believe that there are any material things—do not believe, for instance, that the rattle just dropped from the hand and the visitor just departed from the room are now anywhere at all.

If somebody did behave like this, in what way would he be worse off, and what other beliefs would he be debarred from entertaining? I answer —and this is my principal point—that he would be unable to make valid generalizations, or reliable forecasts of his future experience. He would have to do without the belief in an order in nature, in regular sequences of events, in causal laws. For if I confine myself to what I myself observe or am aware of, I can make no valid generalizations concerning the concomitance or sequence of types of phenomena. I find only that phenomena of one type are quite often accompanied or followed by phenomena of another type, but sometimes not. There is no type of sense-datum A of which it is true that whenever it occurs another type of sense-datum B accompanies or follows or precedes it. And this is the case however complex you make your A and your B. This point has often been overlooked. People know quite well that lightning is always accompanied by thunder, barking by the presence of dogs, that green apples are always sour, and the ground always gets dark and sticky after a heavy fall of rain; and they talk about these as though they were *phenomenal* regularities—as though the seeing of lightning always went along with the hearing of thunder, and so forth. But this is of course not the case. If, as some people have said, it was the business of science to disclose the order or regularity in phenomena, meaning by phenomena what we see and hear and feel, science would be a very unrewarding pursuit. For phenomena are disorderly and irregular, and scientists cannot make them out any different.

Many philosophers have indeed thought that natural regularities could be conceived without the postulation of actual unobserved things and events, if instead we postulate that certain phenomena would occur or would have occurred, given certain unfulfilled conditions. Instead of saying that whenever I hear barking there exists an actual dog, perceived or unperceived, I am to say that whenever I hear barking, I should perceive a dog if certain conditions were fulfilled—if my eyes were open and my sight normal, if there was an adequate amount of light, if I looked in the right direction and there was no opaque obstacle in my line of vision, etc. Such an interpretation in terms of possible phenomena would relieve us of any need to postulate another order of physical events over and above perceptual events, and would in this way be more economical. There are, however, three ways in which phenomenal generalizations of this kind cannot take the place of physical generalizations.

(1) A physical generalization associates one uniform property with another uniform property: I mean that when something is asserted to be universally true of dogs, or pieces of iron, or cases of pneumonia, or falling bodies of a weight of ten pounds, it is assumed that there is some physical property or group of properties which is common to all dogs, pieces of iron, etc. Phenomenal generalizations, however, concern associations between sets of diverse phenomena. If we wish to correlate the auditory phenomenon of barking with visual phenomena we must specify a set of canine sense-data, or views of dogs, which are not all alike in any sensory property, but form one class only in virtue of a very complex set of relations.

(2) A physical generalization applies to *all* cases of a given type, and the study of nature aims at reducing to laws all events and all features of events. But phenomenal generalizations can never apply to all cases of a given type, but only to some of them, namely to those cases in which the supplementary conditions for observation are fulfilled. The physical generalization "There's no smoke without fire" applies to all instances of smoke, whether or not either the smoke or the fire is observed. But the corresponding phenomenal generalization brings under a uniformity-rule only those cases in which both the smoke and the fire are observed. Observed smoke can be correlated with observed fire; but when I observe the smoke but not the fire, the observed smoke is correlated with nothing, and is an instance of no natural law (except in the forced and trivial sense in which a white

cat with brown eyes and quick hearing is an instance of the law that all white cats with blue eyes are deaf); it forms no part of the order of nature.

(3) A phenomenal generalization must always include a reference to conditions of observation, whereas physical generalizations are independent of these. We can say without qualification "Whenever it thunders, it lightens." But we can say "Whenever thunder is heard, lightning is seen" only if we add "provided that there is an observer with adequate eyesight, facing in the appropriate direction, having his eyes open and his view not obscured by any opaque object, etc." This difference does not merely prevent the phenomenal generalization from adequately replacing the physical one. It also means that there can be no generalizations on the phenomenal level which are universally valid. For it is impossible to give in purely phenomenal terms an adequate statement of all the conditions required for perceiving lightning besides the occurrence of lightning. It is curious that the analysis of physical-object statements in terms of sense-data and the analysis of causation in terms of regular sequence should have been so often advocated by the same philosophers. For if we restrict our attention to phenomena, we can find no instances for the regular-sequence concept of cause to apply to.

If, therefore, I am to make reliable generalizations about the course of events, and reliable forecasts about my future experiences, I must suppose that there are unperceived as well as perceived events. Thus the connection between the category of substance and that of cause is, as Kant suggested, not fortuitous but necessary. We do not discover that there are (perfect) regularities in nature, that is, in the physical world, as we discover that there are (imperfect) regularities amongst phenomena. On the contrary, the regularity is essential to the concept of nature; the assumption that the physical world is orderly is inseparable from the assumption that the physical world exists. It is only to the extent that I assume it to be orderly that I have any grounds for believing that there is a physical world at all. This may help to account for our strong inclination to regard physical determinism as a necessary a priori truth.

What, then, is the sort of supposition which will make it possible to believe in regular sequences and concomitances in the world, and to regulate our expectations accordingly? A simple and comprehensive answer cannot be given to this question. The precise character of the suppositions we make about physical objects and processes is subject to variation for different kinds of case, and to modification with the improvement of our knowledge. One can, however, indicate the general line which must be followed.

There are, amongst the events which we are aware of, certain associations of characteristics which, while not invariable, are very common: for example, the association between the sound of barking and the sight of dogs, between this visual appearance of oranges and their characteristic flavour, between the brightness of sunshine and felt warmth, between the kinaesthetic sensations of speech and the sound of my own voice, between the visible immersion of a lump of sugar in a cup of tea and its gradual disappearance, between the various members of the visible sequence black-coal . . . flame . . . red-coal . . . ashes, between the patter of raindrops, the sight of rain falling, the feeling of dampness on exposed parts of the body, and the darkening of the soil or pavement. (These are, of course, examples of several different kinds of association.)

The supposition required has two parts: (1) That to these imperfect phenomenal regularities there corresponds in each case a perfect physical regularity, that is, in each case in which there is a frequent association between phenomenal characteristics there are some corresponding physical characteristics which are invariably associated. Whereas the sound of bark-ing is often but not always accompanied by the sight of a dog, there is some type of event, physical barking, which is always accompanied by the presence of some one type of physical object, a dog. Whereas the visual brightness of sunshine is only sometimes accompanied by a feeling of warmth, there is a physical entity, sunlight, and a physical entity, heat, which always goes with it. Whereas a person may be seen setting off from A and arriving at B without being seen at intermediate places at interme-diate times, physical passage from A to B involves the temporally contin-uous traversing of a spatially continuous path. In general, whenever there is an imperfect but frequent association between a phenomenal characteristic A and a phenomenal characteristic B, there is a thing or process having a characteristic corresponding to A which is invariably associated with a thing or process having a characteristic corresponding to B. Thus whenever I hear barking, there exists a physical dog, whether or not there also occurs the experience of my seeing him.

(2) The existence of the corresponding physical thing, or the occur-rence of the corresponding physical process, is a necessary but not a suffi-cient condition for the awareness of the phenomenal characteristic. There can be no hearing of barks without there being (physical) barks; but there can be barks without the hearing of barks. The further conditions, other than the existence of the dog or the occurrence of the bark, which are required if I am to have the corresponding perception of the dog or the bark, may be called the observation-conditions. Some of these conditions are pretty easy to discover. For instance, if I am to see anything at all, there must be a certain amount of light (but not enough to dazzle), and my vision must not be blocked by any obstacle. Other observation-conditions can only be discovered by much experimental research: for instance, the need for air or some other transmitting medium in the case of hearing, the

need for integrity of the optic nerves in the case of sight. The occurrence of the appropriate sense experience is determined jointly by the corresponding physical process and the relevant observation-conditions. (These conditions, of course, concern the properties of other physical things and processes, so that we cannot say just what they are without knowing something about physical things other than the one to be perceived. Learning about the properties of dogs, and learning about the properties of light and the human sense-organs, go hand in hand.) Thus the assumption of a physical world involves two supposed sets of regularities: an association between one physical characteristic and another, and an association between physical processes together with observation-conditions on the one hand and sense-experiences on the other.

So far, the physical world has been presented as a set of processes which occur independently of perceptions, which are related by laws of sequence and concomitance to other processes, and which together with the relevant observation-conditions determine specific sense-experiences of ours. These are purely relational properties; and nothing has been said so far about any other properties that physical objects may possess. On the view here advocated, namely that the justification of a belief in a physical world is that it makes possible the formulation of laws of nature, the only positive reason for attributing a property to physical objects would be that by assuming physical objects to possess this property we can account for the character of our perceptions, and explain how we come to perceive this rather than that, now rather than then. One way of accounting for the character of our perceptions would be to suppose that the sensory qualities which are present in them (the particular colours, sounds, tastes, etc.) are properties of physical objects, and persist unperceived just as they appear when perceived. This is naïve realism. A completely naïve-realist theory would hold that all sensory qualities are properties of physical objects, and exist independently of perception; other theories are naïvely realistic to the extent that they identify the properties of physical things with those properties which are present in sense-experience.

Now the investigation of the properties of physical things is the business of the science of physics. And contemporary physics is not naïvely realistic in any degree. The properties which it attributes to physical objects are not sensory properties, but hypothetical properties defined by their relations to one another and to certain kinds of perceptions. The reason for this is often misunderstood. Philosophical criticism of naïve realism is apt to concentrate on the "argument from illusion," that is, on the *deceptiveness* of sense-perception. This is the wrong sort of criticism. Our perceptions can sometimes mislead us (that is, lead us to form false expectations about other perceptions to come) only because they also, and more often, lead us to form true expectations; perception could not be systematically misleading. But the question whether our perceptions induce in us true or false expectations is quite independent of the question whether they show us the permanent characteristics of material things. The damaging criticisms of naïve realism rest on this principle: given that the physical object corresponding to a given sense-datum is something which, in conjunction with the relevant observation-conditions, determines the characteristics of that sense-datum, then if a given characteristic can be shown to be determined by the observation-conditions, there can be no reason for attributing it to the corresponding physical object. The successive modifications in our concept of the physical world arise from our increasing knowledge of the dependence of sensory properties upon observation-conditions. The challenge to naïve realism with respect to colours comes from optics. The challenge to naïve realism with respect to space and time comes from relativity-theory. The challenge to naïve realism with respect to beauty and ugliness comes from our understanding of the dependence of aesthetic delight and disgust upon the dispositions and past experiences of the subject.

In abandoning naïve realism, scientific theory only carries further a process which pre-scientific common sense has already begun. The common-sense view of the physical world is by no means a purely naïve-realist view. When I look at an object from different angles and in different lights successively, the sensory properties which appear to me are many and various. Common sense does not hold that all these various sensory properties belong to the physical object and exist apart from my perception. Were that so, there would have to be either a multitude of physical objects or a constantly changing object to possess all these different properties. Common sense holds, on the contrary, that there is but one object with one shape, size, colour, etc., which is unchanging throughout my changing perceptions. This postulation of a single set of physical properties corresponding to a multiplicity of sensory properties is the first and fundamental step away from naïve realism. A Berkeleian analysis, which reverses this step, is a greater affront to common sense and provokes more resistance from it than a Lockean analysis which takes a step or two further in the same direction.

It is a belief of common sense that at least some sensory properties are *not* properties of physical objects, but are due to conditions of observation (quantity and quality of light, distance, defects of vision, etc.). As to whether *any* sensory properties are also physical properties, I am not convinced that common sense has any clear and consistent view. Of course we say that grass is green and roses are red. But does this mean more than that if we look at them under suitable conditions green and red are the colour we shall see? It is not clear to me that common sense is committed to the belief that objects have any colours when unperceived. (Examining the way we talk about the matter is of no help. Given that a certain piece of cloth looks bluish in artificial light and greyish in daylight, are we to presume that its colour changes with changes in the light, and say "It *is* blue in artificial light and grey in daylight," or are we to presume that it has a colour independently of the light, and say "It is really grey, but it looks blue in artificial light?" Ordinary idiom allows us to say either of these things indifferently.) By contrast, there are some properties which common sense does attribute to physical objects apart from perception— size and weight, for instance. When I conclude that this brick must have made that hole in the window, though nobody saw it do so, I credit the brick with having a size and weight at a time when it was not being perceived. But size and weight are not sensory properties. Blueness is a way things look; but heaviness is not a way things look or feel. A thing can, of course, look or feel heavy; but its *being* heavy is something different—it is heavy if it will hold down or make dents in other objects, if you can't lift it with one hand, and so on; and these causal characteristics are no ways of looking or feeling. Properties like size and weight, which common sense does attribute to unperceived objects, bear the same sort of relation to sense-experience as the concepts of modern physics. Thus it seems to me that one can abandon naïve realism in all its forms without abandoning any belief to which common sense is committed.

To sum up. That there are physical objects is a supposition, not a datum. The use of the supposition is to account for the regularities in sensory phenomena, to enable the course of events to be set in a framework of regular sequences and concomitances. It is confirmed by the success we achieve in ordering our experiences by its aid, in making our generalizations continually more extensive and more exact. Being a supposition, and not an inevitable and invariable category of thought, it is subject to modification as we learn more about the conditions under which perception takes place. Scientific concepts are related to sense-experience in a remoter and more complex fashion than common-sense concepts of physical objects. But they are not of an entirely different order. The common-sense concept of "table" is not, like "blue" or "bang" or "stench," a merely phenomenal concept; it is explanatory and theoretical.

For Further Study

Alexander, Samuel. "The Basis of Realism," in *Realism and the Background of Phenomenology*, ed. Roderick M. Chisholm. Glencoe: Free Press, 1961, Ch. 9.

Chisholm, Roderick. "The Theory of Appearing," in *Philosophical Analysis: A Collection of Essays*, ed. Max Black. Englewood Cliffs: Prentice-Hall, 1950.

Lovejoy, A. O. *The Revolt Against Dualism*. LaSalle: Open Court, 1930, Ch. 8, "Dualism and the Physical World."

Monist, The: 51 (April, 1967): 159–304. (A special issue on "British and American Realism, 1900–1930" with articles by Max Fisch, Preston Warren, and others.)

Montague, William Pepperell. "The Story of American Realism," *Philosophy*, 12 (April, 1937): 140–161. (Reprinted in Montague. *The Ways of Things*. New York: Prentice-Hall, 1940.)

Moore, G. E. "The Refutation of Idealism," *Mind*, 12 (1903): 433–453. (Reprinted in Moore. *Philosophical Studies*. London: Routledge & Kegan Paul, 1948.)

Oliver, W. Donald. "Realism: Reborn or Renovated," *Journal of Philosophy*, 53 (July 19, 1956): 457–469. (A critical review of *The Return to Reason*, ed. John Wild.)

Wild, John, ed. *The Return to Reason*. Chicago: Regnery, 1953.

15 Pragmatism and Its Implications

WILLIAM JAMES / What Pragmatism Means *

See the biographical note on p. 47.

SOME YEARS AGO, being with a camping party in the mountains, I returned from a solitary ramble to find every one engaged in a ferocious metaphysical dispute. The *corpus* of the dispute was a squirrel—a live squirrel supposed to be clinging to one side of a tree-trunk; while over against the tree's opposite side a human being was imagined to stand. This human witness tries to get sight of the squirrel by moving rapidly round the tree, but no matter how fast he goes, the squirrel moves as fast in the opposite direction, and always keeps the tree between himself and the man, so that never a glimpse of him is caught. The resultant metaphysical problem now is this: *Does the man go round the squirrel or not?* He goes round the tree, sure enough, and the squirrel is on the tree; but does he go round the squirrel? In the unlimited leisure of the wilderness, discussion had been worn threadbare. Everyone had taken sides, and was obstinate; and the numbers on both sides were even. Each side, when I appeared therefore appealed to me to make it a majority. Mindful of the scholastic adage that whenever you meet a contradiction you must make a distinction, I immediately sought and found one, as follows: "Which party is right," I said, "depends on what you *practically mean* by 'going round' the squirrel. If you mean passing from the north of him to the east, then to the south,

---

* William James, from "What Pragmatism Means," in *Pragmatism* (New York: Longmans, Green, 1907), pp. 43–47, 49–55.

then to the west, and then to the north of him again, obviously the man does go round him, for he occupies these successive positions. But if on the contrary you mean being first in front of him, then on the right of him, then behind him, then on his left, and finally in front again, it is quite as obvious that the man fails to go round him, for by the compensating movements the squirrel makes, he keeps his belly turned towards the man all the time, and his back turned away. Make the distinction, and there is no occasion for any farther dispute. You are both right and both wrong according as you conceive the verb 'to go round' in one practical fashion or the other."

Although one or two of the hotter disputants called my speech a shuffling evasion, saying they wanted no quibbling or scholastic hair-splitting, but meant just plain honest English "round," the majority seemed to think that the distinction had assuaged the dispute.

I tell this trivial anecdote because it is a peculiarly simple example of what I wish now to speak of as *the pragmatic method*. The pragmatic method is primarily a method of settling metaphysical disputes that otherwise might be interminable. Is the world one or many?—fated or free?—material or spiritual?—here are notions either of which may or may not hold good of the world; and disputes over such notions are unending. The pragmatic method in such cases is to try to interpret each notion by tracing its respective practical consequences. What difference would it practically make to any one if this notion rather than that notion were true? If no practical difference whatever can be traced, then the alternatives mean practically the same thing, and all dispute is idle. Whenever a dispute is serious, we ought to be able to show some practical difference that must follow from one side or the other's being right.

A glance at the history of the idea will show you still better what pragmatism means. The term is derived from the same Greek word πρᾶγμα, meaning action, from which our words "practice" and "practical" come. It was first introduced into philosophy by Mr. Charles Peirce in 1878. In an article entitled "How to Make Our Ideas Clear," in the "Popular Science Monthly" for January of that year Mr. Peirce, after pointing out that our beliefs are really rules for action, said that, to develop a thought's meaning, we need only determine what conduct it is fitted to produce: that conduct is for us its sole significance. And the tangible fact at the root of all our thought-distinctions, however subtle, is that there is no one of them so fine as to consist in anything but a possible difference of practice. To attain perfect clearness in our thoughts of an object, then, we need only consider what conceivable effects of a practical kind the object may involve—what sensations we are to expect from it, and what reactions we must prepare. Our conception of these effects, whether immediate or remote, is then for us the whole of our conception of the object, so far as that conception has positive significance at all.

This is the principle of Peirce, the principle of pragmatism. It lay entirely unnoticed by any one for twenty years, until I, in an address before Professor Howison's philosophical union at the University of California, brought it forward again and made a special application of it to religion. By that date (1898) the times seemed ripe for its reception. The word "pragmatism" spread, and at present it fairly spots the pages of the philosophic journals. On all hands we find the "pragmatic movement" spoken of, sometimes with respect, sometimes with contumely, seldom with clear understanding. It is evident that the term applies itself conveniently to a number of tendencies that hitherto have lacked a collective name, and that it has "come to stay." . . .

It is astonishing to see how many philosophical disputes collapse into insignificance the moment you subject them to this simple test of tracing a concrete consequence. There can *be* no difference anywhere that doesn't *make* a difference elsewhere—no difference in abstract truth that doesn't express itself in a difference in concrete fact and in conduct consequent upon that fact, imposed on somebody, somehow, somewhere, and somewhen. The whole function of philosophy ought to be to find out what definite difference it will make to you and me, at definite instants of our life, if this world-formula or that world-formula be the true one.

There is absolutely nothing new in the pragmatic method. Socrates was an adept at it. Aristotle used it methodically. Locke, Berkeley, and Hume made momentous contributions to truth by its means. Shadworth Hodgson keeps insisting that realities are only what they are "known as." But these forerunners of pragmatism used it in fragments: they were preluders only. Not until in our time has it generalized itself, become conscious of a universal mission, pretended to a conquering destiny. I believe in that destiny, and I hope I may end by inspiring you with my belief.

Pragmatism represents a perfectly familiar attitude in philosophy, the empiricist attitude, but it represents it, as it seems to me, both in a more radical and in a less objectionable form than it has ever yet assumed. A pragmatist turns his back resolutely and once for all upon a lot of inveterate habits dear to professional philosophers. He turns away from abstraction and insufficiency, from verbal solutions, from bad *a priori* reasons, from fixed principles, closed systems, and pretended absolutes and origins. He turns towards concreteness and adequacy, towards facts, towards action and towards power. That means the empiricist temper regnant and the rationalist temper sincerely given up. It means the open air and possibilities of nature, as against dogma, artificiality, and the pretence of finality in truth.

At the same time it does not stand for any special results. It is a method only. But the general triumph of that method would mean an enormous change in what I called in my last lecture the "temperament" of philosophy. Teachers of the ultra-rationalistic type would be frozen out, much as the courtier type is frozen out in republics, as the ultramontane type of priest is frozen out in protestant lands. Science and metaphysics would come much nearer together, would in fact work absolutely hand in hand.

Metaphysics has usually followed a very primitive kind of quest. You know how men have always hankered after unlawful magic, and you know what a great part in magic *words* have always played. If you have his name, or the formula of incantation that binds him, you can control the spirit, genie, afrite, or whatever the power may be. Solomon knew the names of all the spirits, and having their names, he held them subject to his will. So the universe has always appeared to the natural mind as a kind of enigma, of which the key must be sought in the shape of some illuminating or power-bringing word or name. That word names the universe's *principle*, and to possess it is after a fashion to possess the universe itself. "God," "Matter," "Reason," "the Absolute," "Energy," are so many solving names. You can rest when you have them. You are at the end of your metaphysical quest.

But if you follow the pragmatic method, you cannot look on any such word as closing your quest. You must bring out of each word its practical cash-value, set it at work within the stream of your experience. It appears less as a solution, then, than as a program for more work, and more particularly as an indication of the ways in which existing realities may be *changed.*

Theories thus become instruments, not answers to enigmas, in which we can rest. We don't lie back upon them, we move forward, and, on occasion, make nature over again by their aid. Pragmatism unstiffens all our theories, limbers them up and sets each one at work. Being nothing essentially new, it harmonizes with many ancient philosophic tendencies. It agrees with nominalism for instance, in always appealing to particulars; with utilitarianism in emphasizing practical aspects; with positivism in its disdain for verbal solutions, useless questions and metaphysical abstractions. . . .

No particular results then, so far, but only an attitude of orientation, is what the pragmatic method means. *The attitude of looking away from first things, principles, "categories," supposed necessities; and of looking towards last things, fruits, consequences, facts.*

So much for the pragmatic method! . . . Meanwhile the word pragmatism has come to be used in a still wider sense, as meaning also a certain *theory of truth.*[1]

[1] For James' account of the pragmatic theory of truth, see pp. 47–49.

JOHN DEWEY / *Ideas at Work* *

See the biographical note on p. 87.

OF ALL PHILOSOPHICAL problems that which concerns the nature and worth of ideas is probably the one that most readily appeals to any cultivated mind. The eulogistic flavor which hangs about the word Idealism is a tribute to the respect men pay to thought and its power. The obnoxious quality of materialism is due to its depression of thought, which is treated as an illusion or at most an accidental by-product; materialism leaves no place where ideas have creative or regulative effect. In some sense the cause of ideas, of thought, is felt to be that of the distinctive dignity of man himself. Serious minds have always desired a world in which experiences would be productive of ideas, of meanings, and in which these ideas in turn would regulate conduct. Take away ideas and what follows from them and man seems no better than the beasts of the field.

It is, however, an old story that philosophers have divided into opposed schools as to the nature of ideas and their power. To the extreme right are those who, under the banner of Idealism, have asserted that thought is the creator of the universe and that rational ideas constitute its structure. This constitutive work, however, is something done once for all by thought in a transcendental aboriginal work. The empirical world in which we live from day to day is crass and obdurate, stubbornly unideal in character because it is only an appearance of the reality of which thought is the author. This philosophic mode of paying reverence to ideas is thus compensatory rather than vital. It has nothing to do with rendering the natural and social environment of our experience a more ideal abode, namely, one characterized by meanings which are the fruits of thought. There are those who would be willing to exchange the thought which constitutes reality once for all for that thinking which by continued particular acts renders our experienced world here and now more charged with coherent and luminous meanings.

At the other pole is the school of sensational empiricists who hold that the doctrine that thought in any mode of operation is originative is an illusion. It proclaims the necessity of direct, first-hand contact with things as the source of all knowledge. Ideas are pale ghosts of flesh and blood

* John Dewey, from "Ideas at Work," in *The Quest for Certainty* (New York: Putnam, 1929), pp. 108–114, 122–124. Used by permission of the publisher.

impressions; they are images, pallid reflections, dying echoes of first hand intercourse with reality which takes place in sensation alone.

In spite of the polar opposition between the two schools, they depend upon a common premise. According to both systems of philosophy, *reflective* thought, thinking that involves inference and judgment, is not originative. It has its test in antecedent reality as that is disclosed in some non-reflective immediate knowledge. Its validity depends upon the possibility of checking its conclusions by identification with the terms of such prior immediate knowledge. The controversy between the schools is simply as to the origin and nature of previous direct knowledge. To both schools, reflection, thought involving inference, is *re*productive; the "proof" of its results is found in comparison with what is known without any inference. In traditional empiricism the test is found in sensory impressions. For objective idealism, reflective inquiry is valid only as it reproduces the work previously effected by constitutive thought. The goal of human thinking is approximation to the reality already instituted by absolute reason. The basic premise is also shared by realists. The essence of their position is that reflective inquiry is valid as it terminates in apprehension of that which already exists. When thinking introduces any modification into antecedent reality it falls into error; in fact, productive origination on the part of mind defines error.

The issue is connected with the analysis of experimental knowing which was begun in the preceding chapter. For the common premise of these philosophical schools, so opposed to one another in most ways, goes back to adoption of the idea about knowledge in relation to what is independently real which, originating in Greek thought, has become engrained in tradition. In our summary of the characteristics of experimental thinking, its second trait was said to be the direction of experiment by ideas, the fact that experiment is not random, aimless action, but always includes, along with groping and relatively blind doing, an element of deliberate foresight and intent, which determines that one operation rather than another be tried. In this chapter we shall, accordingly, consider the implications for the theory of ideas that follow from experimental method. Let us suppose, for the time being, that all that we can know about ideas is derived from the way in which they figure in the reflective inquiries of science. What conception of their nature and office shall we then be led to form?

We shall begin, somewhat abruptly, with a statement of the nature of conceptions which has been framed on the basis of recent conclusions in physical science. . . .

The position of present science on this matter has been stated as follows: "To find the length of an object, we have to perform certain physical operations. The concept of length is therefore fixed when the operations by which length is measured are fixed; that is, the concept of length involves as much as and nothing more than the set of operations by which length is determined. In general, we mean by any concept nothing more than a set of operations; *the concept is synonymous with the corresponding set of operations.*" [1] The same idea is repeated by Eddington in his Gifford Lectures. His statement is as follows: "The vocabulary of the physicist comprises a number of words such as length, angle, velocity, force, potential, current, etc., which we call 'physical quantities.' It is now recognized that these should be *defined* according to the way in which we recognize them when actually confronted with them, and not according to the metaphysical significance which we may have anticipated for them. In the old text-books mass was defined as 'quantity of matter'; but when it came to an actual determination of mass, an experimental method was prescribed which had no bearing on this definition." [2] The adoption of this point of view with respect to the meaning and content of thinking, and as to the validity or soundness of the ideas by means of which we understand natural events, makes possible what has been lacking throughout the history of thought, a genuinely experimental empiricism. The phrase "experimental empiricism" sounds redundant. It ought to be so in fact, since the adjective and the noun should have the same significance, so that nothing is gained by using the two terms. But historically such is not the case. For, historically, empirical philosophies have been framed in terms of sensations or sense data. These have been said to be the material out of which ideas are framed and by agreement with which they are to be tested. Sensory qualities are the antecedent models with which ideas must agree if they are to be sound or "proved." These doctrines have always evoked an abundance of criticisms. But the criticisms have taken the form of depreciating the capacity of "experience" to provide the source and test of our fundamentally important ideas in either knowledge or morals. They have used the weaknesses of sensational empiricism to reinforce the notion that ideas are framed by reason apart from any experience whatsoever; to support what is known in the vocabulary of philosophical systems as an *a priori* rationalism.

From the standpoint of the operational definition and tests of ideas, ideas have an empirical origin and status. But it is that of *acts* performed, acts in the literal and existential sense of the word, deeds done, not reception of sensations forced on us from without. Sensory qualities are important. But they are intellectually significant only as consequences of acts intentionally performed. A color seen at a particular locus in a spectral band is, for example, of immense intellectual importance in chemistry and in astro-physics. But *merely* as seen, as a bare sensory quality, it is the same

---

[1] Bridgman, *The Logic of Modern Physics*, New York, 1927, p. 5. The italics are in the text.

[2] *The Nature of the Physical World*, London and New York, 1928, p. 255. . . .

for the clodhopper and the scientist; in either case, it is the product of a direct sensory excitation; it is just and only another color the eye has happened upon. To suppose that its cognitive value can be eked out or supplied by associating it with other sensory qualities of the same nature as itself, is like supposing that by putting a pile of sand in the eye we can get rid of the irritation caused by a single grain. To suppose, on the other hand, that we must appeal to a synthetic activity of an independent thought to give the quality meaning in and for knowledge, is like supposing that by thinking in our heads we can convert a pile of bricks into a building. Thinking, carried on inside the head, can make some headway in forming the *plan* of a building. But it takes actual operations to which the plan, as the fruit of thought, gives instrumental guidance to make a building out of separate bricks, or to transform an isolated sensory quality into a significant clew to knowledge of nature.

Sensory qualities experienced through vision have their cognitive status and office, not (as sensational empiricism holds) in and of themselves in isolation, or as merely forced upon attention, but because they are the consequences of definite and intentionally performed operations. Only in connection with the intent, or idea, of these operations do they amount to anything, either as disclosing any fact or giving test and proof of any theory. The rationalist school was right in as far as it insisted that sensory qualities are significant for knowledge only when connected by means of ideas. But they were wrong in locating the connecting ideas in intellect apart from experience. Connection is instituted through operations which define ideas, and operations are as much matters of experience as are sensory qualities.

It is not too much to say, therefore, that for the first time there is made possible an empirical theory of ideas free from the burdens imposed alike by sensationalism and *a priori* rationalism. This accomplishment is, I make bold to say, one of three or four outstanding feats of intellectual history. For it emancipates us from the supposed need of always harking back to what has already been given, something had by alleged direct or immediate knowledge in the past, for the test of the value of ideas. A definition of the nature of ideas in terms of operations to be performed and the test of the validity of the ideas by the *consequences* of these operations establishes connectivity within concrete experience. At the same time, by emancipation of thinking from the necessity of testing its conclusions solely by reference to antecedent existence it makes clear the originative possibilities of thinking. . . .

Now so deeply engrained are the conclusions of the old tradition of rationalism versus (sensationalistic) empiricism, that the question will still be raised: What other certification could be given or can now be given for the properties of scientific physical objects save by inferential extension of the universally found properties of all objects of sense perception? Is there any alternative unless we are prepared to fall back upon *a priori* rational conceptions supposed to bring their own sufficient authority with them?

It is at this point that the recent recognition that the conceptions by which we think scientific objects are derived neither from sense nor from *a priori* conceptions has its logical and philosophical force. Sense qualities, as we saw in the previous chapter, are something *to be* known, they are challenges to knowing, setting problems for investigation. Our scientific knowledge is something *about* them, resolving the problems they propose. Inquiry proceeds by reflection, by thinking; but *not*, most decidedly, by thinking as conceived in the old tradition, as something cooped up within "mind." For experimental inquiry or thinking signifies *directed activity*, doing something which varies the conditions under which objects are observed and directly had and by instituting new arrangements among them. Things perceived suggest to us (originally just evoke or stimulate) certain ways of responding to them, of treating them. These operations have been continuously refined and elaborated during the history of man on earth, although it is only during the last few centuries that the whole affair of controlled thinking and of its issue in genuine knowledge, has been seen to be bound up with their selection and determination.

The central question thus arises: What determines the selection of operations to be performed? There is but one answer:—the nature of the problem to be dealt with—and answer which links the phase of experiment now under discussion with that considered in the last chapter. The first effect of experimental analysis is, as we saw, to reduce objects directly experienced to data. This resolution is required because the objects in their first mode of experience are perplexing, obscure, fragmentary; in some way they fail to answer a need. Given data which locate the nature of the problem, there is evoked a thought of an operation which if put into execution may eventuate in a situation in which the trouble or doubt which evoked inquiry will be resolved. If one were to trace the history of science far enough, one would reach a time in which the acts which dealt with a troublesome situation would be organic responses of a structural type together with a few acquired habits. The most elaborate technique of present inquiry in the laboratory is an extension and refinement of these simple original operations. Its development has for the most part depended upon the utilization of physical instruments, which when inquiry was developed to a certain point were purposely invented. In principle, the history of the construction of suitable operations in the scientific field is not different from that of their evolution in industry. Something needed to be done to accomplish an end; various devices and methods of operation were tried. Experiences of success and failure gradually improved the means used. More economical and effective ways of acting were found—that is, operations which gave the desired kind of result with greater ease, less irrelevancy and less ambiguity, greater security. Each forward step was attended with making better tools. Often the invention of a tool suggested operations not in mind when it was invented and thus carried the perfecting of operations still further. There is thus no *a priori* test or rule for the determination of the operations which define ideas. They are themselves experimentally developed in the course of actual inquiries. They originated in what men naturally do and are tested and improved in the course of doing. . . .

For Further Study

Anton, John P. "John Dewey and Ancient Philosophers," *Philosophy and Phenomenological Research*, 25 (June, 1965): 477–499.

Dewey, John. "The Development of American Pragmatism," in *Studies in the History of Ideas*, ed. Department of Philosophy of Columbia University. New York: Columbia U. Press, 1918. Vol. II.

Geiger, George R. *John Dewey in Perspective.* New York: Oxford U. Press, 1958, Ch. 4, "Inquiry, Knowing, and Truth."

Holmes, R. L. "John Dewey's Moral Philosophy in Contemporary Perspective," *Review of Metaphysics*, 20 (September, 1966): 42–70.

Konvitz, Milton R., and Kennedy, Gail (eds.). *The American Pragmatists: Selected Writings.* New York: Meridian, 1960, 413 pp.

Moore, Edward C. *American Pragmatism: Peirce, James, and Dewey.* New York: Columbia U. Press, 1961, Part I, "The Pragmaticism of Charles Peirce."

Peirce, Charles S. *Values in a Universe of Chance: Selected Writings*, ed. Philip P. Wiener. Stanford: Stanford U. Press, 1958, Ch. 6, "How to Make Our Ideas Clear."

Rorty, Amelie, ed. *Pragmatic Philosophy: An Anthology.* Garden City: Doubleday, 1966. (Anchor Book A 538.)

Van Wesep, Hendrikus B. *Seven Sages: The Story of American Philosophy.* New York: Longmans, Green, 1960, "William James: Primitive Pragmatist"; "John Dewey: Promethean Instrumentalist"; "Charles Sanders Peirce: Trail-Blazing Logician."

16 Analytic Philosophy and Its Implications

ALFRED JULES AYER / *The Elimination of Metaphysics* *

Alfred Jules Ayer (1910–   ), a Fellow of the British Academy, taught for a number of years at the University of London and is now professor of logic at Oxford University. In his early work from which we quote, he gave one of the most vigorous defenses of logical positivism. Although he has modified his position considerably in recent years, *Language, Truth and Logic* has acquired the status of a small classic.

THE TRADITIONAL disputes of philosophers are, for the most part, as unwarranted as they are unfruitful. The surest way to end them is to establish beyond question what should be the purpose and method of a philosophical enquiry. And this is by no means so difficult a task as the history of philosophy would lead one to suppose. For if there are any questions which science leaves it to philosophy to answer, a straightforward process of elimination must lead to their discovery.

We may begin by criticising the metaphysical thesis that philosophy affords us knowledge of a reality transcending the world of science and common sense. Later on, when we come to define metaphysics and ac-

* Alfred Jules Ayer, from "The Elimination of Metaphysics," in *Language, Truth and Logic* (New York: Dover, 1952; London: Gollancz, 1946), pp. · 33–35, 38–42, 44–45. Used by permission of the publishers.

count for its existence, we shall find that it is possible to be a metaphysician without believing in a transcendent reality; for we shall see that many metaphysical utterances are due to the commission of logical errors, rather than to a conscious desire on the part of their authors to go beyond the limits of experience. But it is convenient for us to take the case of those who believe that it is possible to have knowledge of a transcendent reality as a starting-point for our discussion. The arguments which we use to refute them will subsequently be found to apply to the whole of metaphysics.

One way of attacking a metaphysician who claimed to have knowledge of a reality which transcended the phenomenal world would be to enquire from what premises his propositions were deduced. Must he not begin, as other men do, with the evidence of his senses? And if so, what valid process of reasoning can possibly lead him to the conception of a transcendent reality? Surely from empirical premises nothing whatsoever concerning the properties, or even the existence, of anything super-empirical can legitimately be inferred. But this objection would be met by a denial on the part of the metaphysician that his assertions were ultimately based on the evidence of his senses. He would say that he was endowed with a faculty of intellectual intuition which enabled him to know facts that could not be known through sense-experience. And even if it could be shown that he was relying on empirical premises, and that his venture into a nonempirical world was therefore logically unjustified, it would not follow that the assertions which he made concerning this nonempirical world could not be true. For the fact that a conclusion does not follow from its putative premise is not sufficient to show that it is false. Consequently one cannot overthrow a system of transcendent metaphysics merely by criticising the way in which it comes into being. What is required is rather a criticism of the nature of the actual statements which comprise it. And this is the line of argument which we shall, in fact, pursue. For we shall maintain that no statement which refers to a "reality" transcending the limits of all possible sense-experience can possibly have any literal significance; from which it must follow that the labours of those who have striven to describe such a reality have all been devoted to the production of nonsense. . . .

. . . It cannot here be said that the author is himself overstepping the barrier he maintains to be impassable. For the fruitlessness of attempting to transcend the limits of possible sense-experience will be deduced, not from a psychological hypothesis concerning the actual constitution of the human mind, but from the rule which determines the literal significance of language. Our charge against the metaphysician is not that he attempts to employ the understanding in a field where it cannot profitably venture, but that he produces sentences which fail to conform to the conditions under which alone a sentence can be literally significant. Nor are we ourselves obliged to talk nonsense in order to show that all sentences of a certain type are necessarily devoid of literal significance. We need only formulate the criterion which enables us to test whether a sentence expresses a genuine proposition about a matter of fact, and then point out that the sentences under consideration fail to satisfy it. . . .

The criterion which we use to test the genuineness of apparent statements of fact is the criterion of verifiability. We say that a sentence is factually significant to any given person, if, and only if, he knows how to verify the proposition which it purports to express—that is, if he knows what observations would lead him, under certain conditions, to accept the proposition as being true, or reject it as being false. If, on the other hand, the putative proposition is of such a character that the assumption of its truth, or falsehood, is consistent with any assumption whatsoever concerning the nature of his future experience, then, as far as he is concerned, it is, if not a tautology, a mere pseudo-proposition. The sentence expressing it may be emotionally significant to him; but it is not literally significant. And with regard to questions the procedure is the same. We enquire in every case what observations would lead us to answer the question, one way or the other; and, if none can be discovered, we must conclude that the sentence under consideration does not, as far as we are concerned, express a genuine question, however strongly its grammatical appearance may suggest that it does. . . .

. . . We say that the question that must be asked about any putative statement of fact is not, Would any observations make its truth or falsehood logically certain? but simply, Would any observations be relevant to the determination of its truth or falsehood? And it is only if a negative answer is given to this second question that we conclude that the statement under consideration is nonsensical.

To make our position clearer, we may formulate it in another way. Let us call a proposition which records an actual or possible observation an experiential proposition. Then we may say that it is the mark of a genuine factual proposition, not that it should be equivalent to an experiential proposition, or any finite number of experiential propositions, but simply that some experiential propositions can be deduced from it in conjunction with certain other premises without being deducible from those other premises alone.

This criterion seems liberal enough. In contrast to the principle of conclusive verifiability, it clearly does not deny significance to general propositions or to propositions about the past. Let us see what kinds of assertion it rules out.

A good example of the kind of utterance that is condemned by our criterion as being not even false but nonsensical would be the assertion that the world of sense-experience was altogether unreal. It must, of course, be admitted that our senses do sometimes deceive us. We may, as the result of having certain sensations, expect certain other sensations to be obtainable which are, in fact, not obtainable. But, in all such cases, it is further sense-experience that informs us of the mistakes that arise out of sense-experience. We say that the senses sometimes deceive us, just because the expectations to which our sense-experiences give rise do not always accord with what we subsequently experience. That is, we rely on our senses to substantiate or confute the judgements which are based on our sensations. And therefore the fact that our perceptual judgements are sometimes found to be erroneous has not the slightest tendency to show that the world of sense-experience is unreal. And, indeed, it is plain that no conceivable observation, or series of observations, could have any tendency to show that the world revealed to us by sense-experience was unreal. Consequently, anyone who condemns the sensible world as a world of mere appearance, as opposed to reality, is saying something which, according to our criterion of significance, is literally nonsensical.

An example of a controversy which the application of our criterion obliges us to condemn as fictitious is provided by those who dispute concerning the number of substances that there are in the world. For it is admitted both by monists, who maintain that reality is one substance, and by pluralists, who maintain that reality is many, that it is impossible to imagine any empirical situation which would be relevant to the solution of their dispute. But if we are told that no possible observation could give any probability either to the assertion that reality was one substance or to the assertion that it was many, then we must conclude that neither assertion is significant. . . . [T]here are genuine logical and empirical questions involved in the dispute between monists and pluralists. But the metaphysical question concerning "substance" is ruled out by our criterion as spurious. . . .

As to the validity of the verification principle, in the form in which we have stated it, a demonstration will be given in the course of this book. For it will be shown that all propositions which have factual content are empirical hypotheses; and that the function of an empirical hypothesis is to provide a rule for the anticipation of experience. And this means that every empirical hypothesis must be relevant to some actual, or possible, experience, so that a statement which is not relevant to any experience is not an empirical hypothesis, and accordingly has no factual content. But this is precisely what the principle of verifiability asserts.

It should be mentioned here that the fact that the utterances of the metaphysician are nonsensical does not follow simply from the fact that they are devoid of factual content. It follows from that fact, together with the fact that they are not *a priori* propositions. And in assuming that they are not *a priori* propositions, we are once again anticipating the conclusions of a later chapter in this book. For it will be shown there that *a priori* propositions, which have always been attractive to philosophers on account of their certainty, owe this certainty to the fact that they are tautologies. We may accordingly define a metaphysical sentence as a sentence which purports to express a genuine proposition, but does, in fact, express neither a tautology nor an empirical hypothesis. And as tautologies and empirical hypotheses form the entire class of significant propositions, we are justified in concluding that all metaphysical assertions are nonsensical. Our next task is to show how they come to be made.

The use of the term "substance," to which we have already referred, provides us with a good example of the way in which metaphysics mostly comes to be written. It happens to be the case that we cannot, in our language, refer to the sensible properties of a thing without introducing a word or phrase which appears to stand for the thing itself as opposed to anything which may be said about it. And, as a result of this, those who are infected by the primitive superstition that to every name a single real entity must correspond assume that it is necessary to distinguish logically between the thing itself and any, or all, of its sensible properties. And so they employ the term "substance" to refer to the thing itself. But from the fact that we happen to employ a single word to refer to a thing, and make that word the grammatical subject of the sentences in which we refer to the sensible appearances of the thing, it does not by any means follow that the thing itself is a "simple entity," or that it cannot be defined in terms of the totality of its appearances. It is true that in talking of "its" appearances we appear to distinguish the thing from the appearances, but that is simply an accident of linguistic usage. Logical analysis shows that what makes these "appearances" the "appearances of" the same thing is not their relationship to an entity other than themselves, but their relationship to one another. The metaphysician fails to see this because he is misled by a superficial grammatical feature of his language. . . .

Among those who recognise that if philosophy is to be accounted a genuine branch of knowledge it must be defined in such a way as to distinguish it from metaphysics, it is fashionable to speak of the metaphysician as a kind of misplaced poet. As his statements have no literal meaning, they are not subject to any criteria of truth or falsehood: but they may still serve to express, or arouse, emotion, and thus be subject to ethical or æsthetic standards. And it is suggested that they may have considerable value, as means of moral inspiration, or even as works of art. In this way, an attempt is made to compensate the metaphysician for his extrusion from philosophy.

I am afraid that this compensation is hardly in accordance with his deserts. The view that the metaphysician is to be reckoned among the poets appears to rest on the assumption that both talk nonsense. But this assumption is false. In the vast majority of cases the sentences which are produced by poets do have literal meaning. The difference between the man who uses language scientifically and the man who uses it emotively is not that the one produces sentences which are incapable of arousing emotion, and the other sentences which have no sense, but that the one is primarily concerned with the expression of true propositions, the other with the creation of a work of art. Thus, if a work of science contains true and important propositions, its value as a work of science will hardly be diminished by the fact that they are inelegantly expressed. And similarly, a work of art is not necessarily the worse for the fact that all the propositions comprising it are literally false. But to say that many literary works are largely composed of falsehoods, is not to say that they are composed of pseudo-propositions. It is, in fact, very rare for a literary artist to produce sentences which have no literal meaning. And where this does occur, the sentences are carefully chosen for their rhythm and balance. If the author writes nonsense, it is because he considers it most suitable for bringing about the effects for which his writing is designed.

The metaphysician, on the other hand, does not intend to write nonsense. He lapses into it through being deceived by grammar, or through committing errors of reasoning, such as that which leads to the view that the sensible world is unreal. But it is not the mark of a poet simply to make mistakes of this sort. There are some, indeed, who would see in the fact that the metaphysician's utterances are senseless a reason against the view that they have æsthetic value. And, without going so far as this, we may safely say that it does not constitute a reason for it.

It is true, however, that although the greater part of metaphysics is merely the embodiment of humdrum errors, there remain a number of metaphysical passages which are the work of genuine mystical feeling; and they may more plausibly be held to have moral or æsthetic value. But, as far as we are concerned, the distinction between the kind of metaphysics that is produced by a philosopher who has been duped by grammar, and the kind that is produced by a mystic who is trying to express the inexpressible, is of no great importance: what is important to us is to realise that even the utterances of the metaphysician who is attempting to expound a vision are literally senseless; so that henceforth we may pursue our philosophical researches with as little regard for them as for the more inglorious kind of metaphysics which comes from a failure to understand the workings of our language.

FRIEDRICH WAISMANN / How I See Philosophy *

Friedrich Waismann (1896–   ) is Reader in the Philosophy of Mathematics at Oxford University. He was associated with the Vienna Circle before going to England. His thinking represents one type of liberalization of earlier logical positivism which has occurred within more recent analytic philosophy.

FROM PLATO to Schopenhauer philosophers are agreed that the source of their philosophizing is wonder. What gives rise to it is nothing recondite and rare but precisely those things which stare us in the face: memory, motion, general ideas. (Plato: What does "horse" mean? A single particular horse? No, for it may refer to *any* horse; *all* the horses, the total class? No, for we may speak of this or that horse. But if it means neither a single horse nor all horses, what *does* it mean?) The idealist is shaken in just the same way when he comes to reflect that he has, in Schopenhauer's words, "no knowledge of the sun but only of an eye that sees a sun, and no knowledge of the earth but only of a hand that feels an earth." Can it be, then, that nothing whatever is known to us except our own consciousness?

In looking at such questions, it seems as if the mind's eye were growing dim and as if everything, even that which ought to be absolutely clear, was becoming oddly puzzling and unlike its usual self. To bring out what seems to be peculiar to these questions one might say that they are not so much questions as tokens of a profound uneasiness of mind. Try for a moment to put yourself into the frame of mind of which Augustine was possessed when he asked: How is it possible to measure time? Time consists of past, present and future. The past can't be measured, it is gone; the future can't be measured, it is not yet here; and the present can't be measured, it has no extension. Augustine knew of course how time is measured and this was not his concern. What puzzled him was how it is *possible* to measure time, seeing that the past hour cannot be lifted out and placed alongside the present hour for comparison. Or look at it this way: what is measured is in the past, the measuring in the present: how can that be?

* Reprinted with permission of The Macmillan Company from *Contemporary British Philosophy: Third Series* ed. by H. D. Lewis. First published in 1956. Friedrich Waismann, from "How I See Philosophy," pp. 449–462, 464–465, 482–483.

The philosopher as he ponders over some such problem has the appearance of a man who is deeply disquieted. He seems to be straining to grasp something which is beyond his powers. The words in which such a question presents itself do not quite bring out into the open the real point —which may, perhaps more aptly, be described as the recoil from the incomprehensible. If, on a straight railway journey, you suddenly come in sight of the very station you have just left behind, there will be terror, accompanied perhaps by slight giddiness. That is exactly how the philosopher feels when he says to himself, "Of course time can be measured; but how *can* it?" It is as though, up to now, he had been passing heedlessly over the difficulties, and now, all of a sudden, he notices them and asks himself in alarm, "But how can that be?" That is a sort of question which we only ask when it is the very facts themselves which confound us, when something about them strikes us as preposterous.

Kant, I fancy, must have felt something of the sort when he suddenly found the existence of geometry a puzzle. Here we have propositions as clear and transparent as one would wish, prior, it seems, to all experience; at the same time they apply miraculously to the real world. How is that possible? Can the mind, unaided by experience, in some dark manner actually fathom the properties of real things? Looked upon in this way, geometry takes on a disturbing air.

We all have our moments when something quite ordinary suddenly strikes us as queer—for instance, when time appears to us as a curious thing. Not that we are often in this frame of mind; but on some occasions, when we look at things in a certain way, unexpectedly they seem to change as though by magic: they stare at us with a puzzling expression, and we begin to wonder whether they can possibly be the things we have known all our lives. . . .

As we all know what time is and yet cannot say what it is, it feels mystifying; and precisely because of its elusiveness it catches our imagination. The more we look at it the more we are puzzled: it seems charged with paradoxes. "What is time? What is this being made up of movement only without anything that is moving?" (Schopenhauer). How funny to have it bottled up! "I've got here in my hand the most potent, the most enigmatic, the most fleeting of all essences—Time." (Logan Pearsall Smith of an hour-glass.) For Shelley it is an "unfathomable sea! whose waves are years," a "shoreless flood," for Proust—well, why not leave something to the reader?

But isn't the answer to this that what mystifies us lies in the *noun* form "the time"? Having a notion embodied in the form of a noun almost irresistibly makes us turn round to look for what it is "the name of." We are trying to catch the shadows cast by the opacities of speech. A wrong analogy absorbed into the forms of our language produces mental discomfort; (and the feeling of discomfort, when it refers to language, is a profound one). "All sounds, all colours . . . evoke indefinite and yet precise emotions, or, as I prefer to think, call down among us certain disembodied powers whose footsteps over our hearts we call emotions" (W. B. Yeats).

Yet the answer is a prosaic one: don't ask what time is but how the *word* "time" is being used. Easier said than done; for if the philosopher rectifies the use of language, ordinary language has "the advantage of being in possession of declensions," to speak with Lichtenberg, and thus renews its spell over him, luring him on into the shadow chase. It is perhaps only when we turn to languages of a widely different grammatical structure that the way towards such possibilities of interpretation is entirely barred. "It is highly probable that philosophers within the domain of the Ural-Altaic languages (where the subject-concept is least developed) will look differently "into the world" and be found on paths of thought different from those of the Indo-Europeans or Mussulmans" (Nietzsche).

It may be well at this point to remind ourselves that the words "question" and "answer," "problem" and "solution" are not always used in their most trite sense. It is quite obvious that we often have to do something very different to find the way out of a difficulty. A problem of politics is solved by adopting a certain line of action, the problems of novelists perhaps by the invention of devices for presenting the inmost thoughts and feelings of their characters; there is the painter's problem of how to suggest depth or movement on the canvas, the stylistic problem of expressing things not yet current, not yet turned into cliché; there are a thousand questions of technology which are answered, not by the discovery of some truth, but by a practical achievement; and there is of course the "social question." In philosophy, the real problem is not to find the answer to a given question but to find a sense for it. . . .

Many are the types of bewilderment: there is the obsessional doubt— can I ever know that other people have experiences, that they see, hear and feel as I do? Can I be sure that memory does not always deceive me? Are there really material objects and not only sense-impressions "of" them? There is the doubtlike uneasiness—what sort of being is possessed by numbers? There is the anxiety-doubt—are we really free? This doubt has taken many different forms one of which I shall single out for discussion— the question, namely, whether the law of excluded middle, when it refers to statements in the future tense, forces us into a sort of logical Predestination. A typical argument is this. If it is true now that I shall do a certain thing tomorrow, say, jump into the Thames, then no matter how fiercely I resist, strike out with hands and feet like a madman, when the day comes I cannot help jumping into the water; whereas, if this prediction is false now, then whatever efforts I may make, however many times I may nerve and brace myself, look down at the water and say to myself, "One, two, three—," it is impossible for me to spring. Yet that the prediction is either true or false is itself a necessary truth, asserted by the law of excluded middle. From this the startling consequence seems to follow that it is already now decided what I shall do tomorrow, that indeed the entire future is somehow fixed, logically preordained. Whatever I do and whichever way I decide, I am merely moving along lines clearly marked in advance which lead me towards my appointed lot. We are all, in fact, marionettes. If we are not prepared to swallow *that*, then—and there is a glimmer of hope in the "then"—there is an alternative open to us. We need only renounce the law of excluded middle for statements of this kind, and with it the validity of ordinary logic, and all will be well. Descriptions of what will happen are, at present, neither true nor false. (This sort of argument was actually propounded by Lukasiewicz in favour of a three-valued logic with "possible" as a third truth-value alongside "true" and "false.")

The way out is clear enough. The asker of the question has fallen into the error of so many philosophers: of giving an answer before stopping to consider the question. For is he clear what he is asking? He seems to suppose that a statement referring to an event in the future is at present undecided, neither true nor false, but that when the event happens the proposition enters into a sort of new state, that of being true. But how are we to figure the change from "undecided" to "true"? Is it sudden or gradual? At what moment does the statement "it will rain tomorrow" begin to be true? When the first drop falls to the ground? And supposing that it will not rain, when will the statement begin to be false? Just at the end of the day, at 12 p.m. sharp? Supposing that the event *has* happened, that the statement *is* true, will it remain so for ever? If so, in what way? Does it remain uninterruptedly true, at every moment of day and night? Even if there were no one about to give it any thought? Or is it true only at the moments when it is being thought of? In that case, how long does it remain true? For the duration of the thought? We wouldn't know how to answer these questions; this is due not to any particular ignorance or stupidity on our part but to the fact that something has gone wrong with the way the words "true" and "false" are applied here.

If I say, "It is true that I was in America," I am saying that I was in America and no more. That in uttering the words "It is true that—" I take responsibility upon myself is a different matter that does not concern the present argument. The point is that in making a statement prefaced by the words "It is true that" I do not *add* anything to the factual information I give you. *Saying* that something is true is not *making* it true: cp. the criminal lying in court, yet every time he is telling a lie protesting, his hand on his heart, that he is telling the truth.

What is characteristic of the use of the words "true" and "false" and what the pleader of logical determinism has failed to notice is this. "It is true" and "it is false," while they certainly have the force of asserting and denying, are not descriptive. Suppose that someone says, "It is true that the sun will rise tomorrow" all it means is that the sun will rise tomorrow: he is not regaling us with an extra-description of the trueness of what he says. But supposing that he were to say instead, "It is true *now* that the sun will rise tomorrow," this would boil down to something like "The sun will rise tomorrow now"; which is nonsense. To ask, as the puzzle-poser does, "Is it true or false *now* that such-and-such will happen in the future?" is not the sort of question to which an answer can be given: which *is* the answer.

This sheds light on what has, rather solemnly, been termed the "timelessness of truth." It lies in this that the clause "it is true that—" does not allow of inserting a date. To say of a proposition like "Diamond is pure carbon" that it is true on Christmas Eve would be just as poor a joke as to say that it is true in Paris and not in Timbuctoo. (This does not mean that we cannot say in certain circumstances, "Yes, it was true in those days" as this can clearly be paraphrased without using the word "true.")

Now it begins to look a bit less paradoxical to say that when a philosopher wants to dispose of a question the one thing he must not do is: to give an answer. A philosophic question is not solved: it *dissolves*. And in what does the "dissolving" consist? In making the meaning of the words used in putting the question so clear to ourselves that we are released from the spell it casts on us. Confusion was removed by calling to mind the use of language or, so far as the use *can* be distilled into rules, the rules: it therefore *was* a confusion about the use of language, or a confusion about rules. It is here that philosophy and grammar meet. . . .

. . . First, we don't *force* our interlocutor. We leave him free to choose, accept or reject any way of using his words. He may depart from ordinary usage—language is not untouchable—if it is only in this way that he can explain himself. He may even use an expression one time in this, another time in that, way. The only thing we insist upon is that he should be aware of what he is doing. If we strictly adhere to this method—going over the argument, asking him at each step whether he is willing to use an expression in a certain way, if not, offering him alternatives, but leaving the decisions to him and only pointing out what their consequences are—no dispute can arise. Disputes arise only if certain steps in this procedure are omitted so that it looks as if we had made an assertion, adding to the world's woes a new apple of discord. This would be the true way of doing philosophy undogmatically. The difficulty of this method lies in presenting the subject in a manner which can easily be taken in—in arranging the cases and the ways in which they are connected through intermediate links so that we can gain a clear synoptic view of the whole.

Second, we do not use arguments in order to prove or disprove any "philosophic view." As we have no views we can afford to look at things as they are.

Next, we only describe; we do not "explain." An explanation, in the sense of a deductive proof, cannot satisfy us because it pushes the question "Why just these rules and no other ones?" only one stage back. In following that method, we do not *want* to give reasons. All we do is to describe a use or tabulate rules. In doing this, we are not making any discoveries: there is nothing to be discovered in grammar. Grammar is autonomous and not dictated by reality. Giving reasons, bound as it is to come to an end and leading to something which cannot further be explained, *ought* not to satisfy us. In grammar we never ask the question "why?"

But isn't the result of this that philosophy itself "dissolves"? Philosophy eliminates those questions which *can* be eliminated by such a treatment. Not all of them, though: the metaphysician's craving that a ray of light may fall on the mystery of the existence of this world, or on the incomprehensible fact that it is comprehensible, or on the "meaning of life"—even if such questions *could* be shown to lack a clear meaning or to be devoid of meaning altogether, they are *not silenced*. It does nothing to lessen the dismay they rouse in us. There is something cheap in "debunking" them. The heart's unrest is not to be stilled by logic. Yet philosophy is not dissolved. It derives its weight, its grandeur, from the significance of the questions it destroys. It overthrows idols, and it is the importance of these idols which gives philosophy its importance.

Now it can perhaps be seen why the search for answers fitting the moulds of the questions fails, is *bound* to fail. They are not real questions asking for information but "muddles felt as problems" (Wittgenstein) which wither away when the ground is cleared. If philosophy advances, it is not by adding new propositions to its list, but rather by transforming the whole intellectual scene and, as a consequence of this, by reducing the number of questions which befog and bedevil us. Philosophy so construed is one of the great liberating forces. Its task is, in the words of Frege, "to free the spirit from the tyranny of words by exposing the delusions which arise, almost inevitably, through the use of a word language."

What, only criticism and no meat? The philosopher a fog dispeller? If that were all he was capable of I would be sorry for him and leave him to his devices. Fortunately, this is not so. For one thing, a philosophic question, if pursued far enough, may lead to something positive—for instance, to a more profound understanding of language. Take the sceptical doubts as to material objects, other minds, etc. The first reaction is perhaps to say: these doubts are idle. Ordinarily, when I doubt whether I shall finish this article, after a time my doubt comes to an end. I cannot go on doubting for ever. It's the destiny of doubt to die. But the doubts raised by the sceptic never die. Are they doubts? Are they pseudo-questions? They appear so only when judged by the twin standards of common sense and common speech. The real trouble lies deeper: it arises from the sceptic casting doubt on the very facts which underlie the use of language, those permanent features of experience which make concept formation possible, which in fact are precipitated in the use of our most common words. Suppose that you see an object in front of you quite clearly, say, a pipe, and when you are going to pick it up it melts into thin air, then you may feel, "Lord, I'm going mad" or something of the sort (unless the whole situation is such that you have reason to suspect that it was some clever trick). But what, the sceptic may press now, if such experiences were quite frequent? Would you be prepared to *dis*solve the connection between different sense experiences which form the hard core of our idea of a solid object, to *un*do what language has done—to part with the category of thinghood? And would you then be living in a phenomenalist's paradise with colour patches and the other paraphernalia of the sense-datum theory, in a disobjected, desubstantialized world? To say in such circumstances, "Look, it's just tabling now" would be a joke (for even in the weakened verb forms "tabling," "chairing" an element of the thing-category lingers on). That is why the sceptic struggles to express himself in a language which is not fit for this purpose. He expresses himself misleadingly when he says that he doubts such-and-such *facts:* his doubts cut so deep that they affect the fabric of language itself. For what he doubts is already embodied in the very forms of speech, e.g. in what is condensed in the use of thing-words. The moment he tries to penetrate those deep-sunken layers, he undermines the language in which he ventilates his qualms—with the result that he seems to be talking nonsense. He is not. But in order to make his doubts fully expressible, language would first have to go into the melting-pot. (We can get a glimmering of what is needed from modern science where all the long-established categories—thing-hood, causality, position—had to be revolutionized. This required nothing less than the construction of some new language, not the expression of new facts with the old one.)

If we look at the matter in this way the attitude of the sceptic is seen in a new light. He considers possibilities which lie far outside the domain of our current experience. If his doubts are taken seriously, they turn into observations which cast a new and searching light on the subsoil of language, showing what possibilities are open to our thought (though not to ordinary language), and what paths might have been pursued if the texture of our experience were different from what it is. These problems are not spurious: they make us aware of the vast background in which any current experiences are embedded, and to which language has adapted itself; thus they bring out the unmeasured sum of experience stored up in the use of our words and syntactical forms.

The question is the first groping step of the mind in its journeyings that lead towards new horizons. The genius of the philosopher shows itself nowhere more strikingly than in the new kind of question he brings into the world. What distinguishes him and gives him his place is the passion of questioning. That his questions are at times not so clear is perhaps of not so much moment as one makes of it. There is nothing like clear thinking to protect one from making discoveries. It is all very well to talk of clarity, but when it becomes an obsession it is liable to nip the living thought in the bud. This, I am afraid, is one of the deplorable results of Logical Positivism, not foreseen by its founders, but only too striking in some of its followers. Look at these people, gripped by a clarity neurosis, haunted by fear, tongue-tied, asking themselves continually, "Oh dear, now does this make perfectly good sense?" Imagine the pioneers of science, Kepler, Newton, the discoverers of non-Euclidean geometry, of field physics, the unconscious, matter waves or heaven knows what, imagine them asking themselves this question at every step—this would have been the surest means of sapping any creative power. No great discoverer has acted in accordance with the motto, "Everything that can be said can be said clearly." And some of the greatest discoveries have even emerged from a sort of primordial fog. (Something to be said for the fog. For my part, I've always suspected that clarity is the last refuge of those who have nothing to say.) . . .

To ask, "What is your aim in philosophy?" and to reply, "To show the fly the way out of the fly-bottle" is . . . well, honour where it is due, I suppress what I was going to say; except perhaps this. There is something deeply exciting about philosophy, a fact not intelligible on such a negative account. It is not a matter of "clarifying thoughts" nor of "the correct use of language" nor of any other of these damned things. What is it? Philosophy is many things and there is no formula to cover them all. But if I were asked to express in one single word what is its most essential feature I would unhesitatingly say: vision. At the heart of any philosophy worth the name is vision and it is from there it springs and takes its visible shape. When I say "vision" I mean it: I do not want to romanticize. What is characteristic of philosophy is the piercing of that dead crust of tradition and convention, the breaking of those fetters which bind us to inherited preconceptions, so as to attain a new and broader way of looking at things. It has always been felt that philosophy should reveal to us what is hidden. (I am not quite insensitive to the dangers of such a view.) Yet from Plato to Moore and Wittgenstein every great philosopher was led by a sense of vision: without it no one could have given a new direction to human thought or opened windows into the not-yet-seen. Though he may be a good technician, he will not leave his marks on the history of ideas. What is decisive is a new way of seeing and, what goes with it, the will to transform the whole intellectual scene. This is the real thing and everything else is subservient to it.

For Further Study

Blanshard, Brand. *Reason and Analysis.* LaSalle: Open Court, 1962, Ch. 7, "Linguistic Philosophy—Some Earlier Forms"; Ch. 8, "Linguistic Philosophy—Some Later Forms."

Carnap, Rudolf. *The Logical Structure of the World.* Trans. by Rolf A. George. Berkeley: U. of California Press, 1967.

Chappell, V. C., ed. *Ordinary Language.* Englewood Cliffs: Prentice-Hall, 1964.

Hallie, Philip P. "Wittgenstein's Exclusion of Metaphysical Nonsense," *Philosophical Quarterly,* 16 (April, 1966): 97–112.

Henle, Paul (ed.). *Language, Thought, and Culture.* Ann Arbor: U. of Michigan Press, 1958, Ch. 1, "Language, Thought, and Culture."

Kaplan, Abraham. *The New World of Philosophy.* New York: Random House, 1961, Lecture Two, "Analytic Philosophy."

Paton, H. J. *The Modern Predicament.* New York: Macmillan, 1955, Ch. 2, "The Linguistic Veto."

Randall, John Herman, Jr. "Metaphysics and Language," *Review of Metaphysics,* 20 (June, 1967): 591–601.

Schlagel, Richard H. "Science, Truth, and Ordinary Language," *Philosophy and Phenomenological Research,* 27 (September, 1966): 27–44.

White, Morton. "New Horizons in Philosophy," *Saturday Evening Post,* 233 (September 17, 1960): 24–25, 70, 72.

17 Existentialism and
Its Implications

JEAN-PAUL SARTRE / What Is
Existentialism? *

Jean-Paul Sartre (1905–   ) is the leading French representative
of atheistic existentialism. While his main philosophical works are
Being and Nothingness and *Critique of Dialectical Reason*, many
know him best through his plays and novels.

. . . WHAT IS MEANT by the term existentialism?

Most people who use the word would be rather embarrassed if they had
to explain it, since, now that the word is all the rage, even the work of a
musician or painter is being called existentialist. A gossip columnist in
Clartés signs himself *The Existentialist*, so that by this time the word has
been so stretched and has taken on so broad a meaning, that it no longer
means anything at all. It seems that for want of an advance-guard doctrine
analogous to surrealism, the kind of people who are eager for scandal and
flurry turn to this philosophy which in other respects does not at all serve
their purposes in this sphere.

Actually, it is the least scandalous, the most austere of doctrines. It is
intended strictly for specialists and philosophers. Yet it can be defined

* Jean-Paul Sartre, from *Existentialism*, trans. Bernard Frechtman (New York: Philosophical Library, 1947), pp. 14–19, 20–24, 25–27, 34–35, 42–44. Used by permission
of the publisher.

easily. What complicates matters is that there are two kinds of existentialist; first, those who are Christian, among whom I would include Jaspers and Gabriel Marcel, both Catholic; and on the other hand the atheistic existentialists, among whom I class Heidegger, and then the French existentialists and myself. What they have in common is that they think that existence precedes essence, or, if you prefer, that subjectivity must be the starting point.

Just what does that mean? Let us consider some object that is manufactured, for example, a book or a paper-cutter: here is an object which has been made by an artisan whose inspiration came from a concept. He referred to the concept of what a paper-cutter is and likewise to a known method of production, which is part of the concept, something which is, by and large, a routine. Thus, the paper-cutter is at once an object produced in a certain way and, on the other hand, one having a specific use; and one can not postulate a man who produces a paper-cutter but does not know what it is used for. Therefore, let us say that, for the paper-cutter, essence—that is, the ensemble of both the production routines and the properties which enable it to be both produced and defined—precedes existence. Thus, the presence of the paper-cutter or book in front of me is determined. Therefore, we have here a technical view of the world whereby it can be said that production precedes existence.

When we conceive God as the Creator, He is generally thought of as a superior sort of artisan. Whatever doctrine we may be considering, whether one like that of Descartes or that of Leibnitz, we always grant that will more or less follows understanding or, at the very least, accompanies it, and that when God creates He knows exactly what He is creating. Thus, the concept of man in the mind of God is comparable to the concept of paper-cutter in the mind of the manufacturer, and, following certain techniques and a conception, God produces man, just as the artisan, following a definition and a technique, makes a paper-cutter. Thus, the individual man is the realisation of a certain concept in the divine intelligence.

In the eighteenth century, the atheism of the *philosophes* discarded the idea of God, but not the [related] notion that essence precedes existence. To a certain extent, this idea is found everywhere; we find it in Diderot, in Voltaire, and even in Kant. Man has a human nature; this human nature, which is the concept of the human, is found in all men, which means that each man is a particular example of a universal concept, man. In Kant, the result of this universality is that the wild-man, the natural man, as well as the bourgeois, are circumscribed by the same definition and have the same basic qualities. Thus, here too the essence of man precedes the historical existence that we find in nature.

Atheistic existentialism, which I represent, is more coherent. It states that if God does not exist, there is at least one being in whom existence precedes essence, a being who exists before he can be defined by any concept, and that this being is man, or, as Heidegger says, human reality. What is meant here by saying that existence precedes essence? It means that, first of all, man exists, turns up, appears on the scene, and, only afterwards, defines himself. If man, as the existentialist conceives him, is indefinable, it is because at first he is nothing. Only afterward will he be something, and he himself will have made what he will be. Thus, there is no human nature, since there is no God to conceive it. Not only is man what he conceives himself to be, but he is also only what he wills himself to be after this thrust toward existence.

Man is nothing else but what he makes of himself. Such is the first principle of existentialism. It is also what is called subjectivity, the name we are labeled with when charges are brought against us. But what do we mean by this, if not that man has a greater dignity than a stone or table? For we mean that man first exists, that is, that man first of all is the being who hurls himself toward a future and who is conscious of imagining himself as being in the future. . . .

. . . When we say that man chooses his own self, we mean that every one of us does likewise; but we also mean by that that in making this choice he also chooses all men. In fact, in creating the man that we want to be, there is not a single one of our acts which does not at the same time create an image of man as we think he ought to be. To choose to be this or that is to affirm at the same time the value of what we choose, because we can never choose evil. We always choose the good, and nothing can be good for us without being good for all.

If, . . . [furthermore], existence precedes essence, and if we grant that we exist and fashion our image at one and the same time, the image is valid for everybody and for our whole age. Thus, our responsibility is much greater than we might have supposed, because it involves all mankind. . . . Therefore, I am responsible for myself and for everyone else. I am creating a certain image of man of my own choosing. In choosing myself, I choose man.

This helps us understand what the actual content is of such rather grandiloquent words as anguish, forlornness, despair. As you will see, it's all quite simple.

First, what is meant by anguish? The existentialists say at once that man is anguish. What that means is this: the man who involves himself and who realizes that he is not only the person he chooses to be, but also a law-maker who is, at the same time, choosing all mankind as well as himself, can not . . . escape the feeling of his total and deep responsibility. Of course, there are many people who are not anxious; but we claim that they are hiding their anxiety, that they are fleeing from it. Certainly, many people believe that when they do something, they themselves are the only ones involved, and when someone says to them, "What if everyone acted that way?" they shrug their shoulders and answer, "Everyone doesn't act that way." But really, one should always ask himself, "What would happen if everybody looked at things that way?" There is no escaping this disturbing thought except by a kind of double-dealing. A man who lies and makes excuses for himself by saying "not everybody does that," is someone with an uneasy conscience, because the act of lying implies that a universal value is conferred upon the lie.

Anguish is evident even when it conceals itself. This is the anguish that Kierkegaard called the anguish of Abraham. You know the story: an angel has ordered Abraham to sacrifice his son; if it really were an angel who has come and said, "You are Abraham, you shall sacrifice your son," everything would be all right. But everyone might first wonder, "Is it really an angel, and am I really Abraham? What proof do I have?"

There was a madwoman who had hallucinations; someone used to speak to her on the telephone and give her orders. Her doctor asked her, "Who is it who talks to you?" She answered, "He says it's God." What proof did she really have that it was God? If an angel comes to me, what proof is there that it's an angel? And if I hear voices, what proof is there that they come from heaven and not from hell, or from the subconscious, or a pathological condition? What proves that they are addressed to me? What proof is there that I have been appointed to impose my choice and my conception of man on humanity? I'll never find any proof or sign to convince me of that. If a voice addresses me, it is always for me to decide that this is the angel's voice; if I consider that such an act is a good one, it is I who will choose to say that it is good rather than bad.

Now, I'm not being singled out as an Abraham, and yet at every moment I'm obliged to perform exemplary acts. For every man, everything happens as if all mankind had its eyes fixed on him and were guiding itself by what he does. And every man ought to say to himself, "Am I really the kind of man who has the right to act in such a way that humanity might guide itself by my actions?" And if he does not say that to himself, he is masking his anguish.

There is no question here of the kind of anguish which would lead to quietism, to inaction. It is a matter of a simple sort of anguish that anybody who has had responsibilities is familiar with. . . .

When we speak of forlornness, a term Heidegger was fond of, we mean only that God does not exist and that we have to face all the consequences of this. The existentialist is strongly opposed to a certain kind of secular ethics which would like to abolish God with the least possible expense. About 1880, some French teachers tried to set up a secular ethics which went something like this: God is a useless and costly hypothesis; we are discarding it; but, meanwhile, in order for there to be an ethics, a society, a civilization, it is essential that certain values be taken seriously and that they be considered as having an *a priori* existence. It must be obligatory, *a priori*, to be honest, not to lie, not to beat your wife, to have children, etc., etc. So we're going to try a little device which will make it possible to show that values exist all the same, inscribed in a heaven of ideas, though otherwise God does not exist. In other words—and this, I believe, is the tendency of everything called reformism in France—nothing will be changed if God does not exist. We shall find ourselves with the same norms of honesty, progress, and humanism, and we shall have made of God an outdated hypothesis which will peacefully die off by itself.

The existentialist, on the contrary, thinks it very distressing that God does not exist, because all possibility of finding values in a heaven of ideas disappears along with Him; there can no longer be an *a priori* Good, since there is no infinite and perfect consciousness to think it. Nowhere is it written that the Good exists, that we must be honest, that we must not lie; because the fact is we are on a plane where there are only men. Dostoievsky said, "If God didn't exist, everything would be possible." That is the very starting point of existentialism. Indeed, everything is permissible if God does not exist, and as a result man is forlorn, because neither within him nor without does he find anything to cling to. He can't start making excuses for himself.

If existence really does precede essence, there is no explaining things away by reference to a fixed and given human nature. In other words, there is no determinism, man is free, man is freedom. On the other hand, if God does not exist, we find no values or commands to turn to which legitimize our conduct. So, in the bright realm of values, we have no excuse behind us, nor justification before us. We are alone, with no excuses.

That is the idea I shall try to convey when I say that man is condemned to be free. Condemned, because he did not create himself, yet, in other respects is free; because, once thrown into the world, he is responsible for everything he does. . . .

As for despair, the term has a very simple meaning. It means that we shall confine ourselves to reckoning only with what depends upon our will, or on the ensemble of probabilities which make our action possible. When we want something, we always have to reckon with probabilities. I may be counting on the arrival of a friend. The friend is coming by rail or streetcar; this supposes that the train will arrive on schedule, or that the streetcar will not jump the track. I am left in the realm of possibility; but possibilities are to be reckoned with only to the point where my action comports with the ensemble of these possibilities, and no further. The moment the possibilities I am considering are not rigorously involved by my action, I ought to disengage myself from them, because no God, no scheme, can adapt the world and its possibilities to my will. When Descartes said, "Conquer yourself rather than the world," he meant essentially the same thing. . . .

. . . You see that it [existentialism] can not be taken for a philosophy of quietism, since it defines man in terms of action; nor for a pessimistic description of man—there is no doctrine more optimistic, since man's destiny is within himself; nor for an attempt to discourage man from acting, since it tells him that the only hope is in his acting and that action is the only thing that enables a man to live. Consequently, we are dealing here with an ethics of action and involvement.

Nevertheless, on the basis of a few notions like these, we are still charged with immuring man in his private subjectivity. There again we're very much misunderstood. Subjectivity of the individual is indeed our point of departure, and this for strictly philosophic reasons. Not because we are bourgeois, but because we want a doctrine based on truth and not a lot of fine theories, full of hope but with no real basis. There can be no other truth to take off from than this: *I think; therefore, I exist.* There we have the absolute truth of consciousness becoming aware of itself. Every theory which takes man out of the moment in which he becomes aware of himself is, at its very beginning, a theory which confounds truth, for outside the Cartesian *cogito*, all views are only probable, and a doctrine of probability which is not bound to a truth dissolves into thin air. In order to describe the probable, you must have a firm hold on the true. Therefore, before there can be any truth whatsoever, there must be an absolute truth; and this one is simple and easily arrived at; it's on everyone's doorstep; it's a matter of grasping it directly.

Secondly, this theory is the only one which gives man dignity, the only one which does not reduce him to an object. The effect of all materialism is to treat all men, including the one philosophizing, as objects, that is, as an ensemble of determined reactions in no way distinguished from the ensemble of qualities and phenomena which constitute a table or a chair or a stone. We definitely wish to establish the human realm as an ensemble of values distinct from the material realm. But the subjectivity that we have thus arrived at, and which we have claimed to be truth, is not a strictly individual subjectivity, for we have demonstrated that one discovers in the *cogito* not only himself, but others as well.

GABRIEL MARCEL / On the Ontological Mystery *

Gabriel Marcel (1889–   ) is a leading French exponent of Christian existentialism. He has expressed his philosophy in several plays and in such books as *Homo Viator; Being and Having;* and his Gifford Lectures, *The Mystery of Being.*

RATHER THAN to begin with abstract definitions and dialectical arguments which may be discouraging at the outset, I should like to start with a sort of global and intuitive characterisation of the man in whom the sense of the ontological—the sense of being—is lacking, or, to speak more correctly, of the man who has lost the awareness of this sense. Generally speaking, modern man is in this condition; if ontological demands worry him at all, it is only dully, as an obscure impulse. Indeed I wonder if a psychoanalytical method, deeper and more discerning than any that has been evolved until now, would not reveal the morbid effects of the repression of this sense and of the ignoring of this need.

The characteristic feature of our age seems to me to be what might be called the misplacement of the idea of function, taking function in its current sense which includes both the vital and the social functions.

The individual tends to appear both to himself and to others as an agglomeration of functions. As a result of deep historical causes, which can as yet be understood only in part, he has been led to see himself more and more as a mere assemblage of functions, the hierarchical interrelation of which seems to him questionable or at least subject to conflicting interpretations.

To take the vital functions first. It is hardly necessary to point out the role which historical materialism on the one hand, and Freudian doctrines on the other, have played in restricting the concept of man.

Then there are the social functions—those of the consumer, the producer, the citizen, etc.

Between these two there is, in theory, room for the psychological functions as well; but it is easy to see how these will tend to be interpreted in relation either to the social or the vital functions, so that their indepen-

* Gabriel Marcel, from "On the Ontological Mystery," in *The Philosophy of Existence* (New York: Philosophical Library, 1949), pp. 1–4, 8–11, 16, 18–19, 28–29. Used by permission of the publisher.

dence will be threatened and their specific character put in doubt. In this sense, Comte, served by his total incomprehension of psychical reality, displayed an almost prophetic instinct when he excluded psychology from his classification of sciences.

So far we are still dealing only with abstractions, but nothing is easier than to find concrete illustrations in this field.

Travelling on the Underground, I often wonder with a kind of dread what can be the inward reality of the life of this or that man employed on the railway—the man who opens the doors, for instance, or the one who punches the tickets. Surely everything both within him and outside him conspires to identify this man with his functions—meaning not only with his functions as worker, as trade union member or as voter, but with his vital functions as well. The rather horrible expression "time table" perfectly describes his life. So many hours for each function. Sleep too is a function which must be discharged so that the other functions may be exercised in their turn. The same with pleasure, with relaxation; it is logical that the weekly allowance of recreation should be determined by an expert on hygiene; recreation is a psycho-organic function which must not be neglected any more than, for instance, the function of sex. We need go no further; this sketch is sufficient to suggest the emergence of a kind of vital schedule; the details will vary with the country, the climate, the profession, etc., but what matters is that there is a schedule.

It is true that certain disorderly elements—sickness, accidents of every sort—will break in on the smooth working of the system. It is therefore natural that the individual should be overhauled at regular intervals like a watch (this is often done in America). The hospital plays the part of the inspection bench or the repair shop. And it is from this same standpoint of function that such essential problems as birth control will be examined.

As for death, it becomes, objectively and functionally, the scrapping of what has ceased to be of use and must be written off as total loss.

I need hardly insist on the stifling impression of sadness produced by this functionalised world. It is sufficient to recall the dreary image of the retired official, or those urban Sundays when the passers-by look like people who have retired from life. In such a world, there is something mocking and sinister even in the tolerance awarded to the man who has retired from his work.

But besides the sadness felt by the onlooker, there is the dull, intolerable unease of the actor himself who is reduced to living as though he were in fact submerged by his functions. This uneasiness is enough to show that there is in all this some appalling mistake, some ghastly misinterpretation, implanted in defenceless minds by an increasingly inhuman social order and an equally inhuman philosophy (for if the philosophy has prepared the way for the order, the order has also shaped the philosophy).

I have written on another occasion that, provided it is taken in its metaphysical and not its physical sense, the distinction between the *full* and the *empty* seems to me more fundamental than that between the *one* and the *many*. This is particularly applicable to the case in point. Life in a world centered on function is liable to despair because in reality this world is *empty*, it rings hollow; and if it resists this temptation it is only to the extent that there come into play from within it and in its favour certain hidden forces which are beyond its power to conceive or to recognise.

It should be noted that this world is, on the one hand, riddled with problems and, on the other, determined to allow no room for mystery. I shall come back to this distinction between problem and mystery which I believe to be fundamental. For the moment I shall only point out that to eliminate or to try to eliminate mystery is (in this functionalist world) to bring into play in the face of events which break in on the course of existence—such as birth, love and death—that psychological and pseudo-scientific category of the "purely natural" which deserves a study to itself. In reality, this is nothing more than the remains of a degraded rationalism from whose standpoint cause explains effect and accounts for it exhaustively. . . .

At this point we can begin to define the distinction between mystery and problem. A mystery is a problem which encroaches upon its own data, invading them, as it were, and thereby transcending itself as a simple problem. A set of examples will help us to grasp the content of this definition.

It is evident that there exists a mystery of the union of the body and the soul. The indivisible unity always inadequately expressed by such phrases as *I have a body, I make use of my body, I feel my body*, etc., can be neither analysed nor reconstituted out of precedent elements. It is not only data, I would say that it is the basis of data, in the sense of being my own presence to myself, a presence of which the act of self-consciousness is, in the last analysis, only an inadequate symbol.

It will be seen at once that there is no hope of establishing an exact frontier between problem and mystery. For in reflecting on a mystery we tend inevitably to degrade it to the level of a problem. . . .

Let us take another illustration, more immediate and more particular, which may shed some light on the distinction between problem and mystery.

Say that I have made an encounter which has left a deep and lasting trace on all my life. It may happen to anyone to experience the deep spiritual significance of such a meeting—yet this is something which philosophers have commonly ignored or disdained, doubtless because it affects only the particular person as person—it cannot be universalised, it does not concern rational being in general.

It is clear that such a meeting raises, if you will, a problem; but it is equally clear that the solution of this problem will always fall short of the only question that matters. Suppose that I am told, for instance: "The reason you have met this person in this place is that you both like the same kind of scenery, or that you both need the same kind of treatment for your health"—the explanation means nothing. Crowds of people who apparently share my tastes were in the Engadine or in Florence at the time I was there; and there are always numbers of patients suffering from the same disease as myself at the health resort I frequent. But neither this supposed identity of tastes nor this common affliction has brought us together in any real sense; it has nothing to do with that intimate and unique affinity with which we are dealing. At the same time, it would be transgression of this valid reasoning to treat this affinity as if it were itself the cause and to say: "It is precisely this which has determined our meeting."

Hence I am in the presence of a mystery. That is to say, of a reality rooted in what is beyond the domain of the problematical properly so called. Shall we avoid the difficulty by saying that it was after all nothing but a coincidence, a lucky chance? But the whole of me immediately protests against this empty formula, this vain negation of what I apprehend with the deepest of my being. Once again we are brought back to our first definition of a mystery as a problem which encroaches upon its own data: I who inquire into the meaning and the possibility of this meeting, I cannot place myself outside it or before it; I am engaged in this encounter, I depend upon it, I am inside it in a certain sense, it envelops me and it comprehends me—even if it is not comprehended by me. Thus it is only by a kind of betrayal or denial that I can say: "After all, it might not have happened, I would still have been what I was, and what I am to-day." Nor must it be said: I have been changed by it as by an outward cause. No, it has developed me from within, it has acted in me as an inward principle. . . .

The world of the problematical is the world of fear and desire, which are inseparable; at the same time, it is that world of the functional—or of what can be functionalised—which was defined at the beginning of this essay; finally, it is the kingdom of technics of whatever sort. Every technique serves, or can be made to serve, some desire or some fear; conversely, every desire as every fear tends to invent its appropriate technique. From this standpoint, despair consists in the recognition of the ultimate inefficacy of all technics, joined to the inability or the refusal to change over to a new ground—a ground where all technics are seen to be incompatible with the fundamental nature of being, which itself escapes our grasp (in so far as our grasp is limited to the world of objects and to this alone). It is for this reason that we seem nowadays to have entered upon the very era of despair; we have not ceased to believe in technics, that is to envisage reality as a complex of problems; yet at the same time the failure of technics *as a whole* is as discernible to us as its *partial* triumphs. To the question: what can man achieve? we continue to reply: He can achieve as much as his technics; yet we are obliged to admit that these technics are unable *to save man himself,* and even that they are apt to conclude the most sinister alliance with the enemy he bears within him.

I have said that man is *at the mercy of his technics.* This must be understood to mean that he is increasingly incapable of controlling his technics, or rather of *controlling his own control.* This control of his own control, which is nothing else than the expression on the plane of active life of what I have called thought at one remove, cannot find its centre or its support anywhere except in recollection.

It will be objected that even those whose faith in technics is strongest are bound to admit that there exist enormous realms which are outside man's control. But what matters is the spirit in which this admission is made. We have to recognise that we have no control over meteorological conditions, but the question is: do we consider it desirable and just that we should have such control? The more the sense of the ontological tends to disappear, the more unlimited become the claims of the mind which has lost it to a kind of cosmic governance, because it is less and less capable of examining its own credentials to the exercise of such dominion.

It must be added that the more the disproportion grows between the claims of the technical intelligence on the one hand, and the persisting fragility and precariousness of what remains its material substratum on the other, the more acute becomes the constant danger of despair which threatens this intelligence. From this standpoint there is truly an intimate dialectical correlation between the optimism of technical progress and the philosophy of despair which seems inevitably to emerge from it—it is needless to insist on the examples offered by the world of to-day. . . .

As against this, hope is what implies credit. Contrary to what was thought by Spinoza, who seems to me to have confused two quite distinct notions, fear is correlated to desire and not to hope, whereas what is negatively correlated to hope is the act which consists in putting things at their worst—an act which is strikingly illustrated by what is known as defeatism, and which is ever in danger of being degraded into the desire of the worst. Hope consists in asserting that there is at the heart of being, beyond all data, beyond all inventories and all calculations, a mysterious principle which is in connivance with me, which cannot but will that which I will, if what I will deserves to be willed and is, in fact, willed by the whole of my being.

We have now come to the centre of what I have called the ontological mystery, and the simplest illustrations will be the best. To hope against all hope that a person whom I love will recover from a disease which is said to be incurable is to say: It is impossible that I should be alone in willing this cure; it is impossible that reality in its inward depth should be hostile or so much as indifferent to what I assert is in itself a good. It is quite useless to tell me of discouraging *cases* or *examples:* beyond all experience, all probability, all statistics, I assert that a given order shall be re-established, that reality *is* on my side in willing it to be so. I do not wish: I assert; such is the prophetic tone of true hope.

No doubt I shall be told: "In the immense majority of cases this is an illusion." But it is of the essence of hope to exclude the consideration of cases; moreover, it can be shown that there exists an ascending dialectic of hope, whereby hope rises to a plane which transcends the level of all possible empirical disproof—the plane of salvation as opposed to that of success in whatever form. . . .

Pessimism is rooted in the same soil as the inability to be at the disposal of others. If the latter grows in us as we grow old, it is only too often because, as we draw near to what we regard as the term of our life, anxiety grows in us almost to the point of choking us; to protect itself, it sets up an increasingly heavy, exacting and, I would add, vulnerable mechanism of self-defence. The capacity to hope diminishes in proportion as the soul becomes increasingly chained to its experience and to the categories which arise from it, and as it is given over more completely and more desperately to the world of the problematical.

Here at last can be brought together the various motifs and thematic elements which I have had to bring out one by one. In contrast to the captive soul we have described, the soul which is at the disposal of others is consecrated and inwardly dedicated; it is protected against suicide and despair, which are interrelated and alike, because it knows that it is not its own, and that the most legitimate use it can make of its freedom is precisely to recognise that it does not belong to itself; this recognition is the starting point of its activity and creativeness.

The difficulties of a philosophy of this sort must not be disguised. It is inevitably faced by a disquieting alternative: Either it will try to solve these difficulties—to give all the answers; in that case it will fall into the excesses of a dogmatism which ignores its vital principles and, I would add, into those of a sacrilegious theodicy, or else it will allow these difficulties to subsist, labelling them as mysteries.

Between these two I believe that there exists a middle way—a narrow, difficult and dangerous path which I have tried to discover. But, like Karl Jaspers in his *Philosophy of Existence*, I can only proceed in this kind of country by calling out to other travellers. If, as it occasionally happened, certain minds respond—not the generality, but this being and that other— then there is a way. But, as I believe Plato perceived with incomparable clarity, it is a way which is undiscoverable except through love, to which alone it is visible, and this brings us to what is perhaps the deepest characteristic of that realm of the metaproblematical of which I have tried to explore certain regions.

For Further Study

Barrett, William. *Irrational Man*. New York: Doubleday, 1958, Part 3, "The Existentialists." (Also Anchor Book A 321.)

Buber, Martin. *I and Thou*. 2nd ed.; New York: Scribner's, 1958.

Desan, Wilfrid. *The Marxism of Jean-Paul Sartre*. Garden City: Doubleday, 1966. (Anchor Book A 507.)

Dufrenne, Mikel. "Existentialism and Existentialisms," *Philosophy and Phenomenological Research*, 26 (September, 1965): 51–62.

Kaufmann, Walter. *Existentialism from Dostoevsky to Sartre*. New York: Meridian, 1956. (Selections from various existentialist thinkers including Kierkegaard, Jaspers, Heidegger, and Sartre.) (Meridian Book M 39.)

Lessing, Arthur. "Marxist Existentialism," *Review of Metaphysics*, 20 (March, 1967): 461–482.

Moore, Asher. "Existential Phenomenology," *Philosophy and Phenomenological Research*, 27 (March, 1967): 408–414.

Olson, Robert G. *An Introduction to Existentialism*. New York: Dover, 1962, esp. Ch. 1, "Value Orientation"; Ch. 2, "The Human Condition."

Sartre, Jean-Paul. *No Exit and Three Other Plays*. New York: Random House, n.d. (Vintage V 16.)

Shinn, Roger L. *The Existentialist Posture*. New York: Association Press, 1959. (Reflection Book, 122 pp.)·

Tillich, Paul. "Existential Philosophy," *Journal of the History of Ideas*, 5 (January, 1944): 44–70.

Warnock, Mary. *The Philosophy of Sartre*. New York: Barnes & Noble, 1965.

18 Agreements and Disagreements

G. J. WARNOCK / Metaphysics as Vision *

G. J. Warnock (1923–   ) teaches philosophy at Oxford University and has written numerous articles in analytical philosophy. Among his books are *Ethics Since 1900*, *Berkeley*, and *Contemporary Moral Philosophy*.

"PHILOSOPHY IS many things and there is no formula to cover them all. But if I were asked to express in one single word what is its most essential feature I would unhesitatingly say: vision."—"There is something visionary about great metaphysicians as if they had the power to see beyond the horizons of their time."—"To say that metaphysics is nonsense *is* nonsense."

These three quotations are taken from a recent article by Dr. F. Waismann.[1] They certainly indicate no disposition to regard metaphysics with contempt, as a pure waste of time, or as the product of some fundamental misunderstanding. To do this, he observes, would be to fail to acknowledge "the enormous part played at least in the past by those systems." We ought now to consider what part they did play—and also, why Dr. Waismann should have been inclined to put in those qualifying words, "at least in the past."

What, roughly at any rate, are we to understand by the notion of meta-

* G. J. Warnock, from "Metaphysics," in *English Philosophy Since 1900* (New York: Oxford University Press, 1958), pp. 136–145. (Home University Library of Modern Knowledge.) Used by permission of the publisher.
[1] *Contemporary British Philosophy*, Third Series, 1956, pp. 447–90. [For selections from this article, see pp. 215–223.]

physical "vision"? Dr. Waismann writes that "what is decisive is a new way of seeing and, what goes with it, the will to transform the whole intellectual scene. This is the real thing and everything else is subservient to it." It is essential here, first of all, to distinguish carefully between a new way of seeing, and the seeing of something new. To see something new, to find out what was not known before, is not an exercise of *metaphysical* vision—even though the effect of this new knowledge may even be to "transform the whole intellectual scene." It may be, for example, that the theory of evolution has done as much as anything in the last hundred years to alter our ways of thinking, of seeing the world and our own place in it; but this of course was a scientific and not a metaphysical theory, supported not so much by arguments or would-be arguments as by an immense variety and range of empirical facts. It is by contrast characteristic of a metaphysical theory that facts should neither be cited in its support nor be brought in evidence against it; it was for this reason that the Positivists were able to object that metaphysical doctrines were "unverifiable"; such a theory consists not in an account of any new facts but in a new account of familiar facts, a new reading, so to speak, of what has already been agreed upon.

But do not some *scientific* theories still come within the scope of such a description? Certainly they do. For example, the heliocentric theory of the planetary system was of exactly this character. It offered a new "way of seeing" astronomical phenomena without, directly at any rate, adding to astronomical knowledge; and no doubt it was for this very reason that it was thought to be of far more than parochial significance—to be, in fact, a revolutionary and even a dangerous shift in the general intellectual landscape. However, though such theories may often be felt to be of very general, and therefore of some philosophical, importance, they themselves are certainly not metaphysical theories. Why not? Is it not because they are insufficiently general? The *direct* concern of the Copernican theory is solely with the movements of planets; its wider implications, if it really has any, are incidental. By contrast a metaphysical theory may be all-embracing, or immediately relevant at least to a very wide range of diverse phenomena. Such a theory as Spinoza's, for example, not only dictates a peculiar way of regarding facts in any field whatever; it was also at any rate intended to have precise moral and even religious consequences as well. It was intended to transform "the *whole* intellectual scene," and to do this *directly*, not merely by implication, or in virtue of some quirk of psychology or association of ideas. And Hegel notoriously had no doubt whatever that there was a Hegelian way of seeing *any* subject-matter, however little in certain cases he may have succeeded in conveying to others what that way was.

"Suppose that a man revolts against accepted opinion, that he feels 'cramped' in its categories; a time may come when he believes, rightly or wrongly, that he has freed himself of these notions; when he has that sense of sudden growth in looking back at the prejudices which held him captive; or a time when he believes, rightly or wrongly, that he has reached a vantage point from which things can be seen to be arranged in clean and orderly patterns while difficulties of long standing dissolve as though by magic." [2] These words describe exactly the situation of, for example, Berkeley. "I wonder not," he wrote, "at my sagacity in discovering the obvious tho' amazing truth, I rather wonder at my stupid inadvertency in not finding it out before." [3] He had the sense, as he freely asserted, of "a vast view of things soluble hereby." It is worth looking into his case a little further.

Berkeley was familiar, mainly through Locke, with a "way of seeing" the world that was chiefly derived from the thriving scientific inquiries of the seventeenth century. Material things were thought of as being atomic in structure, and in character predominantly mechanical. Our knowledge of them was supposed to be founded upon the occurrence in our minds of "ideas" caused ultimately by the mechanical operation of "corpuscles" upon our bodily organs; and it was thought to be at least an open question how far these ideas could be regarded as reliable indications of the actual character of the "external" world. Fundamentally the physical world was thought of as a mechanical system describable in quantitative laws, but known to us only "indirectly," through the mediation of sensory ideas which in some respects almost certainly misled us as to the real character of our physical environment. By this way of seeing things Berkeley felt most violently "cramped." It appeared to him that the interposition of "ideas" could end only in the sceptical overthrow of our claims to any actual knowledge of the physical world. He felt that the logical conclusion of the mechanistic view must be atheism, the idea that matter was God or that there was no god at all. He could not see (and neither could Locke) how on this view the existence and immortality of the soul could be established. And in countless lesser details he thought that he found insoluble difficulties or undesirable conclusions. But then—and as it appears, quite suddenly —he came to see the whole situation differently. He changed, so to speak, his angle of vision. And at once all the problems seemed to disappear, to be replaced by a strange but startlingly simple new picture. Suppose that matter did not exist at all! What would be the advantages of this supposition? It would simply eliminate the problems of scepticism—for then there would be no "external world" as to which we could wonder how far our "ideas" corresponded with it. It would utterly deflate the pretensions of physical science, the "corpuscular philosophy"—for there would be nothing for mechanistic hypotheses to be *true* of, they would have to be presented as, at best, convenient fictions to facilitate prediction. And what

[2] *Ibid.*, p. 483.
[3] *Philosophical Commentaries*, 279.

would be the disadvantages? None surely—for so long as we suppose "ideas" to occur, the course of our actual experience would be exactly the same. And does it matter that there are no longer objects to cause these ideas? On the contrary—the notion that matter could be a true cause was in any case a bad one; and now the way is clear to attribute the occurrence of ideas to their proper origin, the will of God. On this view, then, scepticism is impossible; materialism is impossible; atheism is actually self-contradictory; so far from its being questionable whether the soul exists, there in fact exists *nothing* but "spirits and ideas." Is there not "a vast view of things soluble hereby"? And so far from worrying over the fact that his new view has no ordinary, gross, experimental and factual consequences, Berkeley is particularly pleased to observe that from it Common Sense "receives no manner of disturbance." He believed indeed that his doctrine was capable of proof; but he never for a moment supposed it to be "verifiable."

Here, then, is a fair example of a metaphysical theory. Almost every paragraph that Berkeley wrote was intended to amplify, to defend, to explain, to render more acceptable the "vision" of a theocentric, immaterial universe by which he had seemed able at one stroke to escape from the difficulties and horrors of Locke's scientific, "corpuscular," material world. "The arguments he will offer, the attacks he will make, the suggestions he will advance are all devised for one end: to win other people over to his own way of looking at things, to change the whole climate of opinion. . . . What is decisive is that he has seen things from a new angle of vision. Compared to that everything else is secondary." [4] He is not like a man proving theorems or relating his discoveries; he is like a reformer endeavouring to propagate a cause.

Is there any value in such theories as these? Do such visionary projects of reform ever really succeed? It might be said that such theories may have, and often do have, the purely intrinsic value of admirable intellectual achievements; they speak well, as it were, for the capacities of the human mind; but do they ever make any actual difference? Sometimes they do—but seldom, it seems, quite the difference that their prophets intend. It appears to be most evidently true that, in its simple foundations, our ordinary "way of seeing" the world is absolutely stable and obstinately unshakeable. Such a project as Berkeley's, which really requires us to abandon our notion of things as solid, substantial, enduring, indifferent to the presence or absence of percipient organisms, seems to attack our conceptual habits at so deep a level that it can really have no serious chance of succeeding. It is doubtful how far even Berkeley was able to retain the full sense of his vision for more than an occasional moment; one cannot so easily shake off what is natural to one's species. But we may, in other cases,

4 Waismann, *loc. cit.*

come to see things differently in certain restricted fields—and really come to do so *naturally*, not in visionary moments only or in abstract theory. Dr. Waismann suggests that in the work of Descartes there may be "a prophetic aspect of the comprehensibility of nature, a bold anticipation of what has been achieved in science at a much later date. The true successors of Descartes were those who translated the spirit of this philosophy into deeds, not Spinoza or Malebranche but Newton and the mathematical description of nature." (Here Berkeley can be seen to have been working *against* the main trend of thought in his time.) And similarly the "true successors" of Hegel might be said to be, not the philosophers who elaborated his doctrines into ever-deepening obscurity, but the historians whom he taught to find in the passage of time not merely a succession of independent episodes, but intelligible processes of change, of growth and decay, having certain analogies with the life-cycle of organic beings. Certainly there *may* be fields of inquiry, areas of knowledge, in which some metaphysician's new way of seeing may have the most fruitful and important results. But there may not be. His theory may stand as a mere eccentricity, with some interest perhaps, but no effect on anything whatever. Whether this will be so, he will doubtless be unable to foresee.

Why are there today few, if any, metaphysicians? The answer to this question, I believe, has at least three branches. First, there have never been many real metaphysicians at any time. To be, after all, sufficiently obsessed by a visionary project of intellectual reform to spend years upon its systematization and propagation is, fortunately no doubt, a very rare condition. There may well have been in earlier times a large number of *second-hand* metaphysicians, parasitic expositors of and elaborators on the theories of some truly original figure. But such secondary labours are surely as pointless as they are usually uninteresting. Of what interest would it be to patch up, to amend and expound, the doctrines of Bradley, if really one had no inclination whatever to share the queer view from which his own fervour was derived? It is reasonable enough to abstain from such work as this; for many vastly more interesting problems lie ready to hand. Is it really surprising that most philosophers should find in these other problems their best occupation? They are fortunate today in that so very many quite unmetaphysical problems have been brought into the light.

Second, it can, I think, be reasonably said that the condition of true metaphysical fervour is today more difficult to achieve than was formerly the case; for it depends in large part upon a kind of illusion which, for good or ill and almost certainly for good, is now inevitably rare. Much admirable philosophical work has been done upon the notion of "ways of seeing," of angles of vision, of—to speak more ponderously—alternative conceptual systems. We have become familiar enough with the idea that phenomena may be viewed in more than one way, comprehended within more than one theory, interpreted by more than one set of explanatory concepts. It has thus become almost impossible to believe that some *one* way of seeing, some *one* sort of theory, has any exclusive claim to be the *right* way; the notion of "reality" itself, it would commonly be held, must be given its sense in terms of some particular theory or view, so that the claim that any such theory reveals or corresponds to "reality" can be given a circular justification which is also open, in just the same way, to quite other views as well. But the belief that some new sort of theory is merely *possible*—that some novel set of concepts or categories *could* be employed —is hardly a sufficiently dynamic incentive to engender the production of a true metaphysical theory. If one has not, and one scarcely can have, the initial conviction that a novel "way of seeing" has some *unique* claim to acceptance, one is unlikely to undertake the considerable labour of equipping it in a full metaphysical panoply. Such work is impossible perhaps, and certainly unattractive, to the disillusioned.

Finally, there are no doubt in our "climate of thought" many factors of a more general kind that are in some way unfriendly to the metaphysical temperament. One might perhaps hazard the idea that metaphysical speculation has often arisen from, and often too been a substitute for, religious or theological doctrine. If so, it could be expected to show some decline in a period when very many people neither have, nor appear to be much oppressed by the want of, any serious religious convictions. It is not obvious that, if this were so, it ought to be deplored. It is, on the other hand, quite clear how undesirable it would be for philosophers to *pretend* to suffer from cosmic anxieties by which they were in fact not seriously troubled at all. Metaphysics, like religion, ought not to be manufactured in deference to any supposed requirements of intellectual decorum, or in the pursuit of some once genuine fervour which, in present conditions, would be synthetic or simulated.

ALFRED NORTH WHITEHEAD / The
Task of Speculative Philosophy *

Alfred North Whitehead (1861–1947) was one of the great specula-
tive philosophers of the present century, whose early work was at the
Universities of Cambridge and London in mathematics and logic.
With Russell he wrote *Principia Mathematica*. In 1924 he came
to Harvard University where he had a brilliant career in philosophy.
His philosophical writings include *Science and the Modern World*;
Adventures of Ideas; and *Process and Reality*.

. . . [F]OUR STRONG IMPRESSIONS dominate my mind: First, that the movement of historical, and philosophical, criticism of detached questions,
which on the whole has dominated the last two centuries, has done its
work, and requires to be supplemented by a more sustained effort of constructive thought. Secondly, that the true method of philosophical construction is to frame a scheme of ideas, the best that one can, and unflinch-
ingly to explore the interpretation of experience in terms of that scheme.
Thirdly, that all constructive thought, on the various special topics of
scientific interest, is dominated by some such scheme, unacknowledged,
but no less influential in guiding the imagination. The importance of
philosophy lies in its sustained effort to make such schemes explicit, and
thereby capable of criticism and improvement. . . .

Speculative Philosophy is the endeavour to frame a coherent, logical,
necessary system of general ideas in terms of which every element of our
experience can be interpreted. By this notion of 'interpretation' I mean
that everything of which we are conscious, as enjoyed, perceived, willed, or
thought, shall have the character of a particular instance of the general
scheme. Thus the philosophical scheme should be coherent, logical, and, in
respect to its interpretation, applicable and adequate. Here 'applicable'
means that some items of experience are thus interpretable, and 'adequate'
means that there are no items incapable of such interpretation.

'Coherence,' as here employed, means that the fundamental ideas, in
terms of which the scheme is developed, presuppose each other so that in
isolation they are meaningless. This requirement does not mean that they

are definable in terms of each other; it means that what is indefinable in one such notion cannot be abstracted from its relevance to the other notions. It is the ideal of speculative philosophy that its fundamental notions shall not seem capable of abstraction from each other. In other words, it is presupposed that no entity can be conceived in complete abstraction from the system of the universe, and that it is the business of speculative philosophy to exhibit this truth. This character is its coherence.

The term 'logical' has its ordinary meaning, including 'logical' consistency, or lack of contradiction, the definition of constructs in logical terms, the exemplification of general logical notions in specific instances, and the principles of inference. It will be observed that logical notions must themselves find their places in the scheme of philosophic notions.

It will also be noticed that this ideal of speculative philosophy has its rational side and its empirical side. The rational side is expressed by the terms 'coherent' and 'logical.' The empirical side is expressed by the terms 'applicable' and 'adequate.' But the two sides are bound together by clearing away an ambiguity which remains in the previous explanation of the term 'adequate.' The adequacy of the scheme over every item does not mean adequacy over such items as happen to have been considered. It means that the texture of observed experience, as illustrating the philosophic scheme, is such that all related experience must exhibit the same texture. Thus the philosophic scheme should be 'necessary,' in the sense of bearing in itself its own warrant of universality throughout all experience, provided that we confine ourselves to that which communicates with immediate matter of fact. But what does not so communicate is unknowable, and the unknowable is unknown; and so this universality defined by 'communication' can suffice.

This doctrine of necessity in universality means that there is an essence to the universe which forbids relationships beyond itself, as a violation of its rationality. Speculative philosophy seeks that essence.

Philosophers can never hope finally to formulate these metaphysical first principles. Weakness of insight and deficiencies of language stand in the way inexorably. Words and phrases must be stretched towards a generality foreign to their ordinary usage; and however such elements of language be stabilized as technicalities, they remain metaphors mutely appealing for an imaginative leap.

There is no first principle which is in itself unknowable, not to be captured by a flash of insight. But, putting aside the difficulties of language, deficiency in imaginative penetration forbids progress in any form other than that of an asymptotic approach to a scheme of principles, only definable in terms of the ideal which they should satisfy. . . .

Thus the first requisite is to proceed by the method of generalization so that certainly there is some application; and the test of some success is application beyond the immediate origin. In other words, some synoptic vision has been gained.

In this description of philosophic method, the term 'philosophic generalization' has meant 'the utilization of specific notions, applying to a restricted group of facts, for the divination of the generic notions which apply to all facts.'

In its use of this method natural science has shown a curious mixture of rationalism and irrationalisn. Its prevalent tone of thought has been ardently rationalistic within its own borders, and dogmatically irrational beyond those borders. In practice such an attitude tends to become a dogmatic denial that there are any factors in the world not fully expressible in terms of its own primary notions devoid of further generalization. Such a denial is the self-denial of thought.

The second condition for the success of imaginative construction is unflinching pursuit of the two rationalistic ideals, coherence and logical perfection. Logical perfection does not here require any detailed explanation. . . .

The requirement of coherence is the great preservative of rationalistic sanity. But the validity of its criticism is not always admitted. If we consider philosophical controversies, we shall find that disputants tend to require coherence from their adversaries, and to grant dispensations to themselves. It has been remarked that a system of philosophy is never refuted; it is only abandoned. The reason is that logical contradictions, except as temporary slips of the mind—plentiful, though temporary—are the most gratuitous of errors; and usually they are trivial. Thus, after criticism, systems do not exhibit mere illogicalities. They suffer from inadequacy and incoherence. . . .

In its turn every philosophy will suffer a deposition. But the bundle of philosophic systems expresses a variety of general truths about the universe, awaiting co-ordination and assignment of their various spheres of validity. Such progress in co-ordination is provided by the advance of philosophy; and in this sense philosophy has advanced from Plato onwards. According to this account of the achievement of rationalism, the chief error in philosophy is overstatement. The aim at generalization is sound, but the estimate of success is exaggerated. There are two main forms of such overstatement. One form is what I have termed elsewhere, the 'fallacy of misplaced concreteness.' This fallacy consists in neglecting the degree of abstraction involved when an actual entity is considered merely so far as it exemplifies certain categories of thought. There are aspects of actualities which are simply ignored so long as we restrict thought to these categories. Thus the success of a philosophy is to be measured by its comparative avoidance of this fallacy, when thought is restricted within its categories.

The other form of overstatement consists in a false estimate of logical procedure in respect to certainty, and in respect to premises. Philosophy has been haunted by the unfortunate notion that its method is dogmatically to indicate premises which are severally clear, distinct, and certain; and to erect upon those premises a deductive system of thought.

But the accurate expression of the final generalities is the goal of discussion and not its origin. Philosophy has been misled by the example of mathematics; and even in mathematics the statement of the ultimate logical principles is beset with difficulties, as yet insuperable. . . .

Philosophy will not regain its proper status until the gradual elaboration of categoreal schemes, definitely stated at each stage of progress, is recognized as its proper objective. There may be rival schemes, inconsistent among themselves; each with its own merits and its own failures. It will then be the purpose of research to conciliate the differences. Metaphysical categories are not dogmatic statements of the obvious; they are tentative formulations of the ultimate generalities.

. . . [T]here are certain general truths, about the actual things in the common world of activity, which will be obscured when attention is confined to some particular detailed mode of considering them. These general truths, involved in the meaning of every particular notion respecting the actions of things, are the subject matter for speculative philosophy.

Philosophy destroys its usefulness when it indulges in brilliant feats of explaining away. It is then trespassing with the wrong equipment upon the field of particular sciences. Its ultimate appeal is to the general consciousness of what in practice we experience. Whatever thread of presupposition characterizes social expression throughout the various epochs of rational society, must find its place in philosophic theory. Speculative boldness must be balanced by complete humility before logic, and before fact. It is a disease of philosophy when it is neither bold nor humble, but merely a reflection of the temperamental presuppositions of exceptional personalities.

Analogously, we do not trust any recasting of scientific theory depending upon a single performance of an aberrant experiment, unrepeated. The ultimate test is always widespread, recurrent experience; and the more general the rationalistic scheme, the more important is this final appeal.

The useful function of philosophy is to promote the most general systematization of civilized thought. There is a constant reaction between specialism and common sense. It is the part of the special sciences to modify common sense. Philosophy is the welding of imagination and common sense into a restraint upon specialists, and also into an enlargement of their imaginations. By providing the generic notions philosophy should make it easier to conceive the infinite variety of specific instances which rest unrealized in the womb of nature.

For Further Study

Adams, George P. *Man and Metaphysics*. New York: Columbia U. Press, 1948.

Adler, Mortimer J. *The Conditions of Philosophy*. New York: Dell Publishing Co., 1967, Ch. 10, "Philosophy as a Public Enterprise: Agreement and Progress." (Delta Book 1451.)

Burtt, E. A. *In Search of Philosophic Understanding*. New York: New American Library, 1965. (Mentor Book, 1967, MY765.)

Charlesworth, Maurice. "Metaphysics as Conceptual Revision," *Philosophical Quarterly*, 16 (October, 1966): 308–318.

Collingwood, R. G. *An Essay on Metaphysics*. Oxford: Clarendon Press, 1940, Ch. 7, "The Reform of Metaphysics."

Emmet, E. R. *Learning to Philosophise*. New York: Philosophical Library, 1965, Ch. 6, "Appearance and Reality."

Emmett, Dorothy. *The Nature of Metaphysical Thinking*. New York: St. Martin's, 1956, Ch. 1, "The Problem of Metaphysics"; Ch. 10, "The Contemporary Prospect."

Hampshire, S. N. "Metaphysical Systems," in *The Nature of Metaphysics*, ed. D. F. Pears. New York: St. Martin's, 1960.

Hartshorne, Charles. *Reality as Social Process: Studies in Metaphysics and Religion*. Glencoe: Free Press; Boston: Beacon Press, 1953, Ch. 4, "A Synthesis of Idealism and Realism."

Kaplan, Abraham. *The New World of Philosophy*. New York: Random House, 1961, "Introduction."

Levi, Albert William. *Philosophy and the Modern World*. Bloomington: Indiana U. Press, 1959, Ch. 1, "Multiplicity and Division."

Pepper, Stephen C. "The Root Metaphor Theory of Metaphysics," *Journal of Philosophy*, 32 (1935): 365–374. (See also the author's book, *World Hypotheses*.)

Urban, Wilbur Marshall. *Beyond Realism and Idealism*. London: Allen & Unwin, 1949, Ch. 10, "Realism, Idealism and Philosophia Perennis."

PART **4**

The Realm of Values

19 The Nature of Values

ETHEL M. ALBERT | Facts and Values *

Ethel M. Albert (1918–   ) was associated with the Comparative Study of Values in Five Cultures, Harvard University, 1953–1955, and has been a Fellow at the Center for Advanced Study in the Behavioral Sciences, Stanford, California. She is now a member of the Department of Anthropology at Northwestern University. Her interests include ethnophilosophy, philosophy of the social sciences, and value theory. She is coauthor of *Great Traditions in Ethics*.

NEARLY TWENTY-FIVE CENTURIES AGO, Socrates asked: What is the good? We are still waiting for the answer. It is not as though nobody has tried. From the Academy to the cracker-barrel, philosophers have offered all too many answers. Perhaps the Socratic question is less a directly answerable query than a continuing symbol of perplexity. Its interpretation has varied with times and places and the ingenuity of philosophers, though the framework has remained much the same.

The mold of moral philosophy in occidental culture was cast in ancient Athens. Plato has left us the image of Socrates as the rational man of high principle, his eyes averted from the world as it is, fixed on an Ideal realm where Truth, Goodness and Beauty are somehow one, truly real, absolute and eternal. To the Sophists he left politicking and the dirty business of getting on in the world. They were very happy to inherit this-worldly good. Their acceptance of the rules of the game as all the ethic we need and

* Ethel M. Albert, from "Social Science Facts and Philosophical Values," *The Antioch Review*, 17 (Winter, 1957–58): 406–430. Used by permission of The Antioch Press.

their refusal to be bound by the rule of reason made the Sophists philosophy's pariahs. Aristotle shared Plato's disdain for them, although he could not share Plato's conviction that the Good had to be sought in some better world than this. Rejecting out of hand the relativism and hedonism of the Sophists, Aristotle proposed a "practical science" of ethics, based on knowledge of what different men find good. The true good for man he equated with what the good man—the philosopher—found good.

None of the parties to the disputes in Athens doubted that different people valued different things. The relativity of values at the descriptive level has never been a problem for philosophy. But the Sophists deduced from it that values are essentially relative. Socrates and Aristotle concluded from the same data that lots of people do not know what is really good.

More than two thousand years of discussion of the relationships between what is valued and what is worthy to be valued have yielded many permutations and combinations of the themes proposed by the Athenian philosophers: absolutism vs. relativism; exalted moral idealism vs. interest in the world as it is; rationalism vs. irrationalism; pure theoretical vs. practical ethics; facts vs. values—both what is valued vs. what is valuable and what is valued vs. what is actually done. In the interval, the meaning of each of the basic themes has changed considerably. Relating values to the facts of life, even in the sophisticated form given them by the sciences of human behavior, is a delicate operation.

In the contemporary scene, ethical relativism is a natural point of contact between moral philosophy and the sciences of human behavior. By and large, philosophers who seek knowledge about what is valued tend to be relativists. From the other side, there is the assumption in many places that social science somehow implies ethical relativism. The logic and the assumption would horrify Aristotle, and properly so. Whatever else the facts about values may mean for ethics, they do not logically imply or prove any particular ethical theory.

Let us limit ourselves to anthropology. Cultural relativism was brilliantly expounded by Ruth Benedict as an anthropological principle. The idea that each culture is a unique and integral unit has become associated with a broad ethical relativism, in effect a plea for tolerance for different patterns of culture and for all the races of man. Yet, nineteenth-century chauvinism used what was known about different cultural value systems to construct evolutionary moral scales. Invariably, African or Australian morality was on the lower rungs and European morality at the top. Pure logic does not account for the shift from chauvinism to relativism. It is more likely due to the unforeseen and tragically negative effects of culture contact between Europeans and the so-called simpler peoples. Postwar research in cultural values by anthropologists like Clyde Kluckhohn illustrates another combination of anthropological facts and ethical interpretation. Here, the ideal of respect for different life-ways is maintained, but it is associated with mapping universals in cultures and values. Kluckhohn's approach calls for a review of the fundamental issues of cultural relativism and value relativism.

II

The notion that there's nothing right or wrong but thinking makes it so is better poetry than logic. Several million Bantu, like so many million others, can be wrong. We side with Columbus and against the many who thought the earth was flat, because he had the evidence on his side. In the long run, standards of evidence weigh more heavily than opinion, even majority opinion, when we want reliable knowledge. But in ethics, we do not have norms of right and wrong to compare with those of logic and scientific method in definiteness and universality. Contemporary positivists suggest a qualitative difference between scientific theory and ethical theory as the reason why. Scientific judgments can be verified, they argue, but value judgments cannot, for they are only expressions of emotion. This may in some respects be so, but the followers of John Dewey reject the distinction on principle. They maintain that it closes our further inquiry in ethical theory. Although social-science facts do not imply values logically, they may yield creative suggestions for a sound moral philosophy.

The relativity of values to culture, society, personality and history is different in kind from ethical relativism. The latter deals with the essence or inner nature of values. This is properly speaking a question of the metaphysics of morals. Relativists and absolutists disagree about what value really is. Then, relativists among themselves disagree as to what value is relative to—pleasure, or interest, or attitude, or likes and dislikes—and absolutists disagree among themselves as to which value is absolute—the Idea of the Good, Loyalty, Charity, Benevolence. Few, if any, of the definitions of the metaphysical nature of the good can be used for scientific research.

For the Sophists, the good was relative to pleasure, in the form of roistering, wealth, social position and political power. They assumed that every individual differed from every other in what pleased him. To this highly individualistic hedonism, they matched their "practical" rules: might makes right, self-interest dictates ends, and any means that gets you what you are after is good. Here was radical ethical relativism, morally naked and unashamed. Some two thousand years further along in the history of moral philosophy, Bentham based his utilitarianism on the notion that man's good is pleasure and pain his evil. But his felicific calculus was designed to aid legislatures to make laws that would promote "the greatest happiness of the greatest number." This sociable hedonism is a world away from the moral anarchy of the Sophists.

A mischievous man, Bentham made no provision for qualitative differences among pleasures. Pushpin, he insisted, is as good as poetry. John Stuart Mill attempted to remedy this excessive egalitarianism of pleasures. His solution was borrowed from Aristotle: the tastes of the refined man could show us which are the higher pleasures. It came to very little. What is worse, in defending his relativism, he made an error in reasoning so startling that it finds its way into most logic textbook chapters on fallacies. When something is seen, he argued, it is visible; hence, when something is desired, it is desirable. As any beginning logic student has learned to discern, "visible" means "is or can be seen," while "desirable" means "ought to be desired." The passage from "is" to "ought" is not so easily maneuvered.

About a generation later, John Dewey proposed that the gap between desired and desirable be closed with relevant scientific knowledge. We can judge whether a desire is worthy of satisfaction in the future, once we know the consequences of satisfying it. The biological, psychological and sociological requirements for well-being must be known before what is valuable can be judged from what is valued. He held, moreover, that values must change with the times. What was good for ancient Athens or Galilee is by no means necessarily good for contemporary America or for the world of tomorrow. Value, then, is relative to the on-going of life—a sort of relativistic absolute, or, better yet, the matrix of evaluation.

Ethical relativism based on anthropology and cultural relativism is similar in many ways to Dewey's pragmatic ethics. The good is meant for man, not man for some fixed and culture-bound notion of what is good. Sensitivity to political, social and other conditions of life and to change is characteristic. Values are assumed relative to well-being as defined within each cultural unit. The unwary may mix together metaphysical relativism with cultural relativism. Extreme ethical relativism results, making unwilling bedfellows of the tough-minded Sophists and humanitarian, social-science-minded relativists.

That whatever is valued by any culture is what is really valuable sounds well enough when it goes with an argument for respect and tolerance. It is not so convincing when the logic is carried to the bitter end. It is not easy, just for consistency's sake, to respect and tolerate intolerance and its sometimes fatal consequences, sadism, cannibalism and slavery, as well as such relatively innocent institutions as pushpin, polygamy or paganism. An ethic of anything-goes is hardly any ethic at all.

One remedy for the dilemmas of relativism is to abandon the word "relativism" itself, for the sake of release from the confusions tradition has tied to it. A more direct attack, with a similar goal, uses more of the hair of the dog, in the form of relating specific values to specific cultural, social and personality factors.

III

From the look of things in current research, the conclusion that all values are relative was somewhat hastily drawn. Available data suggest the pedestrian hypothesis that some values are relative and some are not. Some are relative to personality, sex, age, I.Q.; some to social class, economic factors, political position; some to culture, technology, language. Not the least interesting consequence of a hard look at the data is the realization that in our part of the world there is a powerful tendency to overgeneralize and oversimplify. Really, everyone—or nearly everyone—knows, or would not be surprised to learn, that there are some values that all—or nearly all—men have in common, and others that vary, to a greater or lesser degree, according to personality, society, history and culture. The best that can be said for overgeneralizing is that it can keep a brisk fight going for a very long time.

A change in method may help to reduce apparent relativism in values. If we share Kant's fascination with the starry skies above and the moral law within, we may do worse than to examine them both according to the same general principle. Stars or values, if we look only at what immediately meets the eye, we find a helter-skelter scattering. It is all very interesting and pretty but not meaningfully ordered. Without pushing too far a risky analogy, we can nevertheless experiment with looking at values as we do at stars, to find regularities in relationships. Variation in values then becomes an absorbing object of research, rather than occasion for despair for ethical theory.

To begin with the obvious, every known society has a value system—a set of rules and goals that guide conduct and judgments of it. Every known value system represents an ideal, violated in fact at some point by virtually every individual in the society governed by it. The need for inducements for the "do's" and the likelihood of violations of the "don't's" is taken for granted. Rewards and punishments are an integral part of the value system. When a series of value systems is examined, it becomes apparent that within each, absolutism prevails. In some cultures, it is believed that the local system is right for all men, and missionary activity may be engaged in to make it so. In others, it is taken for granted that each nation has its own ideas of the good. Within different cultures, there are different degrees of tolerance for those who hear a different drummer, though the limits of tolerated deviation tend to be small. But the business of social life proceeds on the assumption that the values established in the group are the ones that must be respected and enforced. When an individual begins to doubt his own values, his integration as a personality flags. When a community becomes confused about its customary rules and goals, social disorganization follows, though sometimes as a transition to a revised value system. The absolutism within value systems is part of what makes for relativism in the comparative, external viewing.

The helter-skelter state of values at the descriptive level has, of course, to be the starting-point of the search for regularities. So: here we find monogamy the only approved form of marriage; in other places, it is the unhappy lot of a man too poor to have many wives. In one place, respect for parents means nurturant care until they die of old age; elsewhere, they are dropped out of trees to prevent their after-life being marred by the infirmities of old age. A good spanking is the standby of one community for teaching children how to behave; in another, the sight of a grown person striking a little boy, especially his own, is shocking. In one society, women are little better than workhorses; in another they are tenderly placed on pedestals. Here, milk is considered a perfect food; in other places, it may be as obscene as other bodily discharges. There are hundreds of similar cases.

A quite different statement of the same data can be made. Every culture has its own marriage rules, the requirement that children look after their parents and parents socialize their children, division of labor according to sex, age, position, etc., and rules about what is fit to be eaten. If we raise the question at this point, but which kind of marriage, which interpretation of respect for parents, which method of raising children, is the right one or the best one, we will find ourselves deep in the traditional dilemmas of relativism. It may be precisely because this question is raised too early that it has gone on being asked. It would seem more judicious to be patient and to see what comes of the hypothesis that there is a common basis for value systems, linked to common human activities for which rules must be made, but the specific content of the rules will vary with the culture. Stated the other way round, the specific rules that govern marriage, child-rearing and other basic human-social activities vary with social structures and organization.

There are some quite specific rules that appear to be cultural universals, though here again, the details are variable from one society to another. All societies forbid and punish murder, incest, adultery, theft. All reward or require caring for one's family, helping others, assuming responsibilities, doing as you would be done by. As we should expect, the specific manifestations of "murder" are different in a feudal kingdom from what they are in a democracy. For a king or prince to kill a commoner is not murder. In an egalitarian society, the same act is defined as murder. Still, in no society is every killing a murder. There is a clear distinction between legal killing—as in war or the execution of criminals—and criminal killing, which is murder. In our country, motive figures heavily in differentiating manslaughter from murder. Among the Navaho, no less democratic or morally sensitive, intentions do not count. A man is just as dead whether he was killed accidentally or with intent, in anger or in cold-blooded premeditation. Whatever the details, murder is a serious affair in every community.

Nobody has as yet been able to explain why the incest taboo is universal. The best we have is Freud's ungracious reminder that a taboo is needed only if the primal desire already exists. Something more will have to be learned about the matter, for the specific rules as to whom you may or may not marry vary markedly according to the system of kinship in force. It is fairly certain that anyone called "brother" or "sister" is taboo as a partner. However, this term applies in some places to children of one or both parents only, in others to these and also to the offspring of the parents' brothers or sisters. The royal houses of ancient Egypt, Siam, Hawaii and Madagascar required brother-sister marriage as a religious obligation. These exceptions to the brother-sister incest taboo are of the kind that so frequently crop up in generalizing about specific rules. There is some comfort in the knowledge that there are no known exceptions to the taboos on parent-child marriage. It is also generally true for incest, as for murder, adultery, food taboos and so on, that discovery of violation evokes severe punishment from society, and usually the threat of worse to come from supernatural sources.

When we examine standards of good and bad character, we find a great deal of variation, but we also find that notions familiar in one society appear in others. The Zuñi priest shares with the Supreme Court justice and the African chieftain a well-defined set of realizable ideals, given excellent formulation in Confucius' model of the "superior man." Benevolence and wisdom, dignity and self-control, justice and peacemaking skills, command of the spoken word and sharpness of wit despite the white hairs, moderation and foresight . . . the elder thus defined is known everywhere, his judgment sought when things get out of hand.

No matter how differently cultures define the associated actions, "respectability" and "modesty" are the qualities that girls must have to get the best husbands. The "other kind" usually have to take what's left over. A good wife anywhere is one who looks after her husband, her children and her home. It is, for some reason, more difficult to find a general pattern for good husbands. Young people, no matter how easy-going the child-rearing practices of their society, owe respect to their elders, obedience and gratitude, conformity to the society's norms. Anywhere, envious and jealous people are mistrusted; quarrelsome, irresponsible, wasteful individuals are disapproved; meddlesome and malicious gossips and isolates are feared. Sometimes such people are called "witches." Whatever name is given them, they are not acknowledged as "normal" or acceptable members of the community.

The elements that make up an intercultural base-line morality are, it must be evident by now, tied to the familiar. We are, then, indebted to the flights of radical relativism for the occasion to reconsider the extent to which values are relative and where the relativity is located. The greatest amount of common ground among cultural value systems is, at rock bottom, at the level of prerequisites for social existence. Variation appears when the common list of virtues and vices is made specific for different forms of social, political and other institutions. In this case, the problem of variation in values is no greater than the problem of variation in social forms, personality types and cultural idioms. Variation is perhaps one of the "givens" of social science. In the realm of values, it is at a maximum in philosophical explanations of why murder is wrong or respect for parents right.

Situational relativism in evaluation becomes more manageable when we start out from homely truths. Any system of values has within it different clusters of values that are appropriate for different occasions and circumstances. For example, when a death occurs, the workaday routine is radically transformed. The grief of survivors must be given some expression and practical details of burial and redistribution of property taken care of. Nobody is expected to behave as though nothing has happened. The same kind of adjustment of values is seen in the release from everyday morality at a New Year's Eve party or a Mexican fiesta, a Zuñi Shalako or Scandinavian Midsummer's Night. Rugged individualists work or fight side by side when called to help a neighbor in trouble or to serve their country. This sort of shift of relevant values with changes in circumstances is not casual. It is very clearly controlled by implicit but definite rules. Those who keep the same values despite changes in circumstances are not being "consistent" but deviant.

Orderly variation of much the same kind exists at the level of individual differences. Nobody expects wisdom or even responsibility of children; everybody expects it of mature persons. The village idiot and the court jester enjoy privileges denied ordinary people. Nobody expects generosity from a pauper; everybody criticizes a wealthy man who keeps his wealth for himself. However, a Zuñi will call such a man a witch, whereas our Scrooges are spoken of as misers, and social sanctions vary accordingly. It is nonetheless true of all societies that value judgments and appropriate conduct are relative in a systematic way to age and sex, intelligence level and physical strength, social rank and economic standing. Personality factors and situational changes may combine to change radically the judgment of a particular individual. In Navaho mythology and American sociological studies alike, there is the familiar figure of the peacetime "bad boy" whose very deviance is what enables him to become a hero in times of stress.

In its further reaches, the adjustment of values to life-situations may go very far. Fatalism is a permanent condition of the world-view of many peoples of the world. It becomes an appropriate, if unconsciously adopted, philosophy for a normally self-confident, aggressive man who finds himself in the midst of battle, ignorant of whether or not his number is up.

Comparative study yields a model of realistic, practical ethics among peasants and other "simple" people, tied to a view of life in which fear figures prominently. The realism and practicality, as well as the fear, are perhaps related to the fact that theirs must perforce be an ethic for survival. Aristotle sought a luxury, an ethical system to assure true happiness. He took the precaution of specifying that to be truly happy, a man had first to be assured of a good family name, good health, good looks and a good income. We may do worse than ponder this difference between an ethic of survival and an ethic of happiness.

IV

No matter how often we pick up the question, what is the good? we answer it almost inevitably in terms of the further question whether the good is the same or different for different men. Or, if we ask, what is really right? we almost inevitably come up with one of our culture's stock of answers—custom is king; thinking makes it so; divinity or reason reveals; conscience dictates; respect for life tells us; or even, might makes right. The choice is wide enough, but the alternatives do not seem to settle anything. Not even in a comparative study can we see ourselves as others see us, nor can anyone see the world in perfect objectivity and freedom from his particular cultural world-view. But a redirection and rephrasing of ethical questions and answers may be possible if we consider formulations that occur in other systems of thought.

Though it has to get across ideas to get done the same basic job of guiding conduct and judgments of it, the language of the Navaho, for example, is vastly different from our own. It is primarily a language of verbs, so that what is happening is more central for the Navaho than what things are. It is difficult to say in their language that something "is" good or bad. Rather, it does good or it does harm. Value judgments, like other judgments, are linked by the structure of the language to the contexts of actions and to their consequences. In one case, an action had bad consequences; ergo, it was a bad action. In another case, what we would call the "same" action had good consequences; ergo, it was a good action. The specific judgments are not tied to the specific actions but to the principle that whatever promotes harmony among men is good, whatever destroys it is bad. There is a fixed value placed upon harmony, but judgments of specific situations are relative to fulfilling the ideal.

Perhaps the most instructive quality of the Navaho ethic is a tendency, determined by language, to consider moral and other value qualities *aspects* of action, not different *kinds* of action. There is no problem of reconciling conflicts between moral principles and practical demands. For them, to solve a value problem involves weighing the different components always present in each situation.

Conflicts between moral values and material interests or between moral and aesthetic values are part of the stock in trade of our tradition. Another example of our proclivity for phrasing value issues as conflicts of opposites is revealed in John Ladd's analysis of the Navaho moral code. There, self-interest and altruism are assumed as interdependent. Western ethical theory has taken it for granted that conflict between individual and social good is inherent in human nature. The Navaho in fact largely have a high degree of harmony between individuals and the group, whereas we largely do not. The self-society conflict is one of our culture's problems, not a universal one. It is perhaps intensified by the belief that it is inevitable.

Comparative study makes it clear that the very definition of morality and the inventory of moral problems are tied to a life-way. Europeans who went to Africa and Australia early learned that their own notions of sin were by no means the same as those of the people they visited. They concluded that all these others "have no morals." More relativistically viewed, there are some societies which consider polygamy or premarital child-bearing simply as customs, not as moral issues in the sense in which crimes are singled out as wrong or the golden rule right. Looked at the other way around, our culture manifests a very flesh-bound conception of what moral judgment is relevant to. An adequate drawing of the map of morals, or of values generally, requires more knowledge than our culture can of itself provide.

Professional moral philosophy in the western tradition has been largely the province of saints and gentlemen, social reformers and apologists for some existing moral code. The least common denominator has been devotion to reason as the method of inquiry. Academicism is a frequent outcome of insistence upon logic, but it is neither inevitable nor typical. Plato himself must be numbered among those whose ethical theory was tested in action. His experiment in making a philosopher-king failed, but there are success stories enough. Bentham and Mill had an indisputable effect on British legislation. Marx's philosophy erupts so violently into the daily affairs of men that we forget how much of his life was spent in the library. As for a personal moral philosophy, Socrates' preference for death to dishonor went far beyond lip-service when he drank the hemlock. The great philosophers took their theories seriously enough to put them to the test. Contact between philosophy and the world of action is as much or more a part of the tradition as Sid Caesar's burlesque of the incomprehensible professor.

Establishing meaningful connections between theoretical ethics and the life of our times is, it can hardly be denied, an immense and difficult chore. That such great diversity of cultures should so abruptly have become one world with one common fear makes the doing more urgent, but hardly easier. Responsibility does not lie with any single individual or group. If we want to determine the appropriate role of philosophy, we start with a handicap. So changed are conditions of life and methods of speculation that there is critical uncertainty about the very conception of what moral philosophy is and what use it can be put to. The only statement that can be made with confidence is that it will have to be different in some respects from what has come before. Beyond this, there are only guesses and experiments.

V

Moral philosophy does not have to be a flight from reality. It tends to become that in part because we are given to generalizing too fast and too far. Compared with other moral systems, moreover, our own appears excessively pleased with high ideals that nobody is expected to realize in action. Where high-flown moral idealism is linked to proportionately noble actions —in saints, Chinese sages, and Hindu yogis—all is well. But it is only the exceptional individual who brings his ideals to bear in practical situations, and that often inconsistently. It has been noted often enough that the most eloquent appeals to ideals—rightist or leftist, other-worldly or humanistic—may merely mask hypocrisy. Or, worse yet, they may be put into action through murderous persecution or cruel repression of alternative moralities and ideologies. Sincere conviction can lead almost anywhere.

The solution, if there is one, to our contemporary value problems does not seem to lie in simple borrowing from other cultures where facts and values are on speaking terms, nor in struggling with the inherited questions of our philosophic tradition. The spirit of rational inquiry can be retained, but the letter of its objectives and methods must be revised. A comprehensive and orderly knowledge of what is valued may serve as the reality in which philosophic values can be rooted. This does not mean a crude, earthbound value system. Creativity in moral philosophy, as in art, may be limited by its medium without having its wings clipped. The realities as well as the potentialities of human existence challenge philosophical creativity. Between what is valued and what is worthy to be valued, the philosophical space is very large. Value relativism does not force a choice between anarchy and absolutism. On the contrary, it offers a model for analysis that is a first step toward closing the gap between social-scientific facts and philosophical values.

What is considered good in practical moral situations is always related to some specific individual or group, living in specific social and cultural ways and facing some specific situation. The social sciences are well on their way to documenting what values are actually held in different parts of the world and what solutions are produced for concrete problems. Convergence upon common human solutions for common human problems is becoming evident. One of the principles is already quite clear: values are not the only relevant factors in solving problems, no matter how distinctively moral they may be. Further, it would seem to make sense to ascertain what is actually possible in a situation before deciding what to do about it. When we have the relevant information about the persons, time, place and circumstances, and when we know the real alternatives in the specific case, we find ourselves with fewer and smaller value problems. Real-world difficulties are great enough, but not as problematic as all the possible if's and but's make them appear.

Moral problems are faced at intervals by every individual and group. They are, however, different in kind from a problematic state of moral philosophy. In specific moral problems, the principles are taken as established. What moral philosophy deals with, however, is the validity of those principles. Between these extremes lie other types of problems about principles. If a question of hanging arises in a court of justice, the law decides the appropriate punishment, the court decides whether or not it is to be dealt out in each particular case. It is somewhat more difficult to settle the question whether hanging, or other capital punishment, shall be prescribed by law. Agreement about exactly which punishment fits the crime does not necessarily follow from agreement that justice and social welfare shall be served. Here is a problem in interpreting how wide general principles will be expressed in narrower ones. Of a different sort but hardly less problematic are conflicts between equally important principles in a specific instance. Mercy and justice do not necessarily lead to the same judgment, social welfare does not always coincide with individual good, happiness and duty do not necessarily prescribe the same action. Applied morality in daily life, law and religion require formulas for solutions. These formulas, explicit or not, ultimately satisfactory or not in their results, are a natural but untapped source of knowledge for ethical theory.

In moral philosophy, formal and otherwise, it is the "ultimate" principles of values that have been sought. They are usually given as a simple panacea. Connections between the panacea and the real-life situations it is supposed to deal with are sometimes clear, sometimes not. What has yet to be tried is the building of ultimate principles from the ground up. This requires systematic knowledge of values in operation. First, what is actually valued must be understood in relation to specific societies and individuals. Then, we may look at solutions of daily moral problems where the specific principle is clear. Next, we may risk analysis of the stickier problems where the same principles seem to imply different courses of action, going on to those where action has had to be decided on in spite of conflicts of moral directives. From an analysis of actual solutions, perhaps there will come inspiration for a moral philosophy at the same time intellectually satisfactory and practically meaningful.

It is as well to be candid. Not even the most up-to-date philosophy and social science, separately or together, give us at this moment what we are looking for. From social science, there is not yet enough information about values and their functioning. In philosophy, the realization is still too new that traditional ways of dealing with values are no longer appropriate. When we ask what is good, what is right, what ought to be done, we get no direct replies but only evasions or hypotheses. But at least, and for now at best, there is also hope.

The temptation has been strong to write off as nonsense the whole of moral philosophy, because the questions and proposed answers have been so badly stated. Not a few contemporary philosophers have fallen prey to it. Throwing out the underlying predicament with the badly phrased question does not turn the trick, if, as seems to be the case, there are genuine value problems. It would seem well to seek a way to restate the real predicaments in intelligible form. The Socratic question represents a genuine perplexity, but it is an incomplete question. If we ask simply, what is the good? we can only answer, that depends. When we ask, what is the good in a specific situation, for a specific individual or group with specific characteristics, we may be able to come up with some answers.

For Further Study

Emmet, E. R. *Learning to Philosophise.* New York: Philosophical Library, 1965, Ch. 5, "Value Judgments."

Johnson, Earl S. *Theory and Practice of the Social Studies.* New York: Macmillan, 1956, Ch. 13, "Science and the Value Problem."

Kahler, Erich. *The Tower and the Abyss.* New York: Braziller, 1957, Ch. 6, "Man Without Values."

Keeton, Morris. *Values Men Live By.* New York: Abingdon, 1960.

Maslow, Abraham H. (ed.). *New Knowledge in Human Values.* New York: Harper, 1959, esp. addresses by Hartman, Maslow, and Fromm.

Mumford, Lewis. *The Conduct of Life.* New York: Harcourt, Brace, 1951, esp. Ch. 5, "The Basis of Human Development."

————. *The Myth of the Machine: Technics and Human Development.* New York: Harcourt, Brace & World, 1967.

Nielson, K. "Ethical Relativism and the Facts of Cultural Relativity," *Social Research*, 33 (Winter, 1966): 531–551.

Sellars, Roy Wood. "In What Sense Do Value Judgments and Moral Judgments Have Objective Import?" *Philosophy and Phenomenological Research*, 28 (September, 1967): 1–16.

Werkmeister, W. H. *Man and His Values*. Lincoln: U. of Nebraska, 1967.

Wieman, Henry N. *The Source of Human Good*. Chicago: U. of Chicago Press, 1946, Ch. 3, "Creative Good."

20 Ethics and the Moral Life

ARISTOTLE / Good and the Highest Good *

Aristotle (384–322 B.C.), a student of Plato, founded the Lyceum near Athens. He laid the foundations for much philosophic and scientific thinking. He was the author of important works in metaphysics, logic, ethics, and natural science.

NOW, IF THERE IS SOME OBJECT of activities that we want for its own sake (and others only because of that), and if it is not true that everything is chosen for something else—in which case there will be an infinite regress, that will nullify all our striving—it is plain that this must be the good, the highest good. Would not knowing it have a great influence on our way of living? Would we not be better at doing what we should, like archers with a target to aim at? If so, we must try to get a general idea of what the good is. . . .

. . . As to the name, there is almost complete agreement; for uneducated and educated alike call it happiness, and make happiness identical with the good life and successful living. They disagree, however, about the meaning of happiness: uneducated people give a different answer from that of the theoreticians. The former say it is something plain and obvious, like pleasure, wealth, or honor, and so on. Quite often, the same man gives different answers—when he falls ill, he says it is good health; when he is

* From *The Philosophy of Aristotle* translated by A. E. Wardman and J. L. Creed and edited by Renford Bambrough, © 1963 by Renford Bambrough, published by arrangement with The New American Library of World Literature, Inc. New York. Pp. 286, 288–289, 292–294, 308–310, 369–370.

poor, wealth. They are aware of their own ignorance, and therefore respect those who say it is something marvelous, something beyond them. Some have thought that, quite apart from all these many "goods," there is something else, which is good of itself, and the reason for all these other things being good too. . . .

. . . The uneducated majority appear to think that pleasure is the good or happiness. This view, like those below, is not unreasonable in view of how they live. That is why they admire the life of enjoyment. There are three kinds of life that stand out: this one; the life spent in public affairs; and the life of contemplation. Now, the vast majority show themselves to be absolute slaves in choosing the kind of life lived by cattle. But they get a hearing because many people in high places feel the same as Sardanapallus.

Clever people and men of affairs say that honor is the good, since, roughly, that is the objective of political life. But it seems to be more superficial than what we are looking for, since it rests in the man who gives the honor rather than in him who receives it, whereas our thought is that the good is something proper to the person, and cannot be taken away from him. Also, people seem to pursue honor to prove that they are good; they want to be honored for their excellence by people of good sense and by their acquaintances. So, it is clear from these that excellence is higher than honor, and perhaps one may be more inclined to take this as the objective of political life. But this, too seems to be incomplete. It is possible, even when you have excellence, to sleep or to be inactive throughout your life, and also to suffer great hardship and extreme failure. No one would call such a man happy, unless he were arguing for a paradox. But no more about that; there is enough on the subject elsewhere.

The third life is the life of contemplation. We shall examine it later on. A life of making money is contrary to nature; it is clear that wealth is not the good: it is merely useful, acquired with a view to something else. That is why one might prefer the "goods" mentioned before, since they are admired for their own sake. Yet, not even they will do, although much argument has been made to establish their claim. . . .

Let us return to the good we are looking for and ask what it is. It appears to vary according to the activity or craft: it is different in medicine from what it is in generalship, and so with the rest. Then, what is meant by "the good" in each and every art? It is that toward which all other activities are means. In medicine, this is health; it is victory in generalship, a house in architecture, and so on. In every activity and choice of action, it is the end: everything else that people do, they do because that is their object. If there is an ultimate end in all matters of action, that will be the good in matters of action; or if there is more than one, then the sum of these. By a different approach, then, the argument has reached the same result. But we must try to be still clearer about this.

There seem to be a number of ends. Some of these we choose on behalf of yet another end—like wealth, flutes, and instruments in general. Not all ends, therefore, are ultimate ends, whereas the supreme good is something final. So if there is some one thing that is alone ultimate, this is what we are looking for; and if there are more than one, it will be the most complete or final among these. That which is sought for its own sake is more complete than that which is sought as a means to something else. That which is never sought as a means to something else is more complete than things sought both on their own account and on account of the former. By absolutely final, we mean that which is sought for its own sake, and never as a means to something else. Happiness seems to be something of that sort. We always pursue that for its intrinsic value, never as a means; whereas we pursue honor, pleasure, wisdom, and all the virtues, both for their own sakes (we would want them even if they led to nothing further) and for the sake of happiness, since we think we shall attain happiness by means of them. But no one wants happiness as a means to these other things, or indeed as a means to anything else at all. . . .

It may be that in calling happiness the highest good, we are only stating a platitude. It needs to be defined more clearly still. We might achieve this by ascertaining the specific function of man. In the case of flute players, sculptors, and all craftsmen—indeed, of all who have some function and activity—"good" and "excellent" reside in their function. Now, the same will be true of man, if he has a function peculiar to himself. Do builders and cobblers have functions and activities, but man not, being by nature idle? Or, just as the eye, hand, foot, and every part of the body has a function, similarly, is one to attribute a function to man over and above these? In that case, what will it be? Living is something shared by man even with plants, whereas we are after something specific. Therefore, we must rule out nutritive living, life as growth. Next comes perception; but this too is shared—in this case by horses, cows, and all animals. We are left with a life concerned with action, belonging to the rational part of man. This has two parts: that which obeys reason, and that which has reason and thinks. This kind of life, concerned with action, is itself twofold; and we must take the part that is actually operative, as this is the more correct sense.

The function of man is activity of soul in accordance with reason, or at least not without reason. Now, we say that function is generically the same when we speak of an individual and of an individual good at his job, as in the case of a lyre player and a good lyre player. This is generally true in all cases. Function comes first, and superiority in excellence is superadded. As an example, playing the lyre is the function of the lyre player, playing it well belongs to the good lyre player. If this is so, the good for man proves to be activity of soul in conformity with excellence; and if there is more than one excellence, it will be the best and most complete of these. Also, it requires a complete lifetime: one swallow does not make a spring, nor does a single fine day; similarly, one day or a short time does not make a man blessed or happy.

This is our outline of the good. . . .

. . . It should be said that all virtue, whatever it belongs to, renders that thing good and makes it function well. The virtue of the eye makes the eye good and makes it function well, since it is by the virtue of the eye that we have good sight. Similarly, the virtue or excellence of a horse makes the horse good, good at running and at carrying its rider and at facing the enemy. Now, if this is always the case, the virtue of man will be the disposition through which he becomes a good man and through which he will do his job well. How that will come about, we have already said, but it will be still clearer if we examine the nature of this virtue. . . .

. . . I speak here of moral virtue, since that is concerned with emotions and actions; and excess, deficiency, and the mean occur in these. In feeling fear, confidence, desire, anger, pity, and in general pleasure and pain, one can feel too much or too little; and both extremes are wrong. The mean and the good is feeling at the right time, about the right things, in relation to the right people, and for the right reason; and the mean and the good are the task of virtue. Similarly, in regard to actions, there are excess, deficiency, and the mean.

Virtue is concerned with emotions and actions, where excess is wrong, as is deficiency, but the mean is praised and is right. Both being praised and being right belong to virtue. So virtue is a kind of mean, since it does at least aim at the mean. Also, going wrong happens in many ways (for bad belongs to the unlimited, as the Pythagoreans conjectured, and good to the limited), whereas doing right happens in one way only. That is why one is easy, the other difficult: missing the target is easy, but hitting it is hard. For these reasons, excess and deficiency belong to evil, the mean to good: "There is only one kind of good man, but many kinds of bad."

Virtue, then, is a disposition involving choice. It consists in a mean, relative to us, defined by reason and as the reasonable man would define it. It is a mean between two vices—one of excess, the other of deficiency. Also, virtue discovers and chooses the mean, whereas the vices exceed or fall short of the essential, in the spheres of both emotions and acts. . . .

If happiness is activity in accordance with virtue, then it must be the best activity, i.e., that of the best in man. Whether it is mind or something else that seems naturally to rule and to lead, and to take notice of good and divine things—whether it is itself divine, or the most divine thing in man

—the activity of this in accordance with its own proper virtue will be complete happiness. We have said that this is contemplation, which appears to agree both with our former arguments and with the truth. This is the best activity (mind is the best in us; and "intelligible" things, which are apprehended by the mind, are the best objects in the known world), and also the most continuous. We are better able to contemplate continuously than to *do* anything.

We think it essential that pleasure should be mixed in with happiness, and the most pleasant of activities in accordance with virtue is admittedly activity in accordance with wisdom. Philosophy has pleasures that are marvelous for their purity and permanence. Besides, it is likely that those who have knowledge have a more pleasant life than those who are seeking it. Sufficiency, as people call it, will be associated above all with contemplation. The wise man, the just, and all the rest of them need the necessities of life; further, once there is an adequate supply of these, the just man needs people with and towards whom he may perform just acts; and the same applies to the temperate man, the brave man, and so on. But the wise man is able to contemplate, even when he is on his own; and the more so, the wiser he is. . . .

IMMANUEL KANT / The Right and Our Duty *

Immanuel Kant (1724–1804), one of the great intellects in Western thought, lived all his life in Königsberg, Germany, where he taught in the University. His attempt to answer Hume's skepticism led to a new conception of the nature of human knowledge. He formulated one of the influential types of moral philosophy.

NOTHING CAN POSSIBLY be conceived in the world, or even out of it, which can be called good, without qualification, except a Good Will. Intelligence, wit, judgment, and the other *talents* of the mind, however they may be named, or courage, resolution, perseverance, as qualities of temperament,

* Immanuel Kant, from *Critique of Practical Reason and Other Works on the Theory of Ethics*, trans. Thomas Kingsmill Abbott (London: Longmans, Green, 1909), pp. 9–53 with omissions. Used by permission of the publisher.

are undoubtedly good and desirable in many respects; but these gifts of nature may also become extremely bad and mischievous if the will which is to make use of them, and which, therefore, constitutes what is called *character*, is not good. It is the same with the *gifts of fortune*. Power, riches, honour, even health, and the general well-being and contentment with one's condition which is called *happiness*, inspire pride, and often presumption, if there is not a good will to correct the influence of these on the mind, and with this also to rectify the whole principle of acting, and adapt it to its end. The sight of a being who is not adorned with a single feature of a pure and good will, enjoying unbroken prosperity, can never give pleasure to an impartial rational spectator. Thus a good will appears to constitute the indispensable condition even of being worthy of happiness.

There are even some qualities which are of service to this good will itself, and may facilitate its action, yet which have no intrinsic unconditional value, but always presuppose a good will, and this qualifies the esteem that we justly have for them, and does not permit us to regard them as absolutely good. Moderation in the affections and passions, self-control, and calm deliberation are not only good in many respects, but even seem to constitute part of the intrinsic worth of the person; but they are far from deserving to be called good without qualification, although they have been so unconditionally praised by the ancients. For without the principles of a good will, they may become extremely bad; and the coolness of a villain not only makes him far more dangerous, but also directly makes him more abominable in our eyes than he would have been without it.

A good will is good not because of what it performs or effects, not by its aptness for the attainment of some proposed end, but simply by virtue of the volition, that is, it is good in itself, and considered by itself is to be esteemed much higher than all that can be brought about by it in favour of any inclination, nay, even of the sum-total of all inclinations. Even if it should happen that, owing to special disfavour of fortune, or the niggardly provision of a step-motherly nature, this will should wholly lack power to accomplish its purpose, if with its greatest efforts it should yet achieve nothing, and there should remain only the good will (not, to be sure, a mere wish, but the summoning of all means in our power), then, like a jewel, it would still shine by its own light, as a thing which has its whole value in itself. Its usefulness or fruitlessness can neither add to nor take away anything from this value. It would be, as it were, only the setting to enable us to handle it the more conveniently in common commerce, or to attract to it the attention of those who are not yet connoisseurs, but not to recommend it to true connoisseurs, or to determine its value. . . .

. . . [R]eason is imparted to us as a practical faculty, *i.e.* as one which is to have influence on the *will*, therefore, admitting that nature generally in the distribution of her capacities has adapted the means to the end, its true destination must be to produce a *will*, not merely good as a *means* to something else, but *good in itself*, for which reason was absolutely necessary. This will then, though not indeed the sole and complete good, must be the supreme good and the condition of every other, even of the desire of happiness. Under these circumstances, there is nothing inconsistent with the wisdom of nature in the fact that the cultivation of the reason, which is requisite for the first and unconditional purpose, does in many ways interfere, at least in this life, with the attainment of the second, which is always conditional, namely, happiness. Nay, it may even reduce it to nothing, without nature thereby failing of her purpose. For reason recognizes the establishment of a good will as its highest practical destination, and in attaining this purpose is capable only of a satisfaction of its own proper kind, namely, that from the attainment of an end, which end again is determined by reason only, notwithstanding that this may involve many a disappointment to the ends of inclination.

We have then to develop the notion of a will which deserves to be highly esteemed for itself, and is good without a view to anything further, a notion which exists already in the sound natural understanding, requiring rather to be cleared up than to be taught, and which in estimating the value of our actions always takes the first place, and constitutes the condition of all the rest. In order to do this, we will take the notion of duty. . . .

[The first proposition is: That to have moral worth an action must be done from duty.]

The second proposition is: That an action done from duty derives its moral worth, *not from the purpose* which is to be attained by it, but from the maxim by which it is determined, and therefore does not depend on the realization of the object of the action, but merely on the *principle of volition* by which the action has taken place, without regard to any object of desire. It is clear from what precedes that the purposes which we may have in view in our actions, or their effects regarded as ends and springs of the will, cannot give to actions any unconditional or moral worth. In what, then, can their worth lie, if it is not to consist in the will and in reference to its expected effect? It cannot lie anywhere but in the *principle of the will* without regard to the ends which can be attained by the action. . . .

The third proposition, which is a consequence of the two preceding, I would express thus: *Duty is the necessity of acting from respect for the law.* I may have *inclination* for an object as the effect of my proposed action, but I cannot have *respect* for it, just for this reason, that it is an effect and not an energy of will. Similarly, I cannot have respect for inclination, whether my own or another's; I can at most, if my own, approve it; if another's, sometimes even love it; *i.e.* look on it as favourable to my own interest. It is only what is connected with my will as a principle, by no means as an effect—what does not subserve my inclination, but overpowers it, or at least in case of choice excludes it from its calculation—in other words, simply the law of itself, which can be an object of respect, and hence a command. Now an action done from duty must wholly exclude the influence of inclination, and with it every object of the will, so that nothing remains which can determine the will except objectively the *law*, and subjectively *pure respect* for this practical law, and consequently the maxim that I should follow this law even to the thwarting of all my inclinations. . . .

But what sort of law can that be, the conception of which must determine the will, even without paying any regard to the effect expected from it, in order that this will may be called good absolutely and without qualification? As I have deprived the will of every impulse which could arise to it from obedience to any law, there remains nothing but the universal conformity of its actions to law in general, which alone is to serve the will as a principle, *i.e.* I am never to act otherwise than so *that I could also will that my maxim should become a universal law*. Here, now, it is the simple conformity to law in general, without assuming any particular law applicable to certain actions, that serves the will as its principle, and must so serve it, if duty is not to be a vain delusion and a chimerical notion. The common reason of men in its practical judgments perfectly coincides with this, and always has in view the principle here suggested. Let the question be, for example: May I when in distress make a promise with the intention not to keep it? I readily distinguish here between the two significations which the question may have: Whether it is prudent, or whether it is right, to make a false promise? The former may undoubtedly often be the case. I see clearly indeed that it is not enough to extricate myself from a present difficulty by means of this subterfuge, but it must be well considered whether there may not hereafter spring from this lie much greater inconvenience than that from which I now free myself, and as, with all my supposed *cunning*, the consequences cannot be so easily foreseen, but that credit once lost may be much more injurious to me than any mischief which I seek to avoid at present, it should be considered whether it would not be more *prudent* to act herein according to a universal maxim, and to make it a habit to promise nothing except with the intention of keeping it. But it is soon clear to me that such a maxim will still only be based on the fear of consequences. Now it is a wholly different thing to be truthful from duty, and to be so from apprehension of injurious consequences. In the first case, the very notion of the action already implies a law for me; in the second case, I must first look about elsewhere to see what results may be combined with it which would affect myself. For to deviate from the principle of duty is beyond all doubt wicked; but to be unfaithful to my maxim of prudence may often be very advantageous to me, although to abide by it is certainly safer. The shortest way, however, and an unerring one, to discover the answer to this question whether a lying promise is consistent with duty, is to ask myself, Should I be content that my maxim (to extricate myself from difficulty by a false promise) should hold good as a universal law, for myself as well as for others? and should I be able to say to myself, "Every one may make a deceitful promise when he finds himself in a difficulty from which he cannot otherwise extricate himself"? Then I presently become aware that while I can will the lie, I can by no means will that lying should be a universal law. For with such a law there would be no promises at all, since it would be in vain to allege my intention in regard to my future actions to those who would not believe this allegation, or if they over-hastily did so, would pay me back in my own coin. Hence my maxim, as soon as it should be made a universal law, would necessarily destroy itself.

I do not, therefore, need any far-reaching penetration to discern what I have to do in order that my will may be morally good. Inexperienced in the course of the world, incapable of being prepared for all its contingencies, I only ask myself: Canst thou also will that thy maxim should be a universal law? If not, then it must be rejected, and that not because of a disadvantage accruing from it to myself or even to others, but because it cannot enter as a principle into a possible universal legislation, and reason extorts from me immediate respect for such legislation. I do not indeed as yet *discern* on what this respect is based (this the philosopher may inquire), but at least I understand this, that it is an estimation of the worth which far outweighs all worth of what is recommended by inclination, and that the necessity of acting from *pure* respect for the practical law is what constitutes duty, to which every other motive must give place, because it is the condition of a will being good *in itself*, and the worth of such a will is above everything. . . .

Now all *imperatives* command either *hypothetically* or *categorically*. The former represent the practical necessity of a possible action as means to something else that is willed (or at least which one might possibly will). The categorical imperative would be that which represented an action as necessary of itself without reference to another end, *i.e.*, as objectively necessary.

Since every practical law represents a possible action as good, and on this account, for a subject who is practically determinable by reason, necessary, all imperatives are formulae determining an action which is necessary according to the principle of a will good in some respects. If now the action is good only as a means *to something else*, then the imperative is *hypothetical*; if it is conceived as good *in itself* and consequently as being necessarily the principle of a will which of itself conforms to reason, then it is *categorical*. . . .

There is therefore but one categorical imperative, namely, this: *Act only on that maxim whereby thou canst at the same time will that it should become a universal law.* . . .

If then there is a supreme practical principle or, in respect of the human will, a categorical imperative, it must be one which being drawn from the conception of that which is necessarily an end for everyone because it is *an end in itself*, constitutes an *objective* principle of will, and can therefore serve as a universal practical law. The foundation of this principle is: *rational nature exists as an end in itself.* Man necessarily conceives his own existence as being so: so far then this is a *subjective* principle of human actions. But every other rational being regards its existence similarly, just on the same rational principle that holds for me: so that it is at the same time an objective principle, from which as a supreme practical law all laws of the will must be capable of being deduced. Accordingly the practical imperative will be as follows: *So act as to treat humanity, whether in thine own person or in that of any other, in every case as an end withal, never as means only.* . . .

This principle, that humanity and generally every rational nature is *an end in itself* (which is the supreme limiting condition of every man's freedom of action), is not borrowed from experience. . . .

On this principle all maxims are rejected which are inconsistent with the will being itself universal legislator. Thus the will is not subject simply to the law, but so subject that it must be regarded *as itself giving the law,* and on this ground only, subject to the law (of which it can regard itself as the author). . . .

The conception of every rational being as one which must consider itself as giving in all the maxims of its will universal laws, so as to judge itself and its actions from this point of view—this conception leads to another which depends on it and is very fruitful, namely, that of a *kingdom of ends.*

By a *kingdom* I understand the union of different rational beings in a system by common laws. Now since it is by laws that ends are determined as regards their universal validity, hence, if we abstract from the personal differences of rational beings, and likewise from all the content of their private ends, we shall be able to conceive all ends combined in a systematic whole (including both rational beings as ends in themselves, and also the special ends which each may propose to himself), that is to say, we can conceive a kingdom of ends, which on the preceding principles is possible.

For all rational beings come under the *law* that each of them must treat itself and all others *never merely as means,* but in every case *at the same time as ends in themselves.* Hence results a systematic union of rational beings by common objective laws, *i.e.,* a kingdom which may be called a kingdom of ends, since what these laws have in view is just the relation of these beings to one another as ends and means. It is certainly only an ideal.

A rational being belongs as a *member* to the kingdom of ends when, although giving universal laws in it, he is also himself subject to these laws. He belongs to it *as sovereign* when, while giving laws, he is not subject to the will of any other.

A rational being must always regard himself as giving law either as member or as sovereign in a kingdom of ends which is rendered possible by the freedom of will. He cannot, however, maintain the latter position merely by the maxims of his will but only in case he is a completely independent being without wants and with unrestricted power adequate to his will.

Morality consists then in the reference of all action to the legislation which alone can render a kingdom of ends possible. This legislation must be capable of existing in every rational being, and of emanating from his will, so that the principle of this will is, never to act on any maxim which could not without contradiction be also a universal law, and accordingly always so to act *that the will could at the same time regard itself as giving in its maxims universal laws. . . .*

The practical necessity of acting on this principle, *i.e.* duty, does not rest at all on feelings, impulses, or inclinations, but solely on the relation of rational beings to one another, a relation in which the will of a rational being must always be regarded as *legislative*, since otherwise it could not be conceived as *an end in itself*. Reason then refers every maxim of the will, regarding it as legislating universally, to every other will and also to every action towards oneself; and this not on account of any other practical motive or any future advantage, but from the idea of the *dignity* of a rational being, obeying no law but that which he himself also gives.

JOSEPH FLETCHER / Situation Ethics: The New Morality *

Joseph Fletcher is a professor at Episcopal Theological School in Cambridge, Mass., whose writings in the field of Christian ethics, especially *Morals and Medicine, Moral Responsibility*, and *Situation Ethics* quoted below, have aroused spirited discussion.

THERE ARE at bottom only three alternative routes or approaches to follow in making moral decisions. They are: (1) the legalistic; (2) the antinomian, the opposite extreme—i.e., a lawless or unprincipled approach; and (3) the situational. All three have played their part in the history of Western morals, legalism being by far the most common and persistent. Just as legalism triumphed among the Jews after the exile, so, in spite of Jesus' and Paul's revolt against it, it has managed to dominate Christianity constantly from very early days. . . .

1. LEGALISM

With this approach one enters into every decision-making situation encumbered with a whole apparatus of prefabricated rules and regulations. Not just the spirit but the letter of the law reigns. Its principles, codified in rules, are not merely guidelines or maxims to illuminate the situation; they are *directives* to be followed. Solutions are preset, and you can "look them up" in a book—a Bible or a confessor's manual.

Judaism, Catholicism, Protestantism—all major Western religious traditions have been legalistic. In morals as in doctrine they have kept to a spelled-out, "systematic" orthodoxy. The ancient Jews, especially under the post-exilic Maccabean and Pharisaic leadership, lived by the law or Torah, and its oral tradition (halakah). . . .

Statutory and code law inevitably piles up, ruling upon ruling, because

---

* Joseph Fletcher, from *Situation Ethics: The New Morality* (Philadelphia: The Westminster Press; London: SCM Press; Gütersloh: Gütersloher Verlagshaus; Barcelona: Libres del Nopal, 1966), pp. 17–31 with omissions. Copyright © 1966, W. L. Jenkins. Used by permission of the publishers.

the complications of life and the claims of mercy and compassion combine —even with code legalists—to accumulate an elaborate system of exceptions and compromise, in the form of rules for breaking the rules! . . .

Any web thus woven sooner or later chokes its weavers. Reformed and even Conservative Jews have been driven to disentangle themselves from it. Only Orthodoxy is still in its coils. Something of the same pilpul and formalistic complication may be seen in Christian history. With Catholics it has taken the form of a fairly ingenious moral theology that, as its twists and involutions have increased, resorts more and more to a casuistry that appears (as, to its credit, it does) to evade the very "laws" of right and wrong laid down in its textbooks and manuals. Love, even with the most stiff-necked of system builders, continues to plead mercy's cause and to win at least partial release from law's cold abstractions. Casuistry is the homage paid by legalism to the love of persons, and to realism about life's relativities.

Protestantism has rarely constructed such intricate codes and systems of law, but what it has gained by its simplicity it has lost through its rigidity, its puritanical insistence on moral rules. In fact, the very lack of a casuistry and its complexity, once people are committed to *even the bare principle* of legalistic morality or law ethics, is itself evidence of their blindness to the factors of doubt and perplexity. They have lost touch with the headaches and heartbreaks of life.

What can be worse, no casuistry at all may reveal a punishing and sadistic use of law to hurt people instead of helping them. How else explain burning at the stake in the Middle Ages for homosexuals (death, in the Old Testament)? Even today imprisonment up to sixty years is the penalty in one state for those who were actually consenting adults, without seduction or public disorder! This is really unavoidable whenever law instead of love is put first. The "puritan" type is a well-known example of it. But even if the legalist is truly *sorry* that the law requires unloving or disastrous decisions, he still cries, "*Fiat justitia, ruat caelum!*" (Do the "right" even if the sky falls down). He is the man Mark Twain called "a good man in the worst sense of the word." . . .

Legalism in the Christian tradition has taken two forms. In the Catholic line it has been a matter of legalistic *reason*, based on nature or natural law. These moralists have tended to adumbrate their ethical rules by applying human reason to the facts of nature, both human and subhuman, and to the lessons of historical experience. By this procedure they claim to have adduced universally agreed and therefore valid "natural" moral laws. Protestant moralists have followed the same adductive and deductive tactics. They have taken Scripture and done with it what the Catholics do with nature. Their Scriptural moral law is, they argue, based on the words and sayings of the Law and the Prophets, the evangelists and apostles of the Bible. It is a matter of legalistic *revelation*. One is rationalistic, the other Biblicistic; one natural, the other Scriptural. But both are legalistic. . . .

2. ANTINOMIANISM

Over against legalism, as a sort of polar opposite, we can put antinomianism. This is the approach with which one enters into the decision-making situation armed with no principles or maxims whatsoever, to say nothing of *rules*. In every "existential moment" or "unique" situation, it declares, one must rely upon the situation of itself, *there and then*, to provide its ethical solution. . . .

One form was libertinism—the belief that by grace, by the new life in Christ and salvation by faith, law or rules no longer applied to Christians. Their ultimate happy fate was now assured, and it mattered no more *what* they did. (Whoring, incest, drunkenness, and the like are what they did, therefore! This explains the warning in I Peter 2:16, "Live as free men, yet without using your freedom as a pretext for evil; but live as servants of God." This license led by inevitable reaction to an increase of legalism, especially in sex ethics, under which Christians still suffer today.) The other form, less pretentious and more enduring, was a Gnostic claim to special knowledge, so that neither principles nor rules were needed any longer even as guidelines and direction pointers. They would just *know* what was right when they needed to know. They had, they claimed, a superconscience. It is this second "gnostic" form of the approach which is under examination here.

While legalists are preoccupied with law and its stipulations, the Gnostics are so flatly opposed to law—even in principle—that their moral decisions are random, unpredictable, erratic, quite anomalous. Making moral decisions is a matter of spontaneity; it is literally unprincipled, purely *ad hoc* and casual. They follow no forecastable course from one situation to another. They are, exactly, anarchic—i.e., without a rule. They are not only "unbound by the chains of law" but actually sheer extemporizers, impromptu and intellectually irresponsible. They not only cast the old Torah aside; they even cease to think seriously and *care-fully* about the demands of love as it has been shown in Christ, the love norm itself. The baby goes out with the bath water!

This was the issue Paul fought over with the antinomians at Corinth and Ephesus. They were repudiating all law, as such, and all principles, relying in all moral action choices solely upon guidance in the situation. . . .

Another version of antinomianism, on the whole much subtler philosophically and perhaps more admirable, is the ethics of existentialism. Sartre speaks of "nausea," which is our anxious experience of the *incoherence* of reality. For him any belief in coherence (such as the Christian doctrine of the unity of God's creation and his Lordship over history) is "bad faith." In every moment of moral choice or decision "we have no excuses behind us and no justification before us." Sartre refuses to admit to any *generally* valid principles at all, nothing even ordinarily valid, to say nothing of universal *laws*. . . .

3. SITUATIONISM

A third approach, in between legalism and antinomian unprincipledness, is situation ethics. (To jump from one polarity to the other would be only to go from the frying pan to the fire.) The situationist enters into every decision-making situation fully armed with the ethical maxims of his community and its heritage, and he treats them with respect as illuminators of his problems. Just the same he is prepared in any situation to compromise them or set them aside *in the situation* if love seems better served by doing so.

Situation ethics goes part of the way with natural law, by accepting reason as the instrument of moral judgment, while rejecting the notion that the good is "given" in the nature of things, objectively. It goes part of the way with Scriptural law by accepting revelation as the source of the norm while rejecting all "revealed" norms or laws but the one command— to love God in the neighbor. The situationist follows a moral law or violates it according to love's need. For example, "Almsgiving is a good thing *if* . . ." The situationist never says, "Almsgiving is a good thing. Period!" His decisions are hypothetical, not categorical. Only the commandment to love is categorically good. "Owe no one anything, except to love one another." (Rom. 13:8.) If help to an indigent only pauperizes and degrades him, the situationist refuses a handout and finds some other way. He makes no law out of Jesus' "Give to every one who begs from you." It is only one step from that kind of Biblicist literalism to the kind that causes women in certain sects to refuse blood transfusions even if death results—even if they are carrying a quickened fetus that will be lost too. The legalist says that even if he tells a man escaped from an asylum where his intended victim is, if he finds and murders him, at least only one sin has been committed (murder), not two (lying as well)! . . .

William Temple put it this way: "Universal obligation attaches not to particular judgments of conscience but to conscientiousness. What acts are right may depend on circumstances . . . but there is an absolute obligation to will whatever may on each occasion be right." Our obligation is relative *to* the situation, but obligation *in* the situation is absolute. We are only "obliged" to tell the truth, for example, if the situation calls for it; if a murderer asks us his victim's whereabouts, our duty might be to lie. . . . Situation ethics aims at a contextual appropriateness—not the "good" or the "right" but the *fitting.* . . .

One competent situationist, speaking to students, explained the position this way. Rules are "like 'Punt on fourth down,' or 'Take a pitch when the count is three balls.' These rules are part of the wise player's know-how, and distinguish him from the novice. But they are not unbreakable. The best players are those who know when to ignore them. In the game of bridge, for example, there is a useful rule which says 'Second hand low.' But have you ever played with anyone who followed the rule slavishly? You say to him (in exasperation), 'Partner, why didn't you play your ace? We could have set the hand.' And he replies, unperturbed, 'Second hand low!' What is wrong? The same thing that was wrong when Kant gave information to the murderer. He forgot the purpose of the game. . . . He no longer thought of winning the hand, but of being able to justify himself by invoking the rule." . . .

There are various names for this approach: situationism, contextualism, occasionalism, circumstantialism, even actualism. These labels indicate, of course, that the core of the ethic they describe is a healthy and primary awareness that "circumstances alter cases"—i.e., that in actual problems of conscience the situational variables are to be weighed as heavily as the normative or "general" constants.

The situational factors are so primary that we may even say "circumstances alter rules and principles." It is said that when Gertrude Stein lay dying she declared, "It is better to ask questions than to give answers, even good answers." This is the temper of situation ethics. It is empirical, fact-minded, data conscious, inquiring. It is antimoralistic as well as antilegalistic, for it is sensitive to variety and complexity. . . .

It is necessary to insist that situation ethics is willing to make full and respectful use of principles, to be treated as maxims but not as laws or precepts. We might call it "principled relativism." To repeat the term used above, principles or maxims or general rules are *illuminators.* But they are not *directors.* The classic rule of moral theology has been to follow laws but do it *as much as possible* according to love and according to reason (*secundum caritatem et secundum rationem*). Situation ethics, on the other hand, calls upon us to keep law in a subservient place, so that *only* love and reason really count when the chips are down! [1]

---

[1] [Editors' Note]: This selection by Joseph Fletcher is one of many statements on "the new morality." It has been widely criticized as well as defended. For a collection of critical reactions see Harvey Cox, ed., *The Situation Ethics Debate* (Philadelphia: Westminster Press, 1968).

For Further Study

Adams, E. M. "Classical Moral Philosophy and Metaethics," *Ethics*, 74 (January, 1964): 97–110.

Bell, Daniel, and others. "A Symposium on Morality," *The American Scholar*, 34 (Summer, 1965): 347–369.

Cooper, Neil. "Two Concepts of Morality," *Philosophy*, 41 (January, 1966): 19–33.

Frankena, William K. *Ethics*. Englewood Cliffs: Prentice-Hall, 1963, Ch. 5, "Intrinsic Values and the Good Life." (Foundations of Philosophy Series.)

Haksar, Vinit. "A Scientific Morality?" *Philosophy*, 42 (July, 1967): 245–264.

Hyde, William DeWitt. *The Five Great Philosophies of Life*. New York: Macmillan, 1911, 296 pp. (Also Collier Book AS 129.)

Singer, Marcus G., "Negative and Positive Duties," *Philosophical Quarterly*, 15 (April, 1965): 97–103.

Sumner, L. W. "Normative Ethics and Metaethics," *Ethics*, 77 (January, 1967): 95–106.

"The New Morality: What, Why—and Why Not?" Symposium in *Religion in Life*, 35 (Spring, 1966): 169–229.

Warburg, James. *The West in Crisis*. Garden City: Doubleday, 1959, Ch. 1, "How Civilized Is Our Society?"

Warnock, G. J. *Contemporary Moral Philosophy*. New York: St. Martin's Press, 1967. (C 47075.)

Warnock, Mary. *Existentialist Ethics*. New York: St. Martin's Press, 1967. (E 73250.)

21 Aesthetics and the Philosophy of Art

C. J. DUCASSE / Aesthetics and the Aesthetic Activities *

See the biographical note on p. 133.

FROM ANCIENT TIMES in the history of thought, man has speculated as to the nature of man. His conceptions of its distinctive essence have been many, but the one most often met with today is that man is *Homo Sapiens* —the animal endowed with reason. This conception, it is true, is rather hard to accept when one observes the countless follies of which human beings are guilty. But then, one should bear in mind that no animal, but only a man, can be a fool; for folly is failure to obey the voice of reason, and is therefore possible only to a being possessed of reason.

Besides reason, however, man obviously also has other capacities— among them, in particular, the capacity for artistic creation and for aesthetic enjoyment. Whether or not it depends on the exercise of the reasoning powers is an interesting question, which I shall not attempt to answer. But it would be raised, if in no other way, by Oscar Wilde's remark that there are two ways of disliking art—one, to dislike it; and the other, to like

* C. J. Ducasse, from "Aesthetics and the Aesthetic Activities," *The Journal of Aesthetics & Art Criticism*, 5 (March, 1947): 165–170, 171–172, 174–176. (Presidential address, read at the third annual meeting of The American Society for Aesthetics, September 6, 1946, at the Chicago Art Institute.) Used by permission of the author and The Society.

it rationally. For there are certain persons—historians, philosophers, critics, and other such addicts of rationality—whose relation to art consists, like mine at this moment, in talking and talking about it rather than in practising it or enjoying its products; and one may therefore well wonder whether they really like art. Certainly, it often looks as if their interest in it were of the same ghoulish sort as that with which an inveterate anatomist might be looking at his friends!

In any case, the fact remains that the idea most of us have of the nature of reason is pretty vague—so vague that, by means of it, we should find it difficult to tell a man from an ape if both looked exactly alike and the ape had the parrot's ability to utter words. It is by what we assume reason does, rather than by an abstract notion of what it is, that we recognize its presence in man. For life, in so far as it is specifically human, is marked by certain kinds of activity of which animals seem incapable or capable only in rudimentary degree; and it is chiefly because we have previously been led to believe man the only rational animal, that we now call rational all the activities peculiar to him. Science evidently is one of them. Philosophy, education, religion, are others. So are manufacture and trade. And, as already noted, art and aesthetic experience constitute still another, as distinctively human as any of the rest.

But to carry further profitably our scrutiny of the relation between the aesthetic activities and the nature of man, we must pause here for a moment to say something as to the meaning of the word "art" and of the adjective "aesthetic," which we have already employed several times and will need to use again in the sequel. For both of these words are commonly employed rather loosely as well as in a variety of senses, and if we do not specify with some precision the meaning we attach to them, misunderstandings and confusion inevitably arise.

"Art," in its most inclusive sense, simply means skill; and skill is ability to control a purposive activity well enough to make it attain its intended purpose. We speak, therefore, not only of the fine and the decorative arts, but also of the practical or useful arts, and of the arts of play. But, when art is mentioned without explicit qualification, what most often is meant is *aesthetic art*, which includes not only painting, sculpture, music, poetry, the theater, and the other fine arts, but also the decorative arts. "Art" in this sense is then the name of a certain sort of *creative activity*, namely, activity that creates objects intended for aesthetic contemplation, no matter whether or not they happen to be also objects of practical use.

The word art, however, is often used also to denote the *products* of such creative activity. But it is better to call these products more explicitly *works* of art, for this distinguishes them at once both from the activity itself, which creates them, and from another category of aesthetic objects, namely those that are products or works not of art but of nature.

As regards now the adjective "aesthetic," we find that it cannot be defined quite as simply. It is true that the French aesthetician, Lalo, has proposed to make it synonymous with "beautiful"; but this is too glaring a violation of the linguistic proprieties to be acceptable, since the word "aesthetic" comes from the Greek *aisthetikos*, which means perceptive or perceptible, capable of being apprehended by the senses. In contemporary usage, the adjective "aesthetic" has come to have a meaning both broader and narrower than this—broader in that it is not restricted to sensory perception; and narrower in that not all sensory perception is called aesthetic. Elucidation of that meaning, however, is possible only in the light of a clear understanding of the nature of a certain psychological attitude commonly called the aesthetic attitude, or aesthetic contemplation.

Various descriptions of it have been given by the many writers that have scrutinized it. Most of these descriptions stress in one way or another that it demands surrender for the time being both of scientific curiosity and of preoccupation with moral or practical considerations. Abstraction from the latter in particular is implied by the metaphor "psychic distance," by which Bullough describes the aesthetic attitude; for, in physical matters, it is distance in time or space that typically bars a person from practical participation in events and forces him into the spectator's position.

But we need to understand not only thus what aesthetic contemplation is not, but also what, positively, it is. It consists in the combination of attention with a certain interest: To contemplate aesthetically an object one attends to is to be at the moment interested in, and as it were to listen for, the particular sensations, feelings, moods, emotions, sentiments, or other *directly intuitable* qualities, which the object exhibits or expresses.

The concepts of aesthetic contemplation is of fundamental importance in aesthetics, and it will therefore probably be well to repeat in slightly different and fuller terms the account of it just given in summary form. Attention to an object, then, is aesthetic contemplation in so far as this attention is governed by interest in certain aspects of the object and coupled with receptiveness to them. These aspects are on the one hand the sensible qualities and patterns of qualities, which the object exhibits or perhaps wholly consists of; and on the other, the moods, emotions, sentiments, and other feelings the object expresses. Aesthetic contemplation means, moreover, that the interest one is taking in these aspects of the object is not at the moment scientific or practical interest, but is interest in them for their own sakes—that it is direct and terminal as ordinarily is one's interest in the taste of a piece of candy or in the odor of a rose. Indeed, attentive interest simply in the quality of an odor, or a taste, tone, or color, is itself genuinely aesthetic contemplation, notwithstanding that the object contemplated is then only a very simple one. Aesthetic contemplation,—or for short hereafter, contemplation—is thus not a rare or delicate sort of activity possible only to persons specially gifted. On the contrary, it is one in which all of us engage spontaneously at times—whenever, for instance, we attend to something we are finding beautiful or ugly; or again, whenever we are at the point of reaching a decision of taste.

This brief analysis of aesthetic contemplation was necessary at this place to enable us to clarify the meaning of certain terms, too vague in current usage, which we shall need to employ. One of them is *aesthetic object*, which now we can define as anything taken as object of aesthetic contemplation. Another is *aesthetic feeling*, which means any feeling an object communicates in aesthetic contemplation. Again, the *aesthetic value* of an object is the pleasingness, or the opposite, which it is found to have in aesthetic contemplation. Further, *aesthetic appreciation*, whether analytical or ingenuous, is valuation of an object in terms of the pleasure or displeasure it gives us in the mere contemplation. And *aesthetic art*, we may say, is art—that is, skilled creation—in so far as its products are intended for contemplation rather than for use as implements or as stimuli to curiosity.

Finally, we may now agree that whenever—as for instance in the title of the present address—we speak of *the aesthetic activities*, what we shall be referring to will be three things: one of them, the creating of works of aesthetic art; another, aesthetic contemplation; and the third, aesthetic appreciation—each of these as just characterized.

With these various relatively precise terms at our disposal, let us now return to the question of the place of the aesthetic activities in the life of man. We asserted earlier that they are intrinsic to it, but it might be contended that although only man is capable of them, nevertheless they are accidental rather than essential parts of his life. For after all, the vast majority of human beings never visit museums of art, never participate in or attend symphony concerts or ballets, never read or write poetry, never paint pictures; and yet their lives remain human lives. Hence it might be urged that the aesthetic activities are only a luxury—something it is well enough to have for moments of leisure, but really of little human importance.

To this, however, I must reply that if we call these activities luxuries, then we shall have to redefine man as the animal for whom certain luxuries are necessities. For, in the objection I have just quoted, the basis on which the aesthetic activities were argued to be of little importance in the life of man was far too narrow to support this conclusion.

For one thing, the range of objects aesthetically contemplated and aesthetically enjoyed by human beings comprises not only those to be found in museums, galleries, concert halls, and the like, but a vastly greater number of others—including not only other works of art, but also innumerable things in nature. And, in parenthesis, it may be mentioned that, to

the taste of some of us, many works of nature are aesthetically more rewarding to contemplate than are certain works of art.

But further, the works of aesthetic art include much beyond the products of what are commonly called the fine arts; for whenever, in the creating of an object, the maker introduces some feature simply at the behest of
his taste, then he is at the moment truly an artist, not just an artisan; and
the thing he creates is to that extent truly a work of art, not just an artifact.

Unless this is kept in mind, one cannot get a fair view of the extent to
which human beings actually engage in the creating of works of aesthetic
art. For a fair view of it, moreover, it is also essential to remember that
something may be genuinely a work of aesthetic art and yet be not an
ambitious but only a very humble one. And further, one needs to recall
again and again that the term "work of art" is not synonymous with "*good
work of art*"; for, as pointed out earlier, "work of art" simply means
"product of skill," and skill is something that has degrees. Hence it is
perfectly possible for something to be truly a work of art, and of aesthetic
art, and yet—whether ambitious or humble—to be a poor one rather than
a good one.

If now we bear these remarks in mind and look about us, we then
perceive innumerable works of aesthetic art, which otherwise would have
escaped our notice. Consider, for example, the man who, coming home at
the end of his day's work, gets out the lawn mower and painstakingly clips
his lawn. Why does he do it? Evidently, because, in the context of houses
and streets, he finds the smooth green surface of the close-cut lawn more
pleasing to contemplate than would be rough wild grass. Thus, he is de-
voting time and effort to the end of creating the sort of appearance his
taste demands. Hence, even if only at a humble level, he is in so far a
creative artist as genuinely as the professional landscape architect, or the
mural painter.

But to go even farther, consider that every man who combs his hair or
shaves his chin, every woman who paints her face or stains her nails, and
every person whose purchase of a garment is determined or influenced by
his taste as to colors and shapes, is likewise exercising his taste creatively in
the constructing of some particular sort of personal appearance; and in so
far making that appearance truly a work of aesthetic art. This remains true
irrespective of what may be the factors, social or other, that influence a
person's taste, and irrespective also of the social functions, such, perhaps,
as sex attraction, which an aesthetically pleasing personal appearance performs.

It is only when one thus takes into account such modest and often
rather poor but immensely numerous works of aesthetic art—and not alone
the lofty and excellent ones—that he truly realizes how various are the
possible media of aesthetic art, how nearly universal is the practice of it,

and what enormous amounts of time, effort, and treasure mankind actually devotes to the aesthetic activities. Then, however, the contention that these activities are only an accidental and dispensable feature of human life is seen to be completely untenable. Rather, the inescapable fact is that a life wholly devoid of them would be not human, but only animal.

But my topic is not only the aesthetic activities, but also aesthetics; and to make clear the relation between the two, I must now call attention to another characteristic, in respect to which also man is unique among the animals. Man, namely, is the animal that looks at himself in mirrors! He alone is capable of and interested in observing himself—his physical appearance, his behavior, and his various experiences and activities, mental as well as physical. The human individual is both performer, and spectator of his own performance. He not only thinks, perceives, acts, experiences, wills, feels, desires, and so on, but also watches himself doing so. He is curious about all these manifestations of his life and is capable of studying them, of appraising them, and then to some extent of regulating them.

Among the activities he thus observes in himself are of course those we have called the aesthetic activities, namely, once more, the creation of works of aesthetic art, aesthetic contemplation of them and of other objects, and aesthetic appreciation of the objects contemplated. But what must now be specially emphasized is that to engage concretely in these activities is one thing, and to observe and study them and their products is another and very different thing. The *study* of them is *aesthetics*. It is an intellectual, not an aesthetic activity. It is a manifestation of *curiosity about* the aesthetic activities, but is not itself one of them. This is true even if it is also true that, to be in position to answer some of the questions this curiosity prompts about the aesthetic activities, one must have some time oneself concretely engaged in them. Such, then, is the relation between aesthetics and the aesthetic activities, to which the title of this address refers.

Aesthetics in this inclusive sense, or as we may say, general aesthetics, is much the same thing as what in German is called *Allgemeine Kunstwissenschaft*—an expression which, taken strictly, means general science of art, but in practice covers study of all aspects of aesthetic experience, as well as of art itself and its products.

But if we speak of aesthetics thus as a *science*, we must be clear that, so far as it is one, it is so only in the broad, etymological sense; namely, in that it is a search for *knowledge* properly so-called, as distinguished from groundless or ill-grounded opinions, snap-judgments, mere dogmas, wishful beliefs, and the like. Today, however, the word "science" is often used in a much narrower and more demanding sense, according to which only such branches of knowledge as physics, chemistry, biology, and a few others, would be granted the name of sciences. In this severe sense of the term, science means not merely knowledge, but knowledge that has a certain structure and that, as a result of it, puts into the hands of its possessors certain powers. For instance, in some degree, power to predict particular events and sometimes to control them; and even power to predict, for the given field, natural laws not previously known, but that later observations confirm. Evidently, if the word "science" should be taken in this rather special and highly exacting sense, then no branch of aesthetics could yet really claim the status of a science. Indeed, some of its branches do not even aspire after that status.

On the other hand, aesthetics can truly be called a science in the more elastic sense that it is a systematic search for knowledge properly so called, about the aesthetic activities and their products. This means that the answers it seeks to the questions it asks about them must be answers based on evidence sufficient to establish the truth or probability of those answers. . . .

[Before explaining the nature and function of philosophical aesthetics or the philosophy of art, the author identifies and distinguishes other branches of the general field of aesthetics, namely the physiology of the aesthetic activities, the history and criticism of art, and the sociology, the psychology, and the pedagogy of the aesthetic activities. In connection with his discussion of the history of art, he remarks:]

. . . [O]ne may say without being accused of disparaging the history of art, that probably the large majority of persons who visit the splendid galleries of this institute, or those of museums of art anywhere else, do so for the sake of the aesthetic enjoyment they obtain from the contemplation of the works of art to be found there, and *not* out of interest in the history of art; just as the great majority of persons who listen to symphony concerts do so not because of interest in the history of music, but for the sake of the aesthetic pleasure they gain from listening to the music itself.

Some of us, perhaps, feel that people really ought not to listen to music, or to look at paintings or statuary, in this particular way; that they do so only because they are ignorant of the history of art; that, if they learned it, their appreciation of those works would be greater; and therefore that they *ought* to learn the history of art. But I am afraid that this feeling, if we have it, rests chiefly on the confusion, which I have been attempting to dispel, between aesthetics on the one hand, and on the other, aesthetic contemplation. Aesthetics, as pointed out earlier, is the name of a group of essentially intellectual enterprises, of which the history of art is one, and the typical reward of which is satisfaction of the curiosity that prompted one to engage in them. Contemplation, on the other hand, whether ingenuous or discriminating, is not an intellectual but an aesthetic activity; and its typical reward is enjoyment of the beauty of the object itself, which one contemplates. But for *this*, information of a historical, or technical, or psychological, or philosophical character, about the object, is mostly irrelevant, no matter how interesting in itself or otherwise important such information may be. This is a statement hard indeed to accept for persons, like myself and many others here, whose life-work is, in one way or another, to *talk about* the aesthetic activities, rather than to practice them. But it is true nonetheless, and failure to perceive that it is true is rooted only in the sort of intellectual insularism against which this address is largely directed. It is rooted in the illusion that, because most people expect and get from *contemplation* of works of art a satisfaction different from the intellectual kind of satisfaction the historian finds in the *study* of them, therefore most people are somehow using a wrong method of approach to works of art. It is illusions of this kind that cause us to throw brickbats at the neighbors. Such illusions are not easy to dispel, for there is nothing more difficult to believe than that another person's tastes or interests may be different from ours and yet not be somehow wrong. . . .

. . . [T]here is another part of the field of aesthetics about which we have so far said nothing, although it is one to which the name of aesthetics is sometimes specially applied. I refer to the philosophy of art and of aesthetic experience.

To make clear the nature and significance of the questions it attempts to answer, it is necessary first to dispel a common misconception of what philosophy is. To many persons, the word chiefly connotes speculations about the "Infinite," the "Ultimate," the "Unknowable," the "Transcendent," the "Absolute," and so on—each of these spelled with a capital initial and thought of, as Schopenhauer said, with the sort of feeling one would have if one were going up in a balloon! This popular view of the nature of philosophy is manifest, for example, in the following statement . . . : "It is a fundamental proposition of the philosopher's aesthetic theory that great art should concern itself with ultimate values and meanings—values that are born of the deeper levels of personality—out of experiences that haunt and deeply stir, overpowering, derived from aspirations, infinities." [1]

Now, it is true that, in the writings of some philosophers, passages could be found to account for the belief that that proposition is fundamental in philosophical aesthetics. But most contemporary philosophers that have written on the subject would, I think, join me in denying that that proposition is even generally valid for the philosophy of the aesthetic activities.

As an example of what the philosopher tries to do in this field, I would offer the attempt made earlier in this address to clarify the meaning of certain terms commonly used and indispensable in discussions of art and of aesthetic experience: the term "art" itself, for instance, and the terms

[1] N. B. Zane, *Studies in Appreciation of Art*, Univ. of Oregon Publications. Vol. IV, No. 6, Feb. 1934, p. 69.

"aesthetics," "aesthetic contemplation," "aesthetic value," "aesthetic object," "aesthetic feeling," and so on.

But is this sort of task important? Well, in aesthetics as elsewhere—and perhaps even more than elsewhere—discussions that are carried on in terms that are ambiguous and vague establish nothing. They do not yield anything worthy of the name of knowledge. And since aesthetics, after all, *is* a search for knowledge, discussion carried on in such terms is a waste of time except sometimes indirectly, in a psychological way; that is, except in so far as the participants' own weariness eventually awakens them to the fact that the discussion *is* a waste of time unless and until they pause to find out, fairly definitely, what they mean by the terms they use. For until then, what goes by the name of a discussion is in truth only a Babel, where each speaks a different tongue and one, moreover, that he himself hardly understands!

The task of the philosophical aesthetician, as I conceive it, is to remedy this sort of situation by doing the indispensable thing which everyone else seems too full of passion and in too much of a hurry to pause for; namely, to analyze and state with some precision the objective meaning of the key terms employed in discussions of the aesthetic activities.

But here it might be asked whether it is not up to the psychologist rather than the philosopher to say what, for instance, "aesthetic contemplation" really means. Let us see what the psychologist, proceeding experimentally, would do. He would, we may take it, confront a number of persons with some work of art—say, a painting—and note the responses it actually elicits in them. I happen to have the record of a large number of spontaneous responses so obtained, and, as might be expected, they are of very diverse sorts. One observer liked the painting, which was a farm yard, because it reminded him of a place where he had been happy; another, because he found it a very realistic representation; another, because he liked animals; another, because he thought he had seen that particular farm; another, because the colors were harmonious and bright; another, because the principal objects were in the middle; another, because of the mood it engendered in him; and so on.

But, now that we know how these people actually did respond to a given painting, do we know *eo ipso* what aesthetic contemplation is? Obviously, the question still remains as to *which* of those responses are to be described as *aesthetic* responses, and which as responses of kinds *other than aesthetic*. And, for an answer to *this* question, what we have to observe is evidently something else, namely, language. That is, we have to start from the fact, as a matter of ordinary usage, *some* of those responses would be called aesthetic responses, and others not. And we have then to discover what latent characteristics of them are determining us unawares to call the ones "aesthetic" and to deny this name to the others.

Any answer we offer to this question is a theory of the nature of aesthetic response, i.e., of aesthetic contemplation. It is a conjecture as to what we *mean* when we spontaneously judge a given response to be "aesthetic" response, and a given other non-aesthetic. Moreover, let it be well noted, *anyone* who talks at all about aesthetic contemplation does so on the basis of some assumptions as to its nature. His only choice is as to whether they will remain unconscious, and therefore both vague and dogmatic; or whether on the contrary they will be brought to consciousness, critically scrutinized, and purged of errors and confusions. But since knowledge rather than just opinion is what all branches of aesthetics aim at, the second choice is the one forced upon us; and to do what it demands is the philosopher's task. All other questions of philosophical aesthetics are ultimately of this same general type.

In the light of this description of the nature of philosophical inquiry in matters of aesthetics, it is now evident that we have actually been engaged in it at many points in what has preceded. For example, when we attempted to analyze the meaning of "aesthetic" in the expressions "aesthetic object," "aesthetic feeling," "aesthetic value," and so on. Also, when we analyzed briefly the meaning of the word "art," and that of "aesthetic" art as distinguished from practical and from sportive art. And also, indeed, when we turned from the aesthetic activities themselves to aesthetics; defined the latter as the study of the former; distinguished the principal branches of aesthetics; and defined the nature of each in terms of the types of questions it investigates.

This means that my remarks not only have been *about* aesthetics and the aesthetic activities, but also have themselves constituted an illustration of the nature of the philosopher's own type of activity in the field of aesthetics. But they may thereby perhaps also, in some small measure, have helped to dispel some of the hostilities, confusions, and misunderstandings so common in matters relating to aesthetics. If so, then my remarks will have provided a modest concrete demonstration of the very practical kind of service philosophy is called upon to render in this field. For, it has been rightly said, truth emerges more easily even out of error than it does out of confusion.

For Further Study

Aldrich, Virgil C. *Philosophy of Art*. Englewood Cliffs: Prentice-Hall, 1963, 116 pp. (Foundations of Philosophy Series.)

Beardsley, Monroe. *Aesthetics: Problems in the Philosophy of Criticism*. New York: Harcourt, Brace, 1958, Ch. 12, "The Arts in the Life of Man."

Ducasse, C. J. *Art, the Critics, and You*. Indianapolis: Bobbs-Merrill, 1955. (Library of Liberal Arts LLAS 1.)

Feibleman, James K. "Art: A Definition and Some Consequences," *Personalist*, 48 (Autumn, 1967): 439–452.

Hook, Sidney, (ed.). *Art and Philosophy: A Symposium*. New York: New York U. Press, 1966.

Langer, Susanne K. (ed.). *Reflections on Art: A Source Book of Writings by Artists, Critics, and Philosophers*. New York: Oxford U. Press, 1958. (Also Galaxy Book, 1960.)

Margolis, Joseph (ed.). *Philosophy Looks at the Arts: Contemporary Readings in Aesthetics*. New York: Scribner's, 1962, 235 pp.

Maritain, Jacques. *The Responsibility of the Artist*. New York: Scribner's, 1960, 115 pp.

Sibley, Frank. "Aesthetics and Nonaesthetics," *Philosophical Review*, 74 (April, 1965): 135–159.

Zimmerman, Robert L. "Form, Content, and Categories in Art," *Philosophy and Phenomenological Research*, 25 (December, 1964): 169–179.

22 Oriental Philosophies: Contrasting Values

Selections from Hindu Writings *

The first three selections are from The Upanishads which are parts of the Vedas, India's oldest and most holy writings that appeared in ancient India. The next selection, "Karma," has to do with the law of sowing and reaping. The last is written by a nineteenth-century Hindu seer.

THE INDWELLING BRAHMAN

DISCIPLES INQUIRE within themselves: what is the cause of this universe—is it Brahman? Whence do we come? Why do we live? Where shall we at last find rest? Under whose command are we bound by the law of happiness and its opposite?

Time, space, law, chance, matter, primal energy, intelligence—none of these, nor a combination of these, can be the final cause of the universe, for they are effects, and exist to serve the soul. Nor can the individual self be the cause, for, being subject to the law of happiness and misery, it is not free.

* Selections from the Upanishads are from *The Upanishads, Breath of the Eternal*, by Swami Prabhavananda and Frederick Manchester (New York: New American Library, 1957, Mentor Book MP386). Used by permission of the Vedanta Society of Southern California, copyright holder; "Karma" is from *The Garuda Purana*, Manmatha Nath Dutt, ed. (Calcutta: Society for the Resuscitation of Indian Literature, 1908; "Many Paths to the One God" is from *The Sayings of Sri Ramakrishnan*, compiled by Swami Abhedananda (New York: The Vedanta Society, 1903).

The seers, absorbed in contemplation, saw within themselves the ulti-mate reality, the self-luminous being, the one God, who dwells as the self-conscious power in all creatures. He is One without a second. Deep within all beings he dwells, hidden from sight by the coverings of the gunas—*sattwa, rajas,* and *tamas.* He presides over time, space, and all apparent causes.

This vast universe is a wheel. Upon it are all creatures that are subject to birth, death, and rebirth. Round and round it turns, and never stops. It is the wheel of Brahman. As long as the individual self thinks it is separate from Brahman, it revolves upon the wheel in bondage to the laws of birth, death, and rebirth. But when through the grace of Brahman it realizes its identity with him, it revolves upon the wheel no longer. It achieves immor-tality.

THE REQUIREMENTS OF DUTY

The requirements of duty are three. The first is sacrifice, study, almsgiving; the second is austerity; the third is life as a student in the home of a teacher and the practice of continence. Together, these three lead one to the realm of the blest. But he who is firmly established in the knowledge of Brahman achieves immortality.

The light that shines above the heavens and above this world, the light that shines in the highest world, beyond which there are no others—that is the light that shines in the hearts of men.

Truly has this universe come forth from Brahman. In Brahman it lives and has its being. Assuredly, all is Brahman. Let a man, freed from the taint of passion, worship Brahman alone.

A man is, above all, his will. As is his will in this life, so does he become when he departs from it. Therefore should his will be fixed on attaining Brahman.

The Self, who is to be realized by the purified mind and the illumined consciousness, whose form is light, whose thoughts are true; who, like the ether, remains pure and unattached; from whom proceed all works, all desires, all odors, all tastes; who pervades all, who is beyond the senses, and in whom there is fullness of joy forever—he is my very Self, dwelling within the lotus of my heart.

Smaller than a grain of rice is the Self; smaller than a grain of barley, smaller than a mustard seed, smaller than a canary seed, yea, smaller even than the kernel of a canary seed. Yet again is that Self, within the lotus of my heart, greater than the earth, greater than the heavens, yea, greater than all the worlds.

He from whom proceed all works, all desires, all odors, all tastes; who pervades all, who is beyond the senses, and in whom there is fullness of joy forever—he, the heart-enshrined Self, is verily Brahman. I, who worship the Self within the lotus of my heart, will attain him at death. He who worships him, and puts his trust in him, shall surely attain him.

TO A LAY STUDENT

Let your conduct be marked by right action, including study and teaching of the scriptures; by truthfulness in word, deed, and thought; by self-denial and the practice of austerity; by poise and self-control; by performance of the everyday duties of life with a cheerful heart and an unattached mind.

Speak the truth. Do your duty. Do not neglect the study of the scriptures. Do not cut the thread of progeny. Swerve not from truth. Deviate not from the path of good. Revere greatness.

Let your mother be a god to you; let your father be a god to you; let your teacher be a god to you; let your guest also be a god to you. Do only such actions as are blameless. Always show reverence to the great.

Whatever you give to others, give with love and respect. Gifts must be given in abundance, with joy, humility, and compassion.

If at any time there is any doubt with regard to right conduct, follow the practice of great souls, who are guileless, of good judgment, and devoted to truth.

KARMA

A man is the creator of his own fate, and even in his fœtal life he is affected by the dynamics of the works of his prior existence. Whether confined in a mountain fastness or lulling on the bosom of a sea, whether secure in his mother's lap or held high above her head, a man cannot fly from the effects of his own prior deeds.

This human body entombs a self which is nothing if not emphatically a worker. It is the works of this self in a prior existence which determine the nature of its organism in the next, as well as the character of the diseases, whether physical or mental, which it is to fall a prey to.

A man reaps that at that age, whether infancy, youth or old age, at which he had sowed it in his previous birth. The Karma of a man draws him away from a foreign country and makes him feel its consequence even in spite of his will. A man gets in life what he is fated to get, and even a god cannot make it otherwise.

MANY PATHS TO THE ONE GOD

You see many stars at night in the sky but find them not when the sun rises; can you say that there are no stars in the heaven of day? So, O man!

because you behold not God in the days of your ignorance, say not that there is no god.

As one and the same material, water, is called by different names by different peoples, one calling it water, another eau, a third aqua, and another pani, so the one Sat-chit-ananda, the everlasting-intelligent-bliss, is invoked by some as God, by some as Allah, by some as Jehovah, by some as Hari, and by others as Brahman.

As one can ascend to the top of a house by means of a ladder or a bamboo or a staircase or a rope, so diverse are the ways and means to approach God, and every religion in the world shows one of these ways.

Different creeds are but different paths to reach the Almighty. Various and different are the ways that lead to the temple of Mother Kali at Kalighat (Calcutta). Similarly, various are the ways that lead to the house of the Lord. Every religion is nothing but one of such paths that lead to God.

As the young wife in a family shows her love and respect to her father-in-law, mother-in-law, and every other member of the family, and at the same time loves her husband more than these; similarly, being firm in thy devotion to the deity of thy own choice (Ishta-Devata), do not despise other deities, but honour them all.

Bow down and worship where others kneel, for where so many have been paying the tribute of adoration the kind Lord must manifest himself, for he is all mercy.

The Sat-chit-ananda has many forms. The devotee who has seen God in one aspect only, knows him in that aspect alone. But he who has seen him in manifold aspects is alone in a position to say, "All these forms are of one god and God is multiform." He is formless and with form, and many are his forms which no one knows.

The Vedas, Tantras, and the Puranas and all the sacred scriptures of the world have become as if defiled (as food thrown out of the mouth becomes polluted), because they have been constantly repeated by and have come out of human mouths. But the Brahman or the Absolute has never been defiled, for no one as yet has been able to express it by human speech.

The magnetic needle always points towards the north, and hence it is that the sailing vessel does not lose her course. So long as the heart of man is directed towards God, he cannot be lost in the ocean of wordliness.

Verily, verily, I say unto thee, he who longs for him, finds him. Go and verify this in thine own life; try for three consecutive days with genuine earnestness and thou are sure to succeed.

God cannot be seen so long as there is the slightest taint of desire; therefore have thy small desires satisfied, and renounce the big desires by right reasoning and discrimination.

Knowledge and love of God are ultimately one and the same. There is no difference between pure knowledge and pure love.

The master said, "Everything that exists is God." The pupil understood it literally, but not in the right spirit.

Selections from Buddhist Writings *

The first selection is said to be part of the first sermon ascribed to Gautama Buddha (b. 563 B.C.) and along with the second selection sets forth the four noble truths and the eight-fold path accepted by all Buddhists. The last selection stresses the meditative practices of the Ch'an Zen (Sect) as set forth by the Chinese Buddhist, Hui-neng, Sixth Patriarch, 638–713.

THE FOUNDATION OF THE KINGDOM OF RIGHTEOUSNESS
(From the First Sermon Ascribed to Gautama Buddha)

"This, monks, is the middle path the knowledge of which the Tathagata has gained, which leads to insight, which leads to wisdom, which conduces to calm, to knowledge, to perfect enlightenment, to Nirvana.

"This, monks, is the noble truth of suffering: birth is suffering; decay is suffering; death is suffering; presence of objects we hate is suffering; separation from objects we love is suffering; not to obtain what we desire is suffering.

"In brief, the five aggregates which spring from grasping, they are painful.

"This, monks, is the noble truth concerning the origin of suffering: verily it originates in that craving which causes the renewal of becomings, is accompanied by sensual delight, and seeks satisfaction now here, now there; that is to say, craving for pleasures, craving for becoming, craving for not becoming.

* "The Foundation of the Kingdom of Righteousness" (from the Mahavagga) is from The Life of Gotama the Buddha, E. H. Brewster (London: Kegan Paul, Trench Trubner; New York: Dutton, 1926). "The Aryan Eightfold Path" (from the Maha Satipatthana Sutra) is from Dialogues of the Buddha, trans. T. W. and C. A. F. Rhys-Davids (London: Henry Frowde, Oxford U. Press, 1938). Copyright vested in Pali Text Society. The above selections are also found in The Portable World Bible (New York: Viking, 1944). "Meditation and Calmness" (from the Platform Scripture) is from A Source Book in Chinese Philosophy, trans. and comp. Wing-tsit Chan (Princeton: Princeton U. Press; London: Oxford U. Press, 1963), p. 436. Used by permission of the publishers.

"This, monks, is the noble truth concerning the cessation of suffering. Verily, it is passionlessness, cessation without remainder of this very craving; the laying aside of, the giving up, the being free from, the harbouring no longer of, this craving.

"This, monks, is the noble truth concerning the path which leads to the cessation of suffering. Verily, it is this noble eightfold path, that is to say, right views, right intent, right speech, right conduct, right means of livelihood, right endeavour, right mindfulness and right meditation."

THE ARYAN EIGHTFOLD PATH

The Exalted One said:

"And what, bhikkhus, is the Aryan truth concerning the way that leads to the cessation of ill?

"This is that Aryan eightfold path, to wit, right view, right aspiration, right speech, right doing, right livelihood, right effort, right mindfulness, right rapture [or meditation].

"And what, bhikkhus, is right view?

"Knowledge, bhikkhus, about ill, knowledge about the coming to be of ill, knowledge about the cessation of ill, knowledge about the way that leads to the cessation of ill. This is what is called right view.

"And what, bhikkhus, is right aspiration?

"The aspiration towards renunciation, the aspiration towards benevolence, the aspiration towards kindness. This is what is called right aspiration.

"And what, bhikkhus, is right speech?

"Abstaining from lying, slander, abuse and idle talk. This is what is called right speech.

"And what, bhikkhus, is right doing?

"Abstaining from taking life, from taking what is not given, from carnal indulgence. This is what is called right doing.

"And what, bhikkhus, is right livelihood?

"Herein, O bhikkhus, the Aryan disciple, having put away wrong livelihood, supports himself by right livelihood.

"And what, bhikkhus, is right effort?

"Herein, O bhikkhus, a brother makes effort in bringing forth will that evil and bad states that have not arisen within him may not arise; to that end he stirs up energy, he grips and forces his mind. That he may put away evil and bad states that have arisen within him he puts forth will, he makes effort, he stirs up energy, he grips and forces his mind. That good states which have not arisen may arise he puts forth will, he makes effort, he stirs up energy, he grips and forces his mind. That good states which have arisen may persist, may not grow blurred, may multiply, grow abundant, develop and come to perfection, he puts forth will, he makes effort, he stirs up energy, he grips and forces his mind. This is what is called right effort.

"And what, bhikkhus, is right mindfulness?

"Herein, O bhikkhus, a brother, as to the body, continues so to look upon the body, that he remains ardent, self-possessed and mindful, having overcome both the hankering and the dejection common in the world. And in the same way as to feelings, thoughts and ideas, he so looks upon each, that he remains ardent, self-possessed and mindful, having overcome the hankering and the dejection that is common in the world. This is what is called right mindfulness.

"And what, bhikkhus, is right rapture [or meditation]?

"Herein, O bhikkhus, a brother, aloof from sensuous appetites, aloof from evil ideas, enters into and abides in the first Jhana, wherein there is cogitation and deliberation, which is born of solitude and is full of joy and ease. Suppressing cogitation and deliberation, he enters into and abides in the second Jhana, which is self-evoked, born of concentration, full of joy and ease, in that, set free from cogitation and deliberation, the mind grows calm and sure, dwelling on high. And further, disenchanted with joy, he abides calmly contemplative while, mindful and self-possessed, he feels in his body that ease whereof Aryans declare: 'He that is calmly contemplative and aware, he dwelleth at ease.' So does he enter into and abide in the third Jhana. And further, by putting aside ease and by putting aside malaise, by the passing away of the happiness and of the melancholy he used to feel, he enters into and abides in the fourth Jhana, rapture of utter purity of mindfulness and equanimity, wherein neither ease is felt nor any ill. This is what is called right rapture.

"This, bhikkhus, is the Aryan truth concerning the way leading to the cessation of ill."

MEDITATION AND CALMNESS

"Now, this being the case, in this method, what is meant by sitting in meditation? In this method, to sit means to be free from all obstacles, and externally not to allow thoughts to rise from the mind over any sphere of objects. To meditate means to realize the imperturbability of one's original nature. What is meant by meditation and calmness? Meditation means to be free from all characters externally; calmness means to be unperturbed internally. If there are characters outside and the inner mind is not disturbed, one's original nature is naturally pure and calm. It is only because of the spheres of objects that there is contact, and contact leads to perturbation. There is calmness when one is free from characters and is not perturbed. There is meditation when one is externally free from characters, and there is calmness when one is internally undisturbed. Meditation and calmness mean that external meditation is attained and internal calmness is achieved. The *Wei-mo-chieh* [*so-shuo*] *ching* says, 'Immediately we become completely clear and recover our original mind.' The *P'u-sa chieh ching* (Scripture of Disciplines for Bodhisattvahood) says, 'We are originally pure in our self-nature.' Good and learned friends, realize that your self-nature is naturally pure. Cultivate and achieve for yourselves the Law-body of your self-nature. Follow the Way of the Buddha yourselves. Act and achieve Buddhahood for yourselves."

Selections from Confucian Writings *

It was Mencius (371–289 B.C.?) rather than Confucius himself (551–479 B.C.) who first explicitly stated the view of human nature which was to become standard in Confucianism. Man's original nature is good, and if its innate tendencies (the Four Beginnings) are properly nurtured, men will develop the characteristic human excellences of humaneness, righteousness, propriety, and wisdom.

The *Ta Hsüeh* (The Great Learning) has exercised an influence upon Confucian thought out of all proportion to its brevity. Chu Hsi (1130–1200), the eminent Sung dynasty Neo-Confucian, followed the traditional practice of attributing the basic text, which we translate in full, to Confucius himself, and the appended chapters of commentary, omitted here, to Tseng Tzu, one of Confucius' leading disciples.

Although the *Chung Yung* (The Doctrine of the Mean) is a central Confucian document, its stress on the attainment of a harmonious equilibrium which reflects the cosmic order appealed also to the Taoists and the Buddhists. Integrity (or sincerity) is lauded, not merely as a personal virtue and as a means to self-realization, but as "that by which all things are completed."

The "Hsi Ming" (The Western Inscription) of Chang Tsai (1020–1077) marks a high point in the expression of a mature Confucian view of man and his place in the universe.

---

* The first three selections are translated by Maylon H. Hepp from the *Meng Tzu* (Mencius), 2A.6; from the *Ta Hsüeh* (The Great Learning), "The Text"; and from the *Chung Yung* (Doctrine of the Mean), Chs. 1, 22, and 25. The final selection is from Chang Tsai, "Hsi Ming" (The Western Inscription), in *A Sourcebook in Chinese Philosophy*, trans. and comp. Wing-tsit Chan (Princeton: Princeton U. Press; London: Oxford U. Press, 1963), pp. 497–498. Used by permission of the publishers.

THE FOUR BEGINNINGS

Mencius said, All men have an inherent sense of compassion. The former kings had such a sense, and hence had a compassionate governing of men. By means of this sense of compassion, they practiced compassionate government, ruling the world, as it were, as if rolling it around in their hand.

What I mean by all men having a sense of compassion is this: Suppose people were suddenly to see a child about to fall into a well. They would in every case have a feeling of apprehension and sympathetic concern, not in order to get on intimate terms with the child's parents, nor because they wanted praise from neighbors and friends, nor because they disliked a bad reputation. From this we see that one who lacked a sense of sympathetic concern would not be a man. [In a similar way, I could go on to show that] one who lacked a sense of shame and dislike would not be a man; one who lacked a sense of modesty and humility would not be a man; one who lacked a sense of right and wrong would not be a man.

The sense of sympathetic concern is the beginning of humaneness; the sense of shame and dislike, the beginning of righteousness; the sense of modesty and humility, the beginning of propriety; the sense of right and wrong, the beginning of wisdom. Men have these four beginnings just as they have four limbs. To have these four beginnings and yet to say that one is unable to do anything about the kind of person one becomes is to malign oneself, and to say this about one's ruler is to malign one's ruler.

Everyone who has these four beginnings within himself knows without exception what it takes to enlarge and develop them, just as a fire [knows how to start] burning or a spring to gush out. If one develops them fully, they will be sufficient to protect all within the four seas; if one does not develop them, they will not even suffice to serve one's parents.

THE WAY TO LEARN GREATNESS

The way to learn greatness is to throw light on enlightened virtue, to love the people, and to rest in the highest good. Knowing where to rest, one's goal is determined; this being determined, one can be tranquil; being tranquil, one can be at peace; being at peace, one can plan carefully. Planning carefully, one can achieve one's goal.

Things have roots and branches; affairs have ends and beginnings. By knowing what comes before and what comes after, one keeps near the Way.

The men of old, desiring to throw light on enlightened virtue, first put their states in order. Desiring to put their states in order, they first regulated their families. Desiring to regulate their families, they first cultivated their own selves. Desiring to cultivate their own selves, they first set their hearts right. Desiring to set their hearts right, they first made their thoughts sincere. Desiring to make their thoughts sincere, they first extended their knowledge. Extending knowledge involves inquiring into things.

By inquiring into things, knowledge is achieved. By achieving knowledge, thoughts are made sincere. By making thoughts sincere, the heart is set right. By setting the heart right, the self is cultivated. By cultivating the self, the family is regulated. By regulating the family, states are put in order. By putting states in order, the world becomes peaceful.

From the Son of Heaven to the common people, in every case without exception, cultivating the self constitutes the root. If this root is in confusion, the branches will be in bad condition too. To treat the weighty lightly and the trivial weightily will never do.

ON FULFILLING ONE'S NATURE

What Heaven has bestowed upon man is called his nature. To be in accord with this nature is called the Way. To cultivate the Way is called education. The Way may not be strayed from even momentarily. If it might be strayed from, it would not be the Way.

It is only the man of complete integrity who can fulfil his nature. Being able to fulfil his own nature, he can also fulfil the nature of others. Being able to fulfil their nature, he can also fulfil the nature of things. Being able to fulfil the nature of things, he can contribute to the transforming and nurturing activity of Heaven and Earth. Being able to contribute to their transforming and nurturing activity, he can form with Heaven and Earth a triad.

Integrity is the self's completion [1] and the Way is the self's way. Integrity is the end and the beginning of everything. To lack integrity is to lack all. Therefore, the superior man places the highest value on integrity. Integrity is not merely the completion of the self; it is the completion of all things. The completion of the self is humaneness; the completion of things is wisdom. Such is the virtue of man's nature, and the way in which the outer and the inner are united. Thus whenever things are so arranged, everything is as it ought to be.

MAN AND HIS PLACE IN NATURE

Heaven is my father and Earth is my mother, and even such a small creature as I find an intimate place in their midst.

[1] The Chinese character for "integrity" has the character for "completion" as one of its components, and the two words have identical pronunciations. Thus, the Chinese reads, "Ch'eng is the self's ch'eng."

Therefore, that which fills the universe I regard as my body and that which directs the universe I consider as my nature.

All people are my brothers and sisters, and all things are my companions. . . .

Wealth, honor, blessing, and benefits are meant for the enrichment of my life, while poverty, humble station, and sorrow are meant to help me to fulfillment.

In life I follow and serve [Heaven and Earth]. In death I will be at peace.

Selections from Taoist Writings *

The two most basic documents of philosophical Taoism are the *Tao Te Ching* (Classic of the Way and Its Power), traditionally attributed to Lao Tzu, held to be an older contemporary of Confucius, and the *Nan Hua Chen Ching* by Chuang Tzu, who lived during the fourth century B.C.

While Confucianism, following the emphasis of Confucius himself, is primarily concerned with the relations of individuals within society, Taoism centers on the individual in his relation to the rest of nature. From our Western point of view, Taoism reveals from the outset a metaphysical dimension that was only gradually acquired by Confucianism. Our first selection sets forth the concept of the Tao (Way) as the underlying reality of the universe, manifesting itself in man and nature, but eluding our attempts to classify or categorize it. The second selection deals with the relation between man and nature in one of its most poignant forms: how is the death of the individual related to the ongoing processes of nature? In our third selection, Chuang Tzu faces the perennial philosophical problem of the basis for distinguishing between appearance and reality, between the seeming and the so. He does not solve the problem, but poses it in the concrete terms characteristic of this philosophizing.

* Translated by Maylon H. Hepp from Lao Tzu, *Tao Te Ching* (Classic of the Way and Its Power), Chs. 1, 25, 34, and 41; and from Chuang Tzu, *Nan Hua Chen Ching* (Pure Classic of Nan Hua), Ch. 18, "Perfect Happiness," and Ch. 2, "Discussion on Equalizing Things."

TAO (THE WAY)

If you can talk about it, it is other than the Constant Tao;
If you can name it, it is other than the Constant Name.
Nameless, Tao is the beginning of Heaven and Earth.
Named, it is "Mother" of the ten thousand things.

There is a Thing undifferentiated, yet, complete,
Born before Heaven and Earth.
Silent and vast,
Standing alone, unchanging,
Extending everywhere and yet not in peril.
I do not know its name.
I dub it "Tao."
Pressed for its name, I call it "The Great."

Man patterns himself after Earth;
Earth patterns itself after Heaven;
Heaven patterns itself after Tao;
Tao patterns itself after its own spontaneity.

The great Tao is like a flood;
It can go to left or right.
Since the ten thousand things depend upon it,
Having produced them, it does not abandon them.
Though its merit is complete, it lays no claim to fame.
Though it clothes and nourishes the ten thousand things,
It does not lord it over them.
Since it constantly lacks desires, it may be named "The Small."
Since the ten thousand things return to it, it may be
        named "The Great."
Because it pursues its goal without aggrandizing itself,
It is able to fulfil its greatness.

When a superior person hears about Tao,
He diligently practices it.
When a middling person hears about Tao,
He wavers between keeping it and losing it.
When an inferior person hears about Tao,
He treats it as a big laugh.
If it were not just a big laugh to him,
It would fall short of being the Tao.

REFLECTIONS ON LIFE AND DEATH

When Chuang Tzu's wife died, Hui Tzu came to express his sympathy. There sat Chuang Tzu with his legs spread out, drumming on a bowl and singing.

Hui Tzu said, "Not to weep at the death of someone who has lived with you, raised your children, and grown old would be bad enough. But to drum on a bowl and sing—isn't that just too much?"

Chuang Tzu replied, "Not at all. Right after she died, left alone like this, how could I not feel depressed? But then I reflected on how it all began: originally she lacked life, and not only life but form, and not only form but spirit. Within the confusion and vastness, something changed and there was spirit; spirit changed and there was form; form changed and there was life. Now another change and she is dead, just as the four seasons progress through spring, summer, fall, and winter.

Now that she has lain down to sleep in the Great Room, for me to go around weeping and wailing for her would show that I don't understand what's what. So I stopped."

CHUANG TZU'S DREAM

Once I, Chuang Chou, dreamed I was a butterfly, a butterfly flitting to and fro, aware of my pleasure and expressing myself, not knowing I was Chou. Suddenly I woke up, and there I was, sound and solid Chou. I didn't know whether it had been Chou dreaming he was a butterfly, or now a butterfly dreaming it was Chou. Chou or butterfly—there must be a difference. This is what is meant by "the transformation of things."

For Further Study

Ballou, Robert O., ed. *World Bible*. New York: Viking Press, 1944. (The Viking Portable Library.)

Bodde, Derk. *China's Cultural Tradition*. New York: Rinehart, 1957. (Source Problems in World Civilization series.)

Chan, Wing-tsit. "Neo-Confucianism: New Ideas in Old Terminology," *Philosophy East and West*, 17 (January–October, 1967): 15–35.

Creel, H. G. *Chinese Thought from Confucius to Mao Tse-tung*. New York: New American Library, 1960. (Mentor MD 269.)

Jackson, Barbara Ward. *The Interplay of East and West*. London: Allen & Unwin, 1957, esp. Lecture 3.

Nakamura, Hajime. *Ways of Thinking of Eastern Peoples: India, China, Tibet, Japan.* Ed. by Philip Wiener. Honolulu: East-West Center Press, 1964.

Nikhilananda, Swami. *Hinduism: Its Meaning for the Liberation of the Spirit.* New York: Harper, 1958, esp. Chs. 1, 4, 9.

Northrop, F. S. C. *The Meeting of East and West.* New York: Macmillan, 1946, Ch. 8, "The Meaning of Western Civilization"; Ch. 10, "The Meaning of Eastern Civilization." (Also Macmillan paperback.)

Radhakrishnan, S. *East and West.* New York: Harper, 1956, esp. Lecture 3.

Suzuki, D. T. *Zen Buddhism.* Ed. William Barrett. Garden City: Doubleday, 1956, esp. Ch. 1, "The Sense of Zen"; Ch. 4, "Satori, or Enlightenment." (Anchor Book.)

Welch, Holmes. *Taoism: The Parting of the Way.* Boston: Beacon Press, 1966 (BP 224)

23 Religion: Its Nature and Forms

L. ARNAUD REID / Religion, Science and Other Modes of Knowledge *

L. Arnaud Reid (1895–   ) is Professor Emeritus of the Philosophy of Education at the University of London Institute of Education. Among his many books are *Knowledge and Truth; The Rediscovery of Belief;* and *Ways of Knowledge and Experience.*

THIS ARTICLE is intended to be a sketch-map of some important questions arising out of the relation of religion to science and other modes of knowledge. I shall first describe the several modes as briefly as possible, proceeding subsequently to problems of their relations.

The word "religion" covers a very wide field indeed, and is much more a collocation of phenomena than a single thing. There are the particular great religions; there is religion as conceived by the philosopher, often in very abstract terms (such as "the apprehension of the unconditional" or "belief in the conservation of value"). Or one may think, as many tend to do, of religion in terms of morality. Some people think of it as a matter of "feeling," or "attitude," or subjective experience. Or one may—as again many do—identify religion with belief in certain creeds and dogmas, or

* L. Arnaud Reid, from "Religion, Science and Other Modes of Knowledge," *Hibbert Journal*, 54 (October, 1955): 2–7, 9–14. Used by permission of the publisher, George Allen & Unwin Ltd.

307

(almost), with the carrying out of certain acts such as rituals. Again, there is a difference between what is called "natural" and what is called "revealed" religion. To all this I must add that "religion" is not necessarily a good thing. If may be very bad. Again, religion for some people is an escape, and a sedative. For others it makes for realism and deeper insight into life's challenges. And so on.

One of the great difficulties in all discussions about religion between those who definitely believe in it and those who are, at least, outside the range of definite beliefs is, it would appear, that one must have had some experience of feeling the significance of religion from within if one is to talk about it sensibly, just as if we are to talk about poetry we must have experienced poetry. Otherwise talk becomes empty. This is awkward, because it seems to beg the question. If you already believe, it may be said, how can you think honestly about religion? Won't all your answers be hopelessly biased? So—put in an extreme form—we have the dilemma that, for opposite reasons, neither the believer nor the unbeliever can be objective about religion. I don't think this is an inescapable dilemma. As regards the believer, it may be said that one may enter receptively into an experience at one time, and may critically scrutinise it at another, just as one may love a person and also be objective about him, seeking intelligently to understand more about the person and one's love for him. We should not, therefore, assume that a religiously involved person cannot honestly scrutinise his beliefs—difficult though this is; we know that this does take place. At times, even, people have decided with great pain that they must abandon at least part of their beliefs after scrutiny. And to put the other side, I do not think that inquirers about religion who are not themselves actively and explicitly involved in the life of religion are, or need be, so wholly outside as they think, nor should they perjure their consciences or their intellects. What is required at the outset is the utmost sympathetic imagination, and an openness and readiness to explore intimations which may be more important than one is at once ready to admit.

These labels "religious," "inside religion," "outside religion," . . . are indeed dangerous and often misleading. The word "religious" can mean so many things that in itself, without specification, it means nothing at all. People often repudiate the adjective as applied to themselves, because they assume that "religion" means being a member of a church, or uttering a creed. Without begging questions about the importance of the community of religious life, or of creeds and doctrines, it is a profound mistake to *identify* religion with these things. I believe we ought at the outset to use the term "religion" and "religious" in a very much wider sense. This is both fair to religion, and it is politic, because if we do, far more people will be able to enter sympathetically into the discussion of religion, without feeling that they are being labelled or somehow being jockeyed into a position which they could not honestly sustain.

In pleading at the outset for a broad use of "religion," I am thinking of certain experiences, which I will call "basic" experiences, which I believe are fundamentally religious although they have nothing particularly or directly to do with creeds and churches. There is, primarily, the sense of the mystery of *being*. Here am I, here are we, *existing*: here is a world of nature and persons so amazing that the sense of its very existence at times can overwhelm. Most of the time, like moribunds or half-wits, we do not realise this. Occasionally we do. When we do, we are having an experience which I should call essentially religious.

A special aspect of this is brought out if we think of the meanings of the words "given" and "gift." The world impinges, is *given*. All our powers—of thought, of imagination, and even of love and charity—are, in the end, given to us, are gifts. So is freedom to reject or abuse them, or to choose evil, a gift. We certainly did not make them nor make ourselves. And scientific explanation in terms of history and causes only pushes the problem further back. There is a final mystery here. The realisation of it, not simply as an intellectual *problem*, but as impinging *mystery*, is a religious sense. I do not mean that all this proves the existence of a good God or anything of that kind. The rational account of it, though important, is another matter. It is the experience itself of which I am speaking; this is basic, and, I think, religious. The same religious experience, of the impinging of the ultimate and the mysterious, occurs in the sense of moral obligation—the recognition that we are under obligation to integrity, to respect the truth, to respect persons—obligation which often seems to command us to do what seems entirely contrary to all our inclinations (and which, I am certain, is not reducible to the "super-ego," nor, finally, to the conditioning of society—however these may function as proximate causes). One may, again, experience this basic thing in and through the love of a good person, the source of whose goodness seems to be that his ego serves what is greater than itself.

I am speaking of certain basic experiences, not (here and now) of any theory which explains them. And I am saying that they are not confined to so-called religious people, but are widely shared—indeed I think potentially open for all, if their conditioning and "education" has not been such as to paralyse their capacity for it. This is part of what is sometimes called "natural" religion, as distinct from "special revelation"—but one has, I think, to be very careful about assuming sharp divisions.

This is experience, not theory. But this sort of experience, not in itself linguistic or a language, is always tending to express itself in language, and language of very varied kinds, some of which claims to express truth. (I might for instance *say* of any of the above experiences "That was God speaking to me.") I want to speak now about the "languages" of religion, and in doing this to plead for a very wide use of the term language, as well as for its basis in a kind of knowledge, an experience-knowledge (sometimes called "existential") which is not adequately expressible in language at all.

Our most ordinary use of language is the use in which we employ words in sentences to convey a meaning which we can assume will be understood by other people. The function of language here is to be an instrument for the conveyance of meaning which can be understood by all who talk together. Thus, suppose I say to someone, "Look, there's a jet up there . . . he seems to be climbing fast . . . now he's dropping . . . *now* it looks as though he were going to dive straight into the bowels of the earth." Here the meaning and intention is plain—to convey matter of fact with, perhaps, a certain thrill of horror in the saying of it. Now take religious language. If the psalmist says "If I ascend up into heaven, thou art there: if I make my bed in hell, behold, thou art there" he is not referring to literal climbing or going down; he does not literally mean (if we interpret his intention) that a person, God, is both up and down at the same time. The meaning of his utterance is different. It is the language of poetry. He is speaking of the spiritual not the physical; he is referring, not to the literal fact of God's being in this locality or that, but to his never-leaving presence; he is speaking of his experience and his faith rather than of matter of cold independent fact; and he is worshipping; his language is expressing his feeling, and particularly his sense of reverence and of the transcendent. Religious language often uses the language of propositions which sound—often much more misleadingly than this—like other propositions, which are liable to be misunderstood if it is assumed that their meaning could be stated and perhaps validated in the same way as matter-of-fact propositions. If it were so, then we might, at certain points, legitimately ask for scientific verification of the statements. But if it is not so, and if religious language contains a great deal more than affirmation of literal facts, it is irrelevant, or at least inadequate, to ask for scientific verification in, say, an observation. I am not saying dogmatically and without examination that there are no aspects of religious statements or claims which are not subject to scientific investigation. But we have to be careful to examine *what* is actually being claimed. Until we are pretty sure what exactly religious claims are, the attempt scientifically to assess their validity is premature. If the psalmist speaks of God "who coverest thyself with light as with a garment," he is speaking as a religious poet, although he is also affirming something. If he says, "O Lord, how manifold are thy works! in wisdom hast thou made them all," no one should expect scientific verification of this, because if wisdom and goodness means anything they are not to be observed by the external senses, but by an entirely different sort of perception which is inward.

The languages of religion include many different kinds of things put into words. What is expressed may be of a metaphysical or theological sort. God is Supreme Being, Infinite Being, Cause and Sustainer, Creator, Father . . . or religion may use, as we have seen, the language of sheer poetry. Or it may be myth and symbol: God is shepherd, king, or the Lamb of God upon the heavenly throne, or One "sitting upon a white horse, called Faithful and True, whose eyes were as a flame of fire, on his head many crowns, clothed in a vesture dipped in blood." Much of the extraordinary imagery of religious language seems to be an attempt to express what taken literally is fantastic, contradictory and ridiculous, but which is an attempt to convey the sense of what transcends all statements. (As I shall say in a few moments, the language of science is by its very nature abstract and precise, and is a long way off from this kind of thing.) The language of religion is not only *affirming*: it is *expressing*—expressing reverence, wonder, aspiration . . . it is faith, prayer, worship. Furthermore, if we continue, for the time being, to use language in a very wide sense, there is much "language" of religion that is not verbal at all. The very attitudes of prayer and reverence are not themselves verbal and yet they are significant. Much of sacrament and ritual is the "language" of action rather than language of words. These nonverbal "languages" are expressing or embodying meaning of some kind, and most or all of them are hinting at assertions which in the end claim to be true and as such are open to be assessed as true or false. (I must insist that I am not at the moment concerned to assess truth or falsity, but am simply offering a very impressionistic description.) But I do not believe that any of these languages is, in any proper sense of the word, scientific.

Behind all religious language there is a kind of irreducible awareness which is sometimes called "existential." By "existential" knowledge is meant here knowledge in which we are personally involved and in which we take responsibility—as distinct from the external and contemplative attitude of science and philosophy. The sense of mystery of which I spoke, the "basic experiences" of religion, are "involved" experiences, and we know them in part through our active response to what is given. Again, knowledge of good and evil is "involved" knowledge. We know the goodness of love and the evil of hate by responding and participating; we come to learn more of evil and of good in the experiences and the experiments of moral living—and we could learn nothing at all of the substance of them by external scientific scrutiny. Again, there is a knowledge of persons through friendship and love, the "I-Thou" relationship of which so much recently has been written. Whereas science is essentially objective in its outlook, and the scientific psychologist, for example, may (quite rightly) scrutinise a person in a scientific way, there is an entirely different kind of knowing possible. In truly *meeting* a person, the one-directional relationship of scientific observer to observed is replaced by an inter-activity between persons. As Dr. J. H. Oldham has written: "No amount of research in the laboratory, no amount of solitary thinking, will teach you what love is—or for that matter, hate. You need another person to do that. And when you meet her (or him) you will not learn what love is by any measurements or tests that you may apply, or by psychological observation, however acute, but only by surrender, by committing yourself, which is a totally different attitude from that of counting, measuring, weighing and calculating, all of which you can do without being caught yourself."

In religious cognition, religious people claim, this kind of knowing occurs—knowing of mystery, of good and evil, of communion between man and God. Some think that it is all illusion or hallucination. . . . But at any rate these claims are made, and not now and then but widely, from all sorts of unlikely quarters, and throughout the history of the world. And the claims are not of knowledge of a scientific sort, but of another kind. There may be aspects of all these things which are open to scientific scrutiny; various aspects of religion can be and have been scientifically investigated. But the kind of knowledge, and the kind of claims which may be investigated, are not, in themselves, claims of scientific knowledge, but of other sorts, not to be dismissed lightly but respected.

Scientific knowledge has been repeatedly mentioned. I must now say something about science. In doing so, I should like it to be understood that I am using the word "science" to denote "the sciences" as generally recognised, and as employing recognised ways of testing by sense-evidence. There may be dispute about what ought and ought not to be included in the sciences. I am not concerned with that now. There may be studies which are graduating towards science, but which have not yet become fully scientific. They are not excluded. What I do, however, wish is to avoid using the word in such a wide sense that it is identified with "Scientia," knowledge. This would get us nowhere. And if I say "science," I usually mean "the scientist." . . .

These, then, are four general characteristics of science—to be specific, to be public, to be impersonal, to be concerned with facts. This is about the minimum that I can say. Has, then, science and scientific method any relevance to religion? And is religion relevant to science?

On the first of these questions, "Is science relevant to religion?" I will make some general observations. Science, I have suggested, selects and isolates and carefully defines its subject-matter with the conscious intention of excluding what is irrelevant to its purposes. Science is a self-limiting procedure. And it gives public knowledge independent as far as possible from feeling and private concern or emotion: science again is concerned with facts rather than values. If these things are true, it will follow, first, that if scientific method is applied to religion it will be to selected aspects of religion, abstracted from the rest; it will consider only those aspects of religion which can be expressed in the common and public language which anyone can understand. It must be impersonal, and factual. I do not see how science could very well deal with total religious experiences, or with those of the exceptional religious person, the person of whom we say that he has insight not given to common men—for such claims are not of the kind that can be put into abstract formulae which any competent intellectual person may comprehend, or which can be verified by some sense observation which anyone can make. The most important religious claims are often exceptional and extraordinary. This does not mean of course that they are self-validating: perhaps extraordinary claims of religious insight are in the end only acceptable if they illuminate human experience and help other men to see relations and meaning which they had not seen before. Yet this is certainly not the kind of validation which is subject to what we commonly call "scientific" method. It may for instance be said to be characteristic of the mystic that he sees what the common (and the commonplace) eye cannot. If so, the neutral observations and experiments of science would not be adequate. Again, if religious knowledge is *involved* knowledge, in which the commitment of personality, and some feeling, is a necessary part if the knowledge is to exist at all, then the knowledge of religion is very different from impersonal scientific knowledge. Again, if science is matter-of-fact, religion is much more. It claims insight into good which is not known through scientific scrutiny; and it claims that in religion there is a strange and yet uniquely infinite form of the I-Thou knowledge, in which the Thou of the divine being is not an object to be examined or defined but Thou to be encountered. In human affairs, we said, this I-Thou relationship is in complete contrast to the attitude of science. If in religion anything even approximately analogous to this situation exists—as many claim it does—then the same thing holds.

Some of the aspects of religion to which science may be directed are the factual aspects, of religious experience or behaviour—such as the psychology of worship, or the sociology of organised religion. Or one may apply science (including archaeology and historical criticism) as well as philological acumen to the·interpretation of the holy books. Much has been done in these ways to help religious people to distinguish the essential which remains in religion when the accidental has been disentangled from it. One ought to add, however, that the "facts" of religion are peculiarly difficult to define and isolate, and that without insight into their relation with what is in hand, scientific investigation may be of little worth.

It is perhaps where religion makes, or appears to make, factual statements about the world of man or nature, that science may have much to do with religion and that, in the clash between science and religion, science has frequently beaten religion into retreat. Obvious examples are quasi-scientific assertions, such as that the world was made in six days out of nothing, that in the universe there are three storeys one above the other—heaven, this world, and the regions below the ground—sheol, hell or what you will. If these statements associated with religion are taken to be literal statements of fact, on a par with scientific statements, then few would dispute that science "has it" every time against religion. We may now be said to know that, in any ordinary sense of the word, the world was not made in six days, and is not of a simple three-decker kind. We know from scientific cosmology and biology that processes of evolution have been extremely slow.

On the other hand, it is no modern discovery, but goes back to the earliest Church Fathers, that statements like those about creation are myth and symbol and not to be taken literally. Of the three-decker universe, though it was a current cosmology, it may be doubted whether its *religious* significance was actually more than symbolical; and at any time, however emancipated we are, we find it difficult to avoid speaking of "aspiration," of a person being at the "height" of his career, of sinking through the earth in shame, of "flat" or "pedestrian" thinking or feeling.

But it is extremely important to realise, not only that many of the quasi-scientific statements of religion are symbolic and *not* literal, but that what they symbolise is something which is important, and which, moreover, may have its basis in some literal fact, although such fact may not come within the realm of science. Take, for instance, the sentence, "God created the world in six days." It is not very important to interpret, as for instance St. Thomas Aquinas did, "six days" as six aeons, for, even if it were true, the statement would still be a "myth," without scientific foundation. But, indeed, it seems ridiculous to interpret the meaning of this statement as having anything to do with historical cosmology at all. If "the world" means the universe, from which the idea of time is inseparable, it makes little sense to say that it took a certain *time* to make the time-system of the universe. In fact this particular myth is not even hinting at any even scientifically thinkable statement. Science deals with the phenomena of our experience: science works *within* the given universe. But the statement, "God created the world in six days" is a statement about the universe as a whole, and is, if anything, metaphysical and not scientific. It may easily of course be retorted that, if so, metaphysics is absurd, since no finite being can conceive "the universe as a whole," still less its creation by God "out of nothing." I think such an objection is well justified. But this presses us to the meaning behind the myth; and I would here simply echo the common theological interpretation of the literal intention of this myth as being that the universe was, and is, dependent on God. This is a metaphysical statement (not a scientific one), and, though its full significance is beyond human understanding, it yet does hint at something which is *literally* and not symbolically meant. There is a *literal* difference between saying that the world that we see with our senses and apprehend with our minds is entirely self-contained and self-explanatory, and denying that it is so, and further affirming that all is dependent upon a Being who is not identical with the universe but who made it. Statements like this are a mixture of religion and theology and metaphysics. About their possible justification I shall say a very few words at the end. But if they make any sense at all, they are in the ways I have described, utterly outside strict scientific scrutiny. They are non-phenomenal: Lavoisier may sweep the heavens for ever with his telescope but he will never find God.

The not unconnected controversies between religion and science upon evolution might be similarly treated. I do not suppose that anyone would argue that, say, a Darwinian, or neo-Darwinian, theory of evolution is finally "proved." But at any rate it is respectably thought out and in many ways is borne out by observation. "Natural Selection," for example, may be open to criticism, but it is so far justified because things look like that over a very wide range of observation. And if religious men step into precisely the same field (as they have done in the past) contradicting the scientists on the facts, and even on conservative hypotheses based on facts, they will get their knuckles rapped, and they will deserve all they get. On the other hand if, say, the theory of Natural Selection intrudes illegitimately into metaphysics, and becomes a dogmatic denial that there can be in evolution any divine plan or purpose at all, then equally the scientist is being presumptuous, because he is affirming what cannot be brought to scientific investigation or test. "Purpose," "end," "good" are correlative terms, and, if I am right, science with its self-limitation is not designed to know good. I do not think that the common cliché that philosophy (and religious philosophy) is concerned with *why* things happen, whilst science is concerned with *how* things happen, is entirely short of the mark.

Exactly the same might be said of the determinism which is a necessary and legitimate working postulate in science with its self-limited purposes. Scientifically speaking, all events happen exhaustively as the effects of causes. As Lavoisier can never find God with his telescope, so observation of fact can never discover providence. Nor has it any need of "that hypothesis." But an hypothesis of voluntary initiative ordering nature may have a place in philosophy if not in natural science.

I am not saying that science and religion never conflict, but that often when they seem to, they are saying different things, that when religion seems to be saying scientific things it may be saying something importantly symbolic though not scientifically accessible. Where religion does presume to make plain scientific statements I think it speaks without authority, as do scientists sometimes when, bringing with them all the great prestige of science, they slip into metaphysical, or religious, or anti-religious dogmatism.

We have looked at some of the ways in which science may be relevant or irrelevant to religion. Taking the other side, is religion relevant to science?

I suppose in a very general way it is. Scientific knowledge is a fundamental human activity of the intellect, with which religion, having to do with the whole person, has concern. On the other hand I find it very difficult to see how religious beliefs could have any important determining influence upon scientific procedure: indeed it would even seem that they ought not to. It may be true that in the seventeenth century some of the great pioneers of scientific thought were influenced in the making of their hypotheses by religious ideas, say of harmony and design. But the test of scientific hypothesis is always bound up with experiment and observation, and no religious hypothesis as such could have any special scientific prestige. And I do not see any grounds for saying that, as between a religious scientist and an agnostic, one would be in any way superior to the other, other things being equal. So I should guess that within the field strictly of science itself religion is irrelevant. It is only when philosophical generalisations begin to be made allegedly on a scientific basis, that religion may have something pertinent to say. (This point has already been covered: if, e.g., it is asserted, on a "scientific" basis, that God could not have created the world, that the evidence of nature is against the hypothesis of the divine purpose, or that miracles could *never* take place—then religion or religious philosophy would certainly have something to say. But the conflict here is not between science as such and religion as such, but between metaphysical statements in pseudo-scientific dress, and metaphysical statements of religion.)

It is not my province here to try to prove religion true or false—even if "proof" is the right word—or to consider the classical "proofs" of the existence of God and their relation to religion.

All that I need ask now is whether one would expect the sort of verification applicable to religion to be of a scientific kind. Here again my general answer would have to be "No."

I have spoken of various religious languages, and have broadly distinguished between "expressive" language and the "categorical" language of propositions. (These overlap.) It must be in respect of the categorical elements in its language, that religion is true or false. Prayer, worship, submission, ritual and sacrament are not, properly speaking, true or false, though they are significant. It is the statements, the affirmations of belief contained in them or implied by them or otherwise made, which are true or false. And, as I have tried to show, the kind of statements that these are, is not the kind that can seek the scientific verification of sense observation or experiment, nor the construction into highly abstract scientific (e.g., mathematical) systems. Assertions about God, or about the existence of God, are of a "total" and "massive" kind which is quite different. As I have suggested, the aim of the scientific statement is to be as precise as it possibly can, a precision which is purchased at the voluntarily paid price of excluding everything that is irrelevant. It is such statements which can prescribe experiments and observations to be made. For religious statements and affirmation there is no parallel. They are not precise and scientifically abstract, but general and comprehensive, concerning the whole of things. No crucial scientific experiment could be devised to substantiate the existence of God.

Strictly speaking, "proof" exists nowhere outside mathematics. There is no proof (accurately speaking) in empirical science: there is only progressive verification and substantiation. In philosophy of religion it has, it is true, been a custom to speak of "proofs" or "demonstrations" of the existence of God. This is certainly scholastic language. I think myself it is out of place in philosophy.

Certainly there is a place for argument; a place, for instance, for the traditional arguments for the existence of God (though they have been, and should be, much criticised, and I do not, as I say, think that they are demonstrations). And there is a place for wider philosophical thinking about the nature of God and his relation to the world. But I believe that the purpose of reasoning in religion is secondary and not primary. It is not so much building up syllogistic proofs, but elucidating, making more explicit, analysing, relating, developing, supporting, criticising, sometimes positively and sometimes negatively, the more immediate intimations of the religious knowledge which I have called "existential" knowing. After all, every argument has premises which are not argued, but given; and the conclusions of the arguments contain no more than is in the arguments. If you start right outside religion—from the causal system of nature or from its order and apparent "design," argument may lead you to postulate a First Cause or a Designer. Even supposing such reasoning is completely valid, what you have got at the end of the argument is just a postulated concept which seems necessary to account for causation or apparent "design." If this can be called "God" at all, it is certainly "un dieu des savants et des philosophes" and not the living God of religious experience—the God of Abraham, Isaac and Jacob . . . the Father of Christ, the God of the Hindu or Muslim worshipper. I am certainly not saying that these and other arguments have not an important bearing on religion (though I cannot go into that now). But the only secure start for germinative thinking about religion (as about art, or personal life) is from within the intimations of religion itself. Starting here, there is unlimited scope for religion to develop some better understanding of its own mystery. This is not the contradiction it may seem. Ultimate mysteries are not problems to be solved, and they remain forever mysteries. But all the time they are setting us problems which it is our bounden duty as thinkers to face with all the ability and honesty we can muster. We ought to warn ourselves at the outset, however, that this is essentially a philosophical, and not a scientific, enterprise; and in the philosophy of religion we must not expect to get the accurate and relatively certain conclusions of science, with its self-defined function. We have to be as reasonable as we can be; our main question is: How far, in the matter of religion, can our reasonableness be of a scientific kind?

For Further Study

Ballou, Robert O. *The Nature of Religion.* New York: Basic Books, 1968.

Blanshard, Brand. "The Liberal in Religion," *Humanist,* 28 (May/June, 1968): 11–14.

Brown, Robert McAfee, and Weigel, Gustave. *An American Dialogue: A Protestant Looks at Catholicism and a Catholic Looks at Protestantism.* Garden City: Doubleday, 1960, 216 pp. (Foreword by Will Herberg.)

Hartshorne, M. Holmes. *The Faith to Doubt.* Englewood Cliffs: Prentice-Hall, 1963. (Spectrum Book S-48.)

Hick, John. *Philosophy of Religion.* Englewood Cliffs: Prentice-Hall, 1963. (Foundations of Philosophy Series.)

Hook, Sidney, ed. *Religious Experience and Truth.* New York: New York U. Press, 1961. Part II, "The Nature of Religious Faith."

Madden, Edward H. "Evil and the Concept of a Limited God," *Philosophical Studies,* 18 (October, 1967): 65–70.

Maslow, Abraham H. *Religions, Values, and Peak Experiences.* Columbus: Ohio State U. Press, 1964.

Northrop, F. S. C. *Man, Nature and God.* New York: Pocket Books, 1963. (GC 779.)

Schilling, Harold K. *Science and Religion.* New York: Scribner's, 1962, Chs. 1–3.

Tillich, Paul. *Dynamics of Faith.* New York: Harper, 1958. (Torchbook TB 42.)

24 Religion: Belief in God

ST. THOMAS AQUINAS / The Existence of God *

St. Thomas Aquinas (1225–1274), the great thirteenth-century philosopher and theologian, developed an imposing structure of thought combining Aristotelian and Christian elements. His system, often referred to as *Thomism*, is a dominant one in contemporary Roman Catholic thought.

These selections illustrate Aquinas' usual method of exposition in the *Summa*. He begins each article with a question to which his analysis provides an answer. Then he presents certain objections which may be raised against the position that he is going to defend. As an introduction or text for his own positive view, he next says, "On the contrary . . ." and briefly indicates the trend his fuller discussion will take, often quoting from Scripture or some other authority. He then says, "I answer that . . ." and proceeds to develop his position. The article concludes with detailed replies to each of the objections raised at the outset.

WHETHER IT CAN BE DEMONSTRATED THAT GOD EXISTS?

Objection 1. It seems that the existence of God cannot be demonstrated. For it is an article of faith that God exists. But what is of faith cannot be

* St. Thomas Aquinas, from "The Existence of God," in *Summa Theologica* (New York: Benziger, 1911), Part I, Question 2, Articles 2 and 3. Used by permission of the publisher.

demonstrated, because a demonstration produces scientific knowledge; whereas faith is of the unseen (*Heb*. xi. I). Therefore it cannot be demonstrated that God exists.

Obj. 2. Further, the essence is the middle term of demonstration. But we cannot know in what God's essence consists, but solely in what it does not consist; as Damascene says (*De Fid. Orth*. i. 4). Therefore we cannot demonstrate that God exists.

Obj. 3. Further, if the existence of God were demonstrated, this could only be from His effects. But His effects are not proportionate to Him, since He is infinite and His effects are finite; and between the finite and infinite there is no proportion. Therefore, since a cause cannot be demonstrated by an effect not proportionate to it, it seems that the existence of God cannot be demonstrated.

On the contrary, The Apostle says: *The invisible things of Him are clearly seen, being understood by the things that are made* (*Rom*. i. 20). But this would not be unless the existence of God could be demonstrated through the things that are made, for the first thing we must know of anything is, whether it exists.

I answer that Demonstration can be made in two ways: One is through the cause, and is called *a priori*, and this is to argue from what is prior absolutely. The other is through the effect, and is called a demonstration *a posteriori*; this is to argue from what is prior relatively only to us. When an effect is better known to us than its cause, from the effect we proceed to the knowledge of the cause. And from every effect the existence of its proper cause can be demonstrated, so long as its effects are better known to us; because since every effect depends upon its cause, if the effect exists, the cause must pre-exist. Hence the existence of God, in so far as it is not self-evident to us, can be demonstrated from those of His effects which are known to us.

Reply Obj. 1. The existence of God and other like truths about God, which can be known by natural reason, are not articles of faith, but are preambles to the articles; for faith presupposes natural knowledge, even as grace presupposes nature, and perfection supposes something that can be perfected. Nevertheless, there is nothing to prevent a man, who cannot grasp a proof, accepting, as a matter of faith, something which in itself is capable of being scientifically known and demonstrated.

Reply Obj. 2. When the existence of a cause is demonstrated from an effect, this takes the place of the definition of the cause in proof of the cause's existence. This is especially the case in regard to God, because in order to prove the existence of anything, it is necessary to accept as a middle term the meaning of the word, and not its essence, for the question of its essence follows on the question of its existence. Now the names given to God are derived from His effects; consequently, in demonstrating the existence of God from His effects, we may take for the middle term the meaning of the word "God."

Reply Obj. 3. From effects not proportionate to the cause no perfect knowledge of that cause can be obtained. Yet from every effect the existence of the cause can be clearly demonstrated, and so we can demonstrate the existence of God from His effects; though from them we cannot perfectly know God as He is in His essence.

WHETHER GOD EXISTS?

Objection 1. It seems that God does not exist; because if one of two contraries be infinite, the other would be altogether destroyed. But the word "God" means that He is infinite goodness. If, therefore, God existed, there would be no evil discoverable; but there is evil in the world. Therefore God does not exist.

Obj. 2. Further, it is superfluous to suppose that what can be accounted for by a few principles has been produced by man. But it seems that everything we see in the world can be accounted for by other principles, supposing God did not exist. For all natural things can be reduced to one principle, which is nature; and all voluntary things can be reduced to one principle, which is human reason, or will. Therefore there is no need to suppose God's existence.

On the contrary, It is said in the person of God: *I am Who am* (*Exod.* iii. 14).

I answer that, The existence of God can be proved in five ways.

The first and more manifest way is the argument from motion. It is certain, and evident to our senses, that in the world some things are in motion. Now whatever is in motion is put in motion by another, for nothing can be in motion except it is in potentiality to that towards which it is in motion; whereas a thing moves inasmuch as it is in act. For motion is nothing else than the reduction of something from potentiality to actuality. But nothing can be reduced from potentiality to actuality, except by something in a state of actuality. Thus that which is actually hot, as fire, makes wood, which is potentially hot, to be actually hot, and thereby moves and changes it. Now it is not possible that the same thing should be at once in actuality and potentiality in the same respect, but only in different respects. For what is actually hot cannot simultaneously be potentially hot; but it is simultaneously potentially cold. It is therefore impossible that in the same respect and in the same way a thing should be both mover and moved, *i.e.*, that it should move itself. Therefore, whatever is in motion must be put in motion by another. If that by which it is put in motion be itself put in motion, then this also must needs be put in motion by another, and that by another again. But this cannot go on to infinity, because then there would be no first mover, and, consequently, no other mover; seeing that subsequent movers move only inasmuch as they are put in motion by the first mover; as the staff moves only because it is put in motion by the hand. Therefore it is necessary to arrive at a first mover, put in motion by no other; and this everyone understands to be God.

The second way is from the nature of the efficient cause. In the world of sense we find there is an order of efficient causes. There is no case known (neither is it, indeed, possible) in which a thing is found to be the efficient cause of itself; for so it would be prior to itself, which is impossible. Now in efficient causes it is not possible to go on to infinity, because in all efficient causes following in order, the first is the cause of the intermediate cause, and the intermediate is the cause of the ultimate cause, whether the intermediate cause be several, or one only. Now to take away the cause is to take away the effect. Therefore, if there be no first cause among efficient causes, there will be no ultimate, nor any intermediate cause. But if in efficient causes it is possible to go on to infinity, there will be no first efficient cause, neither will there be an ultimate effect, nor any intermediate efficient causes; all of which is plainly false. Therefore it is necessary to admit a first efficient cause, to which everyone gives the name of God.

The third way is taken from possibility and necessity, and runs thus. We find in nature things that are possible to be and not to be, since they are found to be generated, and to corrupt, and consequently, they are possible to be and not to be. But it is impossible for these always to exist, for that which is possible not to be at some time is not. Therefore, if everything is possible not to be, then at one time there could have been nothing in existence. Now if this were true, even now there would be nothing in existence, because that which does not exist only begins to exist by something already existing. Therefore, if at one time nothing was in existence, it would have been impossible for anything to have begun to exist; and thus even now nothing would be in existence—which is absurd. Therefore, not all beings are merely possible, but there must exist something the existence of which is necessary. But every necessary thing either has its necessity caused by another, or not. Now it is impossible to go on to infinity in necessary things which have their necessity caused by another, as has been already proved in regard to efficient causes. Therefore we cannot but postulate the existence of some being having of itself its own necessity, and not receiving it from another, but rather causing in others their necessity. This all men speak of as God.

The fourth way is taken from the gradation to be found in things. Among beings there are some more and some less good, true, noble, and the like. But "more" and "less" are predicated of different things, according as they resemble in their different ways something which is the maximum, as a thing is said to be hotter according as it more nearly resembles that which is hottest; so that there is something which is truest, something best, something noblest, and, consequently, something which is uttermost being; for those things that are greatest in truth are greatest in being, as it is written in *Metaph. ii.* Now the maximum in any genus is the cause of all in that genus; as fire, which is the maximum of heat, is the cause of all hot things. Therefore there must also be something which is to all beings the cause of their being, goodness, and every other perfection, and this we call God.

The fifth way is taken from the governance of the world. We see that things which lack intelligence, such as natural bodies, act for an end, and this is evident from their acting always, or nearly always, in the same way, so as to obtain the best result. Hence it is plain that not fortuitously, but designedly, do they achieve their end. Now whatever lacks intelligence cannot move towards an end, unless it be directed by some being endowed with knowledge and intelligence; as the arrow is shot to its mark by the archer. Therefore some intelligent being exists by whom all natural things are directed to their end; and this being we call God.

Reply Obj. 1. As Augustine says (*Enchir. xi.*): *Since God is the highest good, He would not allow any evil to exist in His works, unless His omnipotence and goodness were such as to bring good even out of evil.* This is part of the infinite goodness of God, that He should allow evil to exist, and out of it produce good.

Reply Obj. 2. Since nature works for a determinate end under the direction of a higher agent, whatever is done by nature must needs be traced back to God, as to its first cause. So also whatever is done voluntarily must also be traced back to some higher cause other than human reason or will, since these can change and fail; for all things that are changeable and capable of defect must be traced back to an immovable and self-necessary first principle, as was shown in the body of the *Article.*

PAUL TILLICH / Three Interpretations of "God" *

Paul Tillich (1886–1965) was a prominent theologian and philosopher who left Germany at the beginning of the Nazi regime and came to the United States where he taught at Union Theological Seminary, Harvard University, and the University of Chicago. He wrote many books, articles, and sermons. He was especially concerned about the "problem of Being" and the human predicament in this "age of anxiety."

. . . [W]E MAY DISTINGUISH three ways of interpreting the meaning of the term "God." The first one separates God as a being, the highest being, from all other beings, alongside and above which he has his existence. In this position he has brought the universe into being at a certain moment (five thousand or five billion years ago), governs it according to a plan, directs it toward an end, interferes with its ordinary processes in order to overcome resistance and to fulfil his purpose, and will bring it to consummation in a final catastrophe. Within this framework the whole divine-human drama is to be seen. Certainly this is a primitive form of supra-naturalism, but a form which is more decisive for the religious life and its symbolic expression than any theological refinement of this position.

The main argument against it is that it transforms the infinity of God into a finiteness which is merely an extension of the categories of finitude. This is done in respect to space by establishing a supranatural divine world alongside the natural human world; in respect to time by determining a beginning and an end of God's creativity; in respect to causality by making God a cause alongside other causes; in respect to substance by attributing individual substance to him. Against this kind of supranaturalism the arguments of naturalism are valid and, as such, represent the true concern of religion, the infinity of the infinite, and the inviolability of the created structures of the finite. Theology must accept the antisupranatural criticism of naturalism.

The second way of interpreting the meaning of the term "God" identifies God with the universe, with its essence or with special powers within

* Reprinted from *Systematic Theology*, Vol. 2, by Paul Tillich by permission of The University of Chicago Press. Copyright 1957 by the University of Chicago. From "Introduction," pp. 5–10.

it. God is the name for the power and meaning of reality. He is not identified with the totality of things. No myth or philosophy has ever asserted such an absurdity. But he is a symbol of the unity, harmony, and power of being; he is the dynamic and creative center of reality. The phrase *deus sive natura*, used by people like Scotus Erigena and Spinoza, does not say that God is identical with nature but that he is identical with the *natura naturans*, the creative nature, the creative ground of all natural objects. In modern naturalism the religious quality of these affirmations has almost disappeared, especially among philosophizing scientists who understand nature in terms of materialism and mechanism. In philosophy proper, in so far as it became positivistic and pragmatistic, such assertions about nature as a whole were required. In so far as a whole philosophy of life involving dynamic processes developed, it again approached the religious forms of naturalism.

The main argument against naturalism in whatever form is that it denies the infinite distance between the whole of finite things and their infinite ground, with the consequence that the term "God" becomes interchangeable with the term "universe" and therefore is semantically superfluous. This semantic situation reveals the failure of naturalism to understand a decisive element in the experience of the holy, namely, the distance between finite man, on the one hand, and the holy in its numerous manifestations, on the other. For this, naturalism cannot account.

This criticism of the supranaturalistic and the naturalistic interpretations of the meaning of "God" calls for a third way which will liberate the discussion from the oscillation between two insufficient and religiously dangerous solutions. Such a third way is not new.

Theologians like Augustine, Thomas, Luther, Zwingli, Calvin, and Schleiermacher have grasped it, although in a restricted form. It agrees with the naturalistic view by asserting that God would not be God if he were not the creative ground of everything that has being, that, in fact, he is the infinite and unconditional power of being or, in the most radical abstraction, that he is being-itself. In this respect God is neither alongside things nor even "above" them; he is nearer to them than they are to themselves. He is their creative ground, here and now, always and everywhere.

Up to this point, the third view could be accepted by some forms of naturalism. But then the ways part. At this point the terms "self-transcendent" and "ecstatic," which I use for the third way of understanding the term "God," become meaningful. The term "self-transcendent" has two elements: "transcending" and "self." God as the ground of being infinitely transcends that of which he is the ground. He stands *against* the world, in so far as the world stands against him, and he stands *for* the world, thereby causing it to stand for him. This mutual freedom from each other and for each other is the only meaningful sense in which the "supra" in "supranaturalism" can be used. Only in this sense can we speak of "transcendent" with respect to the relation of God and the world. To call God transcendent in this sense does not mean that one must establish a "superworld" of divine objects. It does mean that, within itself, the finite world points beyond itself. In other words, it is self-transcendent.

Now the need for the syllable "self" in "self-transcendent" has also become understandable: the one reality which we encounter is experienced in different dimensions which point to one another. The finitude of the finite points to the infinity of the infinite. It goes beyond itself in order to return to itself in a new dimension. This is what "self-transcendence" means. In terms of immediate experience it is the encounter with the holy, an encounter which has an ecstatic character. The term "ecstatic" in the phrase "ecstatic idea of God" points to the experience of the holy as transcending ordinary experience without removing it. Ecstasy as a state of mind is the exact correlate to self-transcendence as the state of reality. Such an understanding of the idea of God is neither naturalistic nor supranaturalistic. It underlies the whole of the present theological system.

If, on the basis of this idea of God, we ask: "What does it mean that God, the ground of everything that is, can stand against the world and for the world?" we must refer to that quality of the world which expresses itself in finite freedom, the quality we experience within ourselves. The traditional discussion between the naturalistic and the supranaturalistic ideas of God uses the prepositions "in" and "above," respectively. Both are taken from the spatial realm and therefore are unable to express the true relation between God and the world—which certainly is not spatial. The self-transcendent idea of God replaces the spatial imagery—at least for theological thought—by the concept of finite freedom. The divine transcendence is identical with the freedom of the created to turn away from the essential unity with the creative ground of its being. Such freedom presupposes two qualities of the created: first, that it is substantially independent of the divine ground; second, that it remains in substantial unity with it. Without the latter unity, the creature would be without the power of being. It is the quality of finite freedom within the created which makes pantheism impossible and not the notion of a highest being alongside the world, whether his relation to the world is described in deistic or theistic terms.

The consequences of the self-transcendent idea of God for concepts like revelation and miracle (which are decisive for the christological problem) have been fully developed in the part entitled "Reason and Revelation." These do not need restatement, but they do show the far-reaching significance of the ecstatic interpretation of the relation between God and the world.

However, there is one problem which has moved into the center of the philosophical interest in religion since the appearance of the first volume. This is the problem of the symbolic knowledge of God. If God as the ground of being infinitely transcends everything that is, two consequences follow: first, whatever one knows about a finite thing one knows about God, because it is rooted in him as its ground; second, anything one knows about a finite thing cannot be applied to God, because he is, as has been said, "quite other" or, as could be said, "ecstatically transcendent." The unity of these two divergent consequences is the analogous or symbolic knowledge of God. A religious symbol uses the material of ordinary experience in speaking of God, but in such a way that the ordinary meaning of the material used is both affirmed and denied. Every religious symbol negates itself in its literal meaning, but it affirms itself in its self-transcending meaning. It is not a sign pointing to something with which it has no inner relationship. It represents the power and meaning of what is symbolized through participation. The symbol participates in the reality which is symbolized. Therefore, one should never say "only a symbol." This is to confuse symbol with sign. Thus it follows that everything religion has to say about God, including his qualities, actions, and manifestations, has a symbolic character and that the meaning of "God" is completely missed if one takes the symbolic language literally.

But, after this has been stated, the question arises (and has arisen in public discussion) as to whether there is a point at which a non-symbolic assertion about God must be made. There is such a point, namely, the statement that everything we say about God is symbolic. Such a statement is an assertion about God which itself is not symbolic. Otherwise we would fall into a circular argument. On the other hand, if we make *one* non-symbolic assertion about God, his ecstatic-transcendent character seems to be endangered. This dialectical difficulty is a mirror of the human situation with respect to the divine ground of being. Although man is actually separated from the infinite, he could not be aware of it if he did not participate in it potentially. This is expressed in the state of being ultimately concerned, a state which is universally human, whatever the content of the concern may be. This is the point at which we must speak non-symbolically about God, but in terms of a quest for him. In the moment, however, in which we describe the character of this point or in which we try to formulate that for which we ask, a combination of symbolic with non-symbolic elements occurs. If we say that God is the infinite, or the unconditional, or being-itself, we speak rationally and ecstatically at the same time. These terms precisely designate the boundary line at which both the symbolic and the non-symbolic coincide. Up to this point every statement is non-symbolic (in the sense of religious symbol). Beyond this point every statement is symbolic (in the sense of religious symbol). The point itself is

328 RELIGION: BELIEF IN GOD

both non-symbolic and symbolic. This dialectical situation is the conceptual expression of man's existential situation. It is the condition for man's religious existence and for his ability to receive revelation. It is another side of the self-transcendent or ecstatic idea of God, beyond naturalism and supranaturalism.

For Further Study

Altizer, Thomas J. J. and Hamilton, William. *Radical Theology and the Death of God*. Indianapolis: Bobbs-Merrill, 1966.

Cobb, John B., Jr. "Speaking About God," *Religion in Life*, 36 (Spring, 1967): 28–39.

Durfee, Harold A. "The Reformulation of the Question as to the Existence of God," *Philosophy and Phenomenological Research*, 28 (March, 1968): 385–391.

Ewing, A. C. "Awareness of God," *Philosophy*, 40 (January, 1965): 1–17.

Hick, John, ed. *The Existence of God*. New York: Macmillan, 1964 (Macmillan Paperback 164. Problems of Philosophy Series.)

Hudson, W. D. "An Attempt to Defend Theism," *Philosophy*, 39 (January, 1964): 18–28.

Jenkins, David E. *Guide to the Debate About God*. Philadelphia: Westminster, 1966.

MacGregor, Geddes. *God Beyond Doubt: An Essay in the Philosophy of Religion*. Philadelphia: Lippincott, 1966.

Richardson, Alan. "The Death-of-God Theology," *Religion in Life*, 36 (Spring, 1967): 70–79.

Robinson, John A. T. *Honest to God*. Philadelphia: Westminster, 1963, Ch. 2, "The End of Theism?" Ch. 3, "The Ground of Our Being."

Smith, John E. *Reason and God: Encounters of Philosophy with Religion*. New Haven: Yale U. Press, 1961, Part II, "The Present."

Wisdom, John. "Gods," in *Essays on Logic and Language*, ed. Anthony Flew. Oxford: Blackwell and Mott, 1951.

PART 5

The Social Scene

25 Civil Liberties and the Rule of Law

JOHN STUART MILL / *On Liberty* *

John Stuart Mill (1806–1873), an English empiricist, made important contributions not only to nineteenth-century liberalism but also to the moral philosophy of utilitarianism and to inductive logic.

I. INTRODUCTORY

THE OBJECT of this Essay is to assert one very simple principle, as entitled to govern absolutely the dealings of society with the individual in the way of compulsion and control, whether the means used be physical force in the form of legal penalties, or the moral coercion of public opinion. That principle is, that the sole end for which mankind are warranted, individually or collectively, in interfering with the liberty of action of any of their number, is self-protection. That the only purpose for which power can be rightfully exercised over any member of a civilized community, against his will, is to prevent harm to others. His own good, either physical or moral, is not a sufficient warrant. He cannot rightfully be compelled to do or forbear because it will be better for him to do so, because it will make him happier, because, in the opinions of others, to do so would be wise, or even right. These are good reasons for remonstrating with him, or reasoning with him, or persuading him, or entreating him, but not for compelling him, or visiting him with any evil in case he do otherwise. To justify that, the con-

* John Stuart Mill, from *On Liberty* (1859), Parts I–IV with omissions.

duct from which it is desired to deter him, must be calculated to produce evil to some one else. The only part of the conduct of any one, for which he is amenable to society, is that which concerns others. In the part which merely concerns himself, his independence is, of right, absolute. Over himself, over his own body and mind, the individual is sovereign. . . .

. . . When I say only himself, I mean directly, and in the first instance: for whatever affects himself, may affect others *through* himself; and the objection which may be grounded on this contingency, will receive consideration in the sequel. This, then, is the appropriate region of human liberty. It comprises, first, the inward domain of consciousness; demanding liberty of conscience, in the most comprehensive sense; liberty of thought and feeling; absolute freedom of opinion and sentiment on all subjects, practical or speculative, scientific, moral, or theological. The liberty of expressing and publishing opinions may seem to fall under a different principle, since it belongs to that part of the conduct of an individual which concerns other people; but, being almost of as much importance as the liberty of thought itself, and resting in great part on the same reasons, is practically inseparable from it. Secondly, the principle requires liberty of tastes and pursuits; of framing the plan of our life to suit our own character; of doing as we like, subject to such consequences as may follow: without impediment from our fellow-creatures, so long as what we do does not harm them, even though they should think our conduct foolish, perverse, or wrong. Thirdly, from this liberty of each individual, follows the liberty, within the same limits, of combination among individuals; freedom to unite, for any purpose not involving harm to others: the persons combining being supposed to be of full age, and not forced or deceived.

No society in which these liberties are not, on the whole, respected, is free, whatever may be its form of government; and none is completely free in which they do not exist absolute and unqualified. The only freedom which deserves the name, is that of pursuing our own good in our own way, so long as we do not attempt to deprive others of theirs, or impede their efforts to obtain it. Each is the proper guardian of his own health, whether bodily, or mental and spirtual. Mankind are greater gainers by suffering each other to live as seems good to themselves, than by compelling each to live as seems good to the rest.

Though this doctrine is anything but new, and, to some persons, may have the air of a truism, there is no doctrine which stands more directly opposed to the general tendency of existing opinion and practice. Society has expended fully as much effort in the attempt (according to its lights) to compel people to conform to its notions of personal, as of social excellence. . . .

. . . The disposition of mankind, whether as rulers or as fellow-citizens, to impose their own opinions and inclinations as a rule of conduct on others, is so energetically supported by some of the best and by some of the worst feelings incident to human nature, that it is hardly ever kept under restraint by anything but want of power; and as the power is not declining, but growing, unless a strong barrier of moral conviction can be raised against the mischief, we must expect, in the present circumstances of the world, to see it increase.

It will be convenient for the argument, if, instead of at once entering upon the general thesis, we confine ourselves in the first instance to a single branch of it, on which the principle here stated is, if not fully, yet to a certain point, recognised by the current opinions. This one branch is the Liberty of Thought: from which it is impossible to separate the cognate liberty of speaking and of writing. . . .

II. OF THE LIBERTY OF THOUGHT AND DISCUSSION

The time, it is to be hoped, is gone by, when any defence would be necessary of the "liberty of the press" as one of the securities against corrupt or tyrannical government. No argument, we may suppose, can now be needed, against permitting a legislature or an executive, not identified in interest with the people, to prescribe opinions to them, and determine what doctrines or what arguments they shall be allowed to hear. . . . Let us suppose, therefore, that the government is entirely at one with the people, and never thinks of exerting any power of coercion unless in agreement with what it conceives to be their voice. But I deny the right of the people to exercise such coercion, either by themselves or by their government. The power itself is illegitimate. The best government has no more title to it than the worst. It is as noxious, or more noxious, when exerted in accordance with public opinion, than when in opposition to it. If all mankind minus one, were of one opinion, and only one person were of the contrary opinion, mankind would be no more justified in silencing that one person, than he, if he had the power, would be justified in silencing mankind. Were an opinion a personal possession of no value except to the owner; if to be obstructed in the enjoyment of it were simply a private injury, it would make some difference whether the injury was inflicted only on a few persons or on many. But the peculiar evil of silencing the expression of an opinion is, that it is robbing the human race; posterity as well as the existing generation; those who dissent from the opinion, still more than those who hold it. If the opinion is right, they are deprived of the opportunity of exchanging error for truth: if wrong, they lose, what is almost as great a benefit, the clearer perception and livelier impression of truth, produced by its collision with error.

It is necessary to consider separately these two hypotheses, each of which has a distinct branch of the argument corresponding to it. We can never be sure that the opinion we are endeavouring to stifle is a false opinion; and if we were sure, stifling it would be an evil still. . . .

. . . It is a piece of idle sentimentality that truth, merely as truth, has any inherent power denied to error, of prevailing against the dungeon and the stake. Men are not more zealous for truth than they often are for error, and a sufficient application of legal or even of social penalties will generally succeed in stopping the propagation of either. The real advantage which truth has, consists in this: that when an opinion is true, it may be extinguished once, twice or many times, but in the course of ages there will generally be found persons to rediscover it, until some one of its reappearances falls on a time when from favourable circumstances it escapes persecution until it has made such head as to withstand all subsequent attempts to suppress it. . . .

We . . . recognis[e] the necessity to the mental well-being of mankind (on which all their other well-being depends) of freedom of opinion, and freedom of the expression of opinion, on four distinct grounds. . . .

First, if any opinion is compelled to silence, that opinion may, for aught we can certainly know, be true. To deny this is to assume our own infallibility.

Secondly, though the silenced opinion be an error, it may, and very commonly does, contain a portion of truth; and since the general or prevailing opinion on any subject is rarely or never the whole truth, it is only by the collision of adverse opinions that the remainder of the truth has any chance of being supplied.

Thirdly, even if the received opinion be not only true, but the whole truth; unless it is suffered to be, and actually is, vigorously and earnestly contested, it will, by most of those who receive it, be held in the manner of a prejudice, with little comprehension or feeling of its rational grounds. And not only this, but, fourthly, the meaning of the doctrine itself will be in danger of being lost or enfeebled, and deprived of its vital effect on the character and conduct: the dogma becoming a mere formal profession, inefficacious for good, but cumbering the ground, and preventing the growth of any real and heartfelt conviction, from reason or personal experience. . . .

III. OF INDIVIDUALITY, AS ONE OF THE ELEMENTS
OF WELL-BEING

Such being the reasons which make it imperative that human beings should be free to form opinions, and to express their opinions without reserve; and such the baneful consequences to the intellectual, and through that to the moral nature of man, unless this liberty is either conceded, or asserted in spite of prohibition; let us next examine whether the same reasons do not require that men should be free to act upon their opinions —to carry these out in their lives, without hindrance, either physical or moral, from their fellow-men, so long as it is at their own risk and peril. This last proviso is of course indispensable. No one pretends that actions should be as free as opinions. On the contrary, even opinions lose their immunity, when the circumstances in which they are expressed are such as to constitute their expression a positive instigation to some mischievous act. . . . As it is useful that while mankind are imperfect there should be different opinions, so it is that there should be different experiments of living; that free scope should be given to varieties of character, short of injury to others; and that the worth of different modes of life should be proved practically, when any one thinks fit to try them. It is desirable, in short, that in things which do not primarily concern others, individuality should assert itself. Where, not the person's own character, but the traditions or customs of other people are the rule of conduct, there is wanting one of the principal ingredients of human happiness, and quite the chief ingredient of individual and social progress. . . .

IV. OF THE LIMITS TO THE AUTHORITY OF SOCIETY OVER THE INDIVIDUAL

What, then, is the rightful limit to the sovereignty of the individual over himself? Where does the authority of society begin? How much of human life should be assigned to individuality, and how much to society?

Each will receive its proper share, if each has that which more particularly concerns it. To individuality should belong the part of life in which it is chiefly the individual that is interested; to society, the part which chiefly interests society.

Though society is not founded on a contract, and though no good purpose is answered by inventing a contract in order to deduce social obligations from it, every one who receives the protection of society owes a return for the benefit, and the fact of living in society renders it indispensable that each should be found to observe a certain line of conduct towards the rest. This conduct consists, first, in not injuring the interests of one another; or rather certain interests, which, either by express legal provision or by tacit understanding, ought to be considered as rights; and secondly, in each person's bearing his share (to be fixed on some equitable principle) of the labours and sacrifices incurred for defending the society or its members from injury and molestation. These conditions society is justified in enforcing, at all costs to those who endeavour to withhold fulfilment. Nor is this all that society may do. The acts of an individual may be hurtful to others, or wanting in due consideration for their welfare, without going the length of violating any of their constituted rights. The offender may then be justly punished by opinion, though not by law. As soon as any part of a person's conduct affects prejudicially the interests of others, society has jurisdiction over it, and the question whether the general welfare will or will not be promoted by interfering with it, becomes open to discussion. But there is no room for entertaining any such question when a person's conduct affects the interests of no persons besides himself, or needs not affect them unless they like (all the persons concerned being of full age, and the ordinary amount of understanding). In all such cases there should be perfect freedom, legal and social, to do the action and stand the consequences.

HENRY STEELE COMMAGER / The
Pragmatic Necessity for Freedom *

Henry Steele Commager (1902–   ) has taught history at New York University and Columbia University. He has lectured at various institutions in the United States and abroad. He is the author of many books including *The American Mind; Living Ideas in America;* and *Freedom, Loyalty, and Dissent.*

FREEDOM OF SPEECH and of the press—that is, freedom of inquiry, criticism, and dissent—are guaranteed in State and Federal Constitutions now over a century and a half old. It is a sobering fact, however, that each generation has to vindicate these freedoms anew, and for itself. Yet this is not wholly a misfortune; one might almost see in it Providential wisdom. For there are risks in taking things for granted, risks not only of failure to appreciate them but of failure to understand them. Freedoms vindicated anew are more precious than those achieved without effort, and only those required to justify freedom can fully understand it. . . .

How are we to vindicate the claims of freedom? More specifically—for it

* Henry Steele Commager, from "The Pragmatic Necessity for Freedom," in *Civil Liberties Under Attack,* Clair Wilcox (ed.) (Philadelphia: U. of Pennsylvania Press, 1951), pp. 1–3, 7–10. Used by permission of the publisher and the author.

is this that concerns us most nearly—how are we to vindicate the claims of criticism and dissent and nonconformity? There are various ways we might go about such a vindication, some more familiar, some perhaps more persuasive, than others. There is, for example, the constitutional or legal approach to the whole question. We could submit the Bills of Rights, state and federal; recall the long and glorious history of these parts of our Constitutions; cite relevant court decisions—among them some of the most eloquent and moving documents in our literature. A persuasive, even a conclusive, constitutional case could be made out against some of the practices of state and Congressional Un-American Activities Committees, or against such acts as the McCarran Internal Security Bill.

Or there is what we may call the natural rights approach, an approach which could be launched with equal effect from experience or from theory. This approach emphasizes what was once familiar enough to all Americans —and what we are now in danger of forgetting—that government derives its powers from men; that rights of life and liberty are inalienable; that these rights are not something that government graciously confers upon men, but things no government can take away from men. This approach is profoundly concerned with Right—usually with individual right.

This is another way of saying that it is concerned with what must deeply concern all of us—the dignity of man. It is from this basic philosophical principle that the natural rights argument derives much of its strength. For it is becoming increasingly clear that it is respect for the dignity of the individual that most sharply differentiates democratic from totalitarian systems. Granted this basic principle, it follows that any conduct of the state that impairs the dignity of man is dangerous. And any argument for conformity that finds its ultimate sanction in force rather than in reason strikes at the integrity of the individual, and thus at the basic principle of democracy. . . .

But let us turn without more ado to the pragmatic necessity for freedom. What is the argument here? It is the argument of consequences. "The pragmatic method," William James wrote, "starts from the postulate that there is no difference of truth that doesn't make a difference of fact somewhere, and it seeks to determine the meaning of all differences of opinion by making the discussion hinge as soon as possible upon some practical or particular issue."

What, then, are the practical consequences of the attack upon independence of thought, nonconformity, dissent, which is now gathering momentum everywhere in the land? What kind of society will it create? What climate of opinion will it encourage? What will be its effect on science and scholarship, on politics and diplomacy, on security and peace? What, in short, is happening to us and what is likely to happen to us if we persist in penalizing dissent and rewarding orthodoxy?

The first and most obvious consequence is that we shall arrive, sooner or later, at an official standard of orthodoxy or—to use the current term—loyalty. It is, to be sure, one of the more curious features of the current drive against disloyalty and subversion that we so far lack definitions of either term. Yet definitions are in the making—in the making not so much by Congress or the courts, as in the minds of millions of Americans, in the daily press, in the schoolroom, in magazines and books, pulpits and forums and a thousand other vehicles and channels of opinion. If you are going to penalize disloyalty, you must first determine what is loyalty; if you are going to silence nonconformity, you must determine what is conformity—and to what it conforms. If you are going to accept J. Edgar Hoover's "easy test" of an organization: "Does it have a consistent record of support to the American viewpoint?"—you must determine what is the American viewpoint. If you are going to dismiss men from office or from teaching posts for membership in subversive organizations, you must eventually draw up a list not only of those that are subversive but of those that are patriotic. If you are going to silence dangerous ideas you must establish what are safe ideas.

To whom shall we entrust these great and delicate tasks? This is not a rhetorical question; it is an urgently practical one. Who, in our government or our society, is to determine what ideas are safe?

We need not conjure up, here, anything like George Orwell's "Thought Police," or a set of crimes like "Crime Think." It is not necessary to resort to that. The most effective censorship is not, in fact, legal; in a democracy it is—as Tocqueville pointed out—public opinion. It is not that laws may, in the end, cut us off from that body of independent and original thought that we so urgently need; it is that public opinion may create a situation where independence and originality simply do not emerge. That is even more serious. The greatest danger that threatens us is neither heterodox thought nor orthodox thought, but the absence of thought.

The second consequence of penalizing nonconformity, originality, and independence is a very practical one, and it is one whose effects are already being felt in many quarters. It is simply this: first-rate men and women will not and cannot work under conditions fixed by those who are afraid of ideas. Scholars who have to run the gauntlet of legislative investigations of their teaching, their writing, their associations, will look elsewhere for work —or will turn to purely antiquarian research. Scientists who cannot exchange information because of the requirements of security will fail to get essential information—or will refuse to work under conditions that all but guarantee ineffective and inconclusive work. Civil servants or potential government employees, faced with one investigation after another, with the overshadowing danger of smears from House or from Senate, with harassment and suspicion, will prefer employment in private industry.

It will be useful to determine, a generation from now, whether those universities that have purged their faculties are actually stronger than they were before the purges occurred—stronger in those essentials that go to make a university. It will be valuable to discover whether the civil service is, in fact, more loyal—with all the implications of that tremendous word—than the old civil service of the pre-loyalty investigation years. It will be important to know whether science advances as rapidly under the protection of security as it advanced before the days of elaborate security regulations.

A third consequence of the demand for conformity grows out of the first two. It is the development in this country of the kind of society in which freedom of inquiry does not flourish, in which criticism does not flourish, in which originality does not flourish. This is no alarmist bugaboo; it is a development already under way. Already civil servants are afraid to read certain magazines or to join certain organizations. Already teachers hesitate to discuss certain issues in class; just recently the New York City Board of Education sought to reassure them on this: you may discuss communism objectively, it said, as long as you tell pupils how wicked it all is! Already men and women hesitate to join minority parties or "dangerous" organizations, or to agitate for reform. And well they might! Just the other day we read the story of the much-decorated Negro army captain who had been asked to resign from the service because he was charged with reading the *Daily Worker* and because his father was alleged to have fought segregation in public housing. The demand was, to be sure, withdrawn. But how many instances of such official stupidity go undiscovered, unpublicized, and unchallenged? How many soldiers, duly impressed by the risks involved, were dissuaded by this episode from reading anything but the comics? Do we want the kind of army that will read only approved literature?

It is, you see, with the practical consequences to our society of the limitations on freedom that we are concerned. We do not protect freedom in order to indulge error. We protect freedom in order to discover truth. We do not maintain freedom in order to permit eccentricity to flourish; we maintain freedom in order that society may profit from criticism, even eccentric criticism. We do not encourage dissent for sentimental reasons; we encourage dissent because we cannot live without it.

CHARLES FRANKEL / Is It Ever Right to Break the Law? *

Charles Frankel (1917–   ), professor of philosophy at Columbia University, served as Assistant Secretary of State for Educational and Cultural Affairs 1965–1967. He is the author of numerous books including *The Case for Modern Man, The Democratic Prospect*, and *The Neglected Aspect of Foreign Affairs*.

DURING RECENT MONTHS, public events have repeatedly dramatized an old and troublesome problem. A group of students defies the State Department's ban on travel to Cuba; a teachers' union threatens a strike even though a state law prohibits strikes by public employes; advocates of civil rights employ mass demonstrations of disobedience to the law to advance their cause; the Governor of a Southern state deliberately obstructs the enforcement of Federal laws, and declares himself thoroughly within his rights in doing so.

An observer can approve the motives that lead to some of these actions and disapprove others. All, nevertheless, raise the same fundamental question: Does the individual have the right—or perhaps the duty—to disobey the law when his mind, his conscience or his religious faith tells him that the law is unjust?

The question is as old as Socrates. It has regularly propelled men into radical examination of the premises of personal morality and civic obligation and, indeed, of government itself. And it is an interesting question not only for its philosophical implications but because it has always been a painfully practical question as well, and never more so than today.

Our period in history is frequently described as "materialistic" and "conformist," an age in which governments have enormous powers to crush the bodies and anesthetize the minds of their subjects, and in which the great masses of men and women—presumably in contrast with men and women of other times—prefer to play it safe rather than raise questions of basic moral principle. It is to the point to note, however, that massive resistance to law, justified in the name of higher moral principles like "freedom,"

* Charles Frankel, "Is It Ever Right to Break the Law?", *New York Times Magazine*, January 12, 1964, pp. 17, 36, 39, 41. Copyright © 1964 by The New York Times Company. Reprinted by permission of the author and the publisher.

"equality" and "national independence," has been a conspicuous feature of our period, and one of its most effective techniques of social action. Millions of ordinary people with no pretensions to being either heroes or saints have employed it in India, in South Africa, in the resistance movements against the Nazis and in the struggle for equality for Negroes in the United States.

Moreover, such massive resistance to law is by no means confined only to supremely glorious or dangerous causes; nor is it used only by revolutionaries, underdogs or outsiders. During Prohibition, a large number of respectable, conservative Americans dutifully broke the law in defense of what they regarded as an inalienable human right. In this case, doing one's duty happened also to be agreeable and even fashionable, but this does not change the fact that many right-thinking citizens, who today condemn pacifists or integrationists for using illegal methods to advance their cause, have themselves used such methods happily and unashamedly.

When is it justified, then, for the citizen to act as his own legislator, and to decide that he will or will not obey a given law?

An answer that covers all the issues this question raises cannot be given here, nor can a set of principles be proposed that will allow anyone to make automatic and infallible judgments concerning the legitimacy or illegitimacy of specific acts of civil disobedience. Such judgments require detailed knowledge of the facts of specific cases, and such knowledge is often unavailable to the outsider. Nevertheless, it is possible to indicate some of the principal issues that are raised by civil disobedience, some of the more common mistakes that are made in thinking about these issues, and, at least in outline, the approach that one man would take toward such issues.

We can begin, it seems to me, by rejecting one extreme position. This is the view that disobedience to the law can never be justified in any circumstances. To take this position is to say one or two things: either every law that exists is a just law, or a greater wrong is always done by breaking the law. The first statement is plainly false. The second is highly doubtful. If it is true, then the signers of the Declaration of Independence, and those Germans who refused to carry out Hitler's orders, committed acts of injustice.

It is possible, however, to take a much more moderate and plausible version of this position, and many quite reasonable people do. Such people concede that disobedience to the law can sometimes be legitimate and necessary under a despotic regime. They argue, however, that civil disobedience can never be justified in a democratic society, because such a society provides its members with legal instruments for the redress of their grievances.

This is one of the standard arguments that is made, often quite sincerely, against the activities of people like supporters of the Congress of Racial Equality, who set about changing laws they find objectionable by dramatically breaking them. Such groups are often condemned for risking disorder and for spreading disrespect for the law when, so it is maintained, they could accomplish their goals a great deal more fairly and patriotically by staying within the law, and confining themselves to the courts and to methods of peaceful persuasion.

Now it is perfectly true, I believe, that there is a stronger case for obedience to the law, including bad law, in a democracy than in a dictatorship. The people who must abide by the law have presumably been consulted, and they have legal channels through which to express their protests and to work for reform. One way to define democracy is to say that it is a system whose aim is to provide alternatives to civil disobedience. Nevertheless, when applied to the kind of situation faced, say, by CORE, these generalizations, it seems to me, become cruelly abstract.

The basic fallacy in the proposition that, in a democracy, civil disobedience can never be justified, is that it confuses the *ideals* or *aims* of democracy with the inevitably less than perfect accomplishments of democracy at any given moment. In accordance with democratic ideals, the laws of a democracy may give rights and powers to individuals which, in theory, enable them to work legally for the elimination of injustices.

In actual fact, however, these rights and powers may be empty. The police may be hostile, the courts biased, the elections rigged—and the legal remedies available to the individual may be unavailing against these evils.

Worse still, the majority may have demonstrated, in a series of free and honest elections, that it is unwavering in its support of what the minority regards as an unspeakable evil. This is obviously the case today in many parts of the South, where the white majority is either opposed to desegregation or not so impatient to get on with it as is the Negro minority. Are we prepared to say that majorities never err? If not, there is no absolutely conclusive reason why we must invariably give the results of an election greater weight than considerations of elementary justice.

It is true, of course, that one swallow does not make a summer, and that the test of legal democratic processes is not this or that particular success or failure, but rather the general direction in which these processes move over the long run. Still, the position that violation of the law is never justifiable so long as there are legal alternatives overstates this important truth. It fails to face at least three important exceptions to it.

In the first place, dramatic disobedience to the law by a minority may be the only effective way of catching the attention or winning the support of the majority. Most classic cases of civil disobedience, from the early Christians to Gandhi and his supporters, exemplify this truth. Civil disobedience, like almost no other technique, can shame a majority and make it ask itself just how far it is willing to go, just how seriously it really is committed to defending the status quo.

Second, there is the simple but painful factor of time. If a man is holding you down on a bed of nails, it is all very well for a bystander to say that you live in a great country in which there are legal remedies for your condition, and that you ought, therefore, to be patient and wait for these remedies to take effect. But your willingness to listen to this counsel will depend, quite properly, on the nature of the injury you are suffering.

Third, it is baseless prejudice to assume that observance of the law is *always* conducive to strengthening a democratic system while disobedience to the law can never have a salutary effect. A majority's complacent acquiescence in bad laws can undermine the faith of a minority in the power of democratic methods to rectify manifest evils; yet a vigorous democracy depends on the existence of minorities holding just such a faith.

Disobedience to bad laws can sometimes jolt democratic processes into motion. Which strengthens one's hope for democracy more—the behavior of the Negroes in Birmingham who broke municipal ordinances when they staged their protest marches, or the behavior of the police, using dogs and fire hoses to assert their legal authority?

Another factor should also be taken into account. In our Federal system, there are often legitimate doubts concerning the legal validity, under our Constitution, of various state or local ordinances. Disobedience to these laws is in many cases simply a practical, though painful, way of testing their legality. But even where no thought of such a test is involved, there is often present a moral issue which no one can easily dodge—least of all the man whose personal dignity and self-respect are caught up in the issue.

A citizen caught in a conflict between local laws and what he thinks will be upheld as the superior Federal law can sometimes afford to wait until the courts have determined the issue for him. But often he cannot afford to wait, or must take a stand in order to force a decision. This is the situation of many Negro citizens in Southern states as they confront the conflict between local and Federal laws.

Yet there is another side to the story. It would be a mistake to conclude from what has been said that civil disobedience is justified, provided only that it is disobedience in the name of higher principles. Strong moral conviction is not all that is required to turn breaking the law into service to society.

Civil disobedience is not simply like other acts in which men stand up courageously for their principles. It involves violation of the law. And the law can make no provision for its violation except to hold the offender liable to punishment. This is why President Kennedy was in such a delicate position . . . at the time of the Negro demonstrations in Birmingham. He gave many signs that, as an individual, he was in sympathy with the goals of the demonstrators. As a political leader, he probably realized that these goals could not be attained without dramatic actions that crossed the line into illegality. But as Chief Executive he could not give permission or approval to such actions.

We may admire a man like Martin Luther King, who [was] prepared to defy the authorities in the name of a principle, and we may think that he is entirely in the right; just the same, his right to break the law cannot be officially recognized. No society, whether free or tyrannical, can give its citizens the right to break its laws: To ask it to do so is to ask it to proclaim, as a matter of law, that its laws are not laws.

In short, if anybody ever has a right to break the law, this cannot be a legal right under the law. It has to be a moral right against the law. And this moral right is not an unlimited right to disobey any law which one regards as unjust. It is a right that is hedged about, it seems to me, with important restrictions.

First of all, the exercise of this right is subject to standards of just and fair behavior. I may be correct, for example, in thinking that an ordinance against jaywalking is an unnecessary infringement of my rights. This does not make it reasonable, however, for me to organize a giant sit-down strike in the streets which holds up traffic for a week. Conformity to the concept of justice requires that there be some proportion between the importance of the end one desires to attain and the power of the means one employs to attain it.

When applied to civil disobedience, this principle constitutes a very large restriction. Civil disobedience is an effort to change the law by making it impossible to enforce the law, or by making the price of such enforcement extremely high. It is a case, as it were, of holding the legal system to ransom. It can arouse extreme passions on one side or the other, excite and provoke the unbalanced, and make disrespect for the law a commonplace and popular attitude.

Although violence may be no part of the intention of those who practice civil disobedience, the risks of violence are present, and are part of what must be taken into account when a program of civil disobedience is being contemplated.

In short, civil disobedience is a grave enterprise. It may sometimes be justified, but the provocation for it has to be equally grave. Basic principles have to be at issue. The evils being combated have to be serious evils that are likely to endure unless they are fought. There should be reasonable grounds to believe that legal methods of fighting them are likely to be insufficient by themselves.

Nor is this the only limitation on the individual's moral right to disobey the law. The most important limitation is that his cause must be a just one. It was right for General de Gaulle to disobey Marshal Pétain; it was wrong for the commanders of the French Army in Algeria, twenty years later, to disobey General de Gaulle.

Similarly, if it is absolutely necessary, and if the consequences have been properly weighed, then it is right to break the law in order to eliminate inequalities based on race. But it can never be necessary, and no weighing of consequences can ever make it right, to break the law in the name of Nazi principles.

In sum, the goals of those who disobey the law have to lie at the very heart of what we regard as morality before we can say that they have a moral right to do what they are doing.

But who is to make these difficult decisions? Who is to say that one man's moral principles are right and another man's wrong? We come here to the special function that civil disobedience serves in a society. The man who breaks the law on the ground that the law is immoral asks the rest of us, in effect, to trust him, or to trust those he trusts, in preference to the established conventions and authorities of our society.

He has taken a large and visible chance, and implicitly asked us to join him in taking that chance, on the probity of his personal moral judgment. In doing so, he has put it to us whether we are willing to take a similar chance on the probity of our own judgment.

Thomas Hobbes, who knew the trouble that rebels and dissenters convinced of their rectitude can cause, once remarked that a man may be convinced that God has commanded him to act as he has, but that God, after all, does not command other men to believe that this is so. The man who chooses to disobey the law on grounds of principle may be a saint, but he may also be a madman. He may be a courageous and lonely individualist, but he may also merely be taking orders and following his own crowd. Whatever he may be, however, his existence tends to make us painfully aware that we too are implicitly making choices, and must bear responsibility for the ones we make.

This, indeed, may be the most important function of those who practice civil disobedience. They remind us that the man who obeys the law has as much of an obligation to look into the morality of his acts and the rationality of his society as does the man who breaks the law. The occurrence of civil disobedience can never be a happy phenomenon; when it is justified, something is seriously wrong with the society in which it takes place.

But the man who puts his conscience above the law, though he may be right or he may be wrong, does take personal moral responsibility for the social arrangements under which he lives. And so he dramatizes the fascinating and fearful possibility that those who obey the law might do the same. They might obey the law and support what exists, not out of habit or fear, but because they have freely chosen to do so, and are prepared to live with their consciences after having made that choice.

For Further Study

Abraham, Henry J. *Freedom and the Court: Civil Rights and Liberties in the United States.* New York: Oxford U. Press, 1967.

Barth, Alan. *The Price of Liberty.* New York: Viking, 1961.

Brandt, Irving. *The Bill of Rights: Its Origin and Meaning.* Indianapolis: Bobbs-Merrill, 1965.

Fortas, Abe. *Concerning Dissent and Civil Disobedience.* New York: New American Library, 1968. (Signet Special 3-D3581.)

Hook, Sidney. "Neither Blind Obedience nor Uncivil Disobedience," *New York Times Magazine* (June 5, 1966): 52–53, 122, 124, 126, 128.

Knight, Harold V. *With Liberty and Justice for All: The Meaning of the Bill of Rights Today.* Rev. ed.; Dobbs Ferry, N. Y.: Oceana Publications, 1968.

Masotti, Louis H. and Bowen, Don R. eds. *Riots and Rebellion: Civil Violence in the Urban Community.* Beverley Hills, Calif.: Sage Publications, 1968.

Muller, Herbert J. *Issues of Freedom.* New York: Harper, 1960, Chs. 1–5.

Report of the National Advisory Commission on Civil Disorders. Otto Kerner, Chairman. New York: Dutton, 1968; Bantam Books, 1968.

Schlesinger, Arthur Jr. *Violence: America in the Sixties.* New York: New American Library, 1968. (Signet Special 5-D3747.)

Skolnick, Jerome H. and staff. *The Politics of Protest.* New York: Ballantine Books, 1969. (Report to the National Commission on the Causes and Prevention of Violence.)

Stumpf, Samuel E. *Morality and the Law.* Nashville: Vanderbilt U. Press, 1966.

Walzer, Michael. "The Obligation to Disobey," *Ethics*, 77 (April, 1967): 163–175.

26 Individualism and Governmental Control

SIDNEY HOOK / *The State and the General Welfare* *

See the biographical note on p. 1.

THE PHRASE "the welfare state" is one of the most frequently heard battle cries in the American political arena. Since both major parties are committed to some governmental intervention in the economy, they are not as far apart on the issue as they might appear. . . .

It is not easy to say exactly what the welfare state is, for it has been developing slowly for almost a century. To be sure, the preamble to the United States Constitution states that one of its aims is "to promote the general welfare." But this is hardly a sufficient clue to the meaning of the welfare state. Everyone is for "the general welfare"; but there is no such unanimity about the welfare state, which many people consider to be decidedly opposed to the general welfare.

The phrase is most widely used to describe the social policies adopted by the New Deal and Fair Deal in this country and by the Labor party in England when it came to power in 1945. These policies have not been abandoned but have been continued, albeit with diminishing energy, by

* Sidney Hook, " 'Welfare State'—A Debate That Isn't," *New York Times Magazine*, November 27, 1960: 27, 118–119. Copyright © 1960 by The New York Times Company. Reprinted by permission of the author and the publisher.

liberal Republican and Conservative successors to the Democratic and Labor parties.

The unanimity with which these policies have been followed, in fact, is very impressive. It indicates that no matter what any political group *says* about the welfare state, it will have little or no bearing on what it does. If the welfare state is identified with what the New Deal in the United States and Labor in England have done, then it is as certain as anything can be in human affairs that the *direction* in which they have taken the economy will be continued. This direction seems irreversible, for it would be political suicide for the Republicans here or the Tories in England to oppose it.

But if there is agreement on the actual measures taken, there is little agreement on the reasons for these measures, and still less on the social philosophy from which these reasons are derived. The social philosophy behind the welfare state is vague and inchoate. Some of its partisans deny that there is any social philosophy behind it at all. Nonetheless, man is a reason-giving animal even when he doesn't act reasonably.

The basic outlook or commitment of the welfare state is more or less adequately expressed in the complex proposition that it is the responsibility of the government to adopt measures that tend to produce and sustain full employment and, in its absence, to offer some insurance against unemployment; to coordinate policies to strengthen the economy; to provide economic security for the ill, the aged and dependent; to establish minimum standards of compensation and working conditions which are a function of the productive capacity of the country and of our conception of a decent and civilized mode of existence; to protect and insure the health of its citizens against the hazards of accident and disease; to encourage all local efforts to extend and improve the quality and the quantity of education; and to foster, wherever private enterprise fails, the social, economic and educational conditions that make for equality of opportunity.

In fairness to those who say they oppose the philosophy of the welfare state, it should be acknowledged at once that they are not opposed to these ideal ends. They are opposed only to the *state's* attempt to realize them, and thus transform itself into a service agency.

They contend that the chief function of the state is to keep peace and order and to lay down the legal rules of the road within which men may freely pursue their own aims. They insist that the methods used by the state must never interfere with the operations of the market economy or free enterprise system.

Those who criticize the welfare state seek to prove, in an attempt to discredit it, that it has an unsavory genealogy which can be traced to the traditions and practices of Prussian absolutism tempered by a paternalistic concern for the well-being of its subjects. But whatever may have been the case on the European Continent, this is extremely far-fetched in relation to the welfare measures introduced in England and the United States. The influence of Dickens and Bentham was much more profound than that of Bismarck and "the Socialists of the Chair," as the professorial Socialists in German universities were called, in altering British attitudes toward the victims of the industrial revolution and the aged inmates of poorhouses.

In our own country it was not a theory but a condition of acute distress, resulting from the great depression, which resulted in the complex of state actions that define the New Deal. Even before that, precedents had been established, contested by no one, for state aid to needy business men, not only by preferential tariffs but through the establishment of the Reconstruction Finance Corporation. At no time, however, were the needs of business men as acute as the sufferings of impoverished farmers and workers and those dependent upon them, after the economic crisis of the early Thirties.

The legislation that sought to provide for economic security in its various forms was not planned. It did not flow from any doctrinaire theory. Unlike socialism, it showed no hostility to the profit motive. On the contrary, it appealed to the profit motive and avoided the name of socialism like the very plague. It was undertaken as an *ad hoc* measure to meet a temporary emergency—but few things are more lasting than the "temporary."

What explains the wide popular support enjoyed by the philosophy behind the welfare state? No simple answer can be found. To begin with, we must list a vague yet real sense of solidarity with our fellows and a desire to mitigate the suffering of those not responsible for their own plight.

These sentiments are nurtured by the age-old religious feeling that "we are all members one of another" and that but for the grace of God, or nature or chance, we might be in the shoes of those less fortunate than ourselves.

Support for the welfare state, however, is not derived merely from sentiment. Anybody who takes seriously the ideal of "equality of opportunity" finds himself committed to programs of social change through legislation which will restore equality of opportunity where it is missing or enstate it where it has been absent.

Absolute equality of opportunity, of course, is impossible. Nonetheless, it is clear that children of unemployed or widowed parents or those who live in poverty-stricken, depressed areas have not the same opportunity for a good life as those who are brought up in homes which know no serious privation. Nor can those who suffer from disease and poor health, which could be alleviated by proper medical care, enjoy the same opportunities as those who are medically well provided for.

To some, "equality of opportunity" is limited merely to the formal equality of treatment under a given law. They say that just as traffic rules, enforced by an incorruptible police force, show no favor to big cars or small ones in their use of the road, so the laws of the nation provide equal opportunity for the rich and the poor.

Those who accept the philosophy of the welfare state are quick to point out that in most matters the pains and penalties of the law fall with completely different weight on individuals in different social conditions. Something more than mere formal equality before the law is necessary.

There is much opposition to the state's exchanging its traditional role of umpire or judge for the role of a service institution for those in distress. This opposition flows from three sources, ethical, psychological and administrative.

The chief ethical objection to the welfare state is that it has no right to play Santa Claus or Lady Bountiful to the underprivileged at the expense of those who have worked diligently to achieve their property and position. After all, it is said, someone must pay for all the benefits bestowed by the welfare state. If it were a matter of voluntary philanthropy, as in the past, no one could reasonably object. But when the state, in its official capacity, steps in to relieve distress, its philanthropy is really a form of coercion; it robs Peter by taxation to pay Paul—and before long every Tom, Dick and Harry turns to it for relief.

One group wants "just prices," another "just wages," a third "decent housing," a fourth "adequate terms of leisure." The burden of gratifying these demands falls upon the most productive groups in society who are, in effect, punished for their gumption and success.

The second objection to the welfare state is psychological. It is maintained that the normal springs of action, especially initiative and ambition and desire for independence, are gradually eroded by the unearned beneficence of the welfare state.

People come to expect things to be done for them instead of bestirring themselves. The spirit of the pioneer becomes anachronistic. The hard worker becomes suspect as the bosses' tool to increase the pace and output of production. Joy of work and the instinct of workmanship are replaced by the fine arts of boondoggling and featherbedding. The outstretched hand becomes the symbol of the welfare state, "I have a right" its whining motto, and a forward look to the next paid holiday its sustaining faith.

The third argument against the welfare state is administrative. Government becomes too big and too bureaucratic. Economic life becomes burdened with legal forms and red tape, and subject to multiple decrees of special bureaus whose provisions are derived not from equitable principles of law but from the bureaucratic sense of discretion or fitness. Bureaucracies grow in size by Parkinson's well-known law. A whole new class comes into existence with a vested interest in the social problems that originally induced the state to intervene.

What do the advocates of the welfare state reply to this indictment? First, as to the ethical argument. They point out that the lives of members of a community are so intertwined, the services and obligations of one generation to another so difficult to separate, that it is impossible to establish an exact equation between the services rendered to society by any group and the payments received from it.

The same principle that justifies taxing a bachelor for the education of his neighbor's children, and taxing those without cars for the upkeep of roads they do not use, justifies taxing the entire community in order to moderate the poverty and want of the underprivileged, the needy and the indigent.

Carlyle declared long ago that the sickness of any group in a society is a threat to the health of every group. The poor or underprivileged may suffer more from disease and ignorance and delinquencies than those who are better off. But in the long run, everyone suffers to some extent. No one can seriously contend that large-scale unemployment or the genteel poverty which is a continuous function of inflation are matters for which individuals are personally responsible. Welfare measures may be interpreted, therefore, as a socialization of risk in which the community through taxation collects the premiums and distributes the benefits to those who are unlucky.

There are, to be sure, certain obvious abuses—social security benefits sometimes go to those who do not really need them, unemployment insurance to those who have nest eggs, and certain public services to those who can privately afford them. Gross abuses can be remedied, but any attempt to apply a means test to distinguish between the deserving and undeserving would cost more to enforce than the impartial application of a rule to all.

In addition, there is always something humiliating in having to prove one's need, even when it exists. The bread of charity has a bitter taste which it loses when it is distributed as the legitimate benefits of social insurance.

The psychological argument against the welfare state has more weight because everyone, including the recipients of state aid, agrees that self-help is preferable to dependence upon the government. But there is no convincing psychological evidence that most human beings would settle for state aid alone if opportunities existed enabling them to achieve more. Men have always reacted positively to the incentives of higher status and greater rewards. The desire to surpass others is at least as strong as the desire to equal them. There need be no fear, therefore, that mankind necessarily will be leveled to the same plane of privation and mediocrity.

State aid is not incompatible with private and group initiative. For example, I live for part of the year in a rural area where it was unprofitable for private power companies to serve the inhabitants. Because it was sparsely settled, it was impossible for the farmers themselves to raise sufficient capital to electrify the region. With the aid of low-interest loans from the Rural Electrification Administration, a local cooperative finally managed to do the job. The results raised the cultural and economic level of the entire community, and other areas and industries outside the region also benefited greatly.

State aid to cooperative groups and to individuals has stimulated a vast amount of initiative in housing. Sometimes local conditions of scarcity, overcrowding and sanitation make it imperative for municipalities to underwrite public housing. The human costs of waiting for the market to remedy the situation come too high. Slums are more likely to breed a spirit of dependence and defeatism than of lawful enterprise or initiative.

Nor, finally, can it be gainsaid that the welfare state of necessity must be more bureaucratic, since its services are not self-administered. But bureaucracy is a scare word. Large-scale private enterprises have bureaucracies, too. It is the size of an enterprise, not whether it is public or private, that determines the growth of managerial personnel. Those who want to check its growth, and subject it to additional judicial and administrative controls, can succeed only by adding to the number of state officials.

The incontestable fact is that despite, if not because of, the welfare state and its bureaucracy, the nation is today at once both more prosperous and less riven by class conflict than at any previous time. Further, whatever may have been the case when the shibboleth, "That state is best which governs least," was current, today the people do not fear the state as an instrument of oppression.

The state is no longer "they" as opposed to "us." Instead of viewing it as the orthodox Marxists did—as "the executive committee of the ruling class" —or as the robber barons did as a means of looting the public domain— the farmers and workers and business men, the professions, the blue-and white-collar workers, the young and the aged, the veterans and the armed services see the state as a power to be used.

Out of the struggle for its use arise not only compromises between groups but concessions in order to win allies. When the electorate becomes aroused, which unfortunately is not often enough, the consumer is usually the gainer.

The welfare state is neither creeping socialism nor moribund capitalism. It has no coherent philosophy because its policy is one of improvisation to meet evils rather than one of enlightened planning to prevent them. Its wisdom—such as it is—is always *ex post facto*, which is better than doing nothing about social evils in the hope they will disappear of themselves.

But it can safely go much further in anticipating needs on a national and international scale and in planning for them.

It is a profound error, therefore, to pass judgment on the virtues and defects of the welfare state as a whole. What one must appraise are *specific* proposals that the state do this or that on the ground that the welfare of the community and the preservation of its strategic political freedom require that it be done.

Some things are worth doing but not necessarily by the state. If no individuals or groups are willing or able to do what is worth doing, then the possibility should be seriously entertained that the state do it. Such questions cannot be decided merely on the basis of general allegiance or opposition to the welfare state.

If the state is to be our servant and not our master, a certain skepticism toward state power will always be in order because, as the founders of the American Republic realized, the state is always run by men, and men are not angels. But so long as those who rule are responsible to those whom they govern and to whom they must return for a renewal of their mandates, we need not fear delegation of power to the state in this complex world—a delegation which, in many areas, is inescapable in any case. If such delegation results in usurpation of power, it will not be the fault of the welfare state but of the intelligence—or rather, lack of it—of its citizens.

To date, the achievements of the welfare state are many and it can claim credit for the relative material prosperity of our times as compared with many periods of the past. But in a world that requires more and more foresight, more coordination to keep the economy on an even keel and help develop the economies of under-developed countries, more planning to avoid the dangers of war and the loss of freedom, the scope of the welfare state may well be extended. Today, its only alternative is the "illfare" state.

Even those who condemn the welfare state will, in the very interests of national security, have to continue it and carry the policies of intelligent coordination into more fields of our economy. The resources of freedom cannot be mobilized, whether in peace or in the defense of peace, without a newer and better and bigger "New Deal" irrespective of what we call it.

MORRIS R. COHEN / Why I Am Not a Communist *

Morris R. Cohen (1880–1947), an outstanding champion of social and political liberalism, wrote *Faith of a Liberal* and *Law and the Social Order*. For his other activities, see the biographical note on p. 51.

LIKE MANY OTHERS who are not Communists, I hold no brief for the injustices and stupidities of the present capitalist regime. Indeed, I have never ceased to be grateful for the illumination on historic and contemporary social issues which I found in studying Marx's *Das Kapital*. It prepared me to see that the present [1934] general breakdown of capitalist economy is not an unforeseeable accident but a consequence of the private ownership of the machinery of production, whereby the processes of industry are directed for the profit of individual capitalists rather than for the satisfaction of our common needs. . . .

. . . What distinguishes present-day Communists is not, therefore, their professed ultimate goal or their analysis of our economic ills, but their political remedy or program, to wit, the seizure of power by armed rebellion and the setting up of a dictatorship by the leaders of the Communist Party. To be sure, this dictatorship is to be in the name of the *proletariat*, just as the fascist dictatorship is in the name of *the whole nation*. But such verbal tricks cannot hide the brute facts of tyrannical suppression necessarily involved in all dictatorship. . . .

This program of civil war, dictatorship, and the illiberal or fanatically intolerant spirit which war psychology always engenders, may bring more miseries than those that the communists seek to remove; and the arguments to prove that such war is desirable or inevitable seem to me patently inadequate. . . .

One of the reasons that leads communists to ignore the terrific destruction which armed rebellion must bring about is the conviction that "the revolution" is inevitable. In this they follow Marx, who, dominated by the Hegelian dialectic, regarded the victory of the proletariat over the bourgeoisie as inevitable,[1] so that all that human effort can hope to achieve is

* Morris R. Cohen, from "Why I Am Not a Communist," *Modern Monthly* (April, 1934), with omissions. Used by permission of administrator of author's estate.
[1] *Capital*, I, p. 837.

"to shorten and lessen the birth pangs" of the new order.[2] There is, however, very little scientific value in this dialectic argument. . . .

. . . [N]o amount of repetition can make a truth of the dogma that the capitalist class alone rules this country and like the Almighty can do what it pleases. It would be folly to deny that as individuals or as a class they have more than their proportionate share of influence in the government, and that they have exercised it unintelligently and with dire results. But it is equally absurd to maintain that they have governed or can govern without the cooperation of the farmers and the influential middle classes. None of our recent constitutional amendments, not the income tax amendment, not the popular election of the United States Senators, not woman suffrage, neither prohibition nor its repeal, nor any other major bit of legislation can be said to have been imposed on our country in the interests of the capitalist class. . . .

If the history of the past is any guide at all, it is that real improvements in the future will come like the improvements of the past, namely, through cooperation between different groups, each of which is wise enough to see the necessity of compromising with those with whom we have to live together and whom we cannot or do not wish to exterminate. . . .

It is pure fanaticism to belittle the gains which have come to mankind from the spirit of free inquiry, free discussion, and accommodation. No human individual or group of individuals can claim omniscience. Hence, society can only suffer serious loss when one group suppresses the opinions and criticisms of all others. . . .

The communist criticism of liberalism seems to me altogether baseless and worthless. One would suppose from it that liberalism is a peculiar excrescence of capitalism. This is, however, not true. The essence of liberalism, freedom of thought and inquiry, freedom of discussion and criticism, is not the invention of the capitalist system. It is rather the mother of Greek and modern science without which our present industrial order and the labor movement would be impossible. The plea that the denial of freedom is a temporary necessity is one advanced by all militarists. It ignores the fact that when suppression becomes a habit, it is not readily abandoned. . . .

For Further Study

Allen, Frederick Lewis. *The Big Change: America Transforms Itself—1900–1950*. New York: Harper, 1952, Part Three, "The New America."

Brandt, Richard B., ed. *Social Justice*. Englewood Cliffs: Prentice-Hall, 1962. (Spectrum Book.)

[2] *Ibid.*, pp. 13–15.

Ellsworth, R. G., and Harris, S. M. *The American Right Wing: A Report to the Fund for the Republic*. Washington: Public Affairs Press, 1962, 63 pp.

Girvetz, Harry K. *From Wealth to Welfare: The Evolution of Liberalism*. Stanford: Stanford U. Press, 1950, Part One, "Classical Liberalism"; Part Two, "Contemporary Liberalism."

Goldwin, Robert A. *Left, Right, and Center*. Chicago: Rand McNally, 1967. (Paperback.)

Krutch, Joseph Wood. "Life, Liberty and the Pursuit of Welfare," *Saturday Evening Post*, 234 (July 15, 1961): 18–19, 56–58.

Miller, David L. *Individualism: Personal Achievement and the Open Society*. Austin: U. of Texas Press, 1966.

Sanford, Nevitt. *Self and Society: Social Change and Individual Development*. New York: Atherton Press, 1966.

Templin, Ralph T. *Democracy and Nonviolence: The Role of the Individual in World Crisis*. Boston: Porter Sargent, 1965.

27   The Philosophy of History

*CARL L. BECKER / What Are Historical Facts? ***

Carl L. Becker (1873–1945) taught history at Cornell University
for many years. He was the author of numerous books including
*The Heavenly City of the Eighteenth-Century Philosophers; Mod-
ern Democracy;* and *New Liberties for Old.*

HISTORY IS A VENERABLE BRANCH of knowledge, and the writing of history is
an art of long standing. Everyone knows what history is, that is, everyone is
familiar with the word, and has a confident notion of what it means. In
general, history has to do with the thought and action of men and women
who lived in past times. Everyone knows what the past is too. We all have
a comforting sense that it lies behind us, like a stretch of uneven country
we have crossed; and it is often difficult to avoid the notion that one could
easily, by turning round, walk back into this country of the past. That, at
all events, is what we commonly think of the historian as doing: he works
in the past, he explores the past in order to find out what men did and
thought in the past. His business is to discover and set forth the "facts" of
history.

When anyone says "facts" we are all there. The word gives us a sense of
stability. We know where we are when, as we say, we "get down to the

* Carl L. Becker, from "What Are Historical Facts?" *The Western Political Quarterly,* 8 (September, 1955): 327–329, 330–334, 335–336, 337–340. Used by permission
of the publisher.

facts"—as, for example, we know where we are when we get down to the
facts of the structure of the atom, or the incredible movement of the
electron as it jumps from one orbit to another. It is the same with history.
Historians feel safe when dealing with the facts. We talk much about the
"hard facts" and the "cold facts," about "not being able to get around the
facts," and about the necessity of basing our narrative on a "solid foundation of fact." By virtue of talking in this way, the facts of history come in
the end to seem something solid, something substantial like physical matter (I mean matter in the common sense, not matter defined as "a series of
events in the ether"), something possessing definite shape, and clear persistent outline—like bricks or scantlings; so that we can easily picture the
historian as he stumbles about in the past, stubbing his toe on the hard
facts if he doesn't watch out. That is his affair of course, a danger he runs;
for his business is to dig out the facts and pile them up for someone to use.
Perhaps he may use them himself; but at all events he must arrange them
conveniently so that someone—perhaps the sociologist or the economist—
may easily carry them away for use in some structural enterprise.

Such (with no doubt a little, but not much, exaggeration to give point to
the matter) are the common connotations of the words historical facts, as
used by historians and other people. Now, when I meet a word with which
I am entirely unfamiliar, I find it a good plan to look it up in the dictionary and find out what someone thinks it means. But when I have frequently to use words with which everyone is perfectly familiar—words like
"cause" and "liberty" and "progress" and "government"—when I have to
use words of this sort which everyone knows perfectly well, the wise thing
to do is to take a week off and think about them. The result is often
astonishing; for as often as not I find that I have been talking about words
instead of real things. Well, "historical fact" is such a word; and I suspect
it would be worthwhile for us historians at least to think about this word
more than we have done. For the moment therefore, leaving the historian
moving about in the past piling up the cold facts, I wish to inquire
whether the historical fact is really as hard and stable as it is often supposed to be.

And this inquiry I will throw into the form of three simple questions. I
will ask the questions, I can't promise to answer them. The questions are:
(1) What is the historical fact? (2) Where is the historical fact? (3)
When is the historical fact? Mind I say *is* not *was*. I take it for granted
that if we are interested in, let us say, the fact of the Magna Carta, we are
interested in it for our own sake and not for its sake; and since we are
living now and not in 1215 we must be interested in the Magna Carta, if at
all, for what it is and not for what it was.

First then, What is the historical fact? Let us take a simple fact, as simple as the historian often deals with, viz.: "In the year 49 B.C. Caesar crossed the Rubicon." A familiar fact this is, known to all, and obviously of some importance since it is mentioned in every history of the great Caesar. But is this fact as simple as it sounds? Has it the clear, persistent outline which we commonly attribute to simple historical facts? When we say that Caesar crossed the Rubicon we do not of course mean that Caesar crossed it alone, but with his army. The Rubicon is a small river, and I don't know how long it took Caesar's army to cross it; but the crossing must surely have been accompanied by many acts and many words and many thoughts of many men. That is to say, a thousand and one lesser "facts" went to make up the one simple fact that Caesar crossed the Rubicon; and if we had someone, say James Joyce, to know and relate all these facts, it would no doubt require a book of 794 pages to present this one fact that Caesar crossed the Rubicon. Thus the simple fact turns out to be not a simple fact at all. It is the statement that is simple—a simple generalization of a thousand and one facts.

Well, anyhow Caesar crossed the Rubicon. But what of it? Many other people at other times crossed the Rubicon. Why charge it up to Caesar? Why for two thousand years has the world treasured this simple fact that in the year 49 B.C. Caesar crossed the Rubicon? What of it indeed? If I, as historian, have nothing to give you but this fact taken by itself with its clear outline, with no fringes or strings tied to it, I should have to say, if I were an honest man, why nothing of it, nothing at all. It may be a fact but it is nothing to us. The truth is, of course, that this simple fact *has* strings tied to it, and that is why it has been treasured for two thousand years. It is tied by these strings to innumerable other facts, so that it can't mean anything except by losing its clear outline. It can't mean anything except as it is absorbed into the complex web of circumstances which brought it into being. This complex web of circumstances was the series of events growing out of the relation of Caesar to Pompey, and the Roman Senate, and the Roman Republic, and all the people who had something to do with these. Caesar had been ordered by the Roman Senate to resign his command of the army in Gaul. He decided to disobey the Roman Senate. Instead of resigning his command, he marched on Rome, gained the mastery of the Republic, and at last, as we are told, bestrode the narrow world like a colossus. Well, the Rubicon happened to be the boundary between Gaul and Italy, so that by the act of crossing the Rubicon with his army Caesar's treason became an accomplished fact and the subsequent great events followed in due course. Apart from these great events and complicated relations, the crossing of the Rubicon means nothing, is not an historical fact properly speaking at all. In itself it is nothing for us; it becomes something for us, not in itself, but as a symbol of something else, a symbol standing for a long series of events which have to do with the most intangible and immaterial realities, viz.: the relation between Caesar and the millions of people of the Roman world.

Thus the simple historical fact turns out to be not a hard, cold something with clear outline, and measurable pressure, like a brick. It is so far as we can know it, only a *symbol*, a simple statement which is a generalization of a thousand and one simpler facts which we do not for the moment care to use, and this generalization itself we cannot use apart from the wider facts and generalizations which it symbolizes. And generally speaking, the more simple an historical fact is, the more clear and definite and provable it is, the less use it is to us in and for itself. . . .

What then is the historical fact? Far be it from me to define so illusive and intangible a thing! But provisionally I will say this: the historian may be interested in anything that has to do with the life of man in the past—any act or event, any emotion which men have expressed, any idea, true or false, which they have entertained. Very well, the historian is interested in some event of this sort. Yet he cannot deal directly with this event itself, since the event itself has disappeared. What he can deal with directly is a *statement about the event.* He deals in short not with the event, but with a statement which affirms *the fact that the event occurred.* When we really get down to the hard facts, what the historian is always dealing with is an *affirmation*—an affirmation of the fact that something is true. There is thus a distinction of capital importance to be made: the distinction between the ephemeral event which disappears, and the affirmation about the event which persists. For all practical purposes it is this affirmation about the event that constitutes for us the historical fact. If so the historical fact is not the past event, but a symbol which enables us to recreate it imaginatively. Of a symbol it is hardly worthwhile to say that it is cold or hard. It is dangerous to say even that it is true or false. The safest thing to say about a symbol is that it is more or less appropriate.

This brings me to the second question—Where is the historical fact? I will say at once, however brash it sounds, that the historical fact is in someone's mind or it is nowhere. To illustrate this statement I will take an event familiar to all. "Abraham Lincoln was assassinated in Ford's Theater in Washington on the 14th of April, 1865." That *was* an actual event, occurrence, fact at the moment of happening. But speaking now . . . we say it *is* an historical fact. We don't say that it *was* an historical fact, for that would imply that it no longer is one. We say that it *was* an actual event, but *is now* an historical fact. The actual occurrence and the historical fact, however closely connected, are two different things. Very well, if the assassination of Lincoln is an historical fact, where is this fact now? Lincoln is not being assassinated now in Ford's Theater, or anywhere else (except perhaps in propagandist literature!). The actual occurrence, the event, has passed, is gone forever, never to be repeated, never to be again experienced or witnessed by any living person. Yet this is precisely the sort of thing the historian is concerned with—events, acts, thoughts, emotions that have forever vanished as actual occurrences. How can the historian deal with vanished realities? He can deal with them because these vanished realities give place to pale reflections, impalpable images or ideas of themselves, and these pale reflections, and impalpable images which cannot be touched or handled are all that is left of the actual occurrence. These are therefore what the historian deals with. These are his "material." He has to be satisfied with these, for the very good reason that he has nothing else. Well then, where are they—these pale reflections and impalpable images of the actual? Where are these facts? They are, as I said before, in his mind, or in somebody's mind, or they are nowhere.

Ah, but they are in the records, in the sources, I hear someone say. Yes, in a sense, they are in the sources. The historical fact of Lincoln's assassination is in the records—in contemporary newspapers, letters, diaries, etc. In a sense the fact is there, but in what sense? The records are after all only paper, over the surface of which ink has been distributed in certain patterns. And even these patterns were not made by the actual occurrence, the assassination of Lincoln. The patterns are themselves only "histories" of the event, made by someone who had in *his* mind an image or idea of Lincoln's assassination. Of course we, you and I, can, by looking at these inky patterns, form in *our* minds images or ideas more or less like those in the mind of the person who made the patterns. But if there were now no one in the world who could make any meaning out of the patterned records or sources, the fact of Lincoln's assassination would cease to be an historical fact. You might perhaps call it a dead fact; but a fact which is not only dead, but not known ever to have been alive, or even known to be now dead, is surely not much of a fact. At all events, the historical facts lying dead in the records can do nothing good or evil in the world. They become historical facts, capable of doing work, of making a difference, only when someone, you or I, brings them alive in our minds by means of pictures, images, or ideas of the actual occurrence. For this reason I say that the historical fact is in someone's mind, or it is nowhere, because when it is in no one's mind it lies in the records inert, incapable of making a difference in the world.

But perhaps you will say that the assassination of Lincoln has made a difference in the world, and that this difference is now effectively working, even if, for a moment, or an hour or a week, no one in the world has the image of the actual occurrence in mind. Quite obviously so, but why? Quite obviously because after the actual event people remembered it, and because ever since they have continued to remember it, by repeatedly forming images of it in their minds. If the people of the United States had been incapable of enduring memory, for example, like dogs (as I assume; not being a dog I can't be sure) would the assassination of Lincoln be now doing work in the world, making a difference? If everyone had forgotten the occurrence after forty-eight hours, what difference would the occurrence have made, then or since? It is precisely because people have long memories, and have constantly formed images in their minds of the assassination of Lincoln, that the universe contains the historical fact which persists as well as the actual event which does not persist. It is the persisting historical fact, rather than the ephemeral actual event, which makes a difference to us now; and the historical fact makes a difference only because it is, and so far as it is, in human minds.

Now for the third question—When is the historical fact? If you agree with what has been said (which is extremely doubtful) the answer seems simple enough. If the historical fact is present, imaginatively, in someone's mind, then it is now, a part of the present. But the word present is a slippery word, and the thing itself is worse than the word. The present is an indefinable point in time, gone before you can think it; the image or idea which I have now present in mind slips instantly into the past. But images or ideas of past events are often, perhaps always, inseparable from images or ideas of the future. Take an illustration. I awake this morning, and among the things my memory drags in to enlighten or distress me is a vague notion that there was something I needed particularly to remember but cannot—a common experience surely. What is it that I needed to remember I cannot recall; but I can recall that I made a note of it in order to jog my memory. So I consult my little pocket memorandum book— a little Private Record Office which I carry about, filled with historical sources. I take out my memorandum book in order to do a little historical research; and there I find (Vol. I, p. 20) the dead historical fact—"Pay Smith's coal bill today: $1,016." The image of the memorandum book now drops out of mind, and is replaced by another image—an image of what? Why an image, an idea, a picture (call it what you will) made up of three things more or less inseparable. First the image of myself ordering coal from Smith last summer; second, the image of myself holding the idea in mind that I must pay the bill; third, the image of myself going down to Smith's office at four o'clock to pay it. The image is partly of things done in the past, and partly of things to be done in the future; but it is more or less all one image now present in mind.

Someone may ask, "Are you talking of history or of the ordinary ills of every day that men are heir to?" Well, perhaps Smith's coal bill is only my personal affair, of no concern to anyone else, except Smith to be sure. Take then another example. I am thinking of the Congress of Berlin, and that is without doubt history—the real thing. The historical facts of the Congress of Berlin I bring alive in memory, imaginatively. But I am making an image of the Congress of Berlin for a purpose; and indeed without a purpose no one would take the trouble to bring historical facts to mind. My purpose happens to be to convey this image of the Congress of Berlin to my class in History 42, in Room C, tomorrow afternoon at 3 o'clock. Now I find that inseparable from this image of the Congress of Berlin, which occurred in the past, are flitting images of myself conveying this image of the Congress of Berlin to my class tomorrow in Room C. I picture myself standing there monotonously talking, I hear the labored sentences painfully issuing forth, I picture the students' faces alert or bored as the case may be; so that images of this future event enter into the imagined picture of the Congress of Berlin, a past event; enter into it, coloring and shaping it too, to the end that the performance may do credit to me, or be intelligible to immature minds, or be compressed within the limits of fifty minutes, or to accomplish some other desired end. Well, this living historical fact, this mixed image of the coal bill or the Congress of Berlin—is it past, present, or future? I cannot say. Perhaps it moves with the velocity of light, and is timeless. At all events it is real history to me, which I hope to make convincing and real to Smith, or to the class in Room C.

I have now asked my three questions, and have made some remarks about them all. I don't know whether these remarks will strike you as quite beside the mark, or as merely obvious, or as novel. If there is any novelty in them, it arises, I think, from our inveterate habit of thinking of the world of history as part of the external world, and of historical facts as actual events. In truth the actual past is gone; and the world of history is an intangible world, recreated imaginatively, and present in our minds. If, as I think, this is true, then there are certain important implications growing out of it; and if you are not already exhausted I should like to touch upon a few of these implications. I will present them "firstly," "secondly," and so on, like the points of a sermon, without any attempt at coordination.

One implication is that by no possibility can the historian present in its entirety any actual event, even the simplest. You may think this a commonplace, and I do too; but still it needs to be often repeated because one of the fondest illusions of nineteenth century historians was that the historian, the "scientific" historian, would do just that: he would "present all the facts and let them speak for themselves." The historian would contribute nothing himself, except the sensitive plate of his mind, upon which the objective facts would register their own unimpeachable meaning. . . .

Well, for twenty years I have taken it for granted that no one could [any] longer believe so preposterous an idea. But the notion continues to bob up regularly; and only the other day, riding on the train to the meeting of the Historical Association, Mr. A. J. Beveridge, eminent and honored historian, assured me dogmatically (it would be dogmatically) that the histo-

rian has nothing to do but "present all the facts and let them speak for themselves." And so I repeat, what I have been teaching for twenty years, that this notion is preposterous; first, because it is impossible to present all the facts; and second, because even if you could present all the facts the miserable things wouldn't say anything, would say just nothing at all. . . .
. . . It is the historian who speaks, who imposes a meaning.

A second implication follows from this. It is that the historian cannot eliminate the personal equation. Of course, no one can; not even, I think, the natural scientist. The universe speaks to us only in response to our purposes; and even the most objective constructions, those, let us say, of the theoretical physicist, are not the sole possible constructions, but only such as are found most convenient for some human need or purpose. Nevertheless, the physicist can eliminate the personal equation to a greater extent, or at least in a different way, than the historian, because he deals, as the historian does not, with an external world directly. The physicist presides at the living event, the historian presides only at the inquest of its remains. If I were alone in the universe and gashed my finger on a sharp rock, I could never be certain that there was anything there but my conciousness of the rock and gashed finger. But if ten other men in precisely the same way gash their fingers on the same sharp rock, we can, by comparing impressions, infer that there is something there besides consciousness. There is an external world there. The physicist can gash his finger on the rock as many times as he likes, and get others to do it, until they are all certain of the facts. He can, as Eddington says, make pointer-readings of the behavior of the physical world as many times as he likes for a given phenomenon, until he and his colleagues are satisfied. When their minds all rest satisfied they have an explanation, what is called the truth. But suppose the physicist had to reach his conclusions from miscellaneous records, made by all sorts of people, of experiments that had been made in the past, each experiment made only once, and none of them capable of being repeated. The external world he would then have to deal with would be the records. That is the case of the historian. The only external world he has to deal with is the records. He can indeed look at the records as often as he likes, and he can get dozens of others to look at them: and some things, some "facts," can in this way be established and agreed upon, as, for example, the fact that the document known as the Declaration of Independence was voted on July 4, 1776. But the meaning and significance of this fact cannot be thus agreed upon, because the series of events in which it has a place cannot be enacted again and again, under varying conditions, in order to see what effect the variations would have. The historian has to judge the significance of the series of events from the one single performance, never to be repeated, and never, since the records are incomplete and imperfect, capable of being fully known or fully affirmed.

Thus into the imagined facts and their meaning there enters the personal equation. The history of any event is never precisely the same thing to two different persons; and it is well known that every generation writes the same history in a new way, and puts upon it a new construction. . . .

A third implication is that no one can profit by historical research, or not much, unless he does some for himself. Historical knowledge, however richly stored in books or in the minds of professors of history, is no good to me unless I have some of it. In this respect, historical research differs profoundly from research in the natural sciences, at least in some of them. For example, I know no physics, but I profit from physical researches every night by the simple act of pressing an electric light button. And everyone can profit in this way from researches in physics without knowing any physics, without knowing even that there is such a thing as physics. But with history it is different. Henry Ford, for example, can't profit from all the historical researches of two thousand years, because he knows so little history himself. By no pressing of any button can he flood the spare rooms of his mind with the light of human experience.

A fourth implication is more important than the others. It is that every normal person does know some history, a good deal in fact. Of course we often hear someone say: "I don't know any history; I wish I knew some history; I must improve my mind by learning some history." We know what is meant. This person means that he has never read any history books, or studied history in college; and so he thinks he knows no history. But it is precisely this conventional notion of history as something external to us, as a body of dull knowledge locked up in books, that obscures its real meaning. For, I repeat (it will bear repeating) every normal person—every man, woman, and child—does know some history, enough for his immediate purposes; otherwise he would be a lost soul indeed. I suppose myself, for example, to have awakened this morning with loss of memory. I am all right otherwise; but I can't remember anything that happened in the past. What is the result? The result is that I don't know who I am, where I am, where to go, or what to do. I can't attend to my duties at the university, I can't read this paper before the Research Club. In short, my present would be unintelligible and my future meaningless. Why? Why, because I had suddenly ceased to know any history. What happens when I wake up in the morning is that my memory reaches out into the past and gathers together those images of past events, of objects seen, of words spoken and of thoughts thought in the past, which are necessary to give me an ordered world to live in, necessary to orient me in my personal world. Well, this collection of images and ideas of things past is history, my command of living history, a series of images of the past which shifts and reforms at every moment of the day in response to the exigencies of my daily living. Every man has a knowledge of history in this sense, which is the only vital sense in which he can have a knowledge of history. Every man has some knowledge of past events, more or less accurate; knowledge enough, and accurate enough, for his purposes, or what he regards as such. How much and how accurate, will depend on the man and his purposes. Now, the point is that history in the formal sense, history as we commonly think of it, is only an extension of memory. Knowledge or history, insofar as it is living history and not dead knowledge locked up in notebooks, is only an enrichment of our minds with the multiplied images of events, places, peoples, ideas, emotions outside our personal experience, an enrichment of our experience by bringing into our minds memories of the experience of the community, the nation, the race. Its chief value, for the individual, is doubtless that it enables a man to orient himself in a larger world than the merely personal, has the effect for him of placing the petty and intolerable present in a longer perspective, thus enabling him to judge the acts and thoughts of men, his own included, on the basis of an experience less immediate and restricted.

A fifth implication is that the kind of history that has most influence upon the life of the community and the course of events is the history that common men carry around in their heads. It won't do to say that history has no influence upon the course of events because people refuse to read history books. Whether the general run of people read history books or not, they inevitably picture the past in some fashion or other, and this picture, however little it corresponds to the real past, helps to determine their ideas about politics and society. This is especially true in times of excitement, in critical times, in time of war above all. It is precisely in such times that they form (with the efficient help of official propaganda!) an idealized picture of the past, born of their emotions and desires working on fragmentary scraps of knowledge gathered, or rather flowing in upon them, from every conceivable source, reliable or not matters nothing. Doubtless the proper function of erudite historical research is to be forever correcting the common image of the past by bringing it to the test of reliable information. But the professional historian will never get his own chastened and corrected image of the past into common minds if no one reads his books. His books may be as solid as you like, but their social influence will be nil if people do not read them and not merely read them, but read them willingly and with understanding.

It is, indeed, not wholly the historian's fault that the mass of men will not read good history willingly and with understanding; but I think we should not be too complacent about it. The recent World War leaves us with little ground indeed for being complacent about anything; but certainly it furnishes us with no reason for supposing that historical research has much influence on the course of events. The nineteenth century is often called the age of science, and it is often called the age of history.

Both statements are correct enough. During the hundred years that passed between 1814 and 1914 an unprecedented and incredible amount of research was carried on, research into every field of history—minute, critical, exhaustive (and exhausting!) research. Our libraries are filled with this stored up knowledge of the past; and never before has there been at the disposal of society so much reliable knowledge of human experience. What influence has all this expert research had upon the social life of our time? Has it done anything to restrain the foolishness of politicians or to enhance the wisdom of statesmen? Has it done anything to enlighten the mass of the people, or to enable them to act with greater wisdom or in response to a more reasoned purpose? Very little surely, if anything. Certainly a hundred years of expert historical research did nothing to prevent the World War, the most futile exhibition of unreason, take it all in all, ever made by civilized society. Governments and peoples rushed into this war with undiminished stupidity, with unabated fanaticism, with unimpaired capacity for deceiving themselves and others. I do not say that historical research is to blame for the World War. I say that it had little or no influence upon it, one way or another.

It is interesting, although no necessary part of this paper, to contrast this negligible influence of historical research upon social life with the profound influence of scientific research. A hundred years of scientific research has transformed the conditions of life. How it has done this is known to all. By enabling men to control natural forces it has made life more comfortable and convenient, at least for the well-to-do. It has done much to prevent and cure disease, to alleviate pain and suffering. But its benefits are not unmixed. By accelerating the speed and pressure of life it has injected into it a nervous strain, a restlessness, a capacity for irritation and an impatience of restraint never before known. And this power which scientific research lays at the feet of society serves equally well all who can make use of it—the harbingers of death as well as of life. It was scientific research that made the war of 1914, which historical research did nothing to prevent, a world war. Because of scientific research it could be, and was, fought with more cruelty and ruthlessness, and on a grander scale, than any previous war; because of scientific research it became a systematic massed butchery such as no one had dreamed of, or supposed possible. I do not say that scientific research is to blame for the war; I say that it made it the ghastly thing it was, determined its extent and character. What I am pointing out is that scientific research has had a profound influence in changing the conditions of modern life, whereas historical research has had at best only a negligible influence. Whether the profound influence of the one has been of more or less benefit to humanity than the negligible influence of the other, I am unable to determine. Doubtless both the joys and frustrations of modern life, including those of the scholarly activities, may be all accommodated and reconciled within that wonderful idea of Progress which we all like to acclaim—none more so, surely, than historians and scientists.

For Further Study

Boulding, Kenneth E. *The Meaning of the Twentieth Century*. New York: Harper & Row, 1964.

Durant, Will and Ariel. *The Lessons of History*. New York: Simon and Schuster, 1968.

Harrington, Michael. *The Accidental Century*. New York: Macmillan, 1965. (Also Pelican A 880.)

Hocking, William Ernest. *Strength of Men and Nations*. New York: Harper, 1959, Chs. 10–12.

Johnson, A. H. *Whitehead's Philosophy of Civilization*. Boston: Beacon, 1958, Chs. 1–2.

Koch, Adrienne. *Philosophy for a Time of Crisis: An Interpretation with Key Writings by Fifteen Great Modern Thinkers*. New York: Dutton, 1959, Ch. 2, "Toward an Understanding of the Present Crisis."

Lerner, Max. "Why Do Civilizations Die?" *Saturday Review*, 45 (December 1, 1962): 19–21.

Muller, Herbert J. *The Uses of the Past*. New York: Oxford U. Press, 1952, Ch. 2, "The Nature of History."

Ormsby-Gore, Sir David (Lord Harlech.) *Must the West Decline?* New York: Columbia U. Press, 1966.

Schweitzer, Albert. *The Philosophy of Civilization*. New York: Macmillan, 1949, Preface and Chs. 1–5.

Toynbee, A. J. *Civilization on Trial*. New York: Oxford U. Press, 1948, Ch. 2, "The Present Point in History"; Ch. 3, "Does History Repeat Itself?" (Also Meridian Book M52, including the author's *The World and the West*.)

Van Doren, Charles. *The Idea of Progress*. New York: Praeger, 1967.

Walsh, W. H. *An Introduction to Philosophy of History*. London: Hutchinson's U. Library, 1951, Ch. 1, "What Is Philosophy of History?"

28 Philosophy and the Educational Venture

THEODORE M. GREENE / Philosophy and the Life of the Spirit *

Theodore M. Greene (1897–   ) taught philosophy at Princeton University and Yale University for many years before becoming Professor in the Humanities at Scripps College, 1955–1961. He has been visiting professor at a number of colleges in the United States and abroad. Among his books are *Our Cultural Heritage; Liberalism;* and *Moral, Aesthetic, and Religious Insight.*

OURS IS AN AGE of paradox. It seems impossible to describe it save in terms of contradictory opposites. On the one hand, the now familiar charge that we are "hollow men," half-alive in a "wasteland" of spiritual aridity, seems amply justified. Yet, in apparent opposition to this view, violent beliefs are sweeping through our own land and other lands in a mounting wave of irrationalism. How can an age of hollow men be an age of such fervid affirmations?

Or again, ours is an age of unparalleled achievement in many areas— above all, of course, in science and technology, but also, and no less significantly, in the fine arts, in education, in social justice, and in political experience. Man's age-old wish for long life and prosperity seems, at least in our own land, to be more generously granted to more people than ever

* Theodore M. Greene, from "Philosophy and the Life of the Spirit," *The Christian Scholar*, 38 (March, 1955): 31, 32, 33–34, 46. Used by permission of the author.

before in human history. Yet, as W. H. Auden has so eloquently reminded us, ours is also an age of profound anxiety and fear. These fears are not merely the perennial fears of mankind—of hunger and starvation, of disease and war and sudden death. They are, above all, the subtle fears which reflect our great inner spiritual insecurity—the fear of not being loved, or wanted, or respected; the fear that our individual lives will be empty and that all human life may turn out to be meaningless and purposeless. Never has life been longer, safer, and more comfortable for the vast majority of our fellow citizens; yet seldom, in our own short history, have we viewed life with less confidence or more profound perturbation.

Or, once again, ours is an age of miraculously efficient travel and communication. We can circle the globe in a matter of hours and converse by telephone with people at the antipodes. Radio and television enable us to keep in touch with current events in a manner undreamt of fifty years ago. The most secluded farm is no longer isolated, the most distant outpost no longer cut off. Many of us, moreover, live in urban or suburban areas with people all around us. Yet this is the age in which a widely read book by a sociologist is aptly entitled "The Lonely Crowd." We urbanites and suburbanites are experiencing a loneliness unknown to most of our ancestors on isolated farms and distant lands. Hence the paradox of our spiritual isolation, with people all around us and in touch with us, our tragic solitude in the very midst of human bustle and laughter. . . .

. . . What can we do to hasten the rebirth and to safeguard the growth of the living spirit in our times? And, more specifically, what, if anything, can philosophy do today in the role of spiritual midwife and nurse?

. . . As I see it, philosophy has an essential, though a limited, role in every culture and epoch, and especially in our own. For our immediate cultural predicament has been largely brought about by cleavages, isolations, and lonelinesses which are so tragic partly because they are so stupid and so unnecessary. Our most urgent need today is for bridges across these cleavages and chasms, for bonds of community by which we can shatter our isolation and escape our loneliness. We are bedeviled by fanatical either/or's which can be exorcised only by powerful and healing both/and's. Our age is indeed the first atomic age in history; we can destroy mankind today with unprecedented ease. But more crucial, humanly and spiritually, is our cultural "atomicity," that is, the specializations, the segregations, the provincialisms which threaten us on every hand—internationally and nationally, politically and socially, culturally and religiously, publicly and privately. Hence our *most* pressing need today is for whatever will help us to achieve genuine communion in authentic communities, to transcend the chatter of the crowds and to rise to that level of mutual understanding and respect at which alone we can be persons in the company of other persons.

Can philosophy help us towards this goal? Our answer will be Yes, or No, depending upon how we conceive of the genius and task of philosophy. No, if by philosophy we mean a timid rationalistic venture intent only on absolute conceptual precision and clarity—a venture in essence analytic rather than synthetic, positivistic rather than speculative, technical rather than cultural and spiritual. Philosophy, so conceived and practised, has, I must confess, little to contribute to the healing of the nations; indeed, this kind of philosophy is, in my opinion, but one of the many symptoms of our prevalent cultural disease.

But philosophy can also be conceived of and practised, even today, in its more traditional role of bridger of chasms, healer of wounds, mediator and synthesizer. At its creative best, philosophy has always used the language of both/and rather than either/or. Witness Plato's great reconciliation of Heraclitean flux *and* Parmenidean permanence, or Aristotle's partial resolution of Plato's awkward dualisms, or the Thomistic synthesis of Aristotelian reason *and* Christian faith, or Kant's great defence of *both* science and morality, or Whitehead's masterly synthesis of science *and* culture, religion *and* philosophy. This, I submit, has been philosophy's major role in our Western Culture—the irenic role of imaginative interpreter, of bold reconciler, of tolerant peacemaker. Its genius has *not* been that of science, to make new specific discoveries: or of art, to express poignant intuitive insights in the language of beauty; or of government, to legislate and administer; or of business, to minister to our practical needs; or of religion, to provide us with ultimate spiritual light and power. We must be careful, as most of the great philosophers have been, to be modest in our claims of what philosophy can do, even at its powerful best. But, in all caution and humility, we can insist that philosophy *alone*, in its humane, synthetic role, can give mankind what it so desperately needs today, that is, the wider perspectives which are the only possible correctives for the multiple provincialisms which, in combination, are a major source of our misery.

I hardly need enumerate these provincialisms—national and regional, political and social, professional and cultural, secular and religious. All of us are forever stressing the "here and now" at the expense of the "there and then," "my" interests in opposition to "yours," "our" interests in disregard of "theirs." We are perpetually selling our birthright for a mess of pottage, jeopardizing long-range security for immediate comfort, neglecting enduring satisfactions for present pleasures. We are chronically imprudent, incapable even of consistently intelligent selfishness. Our multiple provincialisms also blind us, tragically, to the needs and rights of others and to the limits of our own righteousness. We are unnecessarily callous in the face of human suffering, culpably indifferent to human aspirations, and inexcusably self-righteous. These very human traits do not, of course, endear us to others, nor do they endear others to us. Hence the dissensions and stupidities, the tensions, local, national, and international, the wars and the threats of war, of our immediate present and our foreseeable future.

It would of course be utopian to believe that philosophy as a formal discipline can single-handed correct all these provincialisms and cure mankind of its perennial ills. Indeed, I must accept the Christian verdict that it is utopian to suppose that men will ever be free of these bedeviling provincialisms, ever able to live in complete mutual respect, harmony, and peace. But I am also convinced that utopian optimism and defeatist pessimism are not our only options. I do believe that our human lot can be improved indefinitely by our own efforts if only we go about it with enough energy, intelligence, and wisdom. I also believe that bold creative philosophical thinking is absolutely essential to this venture. . . .

In a word, philosophy is the unique and irreplaceable humane discipline of man's spiritual quest. Without philosophy all loyalties, however lofty and however spiritual, are doomed to provincialism and divisive intolerance. Without philosophy, dogma can only breed dogmatism; the church, ecclesiasticism; reliance on Scripture, Biblicism; ritual, ritualism; faith, fanaticism. Philosophy at its powerful best is, I am utterly persuaded, the *only* corrective for all these spirit-destroying *isms*. Without its purging discipline and enlightening vision the life of the spirit must destroy itself in unbridled, suicidal excess. Philosophy is, now as ever, the essential partner of religion in man's perennial spiritual pilgrimage.

ROBERT ULICH / Education as Cultural Self-Transcendence *

Robert Ulich (1890–   ) is James Bryant Conant, Professor of Education emeritus at Harvard University. His writings include *Conditions of Civilized Living; History of Educational Thought;* and *Three Thousand Years of Educational Wisdom.*

I. THE AFFINITY BETWEEN PHILOSOPHY AND EDUCATION

Whenever philosophy becomes its true self: not merely the exercise of scholarly skill but an attempt to help men in the understanding of themselves and in the mastery of their lives, it meets education. One could even say, it *becomes* education in its highest form. On the other hand, those rightfully entrusted with educational responsibility not only search for better methods of teaching, but also ask fundamental questions such as: What is life's deeper meaning? How can man's greatest good, his freedom of transcendence, of thought, and of choice, be directed for the good of mankind? In the great periods of civilization, those we like to call "classical," both philosophy and statecraft were closely related to the task of education.

II. THE MODERN CONFLICTS IN EDUCATION

In these classical periods, so we believe (perhaps with a slight admixture of hope), the important concerns of life were still interrelated. Today, we think, they are separated and often treated as if incompatible.

Most of our modern philosophical movements remain esoteric schools of thought. In our educational systems we are for, or against, not only one, but several traditions at once. Consequently we have none that could unite us. On the whole, there prevails in modern countries the heritage of rationalism, but on its way to the twentieth century it has lost much of its initial faith and energy. It is, therefore, incapable of fighting successfully modern nationalism, modern relativism, and modern irrationalism with all their relapses into superstition and sentimentality. We are longing for a new community of men, but we cannot produce it. For it needs souls animated and drawn together by the sense of inner kinship. . . .

Modern education suffers from a frightening loss of inner substance. And this loss may become the greater, the more education turns away from the humanities in order to become a "social science" in the superficial sense in which this term is often understood. Even more than has institutional religion, education has served with equal zest in the preparation of war and the preparation of peace; it has been at the command of tyrants as well as of democracies; it has helped to preach fundamentalism and atheism, relativism and agnosticism; and it has been more the instrument of the competitive than of the cooperative trends in society. Except in rare instances, education has been the handmaid of power rather than the conscience of humanity. There are even academic teachers—not to speak of typical government officials—who no longer know the difference between education and propaganda.

III. EDUCATION AS THE GUARDIAN OF SOCIETY

But criticism of our time is easy. Let us not forget the positive values on which it is built and for which, in many parts of the world, our ancestors fought on battlefields and barricades. Unhampered inquiry and discussion, tolerance of divergent opinions even about sacred taboos of society, the liberation of man from need and disease through science and technology, the unfolding of human energies by tearing down the barrier of castes, the emergence of the modern State out of tribal organizations and the petty domains of absolute princes, the gradual winning of the right of public and nondenominational education for all who are able to learn—should all this lead to the end result of a bewildered generation? Even our international situation, frightening though it is, must not be considered merely a burden and a curse. Should we not more often tell ourselves that we live during the period of a momentous transition as difficult as the one from the lawlessness of the Great Migrations to medieval feudalism, from feudalism to absolutism, and from absolutism to the modern nation state? Before us, of course, is the most difficult stretch, that from the old concept of sovereignty (the hangover from absolutism) to a world of freely cooperative nations. Failure in this attempt will lead us into the abyss; success will open up a new era of human development.

But today less than ever will the circumstances alone determine the future; the deciding factor will be whether man is able to live not merely under, but clearly in front of, and, if necessary, as an enemy of the circumstances that surround him.

It is this kind of man which education must create.

With due regard for the psychological and social nature of man, education must help him not merely to "adjust himself to the changing environment" (one of the most confusing slogans of modern pedagogy), or to regard himself as an advanced species of ape, *un singe arrivé*, but to transcend the existing conditions by a vision of things as they should be. Only when man has an inspiring, rather than a depressive image of himself, can education become a directing force in his social evolution.

But how do it?

IV. FUNDAMENTALS OF EDUCATION

When we ponder this question we discover that [certain] . . . general philosophical considerations . . . apply directly to the educational process.

1. . . . [O]nly that person can achieve maturity who unfolds his powers within organically widening circles of experience and realizes that he lives within, and with the help of, the whole of human society. But the more he understands the heights and abysses of experience, the more he sees that all human life, individual as well as social, exists only through its participation in the mysterious process of life. Man, consequently, is responsible not only to himself and his society; he must also try to identify himself with those cosmic forces which, in the light of his best knowledge, are of universally productive rather than of destructive nature.

2. Often the purpose of education has been found in the individual's desire for self-realization. *But what is the individual?* What is the human self? We are here before a mystery which we experience the moment we make ourselves the object of contemplation. The human person, being at the same time within and outside the embrace of the physical creation, being a part of his own reflections, can feel his unity with all that lives and strives, but also his utter loneliness. He can be split within himself. The great philosophies and the great religions have grown out of the endeavor both to understand the depth of this conflict and to find means for its reconciliation. They all arrive at the paradox, that the individual finds himself only by losing himself within a superindividual purpose, or by means of devotion. But is this really a paradox? Yes, if by individuality and self-realization is meant a process of growing egocentricity (which is bound to defeat itself because it leads toward self-isolation and thus toward self-impoverishment). No, if we understand that never does an individual life

become fuller and richer than it does through sharing, sympathy, and love. . . .

3. . . . Only when a teacher or learner feels that the laws of his thinking are a cosmic gift and not his own invention which he can use or misuse according to his choice, can he teach or learn the real nature of reality. For just as no man, so also no fact or event, is in and by itself. It always is a window to a deeper reality. The logic by which we connect our prehensions to each other and to the objective world, this logic works in *all* human minds. In some it works more obscurely, in others more clearly, but it is the result of the same great evolutionary process by which man has emerged from lower forms of life into the state of reflection and self-awareness. Through our common participation in the world of mind we not only feel the unity of human intellects, but we also have the right to hope that there is something like truth within and beyond our searching and learning. . . .

4. But the more we think about thinking and the individual, the more we are driven to reflect not only *on our relation to reality*, but *on the aspects of reality* itself. While engaged in this ontological, this metaphysical endeavor, we stand in the twilight between scientific philosophy and poetry. All human language is symbolic. In and through it man realizes his greatness, but also his limitations. Yet never does he become so aware of the dilemma of human existence as when he discovers that the unity of life, which is a postulate both of science and philosophy, appears to him only in polarities. Wherever man looks around he meets the contrasts of becoming and being, of dependence and freedom, wholeness and singleness, energy and form, birth and death, good and evil. Man cannot prove whether the logos, or the order of thought within and toward which his thinking progresses, is itself related to the ultimate or whether there are spheres of being and non-being totally beyond even our keenest imagination. No philosophical or scientific system has provided the answer. Probably none ever will. But man's metaphysical quest is not useless play; it represents the finest manifestation of man's endeavor to give himself an account of the universe—or the multiverse—within and on which he lives. Though the answers he receives will turn again into questions, only a shallow generation will stop asking. For this asking opens to man's eyes the horizon of infinity without which he loses the realistic knowledge of his finiteness and runs into the danger of wavering between arrogance and despair. An education, therefore, which believes it thrives better without deeper metaphysical interest may produce a materially informed and busy society, but it will be one without depth. Sooner or later even its efficiency will run dry for lack of inspiration. It may be remembered for its quantity, but not for its quality.

5. Such a society will lack the great *ethical impulse*. For a while it may

live prosperously on legality and convention, but neither of them will produce the creative individuals who are the leaven of civilization. . . . The liberating uplift of our existence into the truth of life that comes during the truly moral act—this sense of unity between fragile individuality and creative wholeness—occurs only to the courageous person who knows that there is no self-realization without self-sacrifice. . . .

6. Destiny wishes to give freedom to man by appealing to his *sense of the beautiful* as well as to his sense of the heroic. By virtue of his imagination he is capable of building above the structure of the actual a world of form and rhythm through which the fuller meaning of the actual becomes surprisingly evident. For superficial minds, just as virtue is supposed to be for nothing but usefulness, so art is supposed to be for nothing but pleasure. If one wishes a broad definition—which, however, would apply as well to other fields of culture—then one might give to art not only the title of liberator from the frictions of existence, but also the title of enricher. For art widens the scale of our sensitiveness in teaching us to understand the depth of ideas, to sense the delicacy and color of forms, to feel the roughness or smoothness of lines and surfaces, and to hear the rhythm and melody of sounds. But, more important, it also allows us to project ourselves into scenes and feelings which otherwise would be far beyond our power of emotional and intellectual creation. . . .

7. But thinking in its profound intuitions, metaphysics in its universal contemplation, the moral act in its heroic decision, and aesthetic fulfillment in its vision of the perfect form are, despite all their greatness, confined within the narrow boundaries of human power. What, then, is the meaning of human existence in the vastness of the universe?

Philosophical considerations as such are bound to remain limited by the uncertainties of seeking—even with the vital experiences and visions of truth; it is *the religious experience* which gives man the feeling of unity with the All-Embracing. Also here he can speak only in symbols; also here he may sometimes be tortured by doubt. But whereas discursive language often reminds us painfully of our distance from the core of reality, in religious symbolism lives the deep hope of certainty.

This certainty is grounded in experiences beyond the competence of science and can, therefore, live in peace with it, though only under two conditions.

The first demand which education must raise is that science does not arrogate to itself the right to drive out of man's conscience and consciousness whatever cannot be proved in laboratory fashion, but that it understand itself as only *one* of the means by which man participates in the logos and understands, at least in part, the laws of life.

The second demand of education is that religion itself be careful in distinguishing essential religious meaning from the historically and environmentally conditioned forms of religious expression. There are many profound myths in all religions, but in their literal form many of them can no longer be upheld without arousing the opposition of man's intellectual conscience.

Nor, in spite of the necessity of specific cultural roots, should there be hostility and exclusiveness among the various creeds and denominations. No doubt, with the evolution of cultures there have developed not only more and more rituals and theological disputes, but also a seemingly endless splitting of religions into subreligions, the latter often displaying the highest degree of hostility against each other. Yet there is also hope that with increasing international contact and insight into humanity's inspirations and aspirations a sense of unity might pervade the plurality. More and more will men feel that the call of the Divine is one and the same, though it may resound differently in each of the valleys of the earth. Reality, just as it speaks to mankind in different vernaculars and nevertheless remains the same, speaks to mankind also in different religions. No one, after the first formative years, can deny his origin. So it would be idle for the Christian, or Buddhist, or the follower of Confucius to try to forget whence he comes and to create the language of all religious languages, or the symbolism of symbolisms. He would create nothing but a rootless abstraction. In other words, our Western religious life, our culture, and our education, in order to avoid the danger of contributing to modern man's spiritual lack of heritage, must be of the Judaeo-Christian tradition. We all look at the world along the vista of our own vantage point; this is in the nature of human reason.

The point at issue is whether the boundaries of this vista will open up to increasingly wider insights, or whether they will suddenly close in and shut us up in a narrow conspectus. If the first is the case, the religious mood and mode of living can and will embrace and penetrate whatever happens to us, however far our intellectual discoveries take us. And there will be no conflict but mutual delight in the enrichment of life by new knowledge. For the main factor in religion is not this or that knowledge or cult, but reverential living. Some, throughout their lives, may need to assemble in worship at their holy places, while others may prefer solitude. But just as deep in the Divine may live a young woman who prepares herself for her child; a farmer who looks at his fields as a guardian of the nature which provides for mankind; a scientist who takes away his eyes from the microscope to meditate on the mysteries of life; a young man who plans his future in the hope that thus he may help not only himself but mankind; or a child whose soul is for the first time captured by the harmonies of a great religious hymn.

8. The more such experiences occur in the life of a group and of all mankind, the greater is the hope for the future. Every step in the *organiza-*

tion and disorganization of mankind creates new concepts of man's nature and his goals, new contacts between nations and nations, new interpretations of man's relation to God and the universe. Much more rapidly than our grandfathers anticipated—after a relative quiet of only slightly more than a hundred years—our generation faces probably the most gigantic task ever imposed on humanity. We must bring order on a world-wide basis to the contacts of nations, with most of them in a state of revolution. If in the execution of this task man lacks the energy of transcendence, or the inspiration which helps him to evolve from barbarism toward dignity and freedom, from what source will he derive his strength and directives? He will be told again and again that this is society. Thus that which he tries to change will at the same time be his God. What a paradoxical situation! . . .

Only self-transcendent man who feels himself as a participant in the unending work of the creation will have the courage to create a new education, and through it one more weapon in the struggle for the liberation of humanity.

There can be schools which no longer educate despite the desperate attempts of devoted educators. There can be refined methods of teaching which nevertheless breed barbarism. There can be the cult of Greek and Latin without a humanist tradition, and much learning of modern tongues, yet the spirit does not speak. There can even be ideals which mislead, rather than lead. This, perhaps, is the greatest of all perils. All our endeavors can become achievements only when they grow out of a society wherein the relations of man to himself, his fellow men, his knowledge, and his institutions are enriched by a sense of common belonging. We may often feel lonely and like foreigners whose language is not understood. This is in the nature of human existence. But living as a foreigner all the time is degeneration. Even the highest degree of sophistication does not help; on the contrary, it only aggravates the situation.

The base of education is deeper and wider than the overt educational process. If it fails to recognize this fact, it becomes uprooted and can be used for any purpose. But if it understands itself in its transcendent nature, it can become the bulwark of mankind.

PLATO / The Vision of the Good *

Plato (c. 427–347 B.C.) was a student of Socrates and a teacher of Aristotle. The Academy that he founded endured for more than nine centuries. Few, if any, philosophers have had greater influence on the course of Western thought. He wrote many dialogues of high literary quality, including the *Apology*, the *Symposium*, and the *Republic*, from which we quote.

NEXT, SAID I, here is a parable to illustrate the degrees in which our nature may be enlightened or unenlightened. Imagine the condition of men living in a sort of cavernous chamber underground, with an entrance open to the light and a long passage all down the cave. Here they have been from childhood, chained by the leg and also by the neck, so that they cannot move and can see only what is in front of them, because the chains will not let them turn their heads. At some distance higher up is the light of a fire burning behind them; and between the prisoners and the fire is a track with a parapet built along it, like the screen at a puppet-show, which hides the performers while they show their puppets over the top.

I see, said he.

Now behind this parapet imagine persons carrying along various artificial objects, including figures of men and animals in wood or stone or other materials, which project above the parapet. Naturally, some of these persons will be talking, others silent.

It is a strange picture, he said, and a strange sort of prisoners.

Like ourselves, I replied; for in the first place prisoners so confined would have seen nothing of themselves or of one another, except the shadows thrown by the fire-light on the wall of the Cave facing them, would they?

Not if all their lives they had been prevented from moving their heads.

And they would have seen as little of the objects carried past.

Of course.

Now, if they could talk to one another, would they not suppose that their words referred only to those passing shadows which they saw?

Necessarily.

And suppose their prison had an echo from the wall facing them? When one of the people crossing behind them spoke, they could only suppose that the sound came from the shadow passing before their eyes.

No doubt.

* From *The Republic of Plato*, trans. Francis MacDonald Cornford (New York: Oxford University Press, Inc., 1945), pp. 227–232. Used by permission of the publisher.

In every way, then, such prisoners would recognize as reality nothing but the shadows of those artificial objects.

Inevitably.

Now consider what would happen if their release from the chains and the healing of their unwisdom should come about in this way. Suppose one of them set free and forced suddenly to stand up, turn his head, and walk with eyes lifted to the light; all these movements would be painful, and he would be too dazzled to make out the objects whose shadows he had been used to see. What do you think he would say, if someone told him that what he had formerly seen was meaningless illusion, but now, being somewhat nearer to reality and turned towards more real objects, he was getting a truer view? Suppose further that he were shown the various objects being carried by and were made to say, in reply to questions, what each of them was. Would he not be perplexed and believe the objects now shown him to be not so real as what he formerly saw?

Yes, not nearly so real.

And if he were forced to look at the fire-light itself, would not his eyes ache, so that he would try to escape and turn back to the things which he could see distinctly, convinced that they really were clearer than these other objects now being shown to him?

Yes.

And suppose someone were to drag him away forcibly up the steep and rugged ascent and not let him go until he had hauled him out into the sunlight, would he not suffer pain and vexation at such treatment, and, when he had come out into the light, find his eyes so full of its radiance that he could not see a single one of the things that he was now told were real?

Certainly he would not see them all at once.

He would need, then, to grow accustomed before he could see things in that upper world. At first it would be easiest to make out shadows, and then the images of men and things reflected in water, and later on the things themselves. After that, it would be easier to watch the heavenly bodies and the sky itself by night, looking at the light of the moon and stars rather than the Sun and the Sun's light in the day-time.

Yes, surely.

Last of all, he would be able to look at the Sun and contemplate its nature, not as it appears when reflected in water or any alien medium, but as it is in itself in its own domain.

No doubt.

And now he would begin to draw the conclusion that it is the Sun that produces the seasons and the course of the year and controls everything in the visible world, and moreover is in a way the cause of all that he and his companions used to see.

Clearly he would come at last to that conclusion.

Then if he called to mind his fellow prisoners and what passed for wisdom in his former dwelling-place, he would surely think himself happy in the change and be sorry for them. They may have had a practice of honouring and commending one another, with prizes for the man who had the keenest eye for the passing shadows and the best memory for the order in which they followed or accompanied one another, so that he could make a good guess as to which was going to come next. Would our released prisoner be likely to covet those prizes or to envy the men exalted to honour and power in the Cave? Would he not feel like Homer's Achilles, that he would far sooner "be on earth as a hired servant in the house of a landless man" or endure anything rather than go back to his old beliefs and live in the old way?

Yes, he would prefer any fate to such a life.

Now imagine what would happen if he went down again to take his former seat in the Cave. Coming suddenly out of the sunlight, his eyes would be filled with darkness. He might be required once more to deliver his opinion on those shadows, in competition with the prisoners who had never been released, while his eyesight was still dim and unsteady; and it might take some time to become used to the darkness. They would laugh at him and say that he had gone up only to come back with his sight ruined; it was worth no one's while even to attempt the ascent. If they could lay hands on the man who was trying to set them free and lead them up, they would kill him.

Yes, they would.

Every feature in this parable, my dear Glaucon, is meant to fit our earlier analysis. The prison dwelling corresponds to the region revealed to us through the sense of sight, and the fire-light within it to the power of the Sun. The ascent to see the things in the upper world you may take as standing for the upward journey of the soul into the region of the intelligible; then you will be in possession of what I surmise, since that is what you wish to be told. Heaven knows whether it is true; but this, at any rate, is how it appears to me. In the world of knowledge, the last thing to be perceived and only with great difficulty is the essential Form of Goodness. Once it is perceived, the conclusion must follow that, for all things, this is the cause of whatever is right and good; in the visible world it gives birth to light and to the lord of light, while it is itself sovereign in the intelligible world and the parent of intelligence and truth. Without having had a vision of this Form no one can act with wisdom, either in his own life or in matters of state.

So far as I can understand, I share your belief.

Then you may also agree that it is no wonder if those who have reached this height are reluctant to manage the affairs of men. Their souls long to spend all their time in that upper world—naturally enough, if here once more our parable holds true. Nor, again, is it at all strange that one who comes from the contemplation of divine things to the miseries of human life should appear awkward and ridiculous when, with eyes still dazed and not yet accustomed to the darkness, he is compelled, in a law-court or elsewhere, to dispute about the shadows of justice or the images that cast those shadows, and to wrangle over the notions of what is right in the minds of men who have never beheld Justice itself.

It is not at all strange.

No; a sensible man will remember that the eyes may be confused in two ways—by a change from light to darkness or from darkness to light; and he will recognize that the same thing happens to the soul. When he sees it troubled and unable to discern anything clearly, instead of laughing thoughtlessly, he will ask whether, coming from a brighter existence, its unaccustomed vision is obscured by the darkness, in which case he will think its condition enviable and its life a happy one; or whether, emerging from the depths of ignorance, it is dazzled by excess of light. If so, he will rather feel sorry for it; or, if he were inclined to laugh, that would be less ridiculous than to laugh at the soul which has come down from the light.

That is a fair statement.

If this is true, then, we must conclude that education is not what it is said to be by some, who profess to put knowledge into a soul which does not possess it, as if they could put sight into blind eyes. On the contrary, our own account signifies that the soul of every man does possess the power of learning the truth and the organ to see it with; and that, just as one might have to turn the whole body round in order that the eye should see light instead of darkness, so the entire soul must be turned away from this changing world, until its eye can bear to contemplate reality and that supreme splendour which we have called the Good.

For Further Study

Barnett, George, ed. *Philosophy and Educational Development*. Boston: Houghton Mifflin, 1966. (Paperback 3–00300.)

Blanshard, Brand. "Current Issues in Education," *The Monist*, 52 (January, 1968): 11–27.

Booth, Wayne C., ed. *The Knowledge Most Worth Having*. Chicago: U. of Chicago Press, 1967.

Clark, K. B. "Intelligence, the University, and Society," *American Scholar*, 36 (Winter, 1966–1967): 23–32.

Frankena, William K., ed. *Philosophy of Education*. New York: Macmillan, 1965. (Sources in Philosophy Series.)

Gardner, John W. *Excellence: Can We Be Equal and Excellent Too?* New York: Harper, 1961.

Jaspers, Karl. *Way to Wisdom.* New Haven: Yale, 1960, Ch. 11, "The Philosophical Life." (Yale Paperbound Y-27.)

Monist, The: 52 (January, 1968): 1–132. (A special issue "Philosophy of Education" with articles by William K. Frankena, Brand Blanshard, and others.)

Phenix, Philip H. *Education and the Common Good.* New York: Harper, 1961, Chs. 1–3.

Smith, Huston. "Values: Academic and Human," in *The Larger Learning*, ed. Marjorie Carpenter. Dubuque: Wm. C. Brown, 1960.

Weatherford, Willis D., Jr. *The Goals of Higher Education.* Cambridge: Harvard U. Press, 1960.

Weiss, Paul. *The Making of Men.* Carbondale: Southern Illinois U. Press, 1967.

Whitehead, Alfred North. *The Aims of Education.* New York: New American Library, 1949, Ch. 1. (Mentor M 41.)

Index

Titles in brackets are supplied by the editors.